CELEBRITY GHOSTS AND NOTORIOUS HAUNTINGS

About the Author

Marie D. Jones is a fully trained disaster response/preparedness member of Community Emergency Response Teams (CERT) through FEMA and the Department of Homeland Security, and she is a licensed ham radio operator (KI6YES). She is the author of over fifteen nonfiction books on cutting-edge science, the paranormal, conspiracies, ancient knowledge, and unknown mysteries, including Visible Ink Press' *Demons, the Devil, and Fallen Angels* plus *PSIence: How New Discoveries in Quantum Physics and New Science May Explain the Existence of Paranormal Phenomena; 2013: End of Days or a New Beginning; Supervolcano: The Catastrophic Event That Changed the Course of Human History*; and *The Grid: Exploring the Hidden Infrastructure of Reality*. She is a regular contributor to *New Dawn Magazine*, *FATE*, *Paranoia Magazine* and other periodicals. Jones has been interviewed on over a thousand radio shows worldwide, including *Coast-to-Coast AM*. She makes her home in San Marcos, California, and is the mom to one very brilliant son, Max.

CELEBRITY GHOSTS AND NOTORIOUS HAUNTINGS

MARIE D. JONES

Detroit

Also from Visible Ink Press

Alien Mysteries, Conspiracies, and Cover-Ups
By Kevin D. Randle
ISBN: 978-1-57859-418-4

Ancient Gods: Lost Histories, Hidden Truths, and the Conspiracy of Silence
By Jim Willis
ISBN: 978-1-57859-614-0

Area 51: The Revealing Truth of UFOs, Secret Aircraft, Cover-ups & Conspiracies
By Nick Redfern
ISBN: 978-1-57859-672-0

The Astrology Book: The Encyclopedia of Heavenly Influences, 2nd edition
By James R. Lewis
ISBN: 978-1-57859-144-2

The Bigfoot Book: The Encyclopedia of Sasquatch, Yeti, and Cryptid Primates
By Nick Redfern
ISBN: 978-1-57859-561-7

Conspiracies and Secret Societies: The Complete Dossier, 2nd edition
By Brad Steiger and Sherry Hansen Steiger
ISBN: 978-1-57859-368-2

Control: MKUltra, Chemtrails and the Conspiracy to Suppress the Masses
By Nick Redfern
ISBN: 978-1-57859-638-6

Demons, the Devil, and Fallen Angels
By Marie D. Jones and Larry Flaxman
ISBN: 978-1-57859-613-3

The Dream Interpretation Dictionary: Symbols, Signs, and Meanings
By J. M. DeBord
ISBN: 978-1-57859-637-9

The Government UFO Files: The Conspiracy of Cover-Up
By Kevin D. Randle
ISBN: 978-1-57859-477-1

Haunted: Malevolent Ghosts, Night Terrors, and Threatening Phantoms
By Brad Steiger
ISBN: 978-1-57859-620-1

Hidden Realms, Lost Civilizations, and Beings from Other Worlds
By Jerome Clark
ISBN: 978-1-57859-175-6

The Horror Show Guide: The Ultimate Frightfest of Movies
By Mike May
ISBN: 978-1-57859-420-7

The Illuminati: The Secret Society That Hijacked the World
By Jim Marrs
ISBN: 978-1-57859-619-5

The Monster Book: Creatures, Beasts, and Fiends of Nature
By Nick Redfern
ISBN: 978-1-57859-575-4

The New World Order Book
By Nick Redfern
ISBN: 978-1-57859-615-7

Real Aliens, Space Beings, and Creatures from Other Worlds,
By Brad Steiger and Sherry Hansen Steiger
ISBN: 978-1-57859-333-0

Real Encounters, Different Dimensions, and Otherworldly Beings
By Brad Steiger with Sherry Hansen Steiger
ISBN: 978-1-57859-455-9

Real Ghosts, Restless Spirits, and Haunted Places, 2nd edition
By Brad Steiger
ISBN: 978-1-57859-401-6

Real Miracles, Divine Intervention, and Feats of Incredible Survival
By Brad Steiger and Sherry Hansen Steiger
ISBN: 978-1-57859-214-2

Real Monsters, Gruesome Critters, and Beasts from the Darkside
By Brad Steiger and Sherry Hansen Steiger
ISBN: 978-1-57859-220-3

Real Vampires, Night Stalkers, and Creatures from the Darkside
By Brad Steiger
ISBN: 978-1-57859-255-5

Real Visitors, Voices from Beyond, and Parallel Dimensions
By Brad Steiger and Sherry Hansen Steiger
ISBN: 978-1-57859-541-9

Real Zombies, the Living Dead, and Creatures of the Apocalypse
By Brad Steiger
ISBN: 978-1-57859-296-8

The Religion Book: Places, Prophets, Saints, and Seers
By Jim Willis
ISBN: 978-1-57859-151-0

The Sci-Fi Movie Guide: The Universe of Film from Alien to Zardoz
By Chris Barsanti
ISBN: 978-1-57859-503-7

Secret History: Conspiracies from Ancient Aliens to the New World Order
By Nick Redfern
ISBN: 978-1-57859-479-5

Secret Societies: The Complete Guide to Histories, Rites, and Rituals
By Nick Redfern
ISBN: 978-1-57859-483-2

Supernatural Gods: Spiritual Mysteries, Psychic Experiences, and Scientific Truths
by Jim Willis
ISBN: 978-1-57859-660-7

The UFO Dossier: 100 Years of Government Secrets, Conspiracies, and Cover-Ups
By Kevin D. Randle
ISBN: 978-1-57859-564-8

Unexplained! Strange Sightings, Incredible Occurrences, and Puzzling Physical Phenomena, 3rd edition
by Jerome Clark
ISBN: 978-1-57859-344-6

The Vampire Book: The Encyclopedia of the Undead, 3rd edition
by J. Gordon Melton
ISBN: 978-1-57859-281-4

The Werewolf Book: The Encyclopedia of Shape-Shifting Beings, 2nd edition
by Brad Steiger
ISBN: 978-1-57859-367-5

The Witch Book: The Encyclopedia of Witchcraft, Wicca, and Neo-paganism
by Raymond Buckland
ISBN: 978-1-57859-114-5

The Zombie Book: The Encyclopedia of the Living Dead
By Nick Redfern and Brad Steiger
ISBN: 978-1-57859-504-4

"Real Nightmares" E-Books by Brad Steiger

Book 1: *True and Truly Scary Unexplained Phenomenon*

Book 2: *The Unexplained Phenomena and Tales of the Unknown*

Book 3: *Things That Go Bump in the Night*

Book 4: *Things That Prowl and Growl in the Night*

Book 5: *Fiends That Want Your Blood*

Book 6: *Unexpected Visitors and Unwanted Guests*

Book 7: *Dark and Deadly Demons*

Book 8: *Phantoms, Apparitions, and Ghosts*

Book 9: *Alien Strangers and Foreign Worlds*

Book 10: *Ghastly and Grisly Spooks*

Book 11: *Secret Schemes and Conspiring Cabals*

Book 12: *Freaks, Fiends and Evil Spirits*

Please visit us at visibleinkpress.com

CELEBRITY GHOSTS AND NOTORIOUS HAUNTINGS

Visible Ink Press®
43311 Joy Rd., #414
Canton, MI 48187-2075

Visible Ink Press is a registered trademark of Visible Ink Press LLC.

Most Visible Ink Press books are available at special quantity discounts when purchased in bulk by corporations, organizations, or groups. Customized printings, special imprints, messages, and excerpts can be produced to meet your needs. For more information, contact Special Markets Director, Visible Ink Press, www.visibleink.com, or 734-667-3211.

Managing Editor: Kevin S. Hile
Art Director: Mary Claire Krzewinski
Typesetting: Marco Divita
Proofreaders: Shoshana Hurwitz and Chava Levin
Indexer: Larry Baker

Cover images: Marilyn Monroe (Dell Publications, Inc.), Houdini and Lincoln's ghost (Library of Congress), Amityville House (BrownieCharles99 at Wikicommons), Jim Morrison (Elektra Records), Jean Harlow (MGM Studios), background image (Shutterstock).

Library of Congress Cataloging-in-Publication Data

Names: Jones, Marie D., 1961 – author.
Title: Celebrity ghosts and notorious hauntings / by Marie D. Jones.
Description: first [edition]. | Detroit, MI : Visible Ink Press, 2019. | Includes index.
Identifiers: LCCN 2019016565 | ISBN 9781578596898 (pbk. : alk. paper)
Subjects: LCSH: Ghosts. | Celebrities—Miscellanea.
Classification: LCC BF1471 .J66 2019 | DDC 133.1—dc23
LC record available at https://lccn.loc.gov/2019016565

Printed in the United States of America

10 9 8 7 6 5 4 3 2 1

CONTENTS

Photo Sources [viii]

Introduction [ix]

What Is a Ghost, Anyway? 1
Hollywood Ghosts 27
Movie Sets, Studios, and Soundstages 55
Hollywood Landmarks 69
Historical Ghosts 89
Plantations 99
Ships and Lighthouses 107
Vehicles, Trains, Tracks, and Roadways 129
Bridges, Roads, and Caves 135
Battlefields, Cemeteries, and Churches 159
Museums, Landmarks, Sports, and Theater 183
Hotels, Motels, Inns, Houses, and Castles 201
Prisons, Hospitals, and Asylums 237
Creepy Schools, Colleges, and Universities 261
Planes and Airports 275
Urban Legends and Creepy Encounters 283
Notorious Ghosts, Poltergeists, and Paranormal Hot Spots 301
Being There 337

Further Reading [369]

Index [371]

Photo Sources

ABC Television: pp. 63, 85.
l'Aquatique (Wikicommons): p. 123.
B575 (Wikicommons): p. 271.
Jeffrey Beall: p. 343.
J. T. Blatty: p. 307.
Brunswick Records: p. 39.
Hereward Carrington: p. 313.
Daniel Case: p. 142.
Cbc717: p. 264.
CBS Television: p. 53.
George Chriss: p. 266.
Cline Library, Northern Arizona University: p. 153.
Cmichel67 (Wikicommons): p. 14.
The Day Book: p. 221.
Leslie K. Dellovade: p. 250.
Kevin Dooley: p. 65.
Dun.can (Wikicommons): p. 96.
EmbraerSkyPilot (Wikicommons): p. 117.
Benjamin D. Esham: p. 79.
Federal Aviation Administration: p. 276.
C. S. Fly: p. 191.
Riccardo Ghilardi: p. 32.
C. L. K. Hatcher: p. 255.
Heritage Auctions: p. 90.
Guy Hottel: p. 329.
Internet Archive Book Images: p. 94.
Jan's Cat (Wikicommons): p. 114.
Jengod (Wikicommons): p. 82.
Brian Josephson: p. 15.
Journal of Parapsychology: p. 318.
Library of Congress: pp. 34, 45, 78, 204, 269, 286, 348.
Los Angeles (Wikicommons): p. 248.
MGM Television: p. 58.
Gary Minnaert: p. 70.
Peter Moore: p. 231.
National Park Service: p. 227.
Scott Oldham: p. 101.
Onetwo1 (wikicommons): p. 340.
John O'Neill: p. 72.
Ormr2014 (Wikicommons): p. 322.
Benjamin Radford: p. 284.
Pascal Rehfeldt: p. 232.
Renelibrary (Wikicommons): p. 224.
Revere Senior High School: p. 52.
Rievse (Wikicommons): p. 103.
RKO: p. 30.
Scanpix: p. 42.
Seulatr (Wikicommons): p. 303.
Shutterstock: pp. 2, 5, 7, 8, 10, 13, 18, 20, 23, 24, 28, 36, 47, 48, 61, 75, 125, 133, 137, 146, 150, 156, 161, 163, 166, 171, 172, 177, 181, 185, 188, 194, 206, 207, 211, 213, 215, 219, 229, 238, 241, 244, 257, 288, 293, 320, 323, 326, 332, 362.
Siebbi (Wikicommons): p. 56.
Gage Skidmore: p. 305.
Slate magazine: p. 119.
Smallbones (Wikicommons): p. 202.
Bowie Snodgrass: p. 144.
Brad A. Totman: p. 108.
Tuxyso (Wikicommons): p. 209.
U.S. Army: p. 168.
U.S. Navy: p. 110.
Bill Whittaker: p. 175.
Public domain: pp. 19, 196, 217, 253, 279, 290, 295, 297, 315, 353, 358.

Introduction

People who strive for fame and fortune want to be known. As celebrities, they long to be recognized and admired, even become household names, whether they are movie stars, musicians, writers, politicians, world leaders, fashion models, filmmakers, athletes, or even business leaders and entrepreneurs. From actors to astronauts, senators to starlets, and rock stars to rocket scientists, the world loves a celebrity who has achieved greatness in their field, even if their only claim to fame is fame itself. In today's Internet-obsessed world, anyone can acquire celebrity status with a popular video account or by posting tons of selfies on social networking. And the public eats it up!

We even love famous places, whether they have a historical past or are popular as tourist spots. It might be a local bar, a regional theme park or a national monument popularized via Internet review sites, word-of-mouth or social networking. If the place is said to be haunted, the public interest skyrockets, giving the location itself celebrity, even legendary, status.

Therefore, it makes sense that those people who were well-known in life are also well-known in death. From movie stars of the silent movie era to past presidents, celebrated individuals sometimes become celebrity ghosts, and they haunt their homes, workplaces, and burial places. In turn, those places become famous, even notorious, depending on who and what is haunting it!

No matter where we live, there is sure to be a haunted house that once belonged to a famous figure nearby. Perhaps a movie star of old whose figure is reported hanging out in their old digs, refusing to let go and move on, wanting only to be a star in death as they were in life. Maybe the local steakhouse sits upon a Native American burial ground and is riddled with spirits, becoming the new favorite hot spot of local ghost-hunting groups. Or the downtown courthouse is said to be visited by the ghost of a judge who was shot by a criminal he sent to prison for murder. These ghosts and ghostly places become famous on a local, regional, and national level based upon facts and real people and events, taking on a bigger-than-life quality just as celebrities themselves do.

Because we still don't know for certain what happens to us after we die, we like to think a part of us lives on forever in some form. This applies to the celebrities and famous figures we love or despise, as the case may be. Even their homes and hangouts become the stuff of legends, as do the cemeteries in which they are buried, the institutions and hospitals in which they died, and the places with which they were most associated such as a battlefield, a bank, a bar, a bistro, or a ballpark.

From famous faces to famous places, *Celebrity Ghosts and Notorious Hauntings* documents the many hauntings that involve celebrities and well-known people and locations, including those deemed more "notorious" than famous (think of Lizzie Borden and her penchant for axes, or the hotel on which horror author Stephen King based *The Shining*, or ghosts of executed murderers and serial killers). Fame doesn't always mean something out of Hollywood, but this book also documents haunted movie sets and experiences actors and actresses had while making some of the most well-known horror movies of our time.

We will also look at the famous people themselves who have seen or experienced ghostly apparitions and things that go bump in the night. Every year, more and more celebrities and famous folks come forward with their sometimes terrifying, inexplicable stories of encounters with spiritual entities. From senators and presidents to rock stars and movie stars, famed figures experience the paranormal, too. Some are brave enough to allow their experiences to be made public, despite backlash from skeptics and nonbelievers. But famous people lend a credibility that normal people do not, whether the witness is someone on a popular television show or the mayor of a large city. We give extra weight to the astronaut who reports a UFO, do we not?

But the paranormal doesn't discriminate based on popularity, income level, or career choices. Just as someone's Aunt Jolene or Uncle Barney can haunt the old family homestead, it also makes sense that Elvis might be walking the halls of Graceland, President Lincoln drops in for a ghostly visit of the White House, and Lizzie Borden can be seen floating down the halls of the house where she supposedly gave her mother forty chops with an axe.

Before we explore famous ghosts and ghost witnesses, we take a look at the subject of ghosts and hauntings in general because there are many different types of hauntings people report. Some ghosts know we are there, watching and observing them. Others have no awareness of us or even their own surroundings. Some appear only as voices on a tape recorder, which is known as the Electronic Voice Phenomenon (EVP).

Some of the questions this book will explore include: What is a ghost? An apparition? A poltergeist? Is there any scientific basis for the existence of ghosts? How do they manifest in our reality if they are the spirits of the dead? Is it possible they are something else entirely? What qualifies as a haunted location?

If it involves fame and celebrity, fortune and notoriety, legend and lore, this book will cover it. Our fascination for celebrity is only matched, if not surpassed, by our fascination with the paranormal and supernatural. *Celebrity Ghosts and Notorious Hauntings* combines the best, and spookiest, of both worlds.

Now a note from the author because chances are someone will complain that their favorite haunted location or ghostly sighting wasn't mentioned. Authors are given specific word or page counts they must stick to when writing. While it has been this author's quest to present as much of a variety of celebrity ghosts and notorious hauntings as possible, it is impossible for every single one out there to fit in one book. Or ten. Or fifty! Not to mention the fact that this book focuses on hauntings in the United States, but with a few international cases included for good measure. If a favorite or popular place or case was left out, it was simply because the author ran out of pages. Please be assured that the contents of this book are not comprehensive, but they will give the reader a broad and amazing taste of what is out there.

Let's go exploring....

WHAT IS A GHOST, ANYWAY?

When we think of a ghost, the first thing that comes to mind is the spirit of a dead person. The word "spirit" is interchangeable with "soul," "essence," and "consciousness," which many people believe is the part of us that lives on after physical death. Popular belief holds that if a person wasn't ready to die yet, or died under traumatic circumstances, such as murder or a terrible accident, their "spirit" might not be ready to cross over into the realm of death and leave their loved ones and old life behind. Thus, it hangs around as a ghost that can be seen by the living until it is ready to give up its hold on life (even though its body already has).

In order to believe in ghosts, one would have to also believe in the afterlife, at least if a ghost is the spirit of a dead person. Quite possibly, this would also require a belief in a part of our human "being" that transcends death, such as the mind or consciousness. Most pop culture references to ghosts play upon this explanation, with the ghost as a spirit of someone identifiable who is trapped in a purgatory mid-world until someone comes along to guide them home.

The origins of the word "ghost" are quite telling. The English word "ghost" has roots in the Old English "gast" from a common Germanic "gaistaz." In Old Norse, the word "geisa," like the pre-Germanic "ghoisdo-s," meant "fury, anger … to rage." The word ghost is synonymous with the Old English "spiritus," which means "breath, blast," which then became a part of the more modern meaning as "soul of the deceased" or "spirit of the dead" we have now. But it is interesting how the original association was with anger and rage, as if ghosts are indeed angry at their predicament, caught between the worlds of life and death.

Every culture, religion, and belief system on Earth has a place for ghosts within their ideas, traditions, and rites. Whether or not the ghostly aspect of a

Television shows about ghost hunters have been rising in popularity over the last fifteen years or so.

human being denotes that person's actual soul or something else entirely is still up for debate, but the belief in something that transcends death is widespread.

Recent ghost hunting television shows since the early 2000s have caused our interest in ghosts, which was always strong, to skyrocket, as the possibility of not only hunting them down but communicating with them via a plethora of gadgets and machines meant that anyone could look for a ghost. Proof has been hard to come by, but the chasing is still hugely popular with hundreds of paranormal groups and individuals actively engaging in the sport of ghost hunting at locations with reputations of being actively haunted, such as local hotels, restaurants, mental institutions, prisons, and cemeteries. Some groups even charge people suffering from ghostly activity a fee to "clear" their homes and banish spooky spirits. Others offer the service of assisting the spirits of the restless to find their way across the bridge and into the light, where they may find peace in death or the next go-around at life.

The use of equipment to locate ghosts has created its own cottage industry. Although the equipment has main uses for things other than the gathering of supernatural evidence, those who use it, and even tweak it with their own concepts and inventions, swear it shows something else is out there beyond the realm of the five senses. Using everything from digital cameras, digital tape recorders (to record EVP, or electronic voice phenomena, said to be ghosts verbalizing), thermal imagers, EMF meters to detect electromagnetic field anomalies, barometers, infrared thermometers, K2 meters, and more, those who hunt ghosts look for everything out of the ordinary, usually by taking baseline measurements before an investigation, then comparing them with data obtained during. Other types of equipment include Faraday cages, ghost boxes, dowsing rods, infrasound monitors (infrasound is associated with experiences of paranormal phenomena), and motion sensors. But again, these items operate on the assumption that ghosts operate on our natural laws of physics.

Our passion for the paranormal continues despite not one person "capturing" a ghost in a manner that proves where they come from, what they are, and how they manifest in our world, in accordance with the scientific method. But this type of activity, which is subjective and erratic at best, requires a different type of "scientific proof" because of the nature of its behaviors and characteristics, which may be beyond our current level of understanding. If the soul still has not been proven, and we are still debating whether mind and brain, or consciousness and brain, are the same thing, will we ever know what these spectral visions are?

Of all paranormal phenomena, a belief in ghosts is most accepted mainly because death itself is still a huge unknown. We love to speculate as to what happens to us after we die, and we hope that some part of us continues on, which is at the heart of the love of all things ghostly.

But is this the only explanation possible for ghosts, apparitions, and spirits that millions of people report seeing and interacting with all over the world? Not at all.

Living ghosts can also be associated with time slips and anomalies, where the ghost might be alive but in another timeline such as the future or the past.

First of all, there are different types of ghost sightings reported all over the world.

Living Ghosts

Living ghosts do exist. These are phantom apparitions of people who are alive! They may even be doppelgangers. One potential explanation for living ghosts is the possibility of parallel universes, where we each exist in an infinite number of them. There are times when the veil between worlds is so thin, we see ourselves in another universe or even another person in another universe who is just as alive as they are in this one. Think of how déjà vu feels as though you are experiencing something you've done or said before, even at a location you feel you were in before ... but you know for sure you haven't.

Living ghosts can also be associated with time slips and anomalies, where the ghost might be alive but in another timeline such as the future or the past. Might this be what happens when see ghosts of the Victorian age? Clearly, those ghosts would have passed into the light a long time ago and aren't still hanging on to life! So just maybe, ghosts of another time are not dead at all but alive and well in another temporal dimension where they continue to exist in the same time frame as they had when they lost their lives, dressed in the same clothing, living in the same style houses. This would certainly explain why historical ghosts are seen just as they were when they died and not walking around in modern clothing or driving cars that didn't exist when they were alive.

It is just as exciting to believe that a ghost is someone living in another parallel world or timeline as it is to believe it is a physical manifestation of the essence of a person after they die. It is encouraging to think that death itself might be like transferring from one state of being to another, or one location to another, where we continue on as we did in this reality.

Living ghosts may or may not be aware of us seeing them. Ghosts can be broken up into two main categories when it comes to awareness.

Imprints/Residual Ghosts

Imprints or residual hauntings describe ghosts that appear to be energy imprinted upon a particular location. The ghosts are only seen and experienced in that location and appear to repeat a particular pattern of behavior over and over again. Residual ghosts, because they are described as energy imprints, do not interact with witnesses and are totally unaware they are being observed. They may take on the quality of an image projected from somewhere else, as if the witness is watching a piece of film being played over and over again.

Imprints are often associated with trauma, as in the ghosts of battlefields and other major emotional events, that may have caused the ghostly energy to become permanently a part of the location itself. Paranormal researchers believe that imprint hauntings involve the actual absorption of the traumatic energy expended by those who were alive during the event, i.e., a war, terrible plane crash, or major factory fire, and that the ghosts are trapped in a cycle that plays out for anyone who happens to be around to see it.

Sentient/Intelligent Ghosts

Now we have those ghosts that seem to not only be aware of our presence but motion, gesture, or communicate with us in some way. These spirits are self-aware and do not repeat the same behaviors over and over. They adapt and change according to whoever is in their vicinity and appear to have the free will to move around, even though they may stick to a location, such as a house, motel, or basement that was somehow important to them.

These ghosts may have a reason to hang around. Perhaps they died in a way that has never been properly explained. They might have some unfinished business with family members or colleagues and want to "haunt" those persons because of it. Most appear in a human form, but some paranormal enthusiasts believe they can take on many other shapes or even act similarly to poltergeists and move objects on their own, make noises, and toss things about in the air.

Sentient ghosts are the ones ghost hunters love to attempt to communicate with using their various meters with flashing lights or via recorded voices during questioning. The ghosts may be asked their name, why they are hanging around, and how they were killed. The researchers will then play back the tape and listen for ghostly responses.

Often, these ghosts are easy to get along with and are not violent or destructive. They may just be seeking attention and have a desire to communicate information that could help them find the peace they need to move on. Like imprints, sentient ghosts remain in one particular location, but the difference is, they are not just trapped snippets of energy but feeling entities that have a connection to the location and what happened there and have made the choice to remain there.

Why Do Ghosts Prefer Sad Places?

The question has long been asked why so many ghosts appear in the places that caused them the most suffering. Asylums, prisons, orphanages, hospitals, cemeteries, abusive homes … ghosts are usually found in locations steeped in tragedy, sadness, and death. One might think that the dead would want to hang out in places that bring them peace and joy, such as a tropical island or a beautiful resort, but there is an obvious connection between where someone died and where they linger after death.

We often also ask why there aren't more ghosts in hospitals than anywhere else on Earth since so much death occurs there and why there are always reports of ghosts at cemeteries when the bodies buried there did not die there. These are questions that haunt paranormal researchers night and day, pun intended.

Paranormal researchers suggest that powerful emotions such as despair, death, and extreme suffering cause imprinted energy upon the environments these things took place in. Like imprint ghosts, the energy remains and acts as a magnet to keep the ghosts fixated there, reliving their suffering over and over again, as if somehow there will be release from it. In life, we often grieve and mourn the deaths of loved ones, or heartbreak, in such ways that we feel trapped by our suffering, unable to begin the healing process, so perhaps the same applies after we die. Psychic mediums claim it is their job to help these ghosts finally break free from being stuck in the places they suffered in life and go on to whatever awaits them, i.e., "going toward the light." In the case of cemeteries, the ghosts may simply be unable to accept that they are dead and linger where their physical body is, rotting beneath the earth in a coffin, nonetheless.

Ghosts seem to hang around places marked by tragedy and despair possibly because emotions such as pain, fear, and sadness are more powerful and likely to leave a spiritual imprint at locales such as cemeteries, hospitals, and orphanages.

That may be the best reason we have so far to explain the abundance of ghostly activity in dark, sinister places. If there is something to the science of energy remaining in a closed system, perhaps that energy that was a living person stays in that closed system even after it has changed upon their death. It is just simply stuck there until it either dissipates over time or somehow finds a way out of the closed system.

We don't hear often of happy ghosts that haunt the places they died in unless there is a strong emotional connection to that location that keeps them from wanting to move on. Usually, we assume that happy ghosts want to go on to the next phase of existence and are not trapped by stronger emotions they cannot accept or deal with. They're ready to go into the light and then some, while those who died under horrific circumstances cannot seem to shake off their past as easily.

Historical Ghosts

They can be sentient or behave in a loop, but if there is some historical connection to a famous location or event, these types of ghosts often prove to be the most fascinating. People flock to various locations around the world that have historical significance, and because the buildings or areas are places where many people have perished over time, they tend to get the reputation of being haunted. A historical ghost will appear as he or she lived at the time they died, so they might wander around in Victorian garb or the dress of the 1920s. If the location is a battlefield, the ghosts may be in soldier's uniforms of the time and carry weapons that correspond to what was used in combat. Places that experienced a great deal of trauma, death, and violence over time are the most haunted, with numerous entities involved, but often, an old house dating back two hundred years can be just as active with paranormal phenomena, although it is witnessed by a smaller number of people.

Historical haunted places often become local, state, or national landmarks, preserved in their original state or restored and renovated to look as they once did when they were functional. Many offer public educational tours that often take place on a date that has special meaning to the location or the event. Because we all know our nation's history and have been exposed to these locations via movies, television shows, and news stories, these locations and their resident ghosts tend to become as popular as those of the most famous celebrities and movie stars.

Elementals

Elementals are spirits found in nature and associated with the elements of fire, air, water, and earth. They are often associated with primitive belief systems such as animism, which ascribes a soul/spirit to everything, including inanimate objects such as rocks and waterfalls. More the stuff of myth and legend, there are also elementals that specifically haunt graveyards and cemeteries. Not so much ghosts as entities, spirits, or even beings such as sprites, elementals can be shape-shifters and manifest in forms applicable to the locations they are specifically associated with (water nymph, fire demon, fairy, woodland sprite …).

Many urban legends and Native American legends tell of elementals responsible for the large number of people who go missing every year in forests and mountain landscapes.

Apparitions

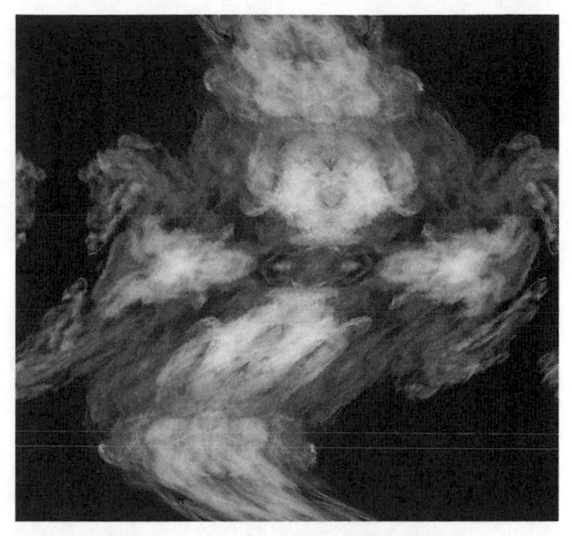

Apparitions are ghosts that don't look like people but, rather, are shapeless fog or mist beings.

Though they are really ghosts, apparitions tend to take on a much more ethereal quality and can look like a mist or a fog that has some semblance of shape to it. They don't have bodies, or even forms, although they can look like a human in the most general sense and are described as transparent. Those who have witnessed apparitions often claim they are disembodied spirits that are of the dead but more of an essence than a form. They can be aware and sentient or behave in a loop as an imprint and often appear as a limb or from the torso up and sometimes appear without their heads. Full-bodied apparitions are a rarity indeed but are sighted on occasion.

Often, apparitions fade into and out of view of the witness, which mimics many UFO sightings. Witnesses often describe them as "flickering," like an image projected from a movie projector onto a screen, and that they are sometimes accompanied by the sound of static or an electrical pop. Maybe these entities are interdimensional in origin and, when the environment allows, are able to move in and out of our world. Maybe we are doing the same in their world!

Poltergeists

Though normally classified separately, poltergeist is German for "noisy ghost," and that is exactly what they are. True poltergeists move objects around, break things, open doors, and cause actual physical trouble to those unlucky enough to encounter them. This kind of activity can be traced to a person, usually a teenage girl, going through hormonal and emotional shifts and may be associated with certain parts of the brain that are also involved in epileptic seizures and déjà vu. The repressed emotions, anger, and sexual energy of the human agent could be finding a way to manifest as physical activity within its immediate environment.

Other poltergeists are said to be the spirits of the dead that form groups and cause all kinds of mischief. This activity can start abruptly, and end just as quickly, and tends to be more frightening than the average ghost because of the ability of the spirits to move objects on the physical plane.

The most common poltergeist reports involve persistent knocking, rapping, doors opening and closing, and beds banging on the floor.

Demons can at times take on ghostly forms, behave like poltergeists, or possess people, animals, and objects.

Demonic Hauntings

Demons can possess people, animals, and objects, and the result looks like a type of haunting. The demons may take on a ghostly form or move objects about, make noises, and bang items, but usually, this form of activity is more harmful. Though incredibly rare, a real demonic haunting involves the possession of a person, often a child, and requires the assistance of a trained exorcist to put an end to the activity. The demons, often called malevolent spirits, can work alone or in groups and often choose to "speak" through a person they possess.

Demons are far more likely to be reported as shape-shifters and can take on a variety of forms from a dark, shadowy figure to a horrifying beast. They are not associated with a dead person and can follow someone they decide to possess from location to location. Often, demons can appear in the form of "attachments" which latch on to an object such as an old clock or a doll and cause chaos for anyone who owns, or comes in contact with, the object.

The only real correlation between a demon and a ghost may be the fact that they exist in a world alongside our own and have found a way to manifest here that we have yet to understand. Yet, some ghosts can display quite hostile behavior, as can poltergeists, causing danger to witnesses involved, so it can be difficult sometimes to discern a ghost from a poltergeist from a demon.

Tulpas and Thought Forms

Tulpas are thought forms or spirits that are created through the power of the mind, often the collective thoughts or intentions of a group of people with the goal of creating their own manifested ghost. The word comes from the Tibetan "sprul-pa," which means emanation or manifestation and is mentioned in Buddhist texts as "mind-made body," or emanations that come from the mind, and can travel via the mind stream into heavenly realms. The actual words "thought form" appear in the 1927 Evans-Wentz translation of the *Tibetan Book of the Dead*. Some Tibetan Buddhists believe that tulpas can possess a human mind, just as a demon might possess a body.

More modern "thought forms" consist of potential apparitions created by groupthink, such as the famous Philip Experiment. A group of Canadian parapsychologists, led by a Dr. A. R. G. Owen, attempted to create a ghost in 1972. The experiment took place in Toronto and involved the members proposing a physical description of the ghost, then using prolonged concentration and focused intention to collectively create the thought form. The ghost even had a background story to make the experiment feel more substantial.

The ghost was named "Philip Aylesford" and had quite a tragic backstory, created in detail, including a tragic death. Using the same techniques as a classic séance, they sat around a table and dimmed the lights. They all had pictures of a castle they believed Philip would have lived in and other objects to add atmosphere. It took a few weeks, but soon, they witnessed an apparition, heard knocks on the table, and got Philip to answer questions that played into his fictional history. Philip couldn't come up with answers to any other questions, leading the group to suggest he was a figment of their own collective unconscious.

Future sessions ended with the table moving of its own volition and even chasing one of them across the room! None of their hands were on the table when this happened. They never did prove if Philip was a real apparition that took the opportunity to show itself (a playful spirit?) or something created out of their own imaginations or subconscious minds.

Paranormal investigators suggest that the expectations of the investigators combined with that of the witnesses could assist in manifesting apparitions. If enough people believe a ghost exists on the premises, their combined belief and focused thought may have more power to make the ghost more real than they think!

Haunted Houses and Objects

The same trauma and emotional distress that may keep a ghost from passing into the light can also keep them entombed within certain objects or locations. We all know what a haunted house is. The house itself is not the origin of the activity (unless the house itself is evil or made from evil wood, plaster, cement, windows, etc.) but harbors the activity within its walls, usually as imprinted energy. A haunted house, or any other building, can be the stomping grounds of ghosts and apparitions that are tied to that building and suffered within its walls. Sometimes, the ghosts are former residents of a house they died violently within. The ghosts may also be tied to the land the house is built upon, which itself can be haunted. It may have once been a cemetery or sacred burial ground or land cursed by Native American tribes. If the house was once something else, say a hospital, prison, or morgue, then the hauntings may come from the older incarnations of the building.

Aside from the misidentification of perfectly normal phenomena, such as creaking wood, hot and cold spots, exposed wiring, EMF fluctuations, faulty lighting, and crooked floorboards, there are hundreds of places the world over with notorious reputations of being home to ghostly activity that doesn't go away after time. Scientists point to such things as electromagnetic anomalies and the presence of infrasound, both natural things, as having a negative effect on people that could be misinterpreted as paranormal activity, including the sense of being watched, seeing shadow figures, and both visual and auditory hallucinations.

Yet, there is also the mistaken idea that any abandoned, old, ugly house is automatically haunted because often, brand-new homes can harbor ghosts as well, and creaky, century-old homes can be haunted by nothing more than mice, termites, and whatever other critters live within the walls.

Can a ghost live inside a doll or object? Those unlucky mortals who have encountered haunted dolls, furniture, paintings, and other objects say yes! Perhaps they do so in the same way a house can harbor the spirits of the dead; an object can if there was some strong association between the object itself and the ghost of the person haunting it. Demons can possess objects, too. A whole new industry has come from the popularity of haunted dolls in particular, with muse-

Ghosts can remain in places such as houses, where they suffered their demise. Haunted places do not always have to be houses, however. They can be almost any kind of place where a tragedy occurred.

ums opening all over the country allowing people to view the "damned" objects, if they dare!

Though a lot of what the public knows and hears about ghosts and haunted locations comes from television shows, novels, and movies, there is a huge body of research and reports by witnesses that makes one wonder ... is it all just the workings of overactive imaginations, or are we living side by side with spirits, whether they are trapped between life and death, the residual part of us that survives physical death, or simply living people from another timeline popping into ours to say hello? Find any neighborhood with an old, abandoned building of any sort, and it is sure to be "haunted," as per the locals. Yet, even brand-new houses can be haunted if they are situated near burial grounds (remember the movie *Poltergeist*?), cemeteries, or on land that once housed a sinister asylum. The land a house or building is constructed on can harbor ghosts and spirits that are trapped there, unable to move on from whatever torments they experienced.

Stories of ghosts and haunted places are as old as time and humanity. Ghosts appear to people of all walks of life and don't discriminate based on age, gender, religion, or color of skin. A great experiment in the popularity of the concept of ghosts is to simply ask five people you know if they've ever seen a ghost. This author did just that at a recent dinner party and was shocked to find that everyone in the crowded room had a story to tell. Just raising the subject led to excitement, and the ghost stories lasted for hours, as everyone clamored to tell their tales, many of whom had never felt comfortable telling anyone before!

And when the ghosts or locations are famous or have some notoriety behind them, we get even more excited still.

There are several popular "theories" that could describe what ghosts are and where they come from.

- Ghosts are the spirits of dead people, still wandering Earth in a sort of in-between state. To many, this theory is the gold standard by which most ghost hunters and paranormal researchers apply their investigative methodologies. It is by far the most popular way to describe a ghost and, for most people, is the most common-sense explanation and the easiest to wrap their minds around. A part of us lives on after death, and for ghosts, that stays fixed to the earthly plane until they are freed to go wherever their next destination is.
- Ghosts may be demons or entities that have a religious origin or are interdimensional entities that are here to terrorize us. This includes demons, shadow people, djinn, and other spirits that possess humans and objects. These particular beings tend to be

evil in nature and clearly harmful, much more so than the average ghost of a dead relative.

- Ghosts are nothing more than manifestations of our own powerful belief or perception and can also be induced via various drugs, especially hallucinogens. The power of suggestion and the power of hysteria could explain the viral nature of ghost sightings and paranormal activity. Could simply telling someone a house is haunted, even if it isn't, mean that they perceive ghosts and other activity simply because they expect to? This is also known as the "is it all in our heads" theory. Have every single one of these reports, over thousands of years of history, simply been fanciful imaginings or hallucinations? Or, is it possible that our brains are somehow responsible for designing these scenarios based upon an external stimulus or influence?
- Ghosts and other apparitions are created by naturally occurring environmental conditions such as electrical, magnetic, or electromagnetic radiation or a combination of external, environmental influences that also may correspond to internal, physiological influences in the human body to create the perfect storm. For years, ghost hunters have used specific pieces of equipment such as EMF meters, barometers, and thermal imaging devices as a means to measure and analyze environmental factors that might be present during a paranormal event, and current research is focusing as well on what goes on in the bodies of the observers of such events.
- Ghosts are the playback of energy, or stored human emotion, trapped within the building or room and somehow captured or "recorded" into the environment. These imprinted ghosts replicate the same actions continually ... like someone pressing rewind and then play repeatedly on a video camera. This theory might also be applied to EVP, or electronic voice phenomena, where words and phrases are captured onto digital voice recorders. The idea is that somehow the ghosts can still speak or that their words have somehow been trapped and imprinted upon the particular location in a never-ending loop.
- Ghosts, spirits, and other "unknowns" are very much alive and active but present in alternate dimensions, parallel universes and timelines, and other realities that exist alongside our own. If there are multiple levels of reality and corresponding forms of life on each of these different levels, we may see so many different manifestations of ghosts, entities, and beings that exist out there in the "multiverse," a term coined in 1895 by American

philosopher and psychologist William James when referring to the hypothetical set of universes and realities. The multiverse theory was expanded by cosmologist Max Tegmark, who postulated a taxonomy of universes beyond our own observable universe, which served as the groundwork for other theories, such as string theory, M-Theory, and Everett's many worlds interpretation. A ghost in another dimension or parallel universe might not be a dead person but a live person in another reality. Ghosts might also be time travelers in different parallel timelines, the past, or the future, and we get little glimpses of them as they were then or will be someday. This theory could also explain the fleeting images reported of ghost cars, planes, and trains that seem to be operating on another level of reality.

Seeing a ghost or experiencing any type of paranormal activity might then be a matter of whether or not our conscious mind is open to it and has the ability to go beyond the five senses of what we call reality in order to then perceive it as a physical manifestation. But it may be the realm of the subconscious, which is responsible for over 90 percent of our thoughts and behaviors, that determines what we are open to. People who claim they believe in ghosts may not, on a subconscious level, want to see one standing at their bedside in the middle of the night!

Is There a Science to Ghosts?

Experiments using photons and other particles on the quantum level have shown that the observer changes the outcome of the results. Until the moment of observation of the particle, there is no real particle to observe. Physicist Paul Davies writes in his book *Superforce* that "in the absence of an observation a quantum system will evolve in a certain way. When an observation is made, an entirely different type of change occurs. Just what produces this different behavior is not clear, but at least some physicists insist that it is explicitly caused by the mind itself." This statement was written in 1984, and since then, more physicists and scientists have conceded the role of the mind in creating the physical reality we "observe" on a daily basis. More and more research is coming to the forefront every day that confirms that the outcomes of quantum phenomena can be modified by consciousness.

Some people might be more likely to see ghosts because their minds (and hopes) are more open to the possibility of life after death.

Arizona State University physicist professor Paul Davies theorized in *Superforce* that consciousness can influence our reality, as evidenced by studies in quantum mechanics.

What is consciousness? A quick look at the dictionary turns up a variety of answers. "Awakened state; the awareness of self and of what one is doing and why; the totality of one's thoughts, feelings, and experiences; a state of knowing the self; cognizance." Consciousness, then, is a state of awareness, of knowing that one exists. We possess consciousness when we are awake and aware of our own existence.

Consciousness is also described as the ability to think and perceive. Thoughts, perception, and consciousness are the key players in understanding the connections between the paranormal and the normal, just as they are the key players in determining the outcome of a quantum physics experiment. The nonlocality experiments of Alain Aspect and his team in 1982 proved that space is nonlocal and that the world is not made up of separate objects that, when put together, make the Universe as we know it. Instead, these groundbreaking experiments showed that the "observer" and the "object being observed" were connected and part of an indivisible whole, with everyone and everything affecting and influencing everything else.

Some physicists look to the realm of superspace, or the Zero Point Field, as the home of the Cosmic Consciousness that observed, and continues to observe, the universe into being. Linked to this cosmic mind is the mind of the individual human who, on a microcosmic scale, observes his or her own reality into being. And synching of vibrations and frequencies, whether those in the electromagnetic field or the human brain, can certainly lead to an experience of something beyond normal, waking consciousness.

Consciousness is the key, and the observer chooses the branch of experience. Physicist Brian Josephson states in his paper "String Theory, Universal Mind and the Paranormal" that "some aspects of mentality involve a realm of reality largely, but not completely, disconnected from the phenomena manifested in conventional physics." He points to the informational aspect of life, and there is a biological character involved with the informational processing of organisms, one that sees life "able to shape its environment in a partnership with it." Two life forms sharing their mental states could account for such phenomena as ESP and telepathy. Many serious parapsychologists suggest greater levels of psi phenomena are reported under laboratory testing conditions when the research subjects have a *vested interest in the outcome of the experiments*. Implied meaning can often make a big difference. Richard S. Broughton, a scientist and former president of the Parapsychological Association, wrote in his presidential address in 1987 about the importance of meaning when working with test subjects. He proposed that researchers ask the question "Whom does psi serve?" when working with subjects, pointing to the "need-serving" nature of psi phenomena and how it might affect the skill levels of individuals.

Cambridge professor and theoretical physicist Brian Josephson published a paper in which he stated the mind could potentially operate in a realm outside of conventional physics.

Obviously, if there is a greater need, often survival-based, for psi, then the psi will show up in a greater amount in the subject. Broughton stated, "Quite a few experiments in ESP and PK [psychokinesis] can be read as providing support for both the need-serving character and its operation at an unconscious level." Test results seem to imply that there are psychological and biological implications to paranormal phenomena and that their functioning significance must be considered.

Thus, if one person has a greater need to display PK, they will display it. That does not mean psi only shows up when there is a desperate need for it, Broughton continues, but that researchers must keep in mind that "probably the primary function of psi is to help the individual survive when faced with serious threats to health and safety, and to gain a competitive advantage in the struggle for survival."

Do we, then, have a choice to be psychic or to see a ghost? Perhaps we do, but on a subconscious level. And when that choice is made on a conscious level, can our brains then sync with the exact frequency necessary to perceive what is considered beyond normal perception? The human brain acts as an amazing filter, accepting and rejecting information and stimuli based upon our survival needs. You could say we operate on a strictly need-to-know basis, with our brain acting as the sentry at the gate, refusing entry to anything that we just plain don't need to understand. People who are able to shift their perception thus shift their need-to-know basis to include *things they did not perceive before*. If you don't need to see it, you won't see it.

On the other hand, phenomena such as ghosts, UFOs, and other entities that take on a nearly physical form may be coming into our consciousness without our consent simply because they have found the operating mechanism for being able to do so. And, on some level, we must be consenting to perceive their presence, just as we tend to see, or not see, what we want to see in daily life.

The RAS and Ghosts

Does the brain filter away things like ghosts that we simply don't have a need to know? There is a part of the brain responsible for just that. The RAS, or reticular activating system, is a cluster of nerves located at the base of the brain stem that serves as a filter to keep out unnecessary information and focus our attention instead on what is important. It really serves as a means to allow us to wade through millions upon millions of bits of information coming at our brains at any given time to find the four dozen bits we need for day-to-day survival.

The RAS not only helps the brain focus on what is important, it also seeks out more of that for the brain to register. For example, if you don't care about pink Cadillacs but then suddenly decide you might want to buy one after seeing one on the road, your brain will now begin to seek out every pink Cadillac it can find, whether on the freeway or in car commercials or ads. This is because the RAS has been activated to filter out all other cars but the one that has now become a priority. Though the RAS was initially probably meant to help humans avoid danger and find the necessary things they needed for survival, such as food, shelter, and allies, it is now attributed with also filtering our beliefs. Another example might have someone deciding to name their baby Ludvig because they don't know any other babies by that name. Suddenly, they begin meeting other parents with a son named Ludvig or see celebrity couples choosing the name Ludvig. What happened? Nothing, really. People have always been naming their sons Ludvig, and only now did it become important to that particular person, and thus, their RAS made sure to seek out corroboration of that importance. (Don't be surprised if, after reading this, you start seeing the name Ludvig turn up everywhere!)

If seeing a ghost becomes a priority or if you have seen a ghost when you had no interest in one before, the RAS will begin to filter *in* more ghostly experiences and items of interest. So, the RAS can both filter out, and filter in, what is important to us at any given time. Like consciousness and perception, the RAS sees what it wants, or needs, to see and doesn't see what is not important. One can only imagine how most people go through their lives filtering out ghosts, aliens, entities, and the presence of other realities simply because their RASs are not allowing their brains to focus on those very things. Ghosts could be all around us, but until it becomes important that we see and interact with them, we might never know it.

EVP AND TALKING GHOSTS

EVP stands for electronic voice phenomena and is a method used by paranormal researchers and ghost hunters to attempt communication with the dead. EVP works by asking questions on a digital recorder and allowing the tape to continue playing. When the questioning is complete, the recording is played back to reveal potential spirit voices that were either recorded unintentionally or in response to the specific questions asked. The voices, if any, are usually embedded in static and white noise and are often just a word or a short phrase.

Scientists claim EVP is nothing more than auditory pareidolia, which is the interpretation of random sounds as voices based upon the expectation of the person listening. This is similar to people seeing faces in wallpaper patterns or in the shapes of clouds. Sometimes, EVP can pick up radio stations and even CB or ham radio operators nearby.

Scientists claim EVP is nothing more than auditory pareidolia, which is the interpretation of random sounds as voices based upon the expectation of the person listening.

Yet, those in the paranormal field claim that Class A EVP are distinct, intelligent responses to questions that can even be verified, such as asking the name of a ghost and getting an actual name that can be corroborated with more research. However, is it possible the EVP is picking up the thoughts of the investigators? Yes, that is a possibility being researched. If ghosts can communicate via digital recorders, why not the living?

In 1982, Sarah Estep founded an organization devoted to further research into EVP, the American Association of Electronic Voice Phenomena (AA-EVP) out of Severna Park, Maryland. Modern ghost hunters, seen on television reality shows, use EVP as a standard method of spirit communication, which is a form of ITC, or Instrumental Trans-Communication, a term coined by Professor Ernst Senkowski in the 1970s, that includes all forms of electronic devices used to speak to the dead—tape recorders, fax machines, television sets, telephones, etc.

One might ask why the voices of spirits can only manifest on tape or some electronic device and not be heard by actual sets of human ears, although in many hauntings, the voices are indeed heard without any assistance. Are ghostly voices coming to us on specific frequencies outside of the range of normal human hearing? Or even within the range? If so, why don't they interrupt our radio and television broadcasts more often? EVP has become so popular, there are few paranormal research groups that don't use it or some form of it, but what is being captured on the recordings? Voices of the dead, thoughts of the researchers themselves, or scattered bits of captured radio station voices that the human mind then shapes into exactly what it wants, or expects, to hear?

GHOST PICTURES—FACT OR FAKED

Nowadays, everyone has a cell phone and can readily photograph a ghost or apparition. But ghost photography wasn't always as easy as point and click. The first ghost photographs were accidental, spotted on pictures of other people or objects as blurred, transparent figures. This was usually attributed to the long exposure time of the film, but it led to an interest in attempting to capture spirits on film.

One of the oldest such photographs is of Prince Arthur, one of Queen Victoria's children. The photo was taken by a man named Roger Fenton in 1854 and shows the ghostly figure of a woman who was said to be his nurse standing by the boy with her arm outraised, as if to steady the child on the box he was standing upon. After that, ghost pictures were sold commercially and became a huge novelty item, even though no one ever attempted to find out whether or not they were real.

Photographers began speculating on how ghost images were made, using varying exposure times and techniques, and it was only a matter of time before fakes and charlatans began claiming the images were real and that they could take pictures of dead loved ones ... for profit, of course. The first serious attempt at spirit photography occurred in the 1860s, when a man named William H. Mumler discovered a technique using double exposure. He began working as a medium who could capture the dead on film and often doctored the negatives. He was busted when he got caught putting real Boston residents in some of the pictures as ghosts!

With everyone these days being an amateur photographer, a lot of "ghost" pictures might be attributed to simply bad technique or deliberate fakery.

The early twentieth century saw spirit photography come of age, with interest by such luminaries as Sir Arthur Conan Doyle and William Crookes. One spiritualist, William Stainton Moses, began referring to the entities in the images as ectoplasm, the fluid stuff that forms into actual spirits. Many early spiritualist photographers were accused of fraud, as ghost photography had a huge and profitable market by then.

Today's ghost hunters use sophisticated camera equipment to try to capture actual ghosts on film or video. Yet, even with that being said, getting a clear ghost image rarely happens. Perhaps they don't like being photographed, or their ethereal nature just doesn't translate well to film.

This portrait of Lady Dorothy Walpole (1686–1726; sister of British prime minister Robert Walpole) is the living image of the woman whose ghost is supposedly that of the Brown Lady of Raynham Hall.

There have been a number of famous ghost photos over the years that do challenge skeptics. The most famous is the Brown Lady of Raynham Hall, written about later in this book. Her image, floating down a staircase as a full-body apparition, has become iconic in the paranormal field.

Another photo shows the ghost of a man named Lord Combermere, who was killed in an accident in London in 1891. At the time the photo was taken, the Lord was being interred several miles away, but the image, taken in the library of the Lord's home, revealed a man resembling him sitting in his favorite chair. The figure's legs were missing, made all the creepier by the fact that Lord Combermere died when his legs were crushed by a carriage.

During a visit to the Bachelor's Grove cemetery in a suburb outside of Chicago, Illinois, the Ghost Research Society of America took a photo at the abandoned graveyard and captured the image of a woman wearing white, old-fashioned clothing and sitting atop a tombstone. Another cemetery ghost was captured on film, this time in Tombstone, Arizona's Boothill Graveyard, where an actor named Terry Ike Clanton took a film photo of a friend, who was dressed as an 1880s cowboy. When he looked at it later, he noticed the figure of a man in the background wearing a black hat and rising out of the ground or kneeling, as no legs could be seen. Clanton tried to recreate the image later but never succeeded.

Another famous ghost picture is that of mechanic Freddie Jackson, who served in the Royal Air Force during World War I. He was tragically killed by an airplane propeller in 1919 and, on the day of his burial, his squadron took a group photo. Jackson's face can be glimpsed behind the fourth airman from the left, in the back row. The photo was made public in 1975 by retired RAF officer Victor Goddard, who had been a member of the same squadron.

One of the most problematic new types of ghost photography involve the infamous orbs that often appear as balls of translucent light in pictures of graveyards or other haunted locations. Though many psychics and paranormal enthusiasts like to believe they are ghost lights or spirits bouncing around in the form of balls of light (and in some cases, they might be!), photographers and skeptics claim they are nothing more than dust or particulate matter captured on camera and are a problem common to digital cameras.

Why Do Ghosts Haunt at Night?

Why is it that most people see ghosts at night? They do appear often during the daytime, but most often, the things that go bump in the night go, well, bump in the night. Is it because we are more afraid when the lights go out and more susceptible to the possibilities of what we might be sharing our space with? Or might there be some actual physiological reasons why things show up when the lights go down? If ghosts and apparitions are translucent and misty, does daylight make it harder to distinguish them from the background?

The human body has long been left out of the equation in terms of modern paranormal research, which has usually focused on external and environmental sources of activity—the actual haunted location, the changes and fluctuations in the electromagnetic field, the weather, and the barometric pressure—and apparitions appear to be totally outside of ourselves in the real and physical sense. Rarely do we think there might be a connection between our own presence, observation, and physiology and that we might play a role in exactly who perceives paranormal phenomena, who doesn't, and when.

According to most paranormal investigators who are out in the field week after week at various haunted locations, a lot of paranormal activity is said to occur during a four-hour time period, from 11 P.M. to 3 A.M., with heavy activity around midnight to 1 A.M., known as the "witching hour." This was said

The time between midnight and 1 A.M. is known as the "witching hour" because that is when paranormal activities are supposedly most frequent. It also happens to be when our fight-or-flight hormone levels are highest.

Continued...

(Continued from previous page)

to be the time witches and demons, even ghosts, were most likely to show up in graveyards and cemeteries. Witches during Medieval times were the most active then, and it was considered a time when the supernatural broke through the veil into the natural world. The late night/early morning hours were times when most people were in bed, not willing to be out in the dark for a number of reasons! The winding down of daily activity could serve as the perfect time for the brain to relax, the mind to chill, and the body to begin the process of entering into sleep mode and the world of dreams.

Our brains have neurotransmitters such as serotonin, dopamine, and norepinephrine, which serve to influence our moods and perceptions, our emotions and emotional states, and even our behaviors and actions. Of those, serotonin is the most powerful, able to change or shift our perceptions based upon existing levels in the body. Serotonin, also known as 5-hydroxytryptamine, is a hormone found in the pineal gland, the digestive tract, blood platelets, and the central nervous system. It is one of the chief hormones regulating cell and organ activity and also regulates our memory, our mode of learning, and, get this, our perception of reality and how we approach it. Altered levels cause depression, even suicidal thoughts, and affect sleep, anxiety, and energy levels. Ninety percent of our serotonin is found in our "second brain," the gut, although we usually associate it with the brain in our skulls!

While there have been anecdotal links between lower levels of serotonin and a more openness to religious and paranormal beliefs, and higher levels have been associated more with objective, empirical views of religion and spirituality, we don't have actual studies. We know that our brain chemicals and hormones do affect us and that they are more or less ample during different times of the day and night.

Melatonin, another powerful and important brain chemical, shares a similar structure with the psychoactive compounds DMT (dimethyltryptamine) and mescaline, both of which are associated with visions, hallucinations, paranormal and religious experiences, and altered states of consciousness. Melatonin levels are regulated by our circadian cycle, which governs sleep and waking states. Melatonin also regulates menstruation cycles in women. Because of its molecular structure being similar to DMT, varying levels can produce extremely intense dreams. Lack of sleep can alter melatonin production, throwing us into a slightly altered waking state. When is the body's peak melatonin production period? Between the hours of 1 A.M. and 3 A.M. Could this have an effect on those up all night in a fearful setting doing a paranormal investigation? If this is when we should be sleeping and dreaming, what happens to that excess melatonin if we don't allow ourselves to sleep during normal hours?

Because melatonin plays such a huge role in the menses of women, some suggest it might even account for the higher rates of psychic ability in women during times of high hormonal activity such as menses, pregnancy, and menopause. This again is purely speculative until more research can be done.

There are a host of other chemicals coursing through our bodies that could affect what we experience, and because the chemical levels in the person standing next to us are different, they may not experience the same thing. This might account for the many investigations where three people see a ghost, and the other four see nothing of the sort. Our bodies may be directly influencing us to perceive what is or isn't there, and all of us have different levels of these hormones and neurotransmitters at any given time. The same goes for the pharmaceuticals we take and the recreational drugs we may engage in, many of

Continued...

(Continued from previous page)

which can alter our reality, willingly or unwillingly.

Two powerful stress hormones that trigger our fight-or-flight response are cortisol and adrenaline. At night, these levels should lower, allowing us the rest we need and enabling our bodies to go into repair mode. But if we are in a situation where our fight-or-flight responses kick in, say late at night having heard a strange sound in the kitchen or on a ghost hunt at the local haunted hotel, we experience a surge in both hormones, which cause blood pressure to rise, pulse to spike, and a host of other responses that would, on any other occasion, allow us to either fight or flee the threat.

Every single organ in our bodies has its own internal clock, which keeps it on a schedule that best serves our health and well-being, unless tampered with. If we look at the witching hours, when brain chemicals and hormones shift down for sleep mode and REM activity, we see that, unless we tamper with them, the parts of the body that are most involved with maintenance, processing and eliminating waste, and removing toxins from the body are the blood vessels and arteries, the gall bladder, and the liver. The gall bladder and liver specifically have the tough job of working between 11:00 P.M. and 3:00 A.M. to process the waste in our bodies and make sure we can eliminate it in the morning. If we are awake during this time, we might experience such symptoms as stomachaches, anxiety, and edginess.

So, we should be sleeping when instead we are walking around dark places looking for ghosts. Our circadian rhythms are knocked out of whack, and our brain chemicals, hormones, and organ responses are as well. The circadian rhythm or cycle is a twenty-four-hour cycle built into our bodies to regulate sleep and being awake, but we can change it and often do. Plants, animals, even fungi and certain bacteria have a circadian cycle. An interesting aspect of this is what happens between the witching hours.... Between the hours of 11:00 P.M. and around 4:00 A.M., our bowel system slows down, going into maintenance mode. Our melatonin secretion begins as we look forward to the lowest body temperature of the day and the deepest of sleep.

Paranormal activity may be a product of our environment, internally and externally, then. Just as a particular location might encourage activity via close proximity to an electromagnetic field, ground water source, or even seismic activity, our own bodies might be the other half of the equation.

The Internet is filled with pages and pages of images said to be ghosts or apparitions, uploaded by those with cell phones and video cameras, but very few pass muster enough to get beyond skeptics with knowledge of photography, lighting, or image distortions. This doesn't mean there are no ghosts, only that whatever it is they are made up of is very difficult to capture as photographic proof. That doesn't stop thousands of people from trying, though, hoping to take that definitive picture that somehow proves the paranormal as real.

Ghostly Personalities

There are three different personalities one might encounter when meeting a ghost at a haunted location.

- Friendly ghosts—These are ghosts that are playful and sometimes even helpful, warning someone of a pending disaster, such as a fire breaking out in the kitchen, or stopping someone from entering a dangerous area. Friendly ghosts can still be frightening to deal with just by the sheer fact they are ghosts, but they do no harm and often coexist peacefully side by side with the living.
- Malevolent ghosts—These are mean, hostile, and sometimes dangerous spirits that seek to terrorize and cause harm. They might be ghosts, poltergeists, or even demonic entities that have the potential to seriously hurt witnesses or destroy homes. They don't want to coexist side by side with the living and usually make it clear they want the living gone from the premises, if not worse. Their anger and violence can be directed toward specific individuals or just outward in general. In the case of demonic possessions, these types of entities won't go away on their own without the help of professional exorcists trained by the Catholic Church.
- Neutral ghosts—These ghosts don't interact with humans at all and instead seem to be unaware of humans altogether. They don't know, or seem to care, they are being observed and appear to be doing the same things over and over again in the same locations, as if trapped in a loop, totally oblivious to any witnesses. They are not friendly, but at least they aren't hostile. They are attached to a specific location, building, or even object, but they do no harm to observers.

Fame and Celebrity

As obsessed as we are with ghosts and the paranormal, it can't hold a candle to our obsession with anything or anyone famous. In today's world of Internet fame, anyone can become a celebrity for any reason, notorious or otherwise. But what is it about celebrities, whether they are movie and television stars, great athletes, or models and rock stars, that has such a hold on us? Why are we addicted to celebrity? In the February 24, 2012, issue of *LiveScience*, Stephanie Pappas writes in "Oscar Psychology: Why Celebrities Fasci-

Not all ghosts are evil by any means. For example, some pet owners feel that their dogs or cats have visited them from the other side.

nate Us" that it may be a combination of humans being social creatures and a fixation on those we deem above us, or at the top of the heap, because that is what we collectively aspire to. It also comes from a sense of knowing someone just because we saw them on television or heard them on the radio. We create a sense of kinship with famous people, even serial killers, simply because we feel like we know who they are.

Psychologist James Houran stated, "Celebrities act like a drug." We get our fix by focusing on what these people are wearing, doing, who they are dating, what they are eating, or any move, big or small, they make. It's a form of worship, just as we might worship a religious or spiritual leader. We feel like famous people are more important than we are, and we naturally want to dissect their lives to find out why. It also plays on our social tendencies to care about other people, and celebrities are open targets for that care. Sadly, they are also open targets for our consternation and gossip! We have a love/hate relationship with celebrities and successful, famous people.

When it comes to the rich, powerful, and famous, there is a natural voyeur in each and every one of us that wants to see how the "other half" lives, especially since they are rich and beautiful, living a lavish lifestyle we can only dream about. It can fill a void within and give us a sense of identity, especially if we are not following our own goals and dreams and have low self-esteem and a weak identity.

We live in a society in which throngs of people practically worship celebrities from movies, television, music, and sports (actor Will Smith takes a photo with fans here), so when a story comes out about a celebrity ghost, we are even more intrigued.

No matter the reasons why, we hand fame and fortune over to anyone nowadays, including reality stars with no real talent to speak of and criminals who get their own television shows, becoming stars in the process. We love celebrities. We love building them up, and we love tearing them down, all to fulfill deeper psychological needs to fill an emptiness within our own lives. We spend billions of dollars buying gossip magazines, watching movies and television shows, and reading juicy memoirs and autobiographies all to get close to these magical, mystical creatures known as stars.

In the April 2014 issue of *Reelrundown.com*, author Sheri Dusseault writes that there is a celebrity worship syndrome called Celebrity Worship Syndrome (CWS). Physiologist John F. Shumaker is quoted as saying "CWS is an obsessive/addictive disorder in which a person becomes involved with the details of a celebrity's personal life." It's the stuff of movies themselves, with average citizens living out the lives of their favorite stars and even harming themselves when their favorite celebrity gets engaged or married!

So, we give any celebrity a place at the top of a pedestal, whether the celebrity deserves it or not, and we worship at the feet of the pedestal until we feel the need to knock the celebrity *off* the pedestal, all of which serves a need to see the best and worst in others and compare ourselves to them. When we fail to measure up, jealousy and envy rear their ugly heads, and we destroy the very things we first worshipped. It must be hard to be rich and famous!

Just as someone might be famous in life, when they die, they take on an almost legendary status in death. Suddenly, the ghost of a celebrity becomes a desirable commodity that people will seek out, and even pay, to see. While your neighbors might pay to see the ghost that haunts the attic of your suburban split-level, who else really cares? But if that ghost was once a president of the United States or a world-famous golfer, you've got yourself a bona fide tourist trap.

The long-lost stars of the past are kept alive by the repeated sightings of their ghosts, haunting old movie sets, or stomping around the mansions they once owned. It's one thing to see the ghost of a total stranger, but to see the ghost of Marilyn Monroe, John Lennon, or Albert Einstein is something special indeed. Sometimes, the mansions these stars lived in themselves become the celebrity, as in the many homes that now give haunted tours to those who hope to catch a glimpse of the former resident, once a glorious star of stage or screen. Buildings and locations associated with events we all recognize also take on famous status simply because they are known to more than just one or two people. The more known the dead person or persons were in life, the more notorious and famous the locations they choose to haunt will be.

The more known the dead person or persons were in life, the more notorious and famous the locations they choose to haunt will be.

A motel on Route Anywhere in Anytown, USA, may have once been just another seedy motel, but after a movie star and her lover were found dead there in Room 15, it becomes a major haunted attraction that is featured in books, movies, and television shows and host to ghost hunters and tourists alike. People will even pay big bucks to stay in Room 15 just in the hopes of catching a glimpse of the ill-fated lovers floating from the bedroom to the kitchenette.

A dusty, musty basement is just a dusty, musty basement, but if a known figure in politics was murdered there, it suddenly becomes a mystical place worthy of being featured on a television reality show, where men and women sit in the dark with various pieces of equipment and hope to encounter, for the cameras, the ghost of the restless celebrity.

It is human nature to love to look up to anyone who has a huge circle of influence, even more so if they are good-looking, rich, and appear on our big or small screens. We think we know these people because we have access to them. Therefore, when they die, we feel just as entitled to have access to their spirits. And just as we are excited to glimpse a star in real life and then tell all our friends about it or post it on social networking, we are thrilled beyond thrilled to glimpse them in death, which brings up the important question—why are there not ghost paparazzi, too?

Rich. Famous. Glamorous. Dead.

In life, we are compelled to watch their every move, whether to judge or to envy their lifestyles, often so different from our own. Yet, the legacy of the famous lives on long after they are buried, often publicly, before crying and adoring fans or smiling and smug enemies. Whether they were once novelists with huge followings, theater actresses with voices of angels, glamourous movie queens, or romantic and iconic men of the big and small screens, the people we celebrate may leave something more behind for us than just souvenirs and signed, glossy, eight-by-ten photographs. They might leave behind their ghosts.

The most famous "famous" ghosts are those in the entertainment fields. Writers, poets, actors and actresses, movie stars and TV starlets, directors and playwrights—we are fascinated by those who entertain us.

Where there is drama, comedy and tragedy, action, thrills, and chills, there are ghosts. Just say the word "Hollywood," and images of old mansions belonging to silent movie stars mix with busy streets filled with aspiring starlets, walking with heads held high and high heels clicking on the pavement. Just think of the City of Angels, and one sees the "Hollywood" sign and conjures up imaginings of what it might be like to be a superstar, living in a massive house in the hills, driving an exotic car, and dining at the most exclusive restaurants, all before going to the set and making entertainment magic.

The entertainment capital of the world is filled with notorious haunted locations, often linked to famous movie stars, rock stars, television icons, and other notable faces that span the history of the town itself. Many current clubs, theaters, studios, production offices, gathering places, cafes, and restaurants were once the offices or homes of celebrities who died tragically, and others are built upon land with its own haunted history—former burial grounds, churches, cemeteries, asylums, and places already ripe with ghostly activity.

Sightings and reports of famous ghosts are common, but there are also many famous celebrities who have their own ghostly encounters to tell about. Many have appeared on popular reality shows featuring movie, television, and music stars who have come in contact with something otherworldly.

The stories of celebrity haunts and hauntings read like a trip down memory lane. These are our icons, our idols, and yet, just like any other human beings, they sometimes refuse to find peace in death.

Elvis Presley

The King of Rock n' Roll, Elvis Presley, achieved unprecedented fame and popularity during his career, and now, even after his death in 1977, people continue to report seeing his ghost in numerous places he once "haunted" in real life. His former Palm Springs home, the Las Vegas Hilton hotel he once performed at, and the old recording facility of RCA Studio B in Nashville, Tennessee … and, of course, Graceland in Memphis, where he can be seen peering out from upstairs windows at the thousands of visitors who come to the grounds. Often, people report hearing music coming from inside the house when it is empty and say the man they see is a ghostly apparition dressed just like the King of Swiveling Hips himself.

Singing legend Elvis Presley's ghost has been reportedly spotted at several locations, including near his grave (shown here) at his Graceland home in Memphis, Tennessee.

The old RCA Studio where he recorded "Heartbreak Hotel" is an alleged haunted hot spot, with people reporting his ghost wandering through the building. If his name is mentioned, ladders fall, lights explode, and there are bangs and noises heard throughout, according to witnesses.

Just as he got around in life, he seems to get around in death! He has even reportedly been seen in local Memphis Burger Kings, leading many to speculate that he may have faked his own death to escape the public eye. It also brings up the possibility that Elvis achieved such an incredible level of fame and notoriety, people think they are seeing him everywhere, mistaking other people for the dead singer. Then again, maybe his ghost is so restless and his spirit so big he cannot be confined to just one location.

The fact that Elvis's ghost is seen in several places, so often, by so many people brings up an interesting question. Is his ghost a big-time restless spirit racking up airline miles as it goes from one location to the next ... or do many Elvises exist in another dimension and in other locations all at the very same time? Theoretical physicists tell us there may be an infinite number of other realities out there, so it's possible at least a dozen have their own Elvis Aaron Presleys wandering about.

What is interesting about Elvis's case was his closeness to his mother, Gladys Presley, and how distraught he was when she died in 1958, just as his career was taking off. It would then make sense that his spirit would not want to linger here in our earthly plane, unable to cross into the light, as many psychics and mediums tell us ghosts are doing when they refuse to "move on," but would prefer to be reunited with his beloved mother, wherever she went to in death. Sadly, the only way to know for sure would be to ask his ghost, and often, spirits don't speak to the living.

Marilyn and the Bombshells

The ghost of the late actress and sex symbol Marilyn Monroe is said to also haunt multiple locations, including her former Brentwood home, her tomb at the Westwood Memorial Cemetery in Los Angeles, California, and the Hollywood Roosevelt Hotel, a location with its own haunted reputation. Witnesses report her image can be seen fading in and out of view in the full-length mirror that once decorated her Hollywood Roosevelt Hotel suite (Room 229), and others have seen her apparition dancing in the ballroom, playing a bugle as she wanders the eighth floor, or posing on the pool diving board for admiring fans. The ghosts of fellow legends Montgomery Clift and Carole Lombard are said to also haunt the same hotel. Clift's spirit can be heard playing the trumpet in Room 928 (as well as reported cold spots and strange noises in the room), and Lombard appears to like frequenting the twelfth floor of the hotel (Lombard is also said to haunt the Oatman Hotel in Arizona near the location of the fatal plane crash that took her life while she was married to Clark Gable, whose ghost also shows up on occasion).

Because she died so tragically, and her life was filled with scandal, many people believe that Marilyn is restless in death, trying to find the peace and acceptance she longed for in life, despite her climb to fame and adoration. Witnesses who have been on the White House tour even report seeing her ghost walking with that of John F. Kennedy, with whom she was romantically involved.

Actress Thelma Todd died at the young age of twenty-nine in 1935 from carbon monoxide poisoning. Her body, which also suffered from an apparent beating, was found in her car in the garage. Was it suicide or murder?

Another beautiful, blonde bombshell who now haunts Hollywood is Jean Harlow. She and her second husband, producer Paul Bern, are often seen roaming the mansion they once owned together. Bern took his own life in the mansions and has a creepy connection to cult leader Charles Manson. The man who purchased the mansion after Paul Bern's death was Jay Sebring, who was later murdered with actress Sharon Tate at her home four years later. Sharon even stayed at the Bern Mansion and saw the ghost of Paul Bern herself, sitting upon her bed!

Thelma Todd was a beautiful actress of old Hollywood. Her body was found in her 1934 Lincoln Phaeton convertible, inside the garage of her Pacific Palisades mansion in 1935, and there is speculation as to whether she was murdered or committed suicide. Thelma appeared in over 120 films between 1926 and 1935, starring with such luminaries as the Marx Brothers, Buster Keaton, Laurel and Hardy, and Jimmy Durante. She was only twenty-nine when she died of accidental carbon monoxide poisoning, and her death has been labeled suspicious ever since. According to *Haunted Hollywood: Tinseltown Terror, Filmdom Phantoms and Movieland Mayhem* by Tom Ogden, she had been drinking heavily when she got into the car and fell asleep. She ran the engine to warm herself up and intended to only run it for a few moments, but she dozed off and was overcome by carbon monoxide fumes in the closed garage.

But when her maid, Mae Whitehead, found the body in the car on Monday morning, Thelma Todd was covered in blood, and there was blood on the seat behind her as well as on the running boards and the floor of the garage. The coroner quickly ruled the death an accidental suicide, but many people at the time wondered if she had been murdered, maybe by a spurned lover, her ex-husband, or even by the Mob. There were even people who claimed to have seen her driving down Vine Street after the alleged time of her death!

Her ghost is said to haunt the old café she last visited before her death, appearing as a diaphanous form that floats down the stairs and glides into an open courtyard, as well as reports of a car engine starting in the garage her body was found in … despite no cars being inside at the time.

The famous and beloved redhead Lucille Ball died at the age of seventy-seven in her home in Beverly Hills. The owners of the home claim it is haunted and that furniture moves around on its own, objects appear and disappear, and there are a spate of loud noises and broken windows to contend with. Could the home be haunted by the comedic queen herself, who appeared so happy and successful in life and chooses to be playful even in death?

Another Hollywood hottie has a different kind of ghost story to tell. Elke Sommer was the German daughter of a Lutheran minister before she became a Hollywood star. She began her career as a model, then a beauty queen, before landing roles in German and Italian films that would make her an international star and sex symbol. She married a man named Joe Hyams, a journalist who covered the top Hollywood stars, and they moved into a Beverly Hills house that happened to be secluded, located on the popular Benedict Canyon Drive. It also happened to be haunted.

The ghostly shenanigans began the night they moved in with bangs, noises, and sounds coming from the first floor, below their master bedroom. It seemed to be coming from the dining room area, and because they never found any signs of break-ins, they assumed it might be the wildlife common to the area. But the sounds continued, and even got louder and more ominous, with tables and chairs moving and glass breaking. Yet, when they went downstairs to investigate, they saw nothing out of place.

This was followed by the sound of voices, and soon, there were telltale marks on the floor and objects moving on their own. As the activity escalated, they both saw the ghost of a man in the dining room. Many of their guests saw the ghost, too! Elke was so scared she got in touch with a local parapsychologist named Thelma Moss. Moss spent the next couple of years visiting the home time and time again. *Life* magazine even got wind and covered the story of the house. One psychic predicted that the house would burn in a fire within a year, starting in the dining room, and causing the occupants to jump out of the second-story window.

Eight months later, it happened. The house's first story was on fire, but Joe managed to get the flames out. They were informed the fire did indeed start in the dining room. The couple moved out soon after, and the home sold over and over to new buyers over a dozen times. The ghosts that lived there just didn't want the company and were determined to drive out anyone who moved in. Sommer went on to tell her full story to the *Saturday Evening Post* and in a 1986 documentary called *Hollywood Ghost Stories*.

Another legendary lady of the silver screen, Joan Crawford, had her own experiences that pushed her to call in an exorcist. It started when her daughter, Christina, claimed to hear the voices of little kids inside the walls of the house they lived in on Bristol Avenue in the ritzy Brentwood area of Los Angeles.

The children's ghosts were said to walk the halls, and when Joan heard them, too, she contacted a priest to perform an exorcism on the home.

Joan died in 1977, and fires would often spontaneously erupt in her bedroom. No cause for them was ever found. Future owners of the house, including performers Anthony Newley and Donald O'Connor, never reported an actual ghost but did claim to sense a presence of something sinister.

Princess Leia and the Ghost

Carrie Fisher will forever be known as Princess Leia in the iconic *Star Wars* movie franchise. Her death caused global mourning to the millions who loved her. But when she was alive, she had her own ghostly encounter in 2005 when her friend, Republican strategist R. Gregory Stevens's fell asleep next to her in bed after a party at her home. He woke up, and the two chatted into the night. She woke up the next morning to find him dead of an overdose.

From then on, she and other guests in the house would hear strange noises, and Fisher insisted she felt Stevens' presence often. Lights would turn on and off, and a toy talking machine would go on and off at night by itself in the closet where her friend's clothing still hung. A psychic later informed her that because Stevens died so young and tragically at the age of forty-two, his spirit was unwilling to accept death and move on.

Actress and author Carrie Fisher (who was best known for playing Princess Leia in the *Star Wars* films) had ghostly encounters with a friend who died in her home.

The Men of Hollywood Legends

Orson Welles is one of those multitalented legends of the big screen, noted for his skills at acting, writing, and directing. His name has become as classic and iconic as his work. Every film student studies the themes behind *Citizen Kane*, and his radio broadcast of H. G. Wells's *War of the Worlds* is itself legendary. Welles loved to hang out at a French restaurant called Ma Maison, which later became Sweet Lady Jane's Bakery, located on Melrose Avenue in Hollywood. Employees of the new bakery report seeing his ghost sitting at a corner table he frequented while alive, dressed to the nines in a black suit and wearing a wide-brimmed hat. Witnesses say that his visible ghost only sticks around for a few seconds, but the distinct smell of cigars and brandy linger on. And no, cigars and brandy are not on the bakery's menu.

Known as an embattled director with a penchant for drink, Welles was the epitome of a restless spirit in life and now in death.

Lon Chaney's face is not as notorious as the many monsters he played on the silver screen during his amazing career. He was a stage and film actor, director, and makeup artist and became known as the "Man of a Thousand Faces." He was a master of pantomime during the silent film era and today is most noted for the 1923 *Hunchback of Notre Dame*, in which he wore a fifty-pound prosthetic hump to play Quasimodo, and as the lead in the 1925 silent film version of *Phantom of the Opera*. After his death in 1973, people began reporting his ghost at the famous Stage 28 at Universal Studios, which in another chapter we will see has a long history of hauntings. The ghost of Chaney has been seen running and walking along the stage, throughout the studio building, and on the catwalks above the stage where *Phantom* was shot. He is even said to be dressed in his full costume! Interestingly, the part of the stage used to film the great "falling chandelier" scene survived several mysterious accidents.

The ghost of Chaney has been seen running and walking along the stage, throughout the studio building, and on the catwalks above the stage where *Phantom* was shot.

Chaney's ghost has also been spotted sitting on a bench near the corner of Hollywood and Vine streets, a frequent haunt of his.

He made *Superman* the legendary and iconic comic book figure that it is, yet George Reeves is not as widely known to today's younger movie audiences. In June 1959, Reeves was found dead with a bullet through his head. It was ruled a suicide, but many people believe Reeves was the victim of murder. His Benedict Canyon home was sold, and the new owners reported his ghost roaming the house in the very room where his body was found. Visitors to the home also report hearing gunshots, screams, and even seeing the full-bodied apparition of Reeves wearing his famous Superman costume.

Rudolph Valentino died young, adding to the legendary quality of this famous and romantic actor, who often bears the title of the world's first Hollywood silver screen heartthrob. His real name was a mouthful—Rodolfo Alfonso Raffaello Pierre Filibert Guglielmi di Valentina d'Antonguella.

The Italian silent film actor changed his name, for obvious reasons, and was considered the great swoon-worthy "lover" figure of the screen, causing women to allegedly faint in the aisles while viewing *The Sheik* in 1921. Valentino died tragically in 1926, at the age of thirty-one, from an infection he contracted during an operation, and people say that his home, named Falcon's Lair, has been haunted since that fateful day. The house in Hollywood was bought later by another actor, Harry Carey, who said he saw Valentino's handsome ghost on many occasions. Millicent Rogers, a noted fashion figure of the era, refused to

The world-renowned escape artist Harry Houdini (shown here in 1905) also believed in the afterlife and promised to contact his wife with a message after his death.

set foot in the mansion after she, too, spotted the ghost of Valentino. Valentino's ghost also appears to witnesses at the Santa Maria Inn, which was his beach home in Ventura County, California, as well as at Paramount Studios famed Studio 5.

Jack Carter was a popular comedian who, along with his wife, was friends with the Sheltons and visited their home often. Turns out the Shelton home was once owned by Conrad Hilton Jr., the son of the Hilton Hotel founder. Hilton Jr. was married to Elizabeth Taylor at one point, who divorced him for being an abusive drinker and gambler, and he was himself a popular socialite and businessman. He once had an affair with his stepmother, actress Zsa Zsa Gabor. He died at the young age of forty-two, in 1949, of an alcohol-related heart attack. The Sheltons had the Carters over one night, and Jack saw the ghost of Conrad Hilton Jr. in the study. Another time, the Carters saw blood appear spontaneously on the clean carpet and the liquor cabinet shake violently. Even later owners of the home reported spectral activity.

Houdini

Harry Houdini was not only an escape artist and magician. Between the years 1919 and 1923, he made silent films and even directed one. Though they were not major successes, it did add to his growing reputation as a star. Houdini also was passionate about debunking séances, reports of ghosts, and communications with the dead. He surely benefited from the publicity as he set about trying to disprove life after death and reveal mediums and psychics as frauds.

But that didn't mean he wasn't personally a believer in the occult and the paranormal. He was and spent a lot of time studying alleged ghost photographs and did hands-on research into the work of psychic photographer Alexander Martin, who he believed was authentic.

He tried to contact the dead himself on many occasions and even made a pact with his wife, Bess, that upon his own death, he would come back and contact her from the "other side." He gave her a private message, and Bess later offered up $10,000 to anyone who could bring the message out. She withdrew the offer after being bombarded with false claims. In January 1928, a psychic named Arthur Ford came forward and said he received the message "Forgive" from Houdini's mother. Bess was thrilled, as Houdini had often wanted a message from his dead mother himself. There was controversy suggesting Bess had revealed the word to a newspaper called the *Brooklyn Eagle* a year before, but later séances revealed a second word, "Rosabelle," and then a third, "Believe." Bess confirmed these as the actual message she and her husband had agreed on, but many would later suggest that Bess and Ford were working together to fool the public.

Message aside, those who have been in his former home claim he has, indeed, returned from the dead in the form of a ghostly apparition.

Pickfair

One of the most well-known celebrity hauntings involved a legend of silent films, Mary Pickford, who cofounded United Artists with Charlie Chaplin and her husband, Douglas Fairbanks. Pickford not only was an actress but also wrote and produced silent films. She was deeply involved in the industry and wasn't one to just sit back and act. She liked the hands-on experience of producing. She and Fairbanks lived on the eighteen-acre Beverly Hills, California, estate that became known as Pickfair. It was designed by the famous architect Wallace Neff and was one of the most famous homes in the world to the elite and wealthy, who often partied there.

During its heyday, the mansion was filled with expensive and often rare furniture, art, and antiques, including a collection of art Pickford and Fairbanks brought back from their many trips to China and the Far East. The interior was designed and redesigned by the best designers in the world, and the home became the social hot spot and place to be for the likes of Charlie Chaplin, the Duke and Duchess of Windsor, Thomas Edison, Amelia Earhart, F. Scott Fitzgerald, H. G. Wells, Franklin D. Roosevelt, Charles Lindbergh, Gloria Swanson, Albert Einstein, and many other notables.

When Pickford and Fairbanks divorced in 1936, Pickford remained in the mansion with her eventual new husband, musician Buddy Rogers. She died in 1979. In her later years, Pickford rarely entertained and usually only for charitable organizations. Pickfair was no more.

Enter the ghosts in 1988, when actress Pia Zadora purchased the home from Los Angeles Lakers owner Jerry Buss. Zadora bought the home with her husband, Meshulam Riklis, and demolished the original structure to build a Venetian-style palazzo to suit her tastes. She was vilified by the public for doing something so awful to such a beloved Hollywood landmark. But there was more to this story than meets the eye.

In 2012, Zadora revealed on an episode of the Bio Channel's *Celebrity Ghost Stories* that she did so because the place was haunted by the laughing ghost of a woman dressed in 1920s attire and not the termite infestation she had originally told the public. She spoke on the show about moving into the home, which was wonderful at first, but then experiencing strange things that terrified her children at night and, eventually, after trying an exorcist who failed to rid the home of the female ghost drove her and her husband to the decision of razing the house. She claimed she would NEVER have torn down the iconic house just because of termites or bad plumbing because those were things you could deal with.

Not so much for the supernatural!

A Foxxy Ghost

Comedian and actor Redd Foxx, who is most known for his role as the cranky Fred Sanford on television's hugely successful series *Sanford and Son*, which ran from 1972 to 1977, haunts Paramount Studios, most notably the notorious Stage 31. It was here Foxx died of a heart attack, and witnesses report hearing his distinct laugh echoing across the stage. Foxx is also said to haunt his former Vegas home, which he lost after a long battle with the IRS over unpaid taxes.

Director Peter Jackson once had a scary encounter with the ghost of a dead actress who had killed herself in London.

The new owners have reported seeing Foxx's ghost walking around in a bathrobe, as well as lights turning on and off and a sliding door opening and closing by itself. The home was purchased by Nevada Aqua Air Systems, and even after employees replaced the sliding door with a wood door that swings, they continue to report the door has a mind of its own.

Lord of the Rings

Famed New Zealand film director Peter Jackson, best known for the *Lord of the Rings* trilogy and *The Hobbit*, had a ghostly encounter in 2009, when he and his wife stayed in an apartment located across from the St. James Theatre in London, England. In an interview with British Channel 4 television, he stated, "I woke up one morning and there was a figure in the room. She was very scary; she had a screaming face, very accusatory. She was a lady about fifty years old." He was terrified as she glided from the foot of the bed, across the room, and vanished into the wall.

When he told his wife, she responded, "Was it the woman with the screaming face?" They had never spoken before about the ghost. They did some research and discovered the screaming woman was known around the theater by others who had seen her. She was once an actress who had taken her own life after she got a terrible review of her vaudeville show. Seems bad reviews and rejection in the entertainment world took their fair share of lives of those with big dreams of lasting success. At least Jackson went on to find great success as a director.

The Shape of Ghosts

Oscar-winning director Guillermo del Toro, who is known for his science fiction and fantasy films, including *The Shape of Water*, told *The Hollywood Reporter*'s Stephen Galloway in the December 21, 2017, issue that he not only saw what he believed was a UFO as a young man, but he witnessed a ghostly apparition while on a trip to a haunted hotel with famous composer Danny Elfman and writer Mike Mignola. He described the ghost as having a "really sad sigh," but that was about the extent of the encounter.

The UFO, on the other hand, was a superfast, classic saucer shape with blinking lights. He felt a primal fear during the sighting, which occurred at the Cerro del Cuatro ("Mountain of the Four") outside of Guadalajara, Mexico, an area well known for its UFO activity.

Ghosts of the Music World

John Lennon's death rocked the world. Whether you loved his music or not, he was one of the most influential figures of the peace movement, and the records he made with the Beatles and as a solo artist have remained iconic and without comparison. He made global headlines when he was shot outside the Dakota Apartments in New York City, where he lived in December 1980. The killer was a young man named Mark David Chapman, who had been stalking Lennon for months and later told police he shot Lennon to become famous.

After Lennon's death, his ghost was said to roam the Dakota building, appearing to bandmates and family. The Dakota building was the setting of the spooky horror film *Rosemary's Baby*, but his ghost also showed up in the recording studio, according to fellow Beatle alumnus Paul McCartney in numerous interviews, including during the recording of "Free as a Bird" in 1995, which was written by Lennon. McCartney, Ringo Starr, and George Harrison felt his playful presence in the form of unexplained noises and equipment acting strangely. The musicians stated they felt Lennon's presence all around them.

Oasis lead singer Liam Gallagher also experienced John Lennon's ghost while recording an unfinished symphony of Lennon's with McCartney. According to Arthur Myers, author of *Ghosts of the Rich and Famous*, a woman named Barbara Garwell, who lived in England and worked with a parapsychologist, claimed Lennon appeared at the foot of her bed at the moment he was shot in New York. Photographer Bob Freeman, who had shot many of the Beatles's album covers, was in Hong Kong at the time and said that a framed picture of John dropped from the wall at the time of his death.

McCartney, Ringo Starr, and George Harrison felt his playful presence in the form of unexplained noises and equipment acting strangely. The musicians stated they felt Lennon's presence all around them.

But it doesn't end there. Lennon, while he was alive, saw a spectral ghost called "The Crying Lady" wandering down the hallways of the Dakota building. He believed in the paranormal enough to tell his first wife, Cynthia, that he would send her a sign when he died, one that would involve a feather. In 1986, she found a dead jackdaw bird wrapped in newspaper tucked behind the fireplace of her home.

Speaking of feathers, during a photo shoot for "Free as a Bird," McCartney reported that a white peacock came over from a nearby farm and visited. The other members of the Beatles agreed it was John making his presence known.

According to "John Lennon's Ghost" in the *Seeks Ghosts* blog post of February 14, 2012, John's ghost was spotted by musician Joey Harrow and his friend Amanda Moores, standing near the door of the Dakota entrance. He was surrounded by an eerie light. Lennon's beloved wife, Yoko Ono, reported seeing John's ghost playing a white piano in the home they shared. Lennon turned to her and said, "Don't be afraid, I am still with you."

Those who loved John Lennon have his music to live on forever, but just maybe, his spirit is also alive and well.

Rock music icon Janis Joplin died of a heroin overdose on October 4, 1970, in Room 105 of the Landmark Hotel in Hollywood. Her ghost has been spotted in the room and other parts of the building, which is now called the Highland Gardens. If you speak her name out loud in the lobby, pictures on the wall will move and doors will slam shut.

Crooner and actor Frank Sinatra loved spending time at the Cal Neva Resort and Casino on the shore of Lake Tahoe, where he owned Lakeview Cabin #5 from 1960 to 1963, when authorities shut down the casino after finding mobster Sam Giancana on the premises. After Sinatra's death, his ghost has been spotted at the cabin, and just two doors down, at Cabin #3, visitors have also reported seeing the ghost of another famous guest who often spent time there: Marilyn Monroe. Her ghost has also been reported in the resort swimming pool she loved to frequent.

Sinatra's ghost may have been haunting his former home in Los Angeles as well, at least according to an encounter country music star Tim McGraw and his four-year-old daughter, Gracie, had. The *Nash Country Daily* reported on March 28, 2017, that Tim and his wife, country music star Faith Hill, had been looking for a home to rent. McGraw visited the former Sinatra home with his young daughter. Sinatra's furniture was still in the house, including his piano. Gracie went to sit down at the piano, choosing to sit at the very end of the piano bench.

There was a photo of Frank Sinatra at the top of the stairs, and when Gracie went upstairs and saw the image, she stopped and said, "Dad, that's the guy." Tim asked her what she meant, and Gracie responded, "That's the guy that was at the piano with me." Then she told her dad that Frank's ghost went into the kitchen and vanished behind a hidden door.

The family was spooked and surprised! But they still ended up renting the house.

The Flamboyant Liberace

The flamboyant pianist and entertainer known to the world as Liberace died from complications of AIDS after a forty-year career in music, movies, television, and stage shows. His real name was Władziu Valentino Liberace, and he was a child prodigy, which few people know about. The son of Polish and Italian immigrants, he was a huge star in Las Vegas, and his ghost is said to haunt the very restaurant he designed, Carluccio's Tivoli Gardens. Few people know that he loved to cook and loved to cook in his restaurant, which was originally called Liberace's Tivoli Gardens. Many who visited after his death have reported hearing a piano playing, experiencing cold spots at the piano, lights going on and off, faucets turning on and off, and bottles falling from shelves.

1950s rock sensation Buddy Holly died in a plane crash with fellow musicians Ritchie Valens and J. P. "The Big Bopper" Richardson Jr. in 1959, an event immortalized in the song "American Pie" by Don McLean.

Buddy Holly

On February 3, 1959, the world lost three true rock legends when a plane crash near Clear Lake, Iowa, took the lives of Buddy Holly, Ritchie Valens, and J. P. "The

Big Bopper" Richardson Jr. The pilot, Roger Peterson, also died. Fans would flock to the crash site for years, many reporting seeing a phantom plane flying overhead and ghostly lights in the field where the plane crashed. Others report hearing Buddy's music near where he is buried at the City of Lubbock Cemetery in Texas and even in his former high school classroom at Lubbock High in the dead of night.

That tragic day would go down in history in one of the biggest hit songs ever written, the 1971 "American Pie" by Don McLean, which was a tribute to the fallen stars and "the day the music died." Yet, the music lives on in the form of recordings and the ghosts of those who died in the crash, like Buddy Holly, who continues to play his songs for anyone alive who will listen.

Jim Morrison

Rock star, poet, idol, enigma. The lead singer of The Doors died of an alleged drug overdose in his apartment in Paris in 1971. His ghost has been spotted around the Paris cemetery where he is buried, and Rhonda Baron, a female fan, stated in *Haunted Rock and Roll: Ghostly Tales of Musical Legends* that his ghost climbed into bed with her on numerous occasions and had sex with her.

Morrison's ghost is also said to haunt the Sunset Sound recording studio. Many dead musicians seem to like hanging out at the studios where they made the music they loved, including Warren Zevon, a singer–songwriter who haunts The Cave, where he spent time making records.

The ghost of rocker Jim Morrison has itself become a legend in the form of a photograph circulating the Internet of Morrison haunting the Pere Lachaise Cemetery in Paris, France, where he was buried. The image shows a man dressed quite like Morrison did when alive. Taken in 1977, it shows rock historian Brett Meisner standing beside Morrison's headstone, where the image is alleged to show up. According to *Rolling Stone* magazine's "Unexplainable Photo Snapped at Jim Morrison's Grave" in the October 16, 2009, issue, the photo is authentic and has not been tampered with, although newer paranormal researchers have attempted to debunk it. Photo experts at the time stated it was not tampered with, and Meisner himself has reported that since that fateful visit, he has been plagued by strange events ever since, including the death of a close friend, the end of his marriage, and strangers approaching him and claiming now they, too, are haunted by Morrison's ghost.

Meisner has claimed the vibe around the photograph turned from positive to negative, and since then, many witnesses have reported seeing the icon's spirit hovering about the gravesite. As for the photo, it is still up for debate, but those who knew Morrison well said his past tragic encounter seeing a Native American ghost after a car accident may have shaped his own beliefs in the existence of the paranormal.

Gram Parsons

Gram Parsons, who played with the Flying Burrito Brothers and often collaborated with Emmylou Harris, his lover, was interested in UFOs and spent a lot of time out in Joshua Tree National Park, California, a desert area known for sightings of aliens. He even ended his life with an overdose of drugs at the Joshua Tree Inn, where witnesses report his spirit haunts Room 8. His best friend, Phil Kaufman, drove to Los Angeles International Airport and stole Parsons's ashes from his family after he was cremated and made sure to fulfill Parsons's last wish of having them spread over the desert landscape. Tourists spending the night at the inn can rent Room 8 in hopes of seeing his ghost. There is even an ad for the inn that states, "Room 8 is haunted—bring your guitar and write songs."

Johnny Horton

One of country music's legends was Johnny Horton, who sang such classics as "The Battle of New Orleans," "North to Alaska," and "Johnny Reb." From the start, Horton was interested in the spirit world and often met with a medium named Bernard Ricks. According to "Growing Up Kilgore: The Johnny Horton Story" for the *Nashville Music Guide*'s August 21, 2012, edition, Horton had a secret code he made with singer/songwriter and good friend Merle Kilgore, like the one Harry Houdini had with his wife. Johnny had a strange feeling he would die and wanted a way to communicate with Merle afterward.

One week later, Johnny was killed by a drunk driver while on his way to a show in College Station, Texas. Years after that, Merle Kilgore was visiting an old friend, radio announcer Bob Lockwood, who introduced Kilgore on the air. Lockwood then went on to play the song "Ring of Fire," which Kilgore had written for Johnny Cash (he cowrote it with Cash's wife, June Carter). During the song, a woman called in to the show saying she was part of a group of psychics that had been together the night before and received an unusual name on their Ouija board. The name? Merle Kilgore.

But that wasn't the whole message. On the Ouija board, the same force or spirit had written the strange message, "The drummer is a rummer and he can't hold the beat." Kilgore heard this and freaked. That was the exact secret code he had created with Horton before his death!

Sid Vicious

Punk rocker and bassist for the legendary Sex Pistols lived in Room 100 of the Chelsea Hotel in New York City with girlfriend Nancy Spungen. In 1978, he was accused of murdering Nancy and died of a drug overdose while out on bail before a verdict was ever reached in the case. People at the hotel report seeing Sid's ghost hanging around the hotel's elevators. Welsh poet Dylan Thomas's ghost has also been seen roaming the halls of the hotel, where he fell into a coma before his death.

Eddie Hinton

Eddie was the troubled guitarist for the Mussel Shoals Sound Rhythm Section. He died in 1995 and was buried in a blue suit. Later, when the Black Keys were recording at the Mussel Shoals Sound Studio, a famous studio in Alabama where big names made their records, including Hinton's band, the members reported seeing an apparition in a blue suit. They also experienced many malfunctions of studio equipment that may have been the ghost of Hinton interfering.

Hank Williams

Country music icon Hank Williams is a busy ghost! He is regarded as one of the most influential musicians of the twentieth century and keeps busy even after his death in 1953 by haunting Nashville's Ryman Auditorium, the former home of the famed Grand Ole Opry. Williams performed there many times, and employees have claimed they've run into his ghost backstage or onstage after the venue has closed. Perhaps he is waiting for his cue to take the stage and perform as he loved to in life.

Jimi Hendrix

Another legend and icon, rock guitarist Jimi Hendrix, died in 1970 at the height of his career as one of the greatest musicians of the twentieth century. His death was considered mysterious because he was staying in London with a woman named Monika Dannemann, who found him in her apartment one morning unconscious and unresponsive. He was taken to the hospital and pronounced dead shortly after, and the cause of death was listed as an overdose of barbiturates and aspiration from his own vomit. His ghost is said to be heard playing guitar around a bronze statue of him that was erected on the Isle of Wight, where he played his final concert.

The ghost of guitarist Jimi Hendrix is said to haunt the Isle of Wight, where he had his final concert.

Hendrix was more than just one of the most celebrated musicians of his time. He was also someone who experienced paranormal phenomena, including UFO sightings. His music and lyrics reflected his beliefs in other worlds and other beings that existed there, and he often spoke in interviews of his interest in UFOs and aliens. According to "Jimi Hendrix's Ghost and His UFO and Alien Encounters" by Paul Seaburn for the April 6, 2017, *Mysterious Universe*, Jimi performed at an extinct volcano in Maui, and those present saw UFOs while Hendrix chilled out between sets in a Hopi tent.

Jimi was once a member of the group Curtis Knight and the Squires. Curtis Knight says the band had an encounter with a landed UFO while near Woodstock, New York, in 1965. Their car got stuck there in a snowstorm, and they all witnessed the UFO land in front of the car, melt the ice, and warm the car enough to get it back on the road. Some people suggest Jimi's out-of-this-world lyrics were the result of too many drugs, but perhaps they were more about his real-life experiences than they could ever have imagined.

Miley Sees a Ghost

Miley Cyrus, the pop singer turned iconic performer, had her own terrifying ghostly encounters during her 2009 London tour. She rented a flat in London and was staying with her family, including her kid sister, Noah, when she heard Noah scream from the bathroom shower. The hot water knob had turned on by itself, burning Noah. Miley later saw a little boy sitting on the sink while she tried to shower. He showed up the next night, too, and, when she did some research into the flat, learned that it was once owned by a family of three. The parents had died, leaving behind a little boy, the same boy she claimed to have seen on the sink.

Ariana Grande ... reported feeling sick and smelling sulfur, a scent often associated with the dead and ghosts, and felt such a sense of negativity....

The Cyrus family left the flat immediately after!

Demi Lovato Sees a Ghost

Pop starlet Demi Lovato claims her home in Texas, where she grew up, is haunted by a little girl named Emily. The ghostly presence and her name were confirmed by a psychic and ghost hunters who came to the home to investigate. Lovato claims she saw Emily many times as a child. The ghost was often seen in the closet, and Lovato would sometimes be talking to the ghost when her mother came into the room. When her mom asked who she was conversing with, Lovato would say quite matter-of-factly, "My best friend, Emily." Imaginary friend or real ghost? Maybe both?

Ariana Grande Sees a Ghost, Too!

Another pop starlet, Ariana Grande, told *Complex* magazine in 2013 about her own encounter in a Kansas City haunted castle and the infamous "Skull Cemetery," said to be the gateway to the Seven Gates of Hell. She reported feeling sick and smelling sulfur, a scent often associated with the dead and ghosts, and felt such a sense of negativity, she rolled down the windows and apologized to the dead buried in the cemetery for disturbing their peaceful slumber.

She took a photo which later showed three faces that were not there, looking just like demons, but when she sent the photo to her manager, the file showed that it couldn't be opened and that it was 666 megabytes in size. She continued to experience weird sounds and sensations afterward and eventually was able to put an end to the strange goings-on by relaxing and not giving in to her fears.

Celebrities Who Have Ghost Encounters of Their Own

Lady Gaga is famous for her music and acting chops and often dresses in bizarre and eye-catching costumes as part of her onstage persona. In May 2010, England's *Mirror* news outlet reported that she had spent a few thousand dollars on an electromagnetic field sweeper and other equipment to remove what she called "bad energy" in the form of dark spirits before her Monster' Ball London concert. Her aide told the *Mirror* they were taking the equipment on the road with them to make sure each location was clear of any spirits and, several months later, held a séance to rid a spirit, whose name was Ryan. Gaga was allegedly annoyed and afraid of the ghost enough to take such measures. No word on whether she still uses the equipment now that her acting career is taking off.

Sting, the singer and former frontman for The Police, claimed he once saw a ghost in the bedroom of an old house he lived in along with his wife, Trudie Styler. In an interview with *The Telegraph*, he claimed they saw a figure standing in the corner with a child one night when they were in bed. Sting woke up and thought his wife was standing with a child. He thought it strange she would be standing there, even more so with a child, but then realized she was right next to him in bed. He got a terrible chill when Trudi then woke up and asked who the woman and child were, standing in the corner. Sting said the figures just vanished into thin air. He also claimed objects would fly around the home, and they would often hear disembodied voices. Yet, he ended the interview with the strange comment, "When you live in old houses you get this energy there. Intellectually, no I don't believe in them (ghosts), but I've experienced them on an emotional level." Pretty sure objects flying around a house on their own goes way beyond the emotional level!

Actress Laura Linney was interviewed by James Corden on *The Late Late Show* and told the story of how she went from ghost skeptic to believer. She was inside The Belasco Theater on Broadway, which had a reputation of being haunted by those who performed and worked there. A chorus girl died at the Theater during a dress rehearsal, and Laura was shocked to see the ghost while she was doing a play with Jane Alexander. She pointed out a woman in the front row of an upper balcony that was supposedly closed off to Jane. The woman had blonde hair and wore a blue dress. Jane saw the woman, too, but when they looked again, the ghost had vanished. Laura later told the house manager she saw a ghost. He replied, "Male or female?" Laura said, "Female." He then said, "Blue dress, blonde hair?" The resident chorus girl ghost was watching the actors from above, wishing she had gotten to the stage before her own tragic death.

Hillary Clinton may not be a movie star, but according to the book *The Choice*, *Washington Post* reporter Bob Woodward wrote that in 1995 the first lady was visited in the White House by her spiritual adviser, Jean Houston, who came to channel Hillary's idol, Eleanor Roosevelt. The ceremony was similar to a séance and allowed Hillary to communicate with Eleanor. At one point, Hillary responded in Eleanor's voice, saying, "I was misunderstood.... You have to do what you think is right ... it was crucial to set a course and hold to it." One has to wonder if Eleanor came back at a later date to give Hillary some advice on how to recover from her loss to Donald Trump in the 2016 presidential election.

Former first lady and U.S. secretary of state Hillary Clinton reportedly hired spiritual adviser Jean Houston to channel Eleanor Roosevelt.

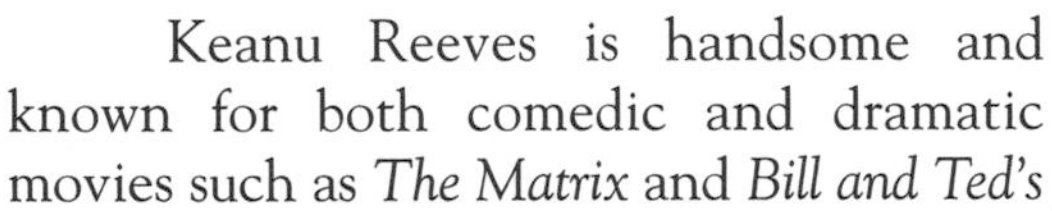

Keanu Reeves is handsome and known for both comedic and dramatic movies such as *The Matrix* and *Bill and Ted's Excellent Adventure*. As a child growing up in New Jersey, he felt the presence of a ghost and saw a man dressed in a white, double-breasted suit with no torso or legs in it. The ghost entered his bedroom, then vanished. Keanu said his nanny also witnessed the strange apparition, and he claims to sometimes still see the man in his dreams.

Actress Alyson Hannigan was no stranger to bizarre and evil entities, having played Willow, the popular character on the *Buffy, the Vampire Slayer* television series for years. She and her husband apparently encountered a ghost in a Los Angeles house they moved into in 2003. A friend saw the ghost first, claiming the ghost followed them out of the house. Alyson stated in an interview the ghost was not intrusive and seemed friendly.

Singer Robbie Williams moved into the house once owned by Beatles drummer Ringo Starr in Los Angeles, according to the *Sunday Post*. The moving men claimed there was a woman sitting in the chair in the house, and they refused to go in! The house was haunted not just by the strange, old woman but by several children, who could be seen and heard playing outside in the garden. Ringo's son, Zak Starkey, once asked Robbie if he had met the children in the garden and the old lady, so clearly, the house had been haunted when Ringo lived in it, too.

Telly Savalas, the bald actor who gained fame playing a lollipop-sucking New York detective named Kojak in the 1970s, had an especially intriguing ghostly encounter years ago, when his car ran out of gas. He had to start walking and wanted a lift to a gas station. A black Cadillac pulled up, and he heard a man's voice ask if he needed a lift, so he said yes. He even loaned Telly a dollar to get gas (this was a long time ago, folks!), and Telly made the man write down his name and phone number so he could pay him back and return the favor. Later, Telly looked up the man's name in the phone book (this was before cell phones, folks!) and found the number. When he called, a woman answered and said she was the man's wife. She told Telly the man had been dead for three years. Telly met her and showed her the handwriting, and she confirmed it was her husband's. She also confirmed her husband owned the clothes Telly said the man was wearing at the time. Telly's catchphrase as Kojak was "Who loves ya, baby?" In this case, it was a nice ghost with a dollar to spare.

She told Telly the man had been dead for three years. Telly met her and showed her the handwriting, and she confirmed it was her husband's.

It's nice to know that there are Good Samaritans out there that will help in times of need, whether they are dead or alive.

Racing legend Dale Earnhardt Jr. recounted an encounter with a ghost on his *The Dale Jr. Download* podcast. He crashed a Corvette in 2004 in Sonoma, California, and the car caught on fire. He felt someone pulling him out of the burning car and thought it was a corner worker by the way the person pulled him from under the armpits. He had no recollection of ever getting out of the car on his own. Everything was moving in slow motion, common during an emergency, and he distinctly felt himself being pulled over the door bars, then being let go. He fell to the ground, and there were many photographs taken of him on the ground but none of him coming out of the car. He asked at the hospital later over and over who helped him so he could thank the person later, but there was no one there. Ghost or angel?

The Blues Brothers

When famous actor and comedian John Belushi, famous for his hilarious movies and stints on *Saturday Night Live*, died in 1982 from a drug overdose, his best friend, Dan Aykroyd, who costarred with Belushi in *The Blues Brothers*, claimed he saw Belushi's ghost haunting the studio they had worked in together—Studio 8H. Aykroyd, also an avid UFO enthusiast, believed Belushi's spirit was trapped in some kind of limbo in the studio.

Aykroyd grew up with a grandfather who was not only a Canadian Mountie but the son of a mystic who was adept at the writings of spiritualists and occultists. Growing up in the old family farmhouse in Ontario, Canada, he was exposed to these things from an early age and went on to have a strong interest in, and appreciation of, the paranormal. In addition to the ghost of Belushi, he also claims he once lived in the house that was once owned by Cass Elliot of the Mamas and the Papas and that the Hollywood house was said to be haunted, according to an interview with him in *Esquire.com*'s October 30, 2013, edition. He reports seeing things moving on their own and doors opening and closing and states even the staff had their own paranormal experiences.

Aykroyd even reports having photographs of himself at the famous Myrtles Plantation, a haunted bed-and-breakfast in South Carolina. In the background of the photos are orb like heads with hair and other swirling images he cannot explain. His avid belief in both ghosts and extraterrestrials have gotten him on television shows and radio shows discussing the spooky subjects with authority. And remember, he did star in *Ghostbusters*!

Michael Jackson's Haunted Cabinet

Did the late Michael Jackson own a haunted cabinet? According to Dan Aykroyd during an interview with *Esquire* magazine in October 2013, mega-superstar Jackson owned a wardrobe that he believed was possessed by spirits. According to Craig and Jane Hamilton-Parker, two mediums and mystic teachers, Jackson also claimed he could communicate with another famous dead musician—Liberace, the flamboyant pianist who died in 1987. In an article titled "Ghosts: Dead Celebrities Make a Comeback!" for a British blog, the couple also report that Michael Jackson had a secret room with moving walls and mirrors, and it was in that room he had his communications with Liberace. Jackson claimed to feel the older man's presence and likened Liberace to a guardian angel.

Ironically, Liberace had his own paranormal experiences, claiming he once owned a piano that belonged to Franz Liszt, the famed classical composer. Liberace felt that he was inspired by the spirit of Liszt to write music on his piano.

The "King of Pop," Michael Jackson was often characterized as a bit quirky. One example might be that he believed he owned a wardrobe that was possessed by spirits.

Ghosts of the Pop World

That same psychic couple also reported on their blog that Roger Daltrey of the British rock band The Who spoke to the spirit of the dead drummer, Keith Moon. Moon died of a drug overdose in 1978, and the band was never the same without his iconic sound and personality. Another pop star, Neil Tennant of the Pet Shop Boys, claimed he communicated with dead spirits and even saw the future while using a Ouija board. He was told, at the age of fifteen during a séance, that he would be famous one day. And the spirit who told him that? None other than the ghost of Oscar Wilde!

Sting, the singer for the rock band The Police, once dealt with a chaotic ghost that haunted his home and flung sharp knives across the kitchen. He also claimed the hanging mobiles in his daughter's bedroom would spin, even when there was no one in the room and the window was closed. Many celebrities see the ghosts of other celebrities, as did Jane Fonda, famed actress, who saw the spirit of her equally famous father, Henry Fonda, who passed away in 1982.

So, Sting's case is a bit more unique, as the alleged poltergeist was not someone identifiable.

The Cursed Car of James Dean

One of the most iconic individuals in entertainment history was James Dean, born James Byron Dean in the town of Marion, Indiana, in 1931. This young and handsome man would soon become one of the greatest movie stars

This replica of James Dean's 1955 Porsche 550 Spyder was on display at a 2013 car show at the Los Angeles Arboretum. The young actor died while driving this car on California's Route 41. Some believed the car to be cursed.

of the Golden Age of Hollywood as well as a sex symbol, and his legend lives on long after his death in a car crash in 1955.

This star of *Rebel without a Cause* doesn't necessarily haunt anyone in ghostly form, but he does have his own urban legend. The car he died in a head-on collision in was a Porsche Spyder he had hoped to one day race. Dean loved living in the fast lane, so he naturally fell in love with the silver-gray 1955 Porsche Spyder, even naming it "Little Bastard." He painted the number 130 on its side and replaced the windshield with a smaller racing shield.

The legend begins when, on September 23, 1955, Dean showed the car to actor Alec Guinness outside a restaurant. Guinness commented that the car had a sinister look to it and told Dean he would die in the car by the same time the next week. In fact, Dean was killed in the car a week later, when he tried to avoid a car making a left turn onto Route 41 heading toward Fresno. The other driver, a Cal Poly student named Donald Turnupseed, crossed over the center line and was slammed into by Dean's car, which was doing upward of 85 miles per hour. Dean was killed instantly from a broken neck and internal injuries. His passenger, mechanic Rolf Wutherich, was injured but survived. Turnupseed suffered minor injuries.

But it was what would come afterward that turned the whole situation into a notorious urban legend that lives on to this day. The wrecked car was taken to the garage of car customizer George Barris, who bought it for $2,500. The Porsche fell on a mechanic during the unloading and broke both his legs. Then, two physicians purchased parts from the car for their own racing cars. One of them died shortly after during a race, and the other was injured in a car rollover.

Fans would break into the garage to try to steal pieces of the wreckage, injuring themselves as a result, which forced Barris to store it away at a garage in Fresno. The garage caught fire, and everything inside was destroyed except for Little Bastard. The car would later be a part of exhibits, including one at a high school, when it fell and broke a student's hip. Then, on a flatbed truck heading toward Salinas, George Barkulus lost control of the truck and was thrown out onto the ground. What killed him, though, was Little Bastard falling off and crushing him to death.

The car would fall off another flatbed truck two years later and cause an accident, and in 1958, a truck carrying wreckage pieces slipped from its hillside parking spot and crashed into a car.

In 1959, the car was on display in New Orleans when it mysteriously broke into eleven pieces. No one knew why. A year later, when the car was heading back to Barris's garage from a trip to Florida, it vanished and hasn't been found since.

Rumors spread that Dean's car was cursed because of his alleged involvement with Satanism and the occult, thanks to his association with a Los Angeles coven and an actress named Maila Nurmi, who starred in *Vampira* and may or may not have cursed Dean. Regardless, his legend as an icon lives on, and as for his car, it may turn up again someday to continue the curse.

There are those who say Dean's ghost haunts the Park Cemetery in Fairmount, Indiana, where his grave sits on a small hill. Because Dean was an avid smoker, there is a legend that says if you leave an unlit cigarette at his grave and walk away, when you return, the cigarette will be lit, and there will be the smell of smoke in the air. Other witnesses report seeing Dean sitting on his gravestone being eternally cool.

Serial Killer Ghosts

Serial killers are notorious in life, and also in death, according to numerous reports. While we might expect their many victims, who died under the most tragic and violent of circumstances, to become ghosts, it isn't often the killers themselves are witnessed. Ted Bundy is one of the worst, having grown up in Tacoma, Washington, as a child. He was nine years old when his family moved to the area, and his bedroom was located on the second floor of the house, where he lived with his mother, stepfather, and four siblings. Bundy may have been fourteen when he killed his first victim, fueled by an obsession with pornography, according to his final interview with a psychologist before his execution in 1989 in the Florida State Prison.

His killing spree, which included rape, torture, and necrophilia, was linked to at least thirty deaths but possibly dozens more and began in 1974, lasting for years and spanning eleven states.

Cell phones and electronics would die or get unplugged from sockets, and the word "leave" was found in the bedroom on the floor with no footprints nearby.

Now his childhood home is haunted, according to those who have experienced the bizarre activity. Cell phones and electronics would die or get unplugged from sockets, and the word "leave" was found in the bedroom on the floor with no footprints nearby. Another time, the words "help me" appeared on a basement window. Furniture has been known to fall over or move on its own.

Two pastors were called in to help cleanse the house, reciting Bible verses as they went from room to room. Christian music was played as they blessed the home. Even real estate agents trying to sell the house were aware of the bizarre activity, which probably sent some buyers running for the hills.

Another haunted serial killer's home is a farm located in La Porte, Indiana, where the bodies of over a dozen victims were buried beneath the farm owned by a notorious killer, Belle Guinness. It is her ghost, and not the ghosts of the victims, locals report seeing wandering about the farm.

Fox Hollow Farm

The same thing happens at the Fox Hollow Farm in Indiana, where another serial killer's ghost is reportedly on the property. Herb Baumeister burned and buried eleven male victims on the farm, discovered in 1996 when his wife led police to investigate the land. The investigation turned up over 5,500 bones and bone fragments from a large burn spot and the compost area. Baumeister fled to Canada, intending to take his own life. His sadistic tendencies began at a young age, when he enjoyed torturing animals and playing with their dead bodies. He was antisocial and, in his teens, was admitted for psychiatric evaluation. He was diagnosed as a schizophrenic and was again institutionalized as an adult for two months in the 1970s. Yet, on the outside, he looked like a normal person, marrying and having three children. He was also the founder of Sav-A-Lot thrift stores. Just goes to show that you never really know your neighbors.

Baumeister never confessed to the crimes he was charged with, but enough evidence existed pointing directly to him. One day after being stopped by a Canadian trooper and eventually let go, he went to Pinery Provincial Park and shot himself with a .357 Magnum, leaving behind a three-page suicide note about family and financial woes being the reason for his suicide. He didn't mention any of the murders he was charged with.

His property was purchased in 2009 by a couple, Rob and Vicky Graves, who knew of the gruesome history of the farm and rented one of the property's apartments to a friend with a dog. Soon after, the man started having horrendous nightmares and began experiencing problems with electrical appliances, which would unplug or malfunction.

The man and his dog were subject to phantom knocks on walls, floors, and doors all through the night, and one knock was so strong it busted the door of its hinges. Others who lived at the estate also reported paranormal activity, including the ghost of Baumeister roaming around the house and the grounds and the feeling of being pushed, prodded, and pulled by unseen hands. One particular apparition wore a red T-shirt and was only visible from the torso up, and dogs on the property would bark wildly at unseen objects or people. The red T-shirt phantom would appear to other witnesses, usually wandering into the woods before vanishing.

Paranormal groups investigating Fox Hollow Farm claim to get active EVP of talkative ghosts, including what may have been Baumeister himself as well as the voices of victims saying things like "Hurry up, he's coming!"

Dahmer and the Tower

No known stories exist of notorious serial killer Jeffrey Dahmer haunting his childhood home, but apparently, the man known as the Milwaukee

A high school yearbook photo of serial killer Jeffrey Dahmer makes it difficult to believe he was a ruthless murderer. His spirit is said to haunt Morrill Tower at Ohio State University.

Monster may be haunting Morrill Tower at Ohio State University. Dahmer is known for raping, murdering, and dismembering seventeen boys and men between 1978 and 1991. He also committed acts of necrophilia and cannibalism. He appeared to have had a normal childhood but as an adolescent began displaying antisocial behavior and an obsession with examining the dead bodies of animals. He committed his first murder in 1978, three weeks after graduating high school, when he picked up a hitchhiker named Steven Hicks and took him back to his father's house to have some beers. Hicks wanted to leave, so Dahmer hit him in the back of the head with a ten-pound dumbbell, then dissected, pulverized, and scattered the man's remains through the backyard. It would be nine years before he killed again.

In 1985, he would go to gay bathhouses to drug and rape men. He was arrested twice for indecent exposure but only given probation. He killed his second victim, Steven Tuomi, in September 1987 in a hotel room. He killed two more victims in 1988, one in 1989, and four in 1990, luring unsuspecting men from bars or soliciting prostitutes, whom he then drugged, raped, and strangled. He also began having sex with the dead bodies and photographing their dismemberments. He kept their perfectly preserved skulls and genitals for display and ate other parts. Eventually, he was arrested for fondling a thirteen-year-old boy, then released, and he then killed four more people and another eight in 1991, claiming later to have drilled holes into their skulls and injected hydrochloric acid or boiling water into their brains to make them like zombies. Eventually, his crimes caught up to him, and he was arrested. His home was filled with the skulls and parts of his victims. Dahmer confessed and told the horrific details of his crimes to the authorities. Dahmer served his time at the Columbia Correctional Institution in Portage, Wisconsin. He was attacked twice by fellow inmates, with the second attempt on November 28, 1994, in the prison showers. Dahmer died on the way to the hospital from severe head trauma.

Dahmer, while in college, lived in Room 541 of Morrill Tower before he dropped out of school and joined the army. Students who now reside there have reported seeing an apparition at the foot of their bed and feeling a strong sense

Famous Fun Ghosts

Hollywood isn't just known for the ghosts of the once famous stars who lived and worked there. Hollywood pop culture is filled with ghosts we have all come to know and sometimes even love. There are hundreds to choose from in movies, television shows, cartoons, and comics, but a few of the most well known are:

- Casper the Friendly Ghost—The sweetly innocent, iconic, cartoon ghost who was very, very friendly and had a lot of friends to boot.
- Slimer—The gross, green ghost of *Ghostbusters* fame who was always hungry and always burping.
- The Ghosts of Christmases Past, Present, and Future—Jacob Marley and the ghosts of Christmas past, present, and future all haunted Ebenezer Scrooge until he changed his hostile ways in the 1843 Charles Dickens classic *A Christmas Carol*.

Comic actor Don Knotts once played a cowardly reporter staying in a haunted house in the 1966 film *The Ghost and Mr. Chicken*.

- Captain Daniel Gregg—Actress Jean Tierney plays a young widow named Mrs. Muir, who seeks peace at a secluded, seaside getaway with her daughter when she discovers it's haunted by the dashing, deceased sea captain played by Rex Harrison in the delightful 1947 romantic fantasy *The Ghost and Mrs. Muir.*
- Hamlet's Father, the King of Denmark—More of a Broadway ghost, the father of Hamlet played an integral role in the Shakespeare classic. He appears three times in the play, all during the night.
- Sam Wheat in *Ghost*—Who can forget the heart-wrenchingly romantic scene of Patrick Swayze's dead character, Sam, creating a clay vase with his despairing wife, played by Demi Moore, in this 1990 film?
- The Creepy Hallway Twins—Stephen King's *The Shining* (1977 horror novel, which was adapted as a 1980 film directed by Stanley Kubrick) is full of ghosts, but none are creepier than two little twin girls who appear at the end of a long hallway and ask little Danny if he wants to play.
- Malcolm Crowe in *The Sixth Sense*—Apparently, Hayley Joel Osment sees dead people, one of which is murdered psychologist Bruce Willis in the 1999 blockbuster thriller directed by M. Night Shyamalan.
- *The Others*—Nicole Kidman starred in this 2001 horror film in which she played a mom trying desperately to protect her children from ghostly entities.
- *The Innocents*—Screen legend Deborah Kerr played a governess dealing with two children and a creepy house full of ghosts and major plot twists in this 1961 British, black-and-white, classic film.

Continued...

(Continued from previous page)

- **Beetlejuice—Don't say his name three times, or you will pay the price! That's what Geena Davis and Alec Baldwin discover as two ghosts who enlist the help of the demon/spirit (played by Michael Keaton) to rid their home of the unwanted new owners.**
- **Mr. Chicken's Ghost—Don Knotts played a reporter challenged to spend a night in an allegedly haunted house that turns out to be, well ... haunted in the 1966 comedy classic *The Ghost and Mr. Chicken*.**

of dread or fear in the room. The university registrar confirms Dahmer was at the college but won't divulge exactly where.

The Killer Writer

Imagine being a journalist and writing about your own heinous crimes. Jack Unterweger covered his own murders in the early 1990s while in Austria and in the state of California. In Austria, he wrote about murders he committed in seven different cities in the country and then in California documented his own murders of three prostitutes. He gained notoriety for his writing, and when he was arrested and jailed, his fans and influential supporters petitioned for his parole on the basis of his journalistic achievements. So much for the deaths and suffering he caused. He killed himself in prison, and his fiancé claimed to have seen his ghost at the foot of her bed the night he died.

Just as ghosts appear to millions of normal folks around the world at any given time, celebrities and stars have their fair share of experiences. These paranormal events level the playing field and make us all quite human when faced with evidence of life after death, or at least ghosts after death, because they don't discriminate based on fame, income, or how many followers you have on social networking. Ghosts seem to be equal-opportunity haunters. Whether the ghosts are of stars themselves or it's the stars seeing the ghosts, we love to read these stories and hear these tales on popular television series such as *A Haunting*, *Celebrity Ghost Stories*, *Celebrity Paranormal Project*, and a host of others that have come and gone or read of their encounters in books and magazines because it makes us feel like the stars we often put up on pedestals are really just like us.

MOVIE SETS, STUDIOS, AND SOUNDSTAGES

What could be worse than making a television show or movie about something scary and having ghostly activity occur on set? For cast and crewmembers, it can be a terrifying blur between reality and the story they are creating and leave a lasting mark on those involved. Some movies seem to be associated with a high level of accidents and problems, and although they may not be paranormal in nature, they still left the cast and crew feeling as though something beyond the normal had occurred.

THE AMITYVILLE SET

During the filming of the 2005 remake of *The Amityville Horror* (the original film was released in 1979), several cast and crewmembers reported waking up at 3:15 A.M., the same time the notorious murders took place at 112 Ocean Avenue in Amityville, Long Island, New York. Those brutal murders were committed in 1974 by a man named Ronald DeFeo Jr., who, while living in the two-story, Dutch Colonial home, claimed he heard voices that urged him to kill his father, mother, two brothers, and two sisters.

According to *Tasteofcinema.com*'s "Ten Famous Movies That Were Haunted on the Set," the house was then purchased by the Lutz family, whose story is documented in the fictional *Amityville* movies. George Lutz, the father, also found himself seeing ghosts and experiencing demonic activity in the house before getting his family out. In the original movie, made in 1979, James Brolin played George Lutz, and Margot Kidder played his wife. In the 2005 remake, Ryan Reynolds played the part of George, and he reported how during filming, he would wake up at 3:15 A.M. just like the character he was portraying. He also reported feeling strange sensations during filming and felt there was something unsettling about the house itself.

Both versions were based on the book by Jay Anson, which Brolin claims he happened to be reading when a pair of pants he had hung up suddenly fell to the floor. He took it as a sign to go ahead and do the movie!

Is Batman Really Cursed?

So, Batman is cursed. That also includes *The Dark Knight* and associated movies, where awful things seem to happen to those involved. Everyone remembers the horrible death of Heath Ledger, who played the Joker in *The Dark Knight*. Allegedly, Ledger was warned not to take the role by Jack Nicholson, but he ignored it and suffered sleepless nights, a battle with depression, and the darkness cast by the film's storyline itself.

On the last page of the script, Ledger wrote the words "Bye, Bye" next to a photo of himself in full makeup. There were on-set accidents involving filming equipment, including the death of a technician during a stunt, and even noted actor Morgan Freeman suffered a car accident and a divorce shortly after filming.

The scariest connection was nothing ghostly at all but continues to perpetuate the curse. On July 20, 2012, a mass shooting occurred during a midnight screening of *The Dark Knight Rises* in Aurora, Colorado. The shooter, James Eagen Holmes, killed twelve people and injured over seventy others during the sold-out premiere that went down in history as one of the deadliest shootings on record.

Actor Heath Ledger, whose brilliant portrayal of the Joker will always be remembered, was warned not to join the cast of *The Dark Knight*. He died of an accidental overdose of medication.

The Making of *The Conjuring*

The story of the Perron family became a popular horror movie that documented the strange goings-on in their Rhode Island home during the 1970s. The actual wife and mother of the Perron family, Carolyn, refused to even visit the movie set with other members of the family. During filming, cast, crewmembers, and actual Perron family members experienced strange winds that would swirl around them but not affect nearby trees. Carolyn experienced an evil presence in her home, and the director, James Wan, stated his dog would growl ferociously at some unseen presence in his office when he was working late at night.

The hotel the actors and crew stayed in caught fire, although everyone safely evacuated.

Both Vera Farmiga and Patrick Wilson, the actors who played the paranormal investigator team of Lorraine and Ed Warren, founders of the New England Society for Psychic Research, experienced their share of strange sensations. Wilson, in an interview with *The Independent* in June 2016, also reported seeing one of the movie's young stars, Joey King, in a doctor's office he was in with his son. King was bruised all over her body, despite not being involved in any stunts. In the film, Lili Taylor's mother awakens with similar unexplained bruising.

Farmiga even reported strange claw marks on her computer that appeared during the filming!

The Crow

Actor Brandon Lee, who was the son of martial arts actor Bruce Lee, became an overnight legend after the release of *The Crow* in 1994 not just because of his haunting performance but because of his untimely death on the movie set. He was struck and killed by a real bullet fragment from a prop gun that accidentally fired eerily during a scene that was a flashback of his character Eric Draven's death. Lee predicted his demise, too, and he believed his entire family was cursed because of bad business dealings with his grandfather. Numerous other injuries were sustained by the crew as well. A carpenter was injured when his crane drove into power lines. An equipment truck caught on fire, and a major storm almost destroyed all of the sets.

The Exorcism of Emily Rose

Star Jennifer Carpenter reported that during the filming of the 2005 movie, in which she portrayed the German woman named Anneliese Michel, who died of poor health after a botched exorcism, her radio would turn on and off. She stated it would turn on loudly, usually when she was trying to sleep in the middle of the night. The song playing on the radio was always Pearl Jam's "Alive," and the lyrics "I'm still alive" would be repeated over and over again, as if on a loop.

Ghost

Though the filming of this movie was pretty much ghost free, it is fun to note that the movie was shot on Stage 19 of Paramount Studios, which has a reputation of being haunted itself, possibly by the ghost of Heather O'Rourke, who starred in the *Poltergeist* movies, which were shot on the same stage!

The Ghost Whisperer

Jennifer Love Hewitt starred in this hugely popular television series about a young woman who communicated with spirits and helped them cross over into the light. But during the filming, Hewitt believed the set was involved in some paranormal activity, especially in 2007. There was video footage taken to back her up of a particular scene where crewmembers noticed a shadow figure behind Hewitt. The shadowy spot showed up on the footage once they replayed it. Cast and crewmembers also reported their clothing being tugged on, lights exploding and moving around on their own, and objects vanishing from one spot and reappearing in another.

The Innkeepers

This 2011 movie was filmed in a haunted location, the Yankee Peddler Inn in Torrington, Connecticut, so the fact that during filming there would be strange activity doesn't come as too much of a surprise. Director Ti West was a skeptic but soon reported doors closing by themselves, television sets turning on and off, lights burning out, and cast and crewmembers having unusually vivid dreams. Actress Sara Paxton even reported waking up at night and sensing a presence in the room with her.

Introducing Dorothy Dandridge

According to Taste of Cinema's "10 Famous Movies That Were Haunted on the Set," actress Halle Berry had a positive ghostly encounter when she was cast as the lead in the 1999 biopic story of Dorothy Dandridge, the first African American ever to be nominated for a Best Actress Oscar. Berry decided to take home the original gown Dandridge wore on her *Ed Sullivan Show* appearance. At her home, Berry reported lights going on and off, doors opening and closing, and that even her housekeeper reported dragging sounds coming from the bedroom.

Actress, singer, and dancer Dorothy Dandridge, who was the first African American woman to be nominated for an Oscar, died in 1965 either from an embolism or an accidental overdose of depression medication. She was only forty-two.

Halle Berry stated that she kept the gown in the den covered in plastic and one day heard a crackling noise. She saw a little baby doll dress floating in front of the Dandridge gown! Berry was so shocked, she ran into her bedroom and hid there. But she felt a true sense of pride and responsibility, once she returned the gown, that she truly understood what Dorothy Dandridge stood for and that her haunting was a positive experience.

On the Set of *The Exorcist*

No movie could have been more associated with curses and hauntings than the one movie most often voted "the scariest movie ever made." *The Exorcist* was released in 1973 based on the best-selling novel by William Peter Blatty and directed by William Friedkin. The box office smash starred Ellen Burstyn as the mother of a possessed girl, played by Linda Blair. On set, the cast and crew reported numerous objects moving on their own, a telephone whose receiver would fall to the floor and float around, and other noisy shenanigans. That was nothing compared to what was to come, including a mysterious fire that burned down the actual set that was the home of the mother and daughter characters. The only room that did not burn was the bedroom where the infamous exorcism of Regan MacNeil, played by Blair, took place that terrified millions of movie-goers.

Burstyn later wrote in her 2006 autobiography of the anxiety many on the set experienced, especially with numerous reported electrical problems.

There were nine deaths associated with *The Exorcist*, including several actors whose characters died in the movie.

There were nine deaths associated with *The Exorcist*, including several actors whose characters died in the movie. There were accidents on set that injured both Ellen Burstyn and Linda Blair, and the film's religious technical advisor, Reverend Thomas Bermingham, was asked to perform a real-life exorcism. While shooting scenes in Iraq, director William Friedkin encountered actual devil worshippers who wanted to know why Friedkin was taking raw meat to a statue of their demon Pazuzu (it was to attract vultures for a particular scene)!

Ghosts in *The Matrix*?

More of a curse than a haunting, bad luck permeated the cast and crew of the huge box office success. Star Keanu Reeves lost his girlfriend, Jennifer Syme, who gave birth to a stillborn child during the filming, then later died in a car accident. Aaliyah, who played Zee in the film and was then twenty-two years of age, died in a tragic plane crash. Gloria Foster, who played the Oracle, died during filming. Reeves had a motorcycle accident that landed him in the hospital and later injured his foot enough to be hospitalized. Reeves also ended up giving up $24 million of his own salary to keep the production afloat. Luckily, the movie was completed and became a big hit, spawning sequels.

The Nun

Released in 2018 as a spin-off prequel to the successful *Conjuring* franchise, *The Nun* was billed as a terrifying ghost story, just as its predecessors. And just as the other franchise films that came out before it, ghastly happenings were reported on set. Director Corin Hardy claimed that while filming a key sequence of scenes called the Corridor of Crosses at an actual fortress in Transylvania, he had set up monitors in a small cell on the side of a long corridor. He went into the room and saw two men sitting around. Presuming them to be sound guys, he said hello and then turned the other way to watch one of his actresses perform her scene.

Despite there being only one way in or out of the cell, in which case they would have had to pass by Hardy while he was directing the scene, when he turned back to the cell to ask the soundmen how they liked the take, it was empty. According to the monitors, the room had been empty all along.

The Omen

A movie about a child who ends up being the Antichrist is bound to be cursed, right? In this case, the original, directed by Richard Donner and released in 1976, and its remake thirty years later, directed by John Moore (release date was 6/6/06!), both had their spooky issues. About two months before the original even began filming, lead actor Gregory Peck's son shot himself in the head in a suicide, and Peck barely escaped a harrowing plane crash when he canceled his reservation at the last minute. Everyone on board the flight died.

David Seltzer, who wrote the screenplay, was in a plane that was struck by lightning, and a few weeks later, producer Mace Neufeld experienced the same thing during a terrifying flight back to Los Angeles. In 2006, director John Moore shot a day's worth of film footage of the scene where the mark of the Devil, 666, is found on the boy, Damien, who is to become the Antichrist. The resulting film footage—about thirteen thousand feet of it—was somehow mysteriously destroyed by the processing lab, whose employees were in tears, lost for an explanation.

But the two most horrific deaths associated with the film involved bizarre coincidences. The animal handler for the original movie, who worked with a scene involving a baboon going crazy, was himself later attacked by a lion and reportedly eaten alive. The worst death occurred when the set designer for the 1976 original, John Richardson, created a scene that depicted a character being decapitated during an automobile accident. That very same year, in Holland, Richardson and his set assistant Liz Moore were in a head-on auto collision, and Moore was cut in half in almost the same way as in Richardson's film depiction. Scarier still, this happened on a Friday the 13th near a road sign that read: "Ommen. 66.6 KM."

The Passion of the Christ

Mel Gibson's powerful and controversial drama depicting the life of Christ had its own alleged curses. Jim Caviezel, who played Jesus, was struck by lightning during filming, and on set, cast and crewmembers reported it appeared as if his whole body was illuminated. But if that wasn't scary enough, director Jan Michelini was also struck twice!

Poltergeist

This 1982 blockbuster horror film was directed by Tobe Hooper and written and produced by Steven Spielberg. The story of a young family who moves into a new home built upon an ancient Indian burial ground and plagued by poltergeist activity raked in millions at the box office and spawned several sequels. It also came with its own fair share of spooky, behind-the-scenes, paranormal activity that had the cast and crew believing the movie was cursed from the first take.

JoBeth Williams played Diane Freeling in the 1982 horror film *Poltergeist*. According to her, she apparently took work home with her, finding pictures on the walls of her home moved at odd angles for no reason.

According to several sources, the corpses used in the infamous pool scene were real skeletons, as they were cheaper to obtain than fake, plastic ones and involved a lot more work to make them. If that didn't set the creep factor high enough, there were strange goings-on while filming, including the near-death of young actor Oliver Robins, who was filming a scene where he was being attacked by a clown. The prop clown had a malfunction and the boy was choking before the crew realized what was happening.

JoBeth Williams, the actress who played the mother of the haunted family, reported that she would find pictures on the wall hanging at strange angles when she got home from filming each day. She would make sure they were straight the next morning, only to come home and find them hanging crooked again that night.

Several actors died close to the time of the movie's filming as well as the two sequels in 1986 and 1988. Julian Beck died of stomach cancer after portraying an evil spirit. Will Sampson, who played the shaman, died of complications from a kidney transplant a year after he attempted to rid the set of the "curse" by performing a makeshift exorcism. Other deaths included Zelda Rubenstein, who played the psychic medium, and Brian Gibson, who directed one of the sequels, although they died years later and of not-so-mysterious causes. Since every movie has a large cast and crew, it is inevitable that some deaths may occur around the same time and close to the filming date.

But it was the mysterious deaths of two young, female actresses that elevated the strangeness sky high. On November 4, 1982, only six months after the filming ended on the first *Poltergeist* movie, actress Dominique Dunn, who played the family's older sister, was found strangled to death in her Hollywood apartment. The murderer was her then boyfriend, John Sweeney. In 1988, actress Heather O'Rourke, who played Carol Anne, the little girl who appears to be at the center of the activity in all three *Poltergeist* movies, died of a septic infection from a bowel blockage.

The Possession

Jeffrey Dean Morgan of "Negan" fame in the hit television series *The Walking Dead* starred in a 2012 horror film with Kyra Sedgwick in which their daughter becomes obsessed with a Dybbuk box, a cursed box that has the power to kill. During the filming of the movie, lights would explode on set for no reason, and there were often chilly breezes that could not be explained during key scary scenes. The storage facility that housed the film's props caught fire mysteriously and burned to the ground, along with the prop Dybbuk box.

Rosemary's Baby

When director Roman Polanski, who was no stranger to controversy himself, made the 1968 hit film *Rosemary's Baby*, he probably had no idea what a cult classic the film would be. It is consistently on many lists of the top ten horror movies of all time. Ironic because the story is about a young, pregnant woman who discovers she has been set up by a Satanic cult to have the Devil's baby! Nor would he and the cast and crew have known of the strange events that would be associated with the making of the iconic horror film, including the mysterious death of film composer Krzysztof Komeda, who died of a brain clot a year after the film was made, or the uremic poisoning and kidney failure of producer William Castle, who received hate mail after the movie's release. As Castle was being admitted to the hospital, he allegedly yelled, "Rosemary, for God's sake, drop the knife!" He died later from a heart attack.

As Castle was being admitted to the hospital, he allegedly yelled, "Rosemary, for God's sake, drop the knife!"

But the really creepy connections came from the setting of the story—the Dakota apartment building in New York City, where Rosemary lived with her husband and her devil-worshipping neighbors. The Dakota apartment building was also where Beatle John Lennon was shot and killed years later. To make matters even spookier, the Beatles released their White Album in 1968, the same year *Rosemary's Baby* was released. The album included the song "Helter Skelter," which was later used by notorious cult leader Charles Manson as a name of the ritualistic killing spree his "family" committed in 1969 ... that included the horrific stabbing of pregnant actress Sharon Tate in her Benedict Canyon home in Los Angeles. Tate was the wife of director Roman Polanski.

Three Men and a Baby's Cardboard Boy

Though it was later debunked, this blockbuster comedy from 1987 gave Hollywood its own urban legend for a while. Starring such big names as Ted

Danson, Tom Selleck, and Steve Guttenberg and directed by Leonard Nimoy ("Spock" of *Star Trek* fame), the movie spawned a huge rumor of the appearance of an apparition of a boy behind a curtain in a window in one scene. The boy, it was alleged, had died of suicide in the same house the movie was filmed at. The story even made the nightly news!

But alas, it was all proved to be sheer nonsense. There was no suicide, and the movie was filmed on a studio soundstage, not in an actual home. As for the "apparition," it turned out to be a large, cardboard stand of Ted Danson's character someone had forgotten to put in its right place! But while it lasted, it was a fun television urban legend.

The Twilight Zone and On-Set Accidents

In 1983, director John Landis's remake of the television classic resulted in one of the most horrific on-set incidents in movie history. During a scene using heavy explosives and a helicopter, actor Vic Morrow and two children actors, who were both illegally hired, were decapitated and crushed when the helicopter spun out of control and crashed to the ground. Landis was suggested by producer Steven Spielberg as being partially responsible, and their working relationship ended after the incident.

Just because a movie set suffered horrific accidents doesn't necessarily mean it was haunted but certainly cursed. The sheer fact that movie and television sets require so many people and equipment, involve dangerous stunts, multiple set pieces, and just plain human error makes these locations ripe for problems. Yet, those that truly seem to have been the stomping grounds of ghosts, apparitions, and poltergeist-like activity add a depth and richness to the acting performances and moods of the movies.

Actor Vic Morrow (shown here on the 1960s TV show *Combat!*) died in a freak 1983 helicopter accident on the set of *The Twilight Zone* movie.

Perhaps just being involved in something scary breeds paranormal activity or makes those involved more aware of it and susceptible to it. Maybe the collective beliefs and expectations of the cast and crew have a role in manifesting actual physical events that haunt them long after the final "and cut!" is called by the director. Maybe the demons are entirely human, as in the case of the 1960 thriller *Psycho*, in which a handyman named Kenneth Dean Hunt who was obsessed with Alfred Hitchcock and his movies murdered Myra Jones, the uncredited body double of star Janet Leigh. Maybe the curse is really an actual bad accident, as in the fire that destroyed most of the sets involved in the making of the Stephen King classic *The Shining*. Interestingly, the Overlook Hotel, which is the setting of the chilling story, burns down at the end of the novel.

One of the most intriguing haunted sets goes back to 1953 and involves a television set used to make a show called *Ding Dong School*, which was a precursor to *Sesame Street*. A Long Island resident named Jerome E. Travers was watching with his three children when they saw a "spectral woman" appear on the screen and heard her voice echoing out from the television. This continued even after the television set was unplugged!!! Reporters flocked to the scene, and the family decided the best way to deal with the haunted television set was to turn it to face the wall as punishment for scaring the children! However, this appears to be more a story of a haunted "television set" than a haunted set where a television show is filmed. Be warned!

Spooky Soundstages and Studios

There are hundreds of haunted places in Hollywood alone, and a few of them are soundstages where the movies we know, and love, were filmed. Whether haunted by the dead ghosts of past performers or those who lost their lives in accidents during filming, these facilities have garnered quite a reputation as notorious as some of the films that were made there.

Charlie Chaplin Studios

Motion picture legend Charlie Chaplin started the studio with his name on it in 1917. Located on La Brea Avenue, the studio had a rich history that included movies and television shows such as *Perry Mason* and *The Adventures of Superman*. Years later, it would change hands, suffer a fire, be broken into lots and partially sold to outside interests, serve as the headquarters for A&M Records, and eventually become the Jim Henson Studio, which it remains today, where the Muppet empire was created.

In 2007, the SyFy Channel series *Ghost Hunters* paid a visit to the now designated historical/cultural monument to investigate stories of cast and crewmembers encountering ghosts and apparitions over the decades. One particular apparition was in the form of a man wearing a top hat and coat, and a female form was often reported walking through doors. Doors opened and closed by themselves, and the ghost of a man with a handlebar mustache was often seen on the soundstage. Voices could be heard coming from the catwalk when no one was around. Other people who have worked at the site reported knocking on glass windows in the children's schoolhouse along with a plethora of reports of people seeing the ghost of Karen Carpenter, the famous singer/musician and half of The Carpenters, who was signed to A&M Records.

The Infamous Stage 28

Stage 28 on the Universal Studios lot in Hollywood is where the 1925 movie *The Phantom of the Opera* was filmed. Since then, weird happenings, including the ghost of Lon Chaney, have been reported there.

Universal Studios has a long history as one of the biggest soundstage and production facilities in world. Over the years, many of its famous stages have been destroyed by fire, demolished, and changed to adapt to the times. One stage in particular, Stage 28, lasted from 1925 to 2014, when it was demolished. But it had quite the reputation for being haunted.

Known as "The Phantom Stage" because one of its biggest claims to production fame, Lon Chaney in the 1925 *The Phantom of the Opera*, used the stage for its Paris Opera House scene, and it became a permanent fixture on the Universal lot. Casts and crewmembers of various films reported ghostly apparitions and strange goings-on, including a black-caped figure running around the catwalk above the stage many attributed to being Lon Chaney's ghost in his performance garb as the Phantom.

Lights turned on and off, and doors opened and closed on their own. In 1925, an electrician fell to his death, and many people later thought it was his ghost that haunted Stage 28. Security guards over time have reported hearing voices when no one was around filming. The soundstage stood up to various earthquakes and fires and hosted tours for the public for years.

Culver Studios

Thomas Ince was a big name in the filmmaking world. In fact, he was considered the "Father of the Western," but few people have ever heard of him. Ince, a silent movie star, started Culver Studios in 1918. The Mansion was the first building to be constructed on the lot. But Ince's death in 1924, on board a yacht owned by none other than William Randolph Hearst, was mysterious. It was Ince's forty-third birthday, and there was a big party on board the *Oneida* with guests such as Louella Parsons, the gossip queen, and Charlie Chaplin. Ince was the guest of honor and missed the boat when it set off from San Pedro, meeting up on the yacht later.

According to the official news stories of the time, Ince partied a bit too hard and died of acute indigestion. But rumor has it that some witnesses on the *Oneida* said they saw Ince being taken off the ship with a bullet hole to his head!

Ince may have gotten caught in the jealous crossfire between Hearst and Chaplin, who were both interested in actress Marion Davies, also on board, and that the bullet may have been meant for Chaplin.

The Culver Studios were said to be haunted by the ghost of Ince, often seen climbing the stairs of the administrative building or walking the catwalk wearing a bowler hat. One special-effects man named Eugene Hilchey was told by the ghost, "I don't like what you're doing to my studio," before the ghost vanished into the walls on Stage 2-3-4.

The studio changed hands over the years, at one time owned by Cecil B. DeMille and then RKO. Today, Culver Studios is a thriving production facility, and although most of it has been rebuilt, much of the original studio is the same as when Ince first envisioned and built it in 1918. Stage 1 was demolished in 1988, and Ince was heard on the catwalks just moments before the wrecking ball struck.

Paramount Pictures Studios

On Los Angeles's famed Melrose Avenue, one of the few streets to ever have its own dramatic television series, sits one of the biggest and most successful movie studios ever built ... and one of the most haunted. Behind the huge, wrought iron gates sits Paramount Studios, the home of many of the most iconic films in history since it was built in 1912. Directors such as Cecil B. DeMille, Steven Spielberg, and Alfred Hitchcock and performers from Elvis Presley to Angelina Jolie and Harrison Ford graced the soundstages and created a legacy of movies and television never to be forgotten. The back lot was home to shows such as *The Brady Bunch* and *Happy Days*, shows that have stood the test of time and become as much a part of history as the place they were filmed.

Paramount Studios has a long history of hauntings and strange goings-on, which have become as legendary as the people who worked there making films. The studio is located next door to another haunted Hollywood location, Hollywood Memorial Park, which serves as the final resting place of some of the biggest stars who ever lived, including Rudy Valentino and Douglas Fairbanks. The Memorial Park is close to Stages 29 through 32, which are said to have been the most often visited by ghostly apparitions, many wearing the clothing of the 1930s and 1940s, including one of Valentino himself walking through the exterior gate into the studio lot (sometimes wearing the white costume from his movie *The Sheik*).

Security guards and other workers state the most active haunted locations were Stages 30 and 31, which were rampant with doors being opened and closed, stage lights flashing on and off, apparitions, and the sounds of footsteps where no one was around. Even after security guards would secure the facilities, they would hear things going on that indicated someone was walking around, but further inspection always revealed there was no one there. Some people suggest that ghosts from the next-door Memorial Park enter the soundstages via the walk-in gates at Lemon Grove, which are only feet from the cemetery. Reports include guards seeing the heads of ghosts peeking through the cemetery wall and then vanishing!

The Hart Building is said to be the most paranormally active location. It is one of the oldest buildings and was once a part of the famous DesiLu Studios started by Desi Arnaz and Lucille Ball. It is in this building the ghost of a woman was seen floating around the upper floors and giving off a very strong scent of flowery perfume.

The Hart Building is also home to slamming doors and lights going on and off, people being touched on the arms and shoulders, and even glowing, red eyes appearing in the bathroom mirror of one section of the studio! The building is small, and the people who work there all know each other by sight, so imagine their shock when one late night, a man and woman left their second-story office together and walked past an old woman. Neither one of them recognized the old woman, and when they turned back to ask if she was lost, she had vanished into thin air!

Some of the folks who worked on the popular TV show *Wings* during the 1990s, which was shot on Stage 19 (where *Happy Days* was shot) reported seeing the ghost of Heather O'Rourke on many occasions. O'Rourke was the child who played Carol Anne in the *Poltergeist* movies and died tragically young. Ironically, O'Rourke guest-starred on some of the final episodes of *Happy Days*. Her ghost could be heard laughing and running across the stage in the dark late at night when the soundstage was empty but for a worker or two. Other locations alleged to be haunted are Stage 25 and the Schulberg Building.

Another famous ghost story involves the "New York" area of the back lot. A security guard there is said to have seen a young man walking around. The guard approached the man and told him he needed to leave. The man smiled at the guard and then proceeded to walk through a wall. When the guard later gave a description of the man in his Incident Report, he described him as looking like Rudolph Valentino, who was buried in the cemetery on the other side of the wall the ghost walked through!

Raleigh Studios

Built in 1914, this studio has a long history of films featuring some of the top stars of the time, including Charlie Chaplin and Frank Sinatra. Stage 5 is a hotbed of paranormal activity. In 1932, an electrician fell to his death from the catwalk above the stage, and many workers have sensed his presence there. Heavy equipment moved on its own, and cold spots would appear out of nowhere. Lights turn on and off and voices could be heard near and around Stage 5.

Three-hundred-pound (136-kilogram) overhead lights would often begin swinging back and forth on their own, according to studio employee Don Kane, who experienced ghostly activity after hours when the soundstage was locked up for the night.

HOLLYWOOD LANDMARKS

All over Hollywood are known and unknown places filled with haunted history. The Hollywood sign has starred in more movies and television shows than most actors. The sign, built by *Los Angeles Times* publisher Harry Chandler, was erected in 1923. It was originally a billboard to advertise his Hollywoodland real estate development. It was supposed to be only for a year or so, but the sign remained standing for another eighty-odd years. People come from all over the world just to see the sign and hike up to take pictures next to it.

The iconic sign has long been associated with a particular ghost that is said to appear to joggers, tourists, and even park rangers alike. High up in the hills above the city of Los Angeles near Griffith Park Observatory sits the sign where, on the night of September 16, 1932, a despairing film starlet named Peg Entwistle jumped to her death from the letter H in the sign. She would be nicknamed by tabloids as "The Hollywood Sign Girl" and unfortunately get the fame in her death she never did in life.

Peg was a starry-eyed actress with big dreams that never quite came true, and the stress and rejection she faced all got to her so much that she ended her life at the one place that most stood for the business she so desired to break into. According to "Is the Hollywood Sign Haunted?" in the October 2014 edition of *Vanity Fair*, writer Valerie Tejeda states that a suicide note was found beside her body and items of her clothing that said, "I am afraid, I am a coward. I am sorry for everything. If I had done this a long time ago, it would have saved a lot of pain. P.E."

The letter H would later fall over in the 1940s, leading some to believe it was Peg who pushed it. As the years progressed, witnesses would see a "disoriented blonde woman" along the jogging path and smell the scent of gardenias, which was Peg Entwistle's favorite perfume. Even the Griffith Park rangers report seeing her ghost near the sign on foggy nights.

Haunted Hollywood Hotels

Throughout Hollywood and Los Angeles are hotels said to house the spirits of famous ghosts. In the last chapter, we looked at the Hollywood Roosevelt Hotel, the most spook-filled of the bunch according to those who dare enter its doors. Located on Hollywood Boulevard, the hotel was named after Theodore Roosevelt and opened its doors to the public on May 15, 1927. It cost $2.5 million, which was a huge amount back then, and quickly became the central point of glamour and glitz for the rich and famous.

The 1929 Academy Awards took place in the hotel's Blossom Room, and the hotel hosted some of the biggest soirees in the entertainment industry. The ghosts of Marilyn Monroe and Montgomery Clift still walk the halls of the renovated hotel. People staying on the ninth floor have often called the front desk to complain about the "trumpet player" in Room 928 or the feel of cold hands on them when no one was around. The ghost of Clift is also reported running his lines in the hallway just outside Room 928.

The comedian and actor John Belushi passed away in Hollywood's iconic Chateau Marmont hotel, and his spirit is said to have been spotted there, even once entertaining a child.

Built in 1929, the Chateau Marmont also claimed iconic Hollywood status to the many stars who stayed there, including Clark Gable, John Lennon, Marilyn Monroe, Greta Garbo, and others. It was the place many Hollywood stars came to have love affairs, drawn to its studding, castlelike appearance and location above the Sunset Strip. It was here in 1982 that comedic actor John Belushi died of an overdose, and his spirit is one of many ghosts that haunt the rooms and hallways. It was originally an apartment building when it opened in 1927. It was seven stories tall and shaped like an L, styled after a Gothic chateau. Belushi died in Bungalow 3, and visitors have reported seeing his ghost and, according to a story in Tom Ogden's 2009 book *Haunted Hollywood*, a young boy staying there heard giggling and when asked why, he said he was laughing at the "funny man" no one else could see. The same boy later saw a picture of Belushi and said that he was the funny man he saw! Other ghostly activity includes windows and doors opening and shutting, cold spots, mysterious voices when no one is around, and footsteps. A few witnesses report seeing disembodied heads floating around and a ghostly woman who floats above a bed!

The Knickerbocker Hotel was built in 1925 and was first a luxury apartment building before becoming a hotel. Located on Ivar Avenue in Hollywood, the hotel was home to dozens of huge stars of yesteryear, and today, witnesses report it is haunted by the likes of Marilyn Monroe and Rudy Valentino. Monroe's ghost is said to favor the ladies' room off the lobby bar, where witnesses have reported seeing a beautiful, blonde ghost with translucent skin looking in the mirror and fixing her makeup. Valentino favors standing in an upper-story window or petting horses in the eight-acre stable. Since the 1970s, the hotel has been a senior residence apartment building, and because it is restricted to tenants, not a lot of ghost sightings have surfaced since.

High above Sunset Boulevard sits the majestic Beverly Hills Hotel. Since it was built and opened in 1912, the hotel hosted royalty, world leaders, and legends in the entertainment industry. Today, the hotel's bungalows are home to the ghosts of Harpo Marx and Sergei Rachmaninoff.

Downtown Los Angeles is home to two of its own haunted hotels. The Figueroa Hotel on South Figueroa Street was a former YWCA residence building in 1925 and in 2015 began many renovations to bring back its original Spanish Colonial splendor. Those who stay there claim to hear strange sounds at night. The elevator will move up and down floors of its own accord without any passengers in it, and lights and televisions in rooms turn on and off.

On Spring Street, the Alexandria Hotel sits. Opened in 1906, it hosted many luminaries from the entertainment industry who often used the hotel as a meeting place. It also hosted Winston Churchill, King Edward VIII, and three presidents—William Howard Taft, Woodrow Wilson, and Theodore Roosevelt. Those who stay there today claim the "lady in black" haunts the halls. She may have been a former resident who died in her room of a broken heart and wears a black veil and hat. Guests Nancy Malone and Lisa Mitchell have seen her walking the hallway and describe her as "gliding" across the floor. They also claim she is not solid but not entirely see-through, according to their account in *Hollywood Haunted: A Ghostly Tour of Filmland* by Laurie Jacobson and Marc Wanamaker.

Haunted Theaters

Hollywood is filled with theaters that host ghosts. The Pantages Theater was once owned by eccentric billionaire Howard Hughes, who purchased the theater in 1949 and is said to haunt the second floor of the building, where he once had offices. Located at the fabled intersection of Hollywood and Vine, this theater was designed by architect B. Marcus Priteca and built by vaudeville impresario Alexander Pantages. By the way, Alexander Pantages has not been reported to haunt the famous theater he built! Most of the ghostly activity occurs in the former offices of Howard Hughes, where people report everything from

The former owner of the historic Pantages Theater in Hollywood, Howard Hughes, has reportedly been spotted on the building's second floor.

doorknobs turning, lights going on and off, filing cabinet drawers opening and closing, the sense of a presence in the room, cold breezes when there was no ventilation system running, and the smell of cigars in the smoke-free offices. A tall man wearing a business suit whom many believe is Hughes has also been seen on the premises.

The former base for RKO, the theater is now home to big Broadway plays and musicals right in the heart of Hollywood. The building sports a wonderful Art Deco design and once was home to vaudeville performers before becoming a movie house during the Great Depression. Between 1949 and 1959, the Pantages Theater was home to the Oscar Awards, and it officially closed as a movie theater in 1977 before reopening as a stage show theater. The ghost of a woman can often be heard singing there and may have been a patron of the theater from 1932 who died in the mezzanine section during a show. Some believe she was herself an aspiring singer who is now living out her dream in death of being a famous performer at the glorious Pantages.

The Avalon Theater was built in 1927 and has been called the Hollywood Playhouse and Palace Theater over the years. Once the host to old-time radio shows and theater revues, the three-floor building on Vine Street is all old Hollywood glamour and also served as a television production studio to such shows as *The Lawrence Welk Show*, *The Dating Game*, *The Jerry Lewis Telethon*, and *This Is Your Life* before becoming a popular nightclub. It also played host to the show *The Hollywood Palace*, which was the first to host the U.S. television debut of the Rolling Stones and the first national network appearance of The Jackson Five.

Over the years, witnesses at the Avalon have reported a male ghost dressed in a tuxedo who may have been a former master of ceremonies and appears in the main theater and several female spirits that some suggest were once performers at the theater. Many of the spirits are said to be most active early in the morning and have appeared before security guards working before the theater opened. In the 1990s, a security guard named Dwayne Soto reported several encounters with ghosts while making his rounds. One was thought to be a male playing jazz on a piano in the comedy room, but when Dwayne went to investigate, the room was empty.

One night after locking up the theater, Dwayne encountered a female presence in the second-floor lobby. He felt as though a breeze were blowing on him and smelled perfume; then, as he headed for the stairs, someone tapped on his shoulder. When he turned to see who, there was no one there. He also witnessed the male ghost in the tuxedo, and his dog reacted to the spirit as well while in the first-floor main theater. The dog ran after the apparition, which vanished on the spot, and the dog sniffed the exact spot on the floor where it disappeared. Dwayne has also seen an older couple dressed in 1930s-style clothing on the theater's main dance floor. He looked up to the balcony and saw this couple talking to one another. He shouted at them, thinking they were people who had gotten into the theater, but the couple ignored him, disappearing only when he went upstairs to the balcony to confront them.

Other Avalon/Palace spirits include a little girl who can be heard crying in a stall in the women's restroom and a playful spirit that loves to tap people on the shoulders. A male ghost wearing a hat has been known to wander the hallway to the basement, and shimmering, blue orbs are seen all over the theater as well as dark, indistinct shapes that float about the club.

The Hollywood Pacific Theater was built in 1927 and also went by the name Warner Pacific Theater, named after the Warner brothers, who built it. It is the largest theater in Hollywood, and some believe one of the brothers haunts the place, namely Sam Warner, who died of a brain hemorrhage during the making of *The Jazz Singer* in 1927. The theater opened to the public a year later, and Sam's ghost was witnessed by many attendees who saw him moving back and forth from the theater to his upstairs offices. He has also been spotted pacing in the lobby, as he was known to do in life. Sam's ghost has even been reported to press elevator buttons and get into and out of elevators to get to his offices instead of the usual ghost method of traveling between walls. People in the theater during quieter times claim they can hear him working up in his office.

Some people say the place was cursed by Sam, who was so angry at not having construction done on the theater in time for the premiere of *The Jazz Singer* in 1928.

Some people say the place was cursed by Sam, who was so angry at not having construction done on the theater in time for the premiere of *The Jazz Singer* in 1928. The security company that watches the building claims the elevator continues to operate of its own volition to this day. The actual theater is supposed to be restored and turned into The Hollywood Entertainment Museum, featuring motion picture, television, radio, and recording arts.

The Silent Movie Theater was built in 1942 and celebrates the history of silent films. But the theater has a long history of hauntings. Actor Lawrence Austin, a former owner of the building, was murdered here by his boyfriend James Van Sickle, who was a projectionist. Van Sickle hired a nineteen-year-old man named Christian Rodriguez to kill Austin on January 17, 1997. A concession counter worker was also shot in that event and told the police what she knew. Employee witnesses claim Austin's ghost roams the place at night after the theater is closed searching for the girl who was there and saw the murder, maybe to thank her. The ghost of the original owner of the theater, John Hampton, has been seen walking on the second floor where he once lived. Hampton died of cancer in 1990, which may have been attributed to the toxic chemicals he was constantly exposed to preserving old films in the bathroom tub of his home above the theater and various film labs around the area.

The Vogue Theater on Hollywood Boulevard opened in 1936. Before that, it was the Prospect Elementary School, where a tragic fire burned it to the ground in 1901, killing twenty-five children and one teacher. The theater then closed until 1992, and a textile factory went up in its place. The factory also burned to the ground a few years later. The Vogue Theater was built on the same site in 1936 as a more modest alternative to the lavish Grauman's Chinese and Egyptian Theaters located further down Hollywood Boulevard.

A paranormal group, the International Society for Paranormal Research, led by parapsychologist Dr. Larry Montz, took over the property. The ISPR, a Los Angeles group founded in 1972, investigated the paranormal activity in the Vogue Theater. Apparently, there were nine resident ghosts, including six children and three adults.

The children were obviously those who died in the fire, and the adults included the teacher, a projectionist who worked in the theater for forty years, and a maintenance engineer who also worked there on occasion. The ISPR team cleared the place of ghosts in 2001 and claim it is no longer haunted. Or is it?

Tourists flock to the famed TCL Chinese Theater (formerly Grauman's Chinese Theater and Mann's Chinese Theater). Named after founder Sid Grauman, who opened the theater in 1927, the place served as a Hollywood hot spot where big stars came for premieres and thousands of fans lined the streets hoping to catch a glimpse of their favorites. The theater was decorated with artifacts that Sid Grauman imported from China, and the forecourt boasts the concrete handprints and footprints of the Hollywood elite. Often, tourists take photos with their own hands in the handprints and never even go inside the actual theater.

One of the most recognizable and famous theaters in the world, TCL Chinese Theater in Hollywood has a forecourt with stars' handprints and footprints as well as the ghost of actor Victor Killian.

Actor Victor Killian's ghost haunts the forecourt area, pacing back and forth as if looking for someone, although he was murdered at a different location. His killer was never found, and those who have seen his dark figure walking the forecourt suggest he might be restless from trying to find the perpetrator. The theater does have its own resident ghost, a man named Fritz who worked at the theater and hanged himself behind the movie screen. His ghost has been witnessed by many people in the theater, but everyone knows him, and he doesn't frighten anyone. Other ghosts that haunt the theater have been reported to move around and make strange noises behind the stage curtains when no one is around except night employees.

Haunted Tourist Hot Spots

The Hollywood Wax Museum on Hollywood Boulevard is frightening enough with its waxy renditions of celebrities. Some don't look much at all like the stars they portray, but others appear ready to jump out and grab you, as they are so realistic. The museum opened in 1965 and has been in operation for decades, with thousands of annual visitors who come to walk the narrow halls and see their favorite movie stars and musicians—well, the waxy kind, anyway. There is even a Horror Chamber room devoted to the figures of great films such as *Dracula* and *Frankenstein*.

Local legend has it that there are also ghosts that walk the halls, which some witnesses claim they've contacted via séances held there, or in photographs that show milky, fuzzy images of something spectral. According to an interview with L.A. *Tourist*, the general manager, Taj Sundher, stated that a reporter with the *National Enquirer* once stayed there overnight on a bit of a dare, only to be found the next day pale and shaking, waiting by the door!

Employees have seen a woman sitting on a bench praying near The Last Supper display, and she vanishes whenever a security guard tries to confront her. No one knows who she is or why she is haunting the wax museum in particular.

The name Wonderland Avenue might sound like a typically glamorous Hollywood locale, but it is the home where famous porn star John Holmes committed four murders. He used a lead pipe to kill four drug dealers in what has become known as the "Four on the Floor" murders, which occurred at 8763 Wonderland Avenue in Los Angeles on July 1, 1981. The victims were drug dealers called "The Wonderland Gang" set up by an organized crime mob boss named Eddie Nash who, along with Holmes, was later tried and acquitted for what LAPD detectives stated was such a brutal, bloody crime, it was considered more gruesome than the Charles Manson-directed Tate–LaBianca murders back in 1969.

Wonderland Avenue is located in Laurel Canyon, an area noted for its many notorious homes and locations, many of which are said to be haunted. Visitors to the Wonderland murder house report being pulled and pushed, having their hair tugged, and witnessing televisions in the home acting strangely. Most of the activity, of course, is at night, even though the actual murders occurred around 8:00 A.M.

Beverly Hills Bermuda Triangle

By Claire Weaver

www.eerieca.com

There's an area in Los Angeles dubbed "The Beverly Hills Bermuda Triangle" that attracts a disproportionately high number of strange events, accidents, and murders.

The Triangle is bordered by N. Linden Drive, Lomitas Avenue, and Whittier Drive in the prestigious 90210 zip code—all quiet streets lined with huge mansions a stone's throw away from the exclusive Los Angeles Country Club. Tall palm trees shade the sidewalks, and children can be heard playing in an elementary school down the street. It's the epitome of an idyllic, upscale neighborhood....

But the history of this small neighborhood is far from serene.

The Beverly Hills Bermuda Triangle earned its name thanks to a high number of unfortunate incidents that have taken place here. The strange events began in 1946 with film producer Howard Hughes, who made his name with movies such as *Two Arabian Knights,* which won the first Academy Award for Best Director of a comedy picture, *The Racket,* and *The Front Page*. Hughes had always had a penchant for planes, and after producing the aviation-themed *Hell's Angels* in 1930, his passion really took off—though his planes had a hard time staying in the sky. Although he set a number of records (the landplane airspeed record in 1935, the transcontinental airspeed record in 1937, and the flight-around-the-world record in 1938), he was involved in several serious crashes.

One such accident happened on July 7, 1946, when Hughes piloted the test flight of a prototype he had designed for the U.S. Army Air Force, the Hughes XF-11. Shortly after takeoff, an oil leak affected the propellers, and the aircraft began to rapidly lose altitude. Hughes attempted to land on the Los Angeles Country Club golf course but couldn't quite make it and instead smashed into a row of nearby houses.

The XF-11 destroyed three houses—and then the fuel tanks exploded, setting fire to a fourth home at 808 N. Whittier Drive. Hughes miraculously survived, though he suffered substantial injuries, including a crushed collarbone, cracked ribs, a collapsed lung, and third-degree burns.

The following year, the Beverly Hills Bermuda Triangle claimed its first official death: that of the infamous New York gangster Bugsy Siegel.

Siegel was one of the leaders of Murder, Inc. (the enforcement arm of the Jewish mob) and a prominent bootlegger during Prohibition. After making a number of enemies in New York in the late 1930s, the East Coast Mob sent him to California to develop syndicate-sanctioned gambling rackets with L.A. family boss Jack Dragna.

Handsome and charismatic, it didn't take Siegel long to infiltrate the highest circles in Hollywood, rubbing shoulders with the likes of Clark Gable, Cary Grant, MGM studio executive and partial namesake Louis B. Mayer, and rising star Frank Sinatra.

His enemies soon caught up with him, however, and on the night of June 20, 1947, as Siegel sat in his girlfriend's Beverly Hills home reading the *Los Angeles Times*, an assassin shot through the window with a .30 caliber semiautomatic carbine, hitting him twice in the head. He died at 801 N. Linden Drive.

In 1966, the strange forces of the Beverly Hills Bermuda Triangle were responsible for bringing an end to popular rock duo Jan & Dean.

Continued...

(Continued from previous page)

William Jan Berry and Dean Ormsby Torrence were the hugely popular surf rock musicians behind hit songs "Surf City," "Drag City," and "Dead Man's Curve." The latter, which tells the tale of a deadly car accident, would come to be viewed as an ominously prescient song for Jan Berry....

On April 12, 1966, Berry was driving his Corvette Stingray down Whittier Drive when he crashed into a parked truck at high speed. His injuries were so severe that first responders initially thought he was dead. He was cut out of the car and rushed to the nearby UCLA Medical Center, where he spent several weeks in a coma with severe injuries to the head and brain.

Eccentric millionaire Howard Hughes had a passion for airplanes. It is said that when he crashed a Hughes XF-11 in the Los Angeles area, it created a kind of "Bermuda Triangle," where mysterious deaths occurred.

Berry survived the accident but suffered permanent brain damage that left him partially paralyzed and impaired his speech. Thanks to the Beverly Hills Bermuda Triangle, the career of Jan & Dean was over.

On November 16, 2010, at about 12:28 A.M., Hollywood publicist Ronni Chasen was shot four times in her car as she waited for the light to change at the intersection of Whittier Drive and Sunset Boulevard. She careened into a street light and died in front of 815 N. Whittier Drive.

No shell casings, live rounds, or weapons were recovered at the intersection, leading many to speculate that this was a professional hit. An article in the *New York Post* referenced Hollywood rumors that Chasen's murder was somehow linked to the gambling debts of her brother, Larry Cohen, though the rumors were never confirmed.

Eight months after the shooting, Beverly Hills Police closed the case, concluding that Chasen was killed in a random robbery gone wrong. They'd received a tip-off that an impoverished ex-felon by the name of Harold Smith had bragged about shooting Chasen and "getting $10,000 for it." Smith committed suicide when confronted by police.

In 2016, *The Hollywood Reporter* reviewed the Beverly Hills Police Department case files, concluding there is overwhelming reason to doubt the investigation's core findings. The case, however, was never reopened.

Chasen's death added to the ongoing legacy of one of the most eerie and sinister locations in Los Angeles. Many locals wonder, when will the Beverly Hills Bermuda Triangle strike again?

Another terrifying house sits at 11547 Braddock Drive in Culver City to the south of L.A. Known as the "Entity House," this was the home of Doris Bither, the victim of a very violent ghost or poltergeist that would throw objects, physically attack her, and even follow her and her family when they tried to get away from the home. The activity later inspired a terrifying movie called *The Entity* in 1981, with Barbara Hershey as the victimized homeowner.

Another potential paranormal triangle, although it's more like just a corner, is located about a mile away from the Hollywood business district in a residential area off Sierra Bonita Avenue. Known as Nichols Canyon, those who live there have reported dozens of sightings of Native American ghosts, even a covered wagon, crossing the street intersection. Sometimes, the Native American ghosts appear in their living rooms! One man encountered several Native Americans in war paint in 1968 while driving on Hollywood Boulevard. They were on horseback, and he had to swerve his car to avoid hitting them, causing him to hit a tree instead.

Boris and Bella

Two of the biggest legends in Hollywood have a ghostly association of their own. Boris Karloff, who played Frankenstein, and Bela Lugosi, known for his portrayal of Dracula, live on in the form of ghosts at their respective homes. Boris Karloff loved to garden, and his gardens were so gorgeous friends often asked to have their ashes spread among the roses. Boris was all for it, and now, his gardens are said to be haunted by the presence of those same friends, according to tourists and visitors to the location. Bela Lugosi loved cigars, and after he died of a heart attack in 1956, his spirit decided to give a little performance for mourning fans when the hearse carrying his casket began driving itself as it passed by Bela's apartment. The driver didn't gain control back until the self-driving hearse passed by Lugosi's favorite cigar shop, a place he haunted in life on numerous occasions.

The Hollywood Tower Hotel in Disneyland is modeled after the real hotel in Hollywood, California, where celebrity ghosts are said to roam the rooms and hallways.

Tower of Terror

If you've ridden the Twilight Zone Tower of Terror ride at Disney's Hollywood Studios, you may not be aware that the ride is based on a real location—the Hollywood Tower Hotel. Built in the 1930s within view of the Hollywood sign, this twelve-story tower boasted bold designs, a top-notch restaurant, a dance hall, and a famous lounge. It wasn't until one fateful night when five people got into an elevator that everything changed.

It was Halloween night in 1939 and all the main elevators were not working when the five hotel guests got on the maintenance elevator in the Tip-Top Lounge. While the elevator was descending floors, lightning struck the hotel and hit the elevator shaft area, plunging the elevator car down out of control and killing all five occupants on impact. The owner of the hotel, Dewey Todd Sr., closed the hotel doors immediately afterward and to this day, witnesses report the place is haunted by those very same five elevator passengers who dropped to their deaths that night.

The tower did reopen later, and people have been living there for decades. The same hotel has been home to many movie stars, including Humphrey Bogart and Errol Flynn, and Carmen Miranda held her wedding in the hotel's lobby. In the late Seventies and into the Eighties, the hotel was overrun with drug users and went into decline. There were a host of murders and suicides and Mafia activity resulting in bodies being thrown off the top of the building, adding to the cadre of ghosts said to have haunted the hotel's rooms and hallways, including a spectral figure on the fourth floor and a male apparition in Thirties-era clothing on the seventh floor who has been spotted staring out at the Hollywood Hills in the distance.

Forever Cemetery

Hollywood Forever Cemetery could be called the final home of many famous celebrities. Buried on the grounds are some of the biggest names in the entertainment industry of the past. The owner of the still active cemetery was featured recently on television's *Six Feet Under*. Buried there are such luminaries as Douglas Fairbanks, Peter Lorre, Tyrone Power, Charlie Chaplin, and even punk guitarist Johnny Ramone. Director Cecil B. DeMille has a large tomb there with stone sarcophagi reminiscent of the Egyptian sets he created for *The Ten Commandments*.

The man who donated Griffith Park, Griffith J. Griffith, is buried there as well as mobster Bugsy Siegel, who was murdered at his girlfriend's mansion in the Beverly Hills Triangle!

Visitors to the grounds report numerous ghosts roaming around and often moving between the cemetery and adjoining entrance to Paramount Studios on the Lemon Grove side, especially Rudolph Valentino, who died at the age of thirty-one and was buried there. But many people also report seeing the ghost of a mysterious woman in black, who leaves flowers at his grave on the anniversary of his death.

Clifton Webb's ghost has been seen around the Abbey of the Psalms mausoleum, sometimes wearing a suit. People report seeing strange lights nearby, smelling strong men's cologne, and hearing whispers from within the mausoleum. Webb also may haunt a chair! Rumors state his ghost is attached to an old, throne-style chair that was given to his old friend, psychic Kenny Kingston. Kingston reported the chair moved on its own during some of his séances despite being kept behind velvet ropes.

A woman named Virginia Rappe is said to haunt her grave there, and visitors report a distinct, cold chill. Rappe was a young woman who died at the age of twenty-six of mysterious causes and was involved in a scandal with comedian and actor Roscoe "Fatty" Arbuckle, whose career was destroyed by unsubstantiated allegations that he raped Rappe at a party.

Marion Davies, the mistress of William Randolph Hearst, is also buried here, and people have reported seeing Hearst's ghost roaming near her grave site as if he is looking for her or watching over her. Davies, who died of cancer in 1961, was with Hearst when he lost all his wealth, so perhaps, he feels as loyal to her in death as he may have in life.

The actor who played Alfalfa in the original *Our Gang* series, Carl Dean Switzer, also haunts the cemetery. He died under mysterious circumstances of a gunshot wound. Also buried here is the legendary Tyrone Power, who was an on-screen swashbuckler and romantic leading man. Sadly, he died in November 1958, hoping to one day have a son. He left behind a pregnant wife, Deborah Ann Montgomery Minardos, who indeed gave birth to his son, Tyrone Power Jr., in January 1959.

Ghostly Locations around Town

Do you remember watching the Aaron Spelling television series *Fantasy Island*? Ricardo Montalbán played the mysterious Mr. Roarke, who helped make your wishes and dreams come true at his lavish island. The show was filmed at the Los Angeles County Arboretum and Botanical Gardens off of Highway 201 near Pasadena, California. Other shows filmed there include *Tarzan*, *Anaconda*, and *Jurassic Park*.

The 127-acre garden and historical site included an older home that was where Chief Buffalo Child Long Lance committed suicide years before in 1932. Chief Buffalo, who wrote an autobiography in 1928 discussing his Blackfoot heritage, was a reporter who was very outspoken in his criticisms of the U.S. government and its treatment of Native Americans. He even starred in a movie called *The Silent Enemy*, which portrayed tribal life. But he held a deep, dark secret, one that was exposed while the movie was filming.

Turns out that Chief Buffalo was really Sylvester Clark Long, a man born to former slaves in North Carolina. He didn't have a drop of Blackfoot Indian

Some scenes from the television show *Fantasy Island* were shot at Queen Anne Cottage at the Los Angeles Arboretum. The ghost of Chief Buffalo has been seen in the area, according to arboretum visitors and the crew from the TV show.

in him, and when his secret came out, he began drinking and was abandoned by his friends and colleagues. In 1932, at the home on the property of the Arboretum, he shot himself. But even today, people visiting the gardens, as well as former cast and crewmembers of the *Fantasy Island* show, insist they've seen his ghost. Some claim they even spoke with him and that he could be seen in the crowd in some scenes of the show!

Another haunted hot spot is located in Laurel Canyon, a place ripe with urban legends. The ghost of the great escape artist haunts his former mansion, known appropriately as "Houdini Mansion," which sits atop a stone staircase amid overgrown brush. The four-story mansion was built back in 1915, where the home suffered through the Laurel Canyon Fire of 1959, as well as lack of care, even becoming a boardinghouse for actors out of work. The isolated location gave rise to many urban legends at the time, and many witnesses claim he roams the grounds in death. Others claim the man seen wandering the property is a murder victim from long before Houdini was associated with the mansion. Either way, it adds to the haunted flavor of Laurel Canyon and has become a favorite destination for ghost hunters on the prowl for proof of the afterlife.

Ghosts aren't usually a laughing matter, but the Sunset Strip in Hollywood boasts a haunted comedy club with quite a history. A popular hot spot opened in the 1940s called Ciro's and later became the famous Comedy Store, where top comedians perform to sold-out crowds. But the ghosts of Ciro's remain, haunting the Belly Room, a smaller, second-floor venue, and the large showroom, usually after hours, when security guards hear banging on piano keys, moving chairs that slide across the stage, lights turning on and off, and even chairs that pile on top of one another!

Then, everything suddenly went black as the lights went out in the entire club. When the lights came back on, many thought it was all part of the act, but Kinison insisted it wasn't.

Even some of the current waitresses have reported unusual activity, according to *8 Hollywood Haunts That Are Seriously Haunted* by Laurie Jacobson for *Britannica.com*. One waitress would open the Belly Room and arrange the chairs and candles, then she would leave, only to return a few moments later to find the door locked, the candles out, and the lights off. Then she would go back and find everything just as she left it! Security guard Blake Clark often heard piano music coming from upstairs, but when he ran up to see if someone got locked in the club after hours, he would find the room empty.

One of the most intriguing encounters at the Comedy Store occurred in the fall of 1986, when stand-up comic Sam Kinison was performing. According to *Haunted Hollywood* by Tom Ogden, Kinison was onstage in the Main Room when he heard voices that were not coming from the crowd. Kinison had also experienced light and sound issues while at the Comedy Store, so when he heard the voices, he wasn't surprised. He stopped the show, and the crowd noticed something was amiss. Kinison then began addressing the voices, telling them they were pissing him off and that if they wanted to play, they needed to reveal themselves to the audience. Then, everything suddenly went black as the lights went out in the entire club. When the lights came back on, many thought it was all part of the act, but Kinison insisted it wasn't.

Then there is the Pink Palace at 1220 Bel Air Drive, a huge, pink mansion that was once home to the likes of Rudy Vallee, Ringo Starr, Engelbert Humperdinck, and its most famous resident, Jayne Mansfield. According to *Haunted Hollywood: Tinseltown Terrors, Filmdom Phantoms and Movieland Mayhem* by Tom Ogden, the Spanish Mediterranean-style mansion was built in 1929 in the swanky Holmby Hills section of Beverly Hills and sported forty rooms total as well as rooms for the staff and a guesthouse. Mansfield was a big, buxom, blonde bombshell and a hugely popular star of the era, and she wanted the house and the walls around it to be pink. She even had her initials carved in wrought iron on the huge entry gate.

As her career rose and fell, she continued to make movies and television appearances and went through her fair share of marriages. She met her end in a car crash when the Buick she was in crashed into a truck in a deep fog at a high speed, killing Mansfield, who was in the front-seat, the car's driver, Ronnie Harrison, and another front seat passenger, Sam Brody. Her three children were in the back seat sleeping and survived the crash with minor injuries.

Later, the Pink Palace became the home of Mama Cass Elliot, then Ringo Starr, who tried to paint over the pink only to find that the pink color could not be covered over! It would bleed back through any color put over it. In 1976, Engelbert Humperdinck, the famous Welsh singer, bought the mansion and restored it to its original pink, then put it on the market in the 1990s. In 2002, he finally sold it to Roland Arnall, a financier who owned a couple of other properties on the cul-de-sac. But it was Humperdinck who reported sensing Jane's ghost and even smelling her favorite rose petal perfume throughout the mansion. He even saw her ghost in a long, black dress. The mansion is no longer there, but Jayne's spirit remains.

One of the richest families in the 1920s in Los Angeles was the Doheny family. One of the clan, Ned Doheny Jr., died tragically at the age of thirty-six after he and his father, Ned Doheny Sr., were involved in a bribery scandal called the Teapot Dome Scandal with President Warren G. Harding. Ned Jr. was murdered, and his assistant and close friend, Hugh Plunkett, was also murdered, although some claim he committed suicide. It all took place at the Greystone Park, where the Doheny Mansion was built in 1928, and is now said to be home to the ghosts of the two dead men.

The 46,000-square-foot, fifty-five-room, Tudor-style mansion cost $3 million at the time it was built. Ned Jr. moved in with his wife and five children only a scant five months before he was found dead of a gunshot wound. Hugh Plunkett was blamed for the murder in the local media, which stated Plunkett went nuts, shot his boss, then shot himself, but a homicide detective named Leslie T. White later wrote a book called *Me, Detective* in which he claimed to have doubted the official story.

He claimed police found the evidence of the crime scene had been tampered with by the family and Ned's physician and that the bodies had even been moved to cover up the real cause of death. There were contradicting claims by family witnesses and the actual evidence found at the scene, and White thought a real investigation should have taken place before it was declared solved only one day after the crime. Some witnesses claimed to have heard an argument with a female behind closed doors before gunshots rang out, suggesting Lucy was involved. And because Ned's death was said to be a murder and not a suicide, he was not buried with his family and instead was buried at Forest Lawn in Glendale, California.

Later, a Chicago man named Henry Crown bought the home and leased it out to film studios in the area, and it was used in many films of the time. The grounds became a city park in 1971, and the mansion was listed as a historical place in 1976. For decades, the two murders remained truly an unsolved mystery, and dozens of witnesses claim to have experienced ghostly activity on the grounds, including the apparition of a man walking the hallways near the room where the murders occurred and even a pool of blood that appears and disappears on the floor of the murder room.

Four Oaks Restaurant was originally built in the 1880s as a café and inn catering to cowboys and animal herders heading to market. Later, its upstairs dining area was used as a brothel, while downstairs in the bar, bootlegged booze was served. Now, a lovely restaurant sits where there was once a huge oak tree with four separate trunks, later cut down to make a parking space but remembered in place that bears its name and its ghosts. In their book *Hollywood Haunted: A Ghostly Tour of Filmland*, authors Laurie Jacobson and Marc Wanamaker tell the haunted history of the restaurant.

The *Adventures of Ozzie and Harriet* featured the Nelson family (clockwise from top left: Harriet, David, Ricky, and Ozzie). After Ozzie passed away, the new owners of the Nelson house reported ghostly occurrences there.

In 1989, Peter Roelant bought the place from actor Jack Allen, who had found interesting items buried in the house during a renovation and even uncovered a secret passageway. After the renovation was done, a busboy who was there after hours encountered a large, glowing figure standing on the other side of the room he was in. He quit the very next day! Jack, the owner at the time, didn't think much of the incident, even staying at an apartment at the restaurant. Big celebrities such as Steve McQueen, Vincent Price, and Elke Sommer were locals who liked to spend time at the café.

But one late evening, something startled Jack. He got out of bed and was about to go check it out when his bedroom door flew open to reveal a glowing figure standing there. Jack screamed for it to go away, and the figure eventually disappeared, never to appear again. Today, the lovely café is free from ghostly endeavors so far.

Jacobson and Wanamaker write about another intriguing haunted location in their book, and it's not one that might first come to mind when the word "ghost" is mentioned. The clean-cut image of Ozzie and Harriet Nelson apparently went beyond their television show, *The Adventures of Ozzie and Harriet*, in the 1950s, at least when it came to their house. The lovely home they lived in for twenty-five years was a two-story colonial located at the base of the Hollywood Hills. The couple raised their two sons there, and the house was used as a model for the home in the television show, including exterior shots.

After Ozzie's death in 1975, Harriet sold the house, and the new owners experienced strange activity such as footsteps, lights turning on and off, and doors opening and closing. They contacted Dr. Barry Taff, a parapsychologist, who came to the home to investigate. He learned that the female owner was experiencing sexual activity courtesy of a ghost, who would caress and kiss her at night. She would wake from sleep and find the covers pulled down, but no one was around. Even though Taff told her this was common paranormal activity, she moved out.

A painter working on the home in 1994 heard footsteps and witnessed a ghostly apparition while in the empty house but was unable to identify the ghost.

Beverly Glen, which connects the San Fernando Valley to West Los Angeles, is one of the oldest canyon areas in the city, with its own winding road lined with woods filled with sycamores and oaks. At the top of the glen is the famous Mulholland Drive. During the 1800s, the road boasted small inns and roadhouses. One in particular was converted more recently into apartments and is home to paranormal activity associated with a husband and wife, a killer and his victim.

Residents of the apartment building report noises and footsteps running upstairs as well as heavy breathing and cold spots. The appearance of a headless man dressed in yellow has spooked more than one resident. The figure would appear in a yellow cape and glow, with no head to speak of, and would stand by the side of the road visible out the apartment windows.

The building was once divided into three floors when it served as an inn, and, around the turn of the century, a wealthy man arrived with his pretty wife for a night at the theater. They stayed overnight at the inn, and afterward, the wife would often arrive alone. She fell in love with a young man who was known for wearing yellow, and when the husband found out, he charged up the stairs and cut off the young man's head with a scythe as his wife watched in horror. The man was later executed for the murder.

Some say the headless ghost is the young man standing in wait for his married lover. The sound of someone running up the stairs is clearly the wealthy husband coming to catch his wife and her lover in the throes of passion, a passion that caused them all such tragedy. The stuff ghost stories are made of.

Another popular hot spot is Barney's Beanery, an eatery on Santa Monica Boulevard that has been a Los Angeles fixture since 1927. A male ghost haunts the place, seen often in a white shirt in the cellar as well as in the rooftop office. Waiters report feeling a sensation of something brushing past them, the sound of beer kegs scraping across the floor, and even knives spinning in the kitchen on their own! Perhaps, these are the ghosts of three men who had been murdered in the bar and restaurant in its early years.

Waiters report feeling a sensation of something brushing past them, the sound of beer kegs scraping across the floor, and even knives spinning in the kitchen on their own!

On West Sunset Boulevard, a pub called The Cat & Fiddle reigned as a popular spot until it closed in 2014. Housed inside the Thompson building, this pub offered British fare when it opened in 1984. It had been located in the notoriously haunted Laurel Canyon area for two years prior and, in its earlier years, hosted a number of mobsters, including one who was killed in 1930. Gunfights broke out during a mob party, resulting in one man being shot to death. These deaths might explain the paranormal shenanigans reported there such as glasses flying around and falling from shelves, lights going on and off, and the saloon doors swinging open and closed as well as the pub's jukebox turning itself on. A male ghost has been reported smoking a cigarette, leaning against the wall at the front gate, or heading upstairs to the office.

Traveling Ghosts

One interesting thing comes to mind when reading of these celebrity ghost sightings. Many times, the particular star's ghost is seen in numerous places, often at the same time! The ghost of a dead actor might haunt his former mansion, the theater he loved to perform in, the place where he tragically died, *and* the cemetery his body is buried at—even his favorite restaurant, to boot. Rarely do we hear about ghosts of average, normal people haunting multiple locations, suggesting that either celebrity ghosts do a lot of traveling in death just as they did in life, or there is something else going on that may have to do with recognition … and fame.

Could it be that we are so enamored and fascinated with these people, even after they leave this Earth, that we imagine them into existence? What might we, the observing fans, have to do with their appearances? Do we expect to see ghosts of famous people where they once lived and worked? Our collective love and often adoration of the rich and famous creates a power all its own that brings about the physical manifestation of our favorite actors, musicians, and performers. It may be a collective endeavor, just as celebrity worship is a collective endeavor that results in the popularity of gossip magazines and television shows.

We see not only what we want to see but what we expect to see, and that includes Elvis in his studio, at Graceland, and even at the local Burger King chowing down on junk food.

Fame, Fortune, and Ghosts

Billionaire Howard Hughes wasn't the only tycoon to haunt his favorite place (Pantages Theater) after death. Frank Winfield Woolworth wasn't an actor or a musician. As the store tycoon and millionaire founder of Woolworth's five-and-dime stores, he certainly was a household name for many. Those who lived in Glen Cove, a suburb of Long Island, New York, where Woolworth owned a mansion, claim there was more to the man than the public imagined. In fact, residents who knew of the mansion, Winfield Hall, told author Arthur Myers in *Ghosts of the Rich and Famous* of everything from apparitions to strange, ghostly music to all kinds of paranormal activity.

Many séances were held at the great mansion after Woolworth died of septic poisoning in 1919, only two years after he had Winfield built, including those organized by Fran Tucciardo and Monica Randall, a native of the region, who wrote about them in her 1987 book *The Mansions of Long Island's Gold Coast*. During séances led by Fran, the ghost of Woolworth himself would appear, angry that his library was going to be remodeled. Monica learned as a child of the hauntings at Winfield and during her own séances even encountered the ghost of Woolworth's daughter, Edna, who had taken her own life. Monica also revealed Woolworth's association with the occult, stating that he filled the house with carvings that represented demons and occult symbolism.

But others, including the official historian of Glen Cove, Dan Russell, believe the occult connection is untrue. Tours of the mansion continued to turn up eyewitness accounts of ghosts and strange activity, even reports by grounds staff, night watchmen, and gardeners. Today, the mansion is owned by the Pall Corporation, a company that makes industrial filters, and uses the home as their headquarters. According to Arthur Myers, the secretaries get a kick out of the secret passageways and interesting angel symbolism on the ceiling!

No word as to whether or not any shoppers at Woolworth stores have ever encountered Frank's ghost roaming the aisles.

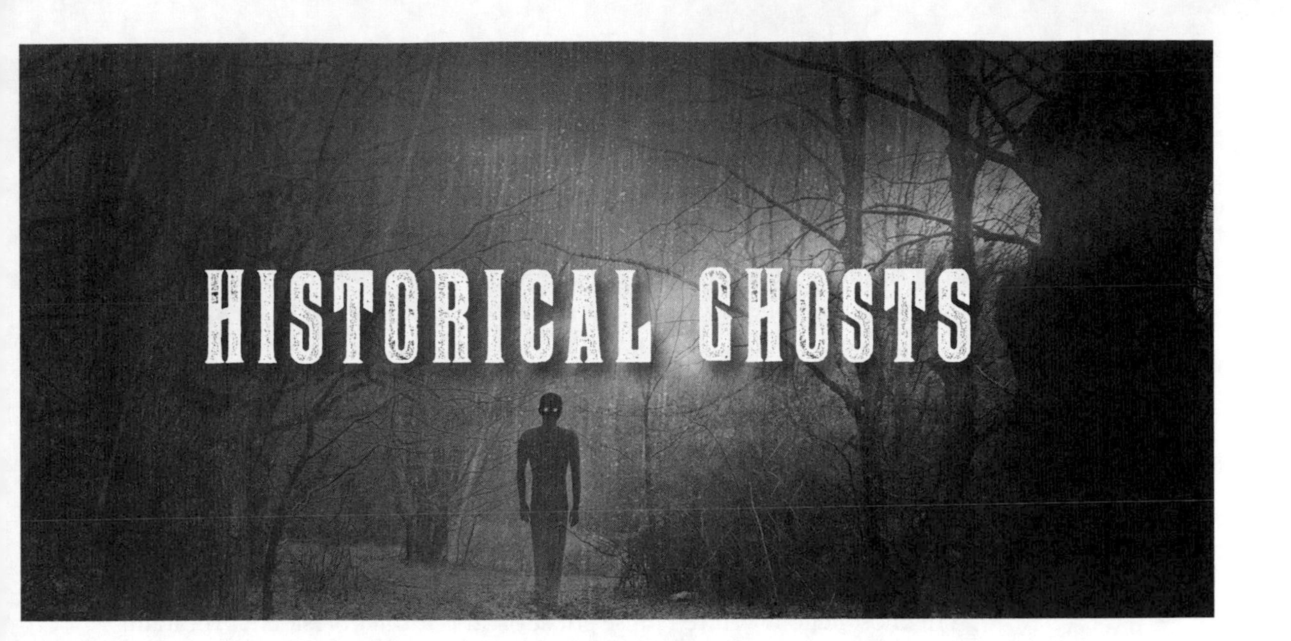

Fame isn't just reserved for movie and television stars, and ghost sightings aren't, either. In fact, there are just as many intriguing accounts of people seeing ghosts of historical figures from politicians to judges to scientists to inventors to religious figures to mass murderers. If a person had some semblance of notoriety, good or bad, in life, they carried that over into death in the form of otherworldly apparitions haunting their favorite, or not-so-favorite, places. If their death happened to be traumatic, as in the case of murder or suicide, there was even more chance their spirits would be witnessed roaming Earth, unable to give up the life they left behind so long ago and step into the light.

When it comes to historical hauntings, our first thoughts usually go to politicians and military leaders who lost their lives to an assassin's bullet or in the heat of war on a battlefield. A senator, general, or even prime minister may not garner the same fan base as a movie idol or pop star, but their importance to the evolution of our country, and even the world, ensures they, too, will be remembered long after the time of their deaths. The more powerful these men and women were in life, the more famous their ghosts become in death.

While many people in the ancient past saw and wrote about ghostly encounters, we focus a bit more on modern historical times, when we have better records of the details of sightings and reports. But who would argue that the ghosts of religious figures, knights, emperors, queens and kings, princes and princesses, pharaohs, prophets, oracles, and high priests roamed the areas important to them in spirit form and probably still do!

Dead Presidents

Presidents who once walked the rooms of the White House may in their deaths still be walking them. Rumors of ghostly apparitions abound not just from tourists but from those who worked in the White House and halls of Congress throughout history. Their stories have no doubt prompted even more of an interest in historical ghosts and driven thousands of tourists to attempt to get a glimpse themselves of these spectral leaders. Could it be because these men and women were of such great importance that their influence lives on to this day in the form of ghost sightings? Are they actual ghosts or products of our viral imaginations?

Yet, even presidents claim to see and experience ghostly sightings of leaders who came before them, as we shall see.

Abraham Lincoln

The most famous White House ghost of all is former president Abraham Lincoln. In fact, Lincoln is called the "White House Ghost" and has appeared to not only regular folks but many political leaders and figures who admit seeing his stately figure long after his death in 1865.

Lincoln was the nation's sixteenth president. He began as a self-taught lawyer and legislator known for speaking against slavery. He was elected in November 1860, just prior to the start of the Civil War, and his Emancipation Proclamation was instrumental in the abolition of slavery when it was made law in January 1863 (the Thirteenth Amendment to the U.S. Constitution outlawing slavery would occur shortly after Lincoln's death in 1865). Many remember him as a great military strategist and orator, and his Gettysburg Address, made during the dedication of the National Cemetery at Gettysburg, Pennsylvania, is considered one of the greatest and most widely quoted speeches of all time despite being only 272 words long.

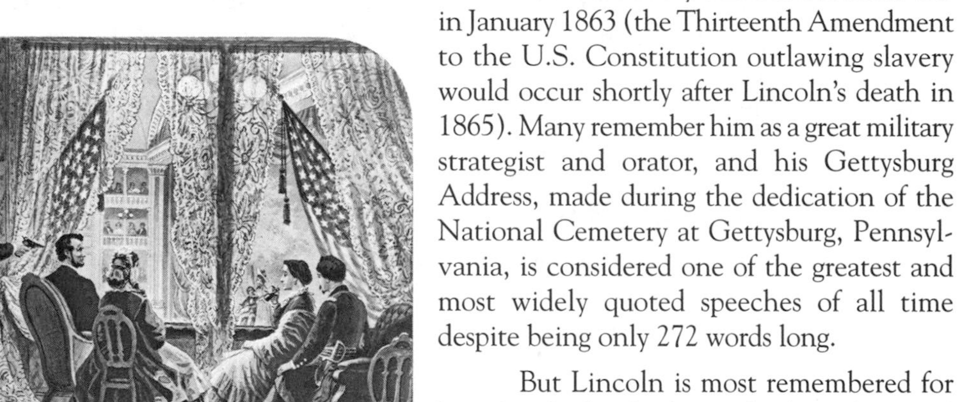

Most Americans are familiar with how President Lincoln was assassinated while attending Ford's Theatre, but did you know his ghost later appeared before his wife, Mary, as well as first ladies Eleanor Roosevelt and Lady Bird Johnson?

But Lincoln is most remembered for how he died, which was both violent and tragic. He was assassinated by a man named John Wilkes Booth in April 1865, just as the Union was on the verge of achieving victory in the Civil War. Booth was an actor and a known Confederate sympathizer, and he shot the president in the back of the head during a performance at the famous Ford's Theatre in Washington, D.C.

Lincoln died the next day, never regaining consciousness. But if Booth had hoped to destroy Lincoln's power and influence as a leader, he failed miserably. Despite being born to humble roots in a one-room log cabin in Hardin County, Kentucky, Abraham Lincoln made a huge mark on American politics and became even more iconic in his death than he was in life. He is regarded as one of the greatest U.S. presidents to this day.

The ghost of Abraham Lincoln is alleged to have appeared to his wife, Mary Todd Lincoln, in a photograph taken by spirit photographer William H. Mumler around 1869, according to the book *Ghosts Caught on Film* by Melvin Willin. The photo, which many now believe to be a hoax, shows Lincoln standing behind his wife, who is sitting, with his hand rested upon her shoulder.

The history of Lincoln ghosts continues with sightings of Abraham Lincoln's young son, Willie, who died at the age of eleven in the White House from typhoid.

Eleanor Roosevelt was reported to have encountered the ghost of Lincoln, or at least his presence, during her time at the White House. She used the Lincoln Bedroom as her study and would feel Lincoln's presence late at night while she was up working.

Because press secretaries spend so much time roaming the White House, it isn't surprising to find that James Hagerty, who served as press secretary to President Dwight Eisenhower, and Liz Carpenter, press secretary to Lady Bird Johnson, both claimed to have been in the presence of Lincoln's ghost on several occasions. Former seamstress Lillian Rogers Parks once investigated strange sounds of someone walking on the upper level of the White House. Other staff members at the time would tell her it was just "Old Abe" pacing the floor.

Lady Bird Johnson herself saw Lincoln's ghost one night while she was watching a television program about his death!

Lincoln's former bedroom has been the location of spectral footsteps and strange knocking on the door, even heard by the likes of Margaret and Harry Truman. Lincoln's figure has been reported seen lying on the bed he once slept in, and his apparition has been reported wearing the coat and top hat he was so famous for. Because of his choice of haunting location, many a president and staff member have claimed to have seen Lincoln's ghost, including Theodore Roosevelt, Grace Coolidge, Herbert Hoover, and Maureen Reagan, who, along with her husband, saw Lincoln's ghost standing at the fireplace. British Prime Minister Winston Churchill visited the White House often during World War II and would take late baths while drinking scotch, often encountering Lincoln standing beside the fireplace, leaning against the mantle, or sitting in a chair by the fireplace, watching him smoke his cigars. Most of the Lincoln ghost sightings occurred in the Lincoln Bedroom or the Yellow Oval Room, the same place the ghost of Thomas Jefferson is often seen and heard playing his violin.

In 1942, Queen Wilhelmina of the Netherlands answered a knock on the door of the bedroom she was staying in at the White House, only to open it and see Lincoln's ghost standing there before her wearing a coat and top hat. She fainted at the sight.

Outside of the White House, Lincoln's ghost often appeared at his gravesite in Springfield, Illinois, and at the house in Loudonville, New York, where a woman who was present during his assassination at Ford's Theatre lived.

The history of Lincoln ghosts continues with sightings of Abraham Lincoln's young son, Willie, who died at the age of eleven in the White House from typhoid. Willie's ghost has appeared to staff members of the Grant Administration during the 1870s as well as to President Lyndon Johnson's daughter Lynda Bird Johnson, who claimed to have talked to the child's ghost, according to *Historic Haunted America* by Beth Scott and Michael Norman.

Haunted White House

Abigail Adams, married to second president John Adams, used to hang laundry out to dry in the East Room of the White House because it was warm and dry. After her death, her ghost has been reported in the same room wearing her cap and lace shawl, arms outstretched as if holding a pile of laundry. As recently as 2002, according to *Ancestry.com*'s "Ghosts of Presidents Past: Who's Haunting the White House?", staff members report smelling wet clothing and the scent of lavender in the room. One of the witnesses who saw Adams's ghost is none other than President William Howard Taft, who saw her ghost float through doors on the second floor and act out mannerisms as if hanging up laundry to dry.

The ghosts of Andrew Jackson and Harry Truman also haunt the White House. Andrew Jackson's apparition made an appearance during a séance in the early 1860s held by Mary Todd Lincoln, who was then first lady. She was a big believer in life after death and the occult and often held séances to communicate with her dead sons. She claimed to have heard Jackson moving around in a hallway and swearing, especially in or near the Rose Room, which was his bedroom while in office.

Another first lady who has haunted the White House is the wife of President James Madison. Dolley Madison planted the famous rose garden in the early 1800s, and after her death, First Lady Ellen Wilson demanded the garden be dug up. But garden workers claimed the ghost of Dolley Madison would appear and refuse to let them dig up her beloved garden. Often, staff have reported the scent of roses inside the White House, attributing them to Dolley and her love for her precious rose garden.

Reagan's Ghostly Encounter

According to reporter Joan Gage in her December 31, 2013, *Huffington Post* blog entry titled "Ronald Reagan's White House Ghost Story," the former president, known as a brilliant storyteller, recounted at a dinner his story of hearing Rex, his Cavalier King Charles Spaniel and first dog, barking at the Lincoln Bedroom and refusing to enter the room. The president also stated he was watching television with his wife, Nancy, when Rex began standing on his two hind legs and barking at something overhead on the ceiling. He wondered if the dog was responding to some high-pitched noise they could not hear or, perhaps ... a ghost. Maybe even the ghost of Abe Lincoln himself. Reagan's daughter, Maureen, and her husband saw the ghost of Lincoln in the Lincoln Bedroom staring out the window. They could see through the ghost!

Mamie's Ghost

Before Dwight "Ike" Eisenhower became president in 1952, he lived with his wife, Mamie, in a farmhouse adjacent the Gettysburg battlefield. Though the place was run-down when they moved in, they came to prefer staying there as a retreat. After their time in the White House, they retreated back to the "Gettysburg house" until Ike's death in 1969 and Mamie's death in 1979. The U.S. Department of the Interior made it a National Historic Landmark shortly afterward, but ever since Mamie's death, strange things have been reported at the farmhouse. Park rangers working at the farmhouse reported hearing thumping noises and seeing apparitions of Mamie, usually in the living room area, even hearing music coming from an empty guest room in the farmhouse.

A respected psychic named Anne Gehman investigated the farmhouse in 1982 and spoke with the rangers, even admitting to communicating herself with the spirit of Mamie's maid, Rose Wood. Other farmhouse spirits Gehman reported during her time there included a little boy and a Native American spirit who encouraged her to have the Park Service acknowledge the area's historical importance, which they did. Mamie was specifically quite concerned that the garden behind the house would be torn up for a possible parking lot and voiced her opposition to Gehman during one communication!

A Deadly Duel

Aaron Burr was the third vice president and presided under Thomas Jefferson. Most people know him instead for his deadly duel at Weehawken on the New Jersey side of the Hudson River with Alexander Hamilton on July 11, 1804. Burr mortally wounded Hamilton, who, along with being the treasury secretary, was one of the Founding Fathers of the nation and chief of staff to George Washington. Burr was tried for treason but acquitted. Yet, his name will always be associated with that fateful treasonous label. During his VP campaign, he worked out of his carriage house located at 17 Barrow Street in New York City. After his death, that location became the One if by Land, Two if by Sea restaurant, and staff and visitors alike claim all kinds of paranormal activity there, including chairs being pulled out from under patrons and dishes flying through the air in the kitchen area.

One of the most famous gun battles in American history was the 1804 duel between Alexander Hamilton and Aaron Burr. Hamilton was mortally wounded. His ghost is said to haunt a restaurant that was built on the spot where he met his fate as well as the home of the former doctor who treated him.

Burr's own daughter, Theodosia Burr, is said to have perished when she boarded a ship called the *Patriot* in December 1812 that sank off the coast of Cape Hatteras, North Carolina, during a terrible storm. She was on her way to see her father when the ship went down, and rumors abounded that pirates may have boarded the boat, forced the passengers and crew to walk the plank, then sank the ship after taking all valuables.

There was a legend long after claiming Theodosia survived with her only possession, a portrait of herself, and was cared for by a local fisherman and his wife until her death. In fact, she may have walked into the ocean holding the portrait, not wanting to part with it. Many people reported seeing her ghost walking along the shoreline. The portrait washed up on the beach. Today, that portrait is said to belong to members of the Burr family.

It wasn't just his daughter who became a ghost. Burr seemed to have been surrounded by spirits! Later, at the age of seventy-seven, Burr married a woman named Eliza Jumel, who was a wealthy widow that many believed had killed her first husband (his ghost was reported to haunt the mansion she lived in with Burr). Eliza and Aaron Burr separated after only a few months when she suspected his land speculation deals were responsible for much of the loss of her money. Interestingly, Burr died on the same day his divorce to Eliza was finalized: September 11, 1836. Eliza herself may have haunted the same mansion after she died at the age of ninety-three.

Hamilton is said to haunt his former home in Greenwich Village, where newer visitors have reported poltergeist-like activity, as well as the home of his doctor, John Francis, who treated him when he was mortally wounded by Burr. This house, located at 27 Jane Street in New York City, was haunted according to a later resident, Jean Karsavina, who lived there from 1939. Hamilton died during his attempts to recover from the gunshot wound while in his own bed in his home at 80 Jane Street, just a few doors down from the Francis home.

According to noted paranormal researcher Hans Holzer in his book *Famous Ghosts: True Encounters with the World Beyond*, the 80 Jane Street home no longer exists, but the 27 Jane Street home of Hamilton's former doctor does, and Karsavina reported hearing footsteps, creaking doors opening and closing, creaking on the stairs, and the unexplained flushing of a toilet! She has witnessed blurred shapes and a shadowy apparition wearing early nineteenth-century garb and white trousers that would walk in and out of her room.

Today, both Burr and Hamilton have found renewed fame in the blockbuster Broadway musical *Hamilton*, putting a modern spin on their long and tumultuous history in life and in death.

Famous Foreign Ghosts

Adolf Hitler needs no introduction. The man who caused so much death and suffering and ended the lives of millions is said to haunt the ruins of his former Bavarian mountain retreat home. Witnesses claim his ghost looks as if it is grieving or in a state of despair and is often seen sitting in an armchair and gazing out to the mountains. Some report even hearing his voice shouting orders to his men.

Henry VIII, the English monarch once married to Anne Boleyn, is said to haunt the Windsor Castle halls, dragging his ulcerated leg or pacing in the Cloisters. Boleyn is even more active, with her ghost appearing in many of the castle windows and in the Dean's Cloister. Boleyn, who was Henry's second of six wives, died in a most horrible way. After she was unable to bear her husband a son and heir, she was tried on charges of adultery and incest and beheaded on the Tower Green inside the Tower of London.

Her headless figure is reported even now moving from the Queen's House to the Chapel Royal of St. Peter ad Vincula, where her remains are buried.

Tower sentries witnessed her ghost wearing a cloak with an empty hood or pacing the Green, holding her head under her arm. She is also said to haunt her birthplace in Norfolk and arrives in a carriage pulled by six headless horses driven by a headless coachman. In addition, she haunts her childhood home of Hever Castle, where she often appears on a bridge on Christmas Eve. Other known haunts of hers include Sallie Church and Marwell Hall. Her spirit is clearly restless and active perhaps because of the horrific way she met her death at the hands of the man she loved.

English explorer and writer Sir Walter Raleigh is most famous for trying to bring the colonists to the New World of America in the 1580s. The colonists landed at a place called Roanoke Island in Virginia. Several years later, he returned with another group of settlers. A man named John White returned to England to find supplies to bring back within a year, but it was several years before the supplies could get to Roanoke. When they did arrive, the entire settlement was gone. They had vanished as if into thin air.

Theories abound to this day about where the Roanoke colony disappeared to. Some "conclusions" have been put forth in books, movies, and television shows but are always disputed because of lack of evidence. No one knows where they went, although they may have ended up on another island, where they perished due to elements and starvation or at the hands of natives.

Sir Walter Raleigh was involved years later in an alleged plot against King James I and was banished to the Tower of London. He was released thirteen years later and went to South America for a short time, then back to London, where he was then arrested, tried, and found guilty. He was beheaded.

The Tower of London has served as a palace and prison for centuries—although its prison days ended in the 1950s. Sir Walter Raleigh, who was once a captive there, is said to still linger in spirit form.

His ghost is said to haunt the Tower of London near the cell he was kept in. The Tower is also said to be home to the ghosts of two little princes, Edward V and his brother Richard, the Duke of York, who were also banished there in 1483 after the death of their father at the hands of their protector uncle, the Duke of Gloucester, during attempts to keep the boys from the throne. In 1674, the remains of two skeletons were found in the White Tower under a stairway to the chapel and reburied in Westminster Abbey on order of then King Charles II. The skeletons are said to be those of the two young boys who thought they would be kings one day.

Russian's capital city of Moscow is home to the iconic Kremlin, a fortified complex that has a reputation of being haunted by old Soviet Russian leaders. The Russian Revolution of 1917 left many ghosts to roam the halls of this imposing building, made of various towers, four palaces, and five cathedrals, including the famous Saint Basil's Cathedral. In the eleventh century, the entire complex was fortified and later was expanded upon, then rebuilt by Catherine the Great during the Imperial period. It has been the site of various assassinations, deaths, murders, and tragedies, and Vladimir Lenin and Joseph Stalin are among the ghosts said to stalk the vast hallways.

The most haunted plantation in the United States may also be one of the most haunted homes in general. Witnesses report at least nine different ghosts haunting the grounds of Myrtles Plantation, a twenty-eight-room Creole cottage bed-and-breakfast located in St. Francisville, Louisiana. Thirty miles north of Baton Rouge, this historical place has spawned a number of books and television shows. Though it has been used as an inn from 1980 on, when it was purchased by a couple who documented their experiences with ghostly apparitions and strange noises in the book *The Myrtles Plantation: The True Story of America's Most Haunted House*, the location has a much richer history going back over 220 years.

Built around 1796, the once working plantation sports a number of ghosts that haunt the grounds, resulting in everything from apparitions to shaking clocks to floating beds, opening and closing doors, and footsteps running up and down the hallways. One of those ghosts is of a young slave girl named Chloe, who was hanged on the plantation around 1823 after poisoning the wife and daughters of the slave owner, who made sexual advances toward her. Though skeptics claim the wife and daughters died of yellow fever, the legend still holds that they were killed by Chloe, who after her hanging decided to stick around and haunt the grounds. Another version of the story has Chloe killing the owner's daughters by accident, having intended to poison them just enough to then nurse them back to health. As a result, she was killed by other slaves who turned on her and tossed her body in the nearby river.

Another ghost, William Winter, was a lawyer who resided on the plantation from 1865 to 1871. He was shot on the porch and went into the house, trying to climb the stairs and find his wife. He died on the seventeenth step, and witnesses today report they can hear his "dying steps" on the stairwell. Though none of the ghostly activity at Myrtles poses any danger to those who dare to stay there, it is still quite unsettling, and the current owners offer tours of the plantation to anyone who hopes to run into one of the many ghosts reported to have died there.

Oak Alley

There is something about Bayou Country. In the town of Vacherie, Louisiana, sits the Oak Alley Plantation, built back in 1837. Known for its wonderful architectural features, this haunted location sports a ghost of a young woman with long, dark hair roaming the hallways and crying. Her sobs are said to echo throughout the mansion. Things move of their own accord, and apparitions appear and then vanish into thin air. Some witnesses believe they've seen the very last caretaker who lived on the plantation—Mrs. Stewart. She died in 1972.

Oak Alley has been investigated by ghost hunters, psychics, and clairvoyants alike, and during one investigation in 2003, the International Society for Paranormal Research used thermal imaging cameras and spotted ghosts of Confederate soldiers standing near the property, a six-year-old boy, a young girl, and the women who originally ran the mansion according to historical records. The team even encountered a candle tossed across a room in the dining room of the mansion, and rocking chairs are alleged to rock wildly on their own.

Magnolia Plantation

Also in Louisiana, the Magnolia Plantation in Natchitoches has a dark, dark past filled with torture and abuse of slaves. There are historical records of the many torture devices that are still on display there, speaking to a past of brutality toward those who served the wealthy, white owners. Once a cotton and tobacco plantation, several parts of the grounds remain the same as they did in 1830, including the main house, the slave quarters, the slave hospital, the store, and the blacksmith shop.

The plantation was built in 1830 by Ambrose Lecomte II and his wife, Julia Buard. It once covered over 5,000 acres (2,000 hectares) and used slave labor to clear woods for cotton fields that helped the family amass enough wealth to buy two additional plantations. Magnolia was the home base, and even until the 1970s, there were still workers picking cotton there until the demise of the operation in the 1980s. The store closed down in 1990, and the entire property was eventually donated to the National Park Service in 1994, which saved it from absolute ruin.

The plantation is known for ghosts of the slaves who suffered and died there from journal entries of the Lecomte family themselves reporting ghostly figures to visitors today seeing the face of a slave named Union Major in the horrific place called the "Dying Room" and other ghostly activity around the grounds, including

The mansion at Oak Alley Plantation, built in the 1830s, is a National Historic Landmark. It is also a hot spot for spooky spirits!

Civil War soldiers who died there and were buried in shallow graves. Some of the ghosts crawl around on all fours. Voices have been reported in empty rooms, and the location has become a popular destination for ghost hunters and researchers, who report that motion detectors pick up activity when there is no one around.

Perhaps it was the torture devices such as leg stocks and records of starvation that drove the slaves not only to their deaths but to haunt the place afterward, still in torment. But there are also records that the slaves resorted to voodoo as a way to cast evil spells on the slave owners, evident in the ornate crosses the slaves were forced to make for the graves of the family members. Those crosses sported symbols associated with voodoo right alongside Christian symbols. The main house is not the original but an exact replica rebuilt in 1897, although the wood used was taken from slave quarters. The ghosts of the slaves were imprinted upon the wood that was used to keep them from freedom.

San Francisco Plantation

The most opulent plantation on the Mississippi River, the Garyville, Louisiana, plantation is an amazing architectural example of ornate style and riverboat tradition. Built in 1854 by a rich sugar planter, Edmond Bozonier-

Marmillion, the main house is colorful and unique, sitting under gorgeous, live oak trees. It is also furnished and decorated with hand-painted ceilings, faux marble pieces, and one of the finest collections of antiques in the United States.

The plantation house has fourteen rooms, and the grounds include historic outbuildings such as a slave cabin and schoolhouse dating back to the 1830s and 1840s. Today, the beautiful grounds are home to weddings, receptions, and craft festivals, and in 1974, the plantation was declared a National Historic Landmark. But it has more than just unique style and appeal. It has ghosts.

One in particular, the ghost of Charles Marmillion, who was the son of the original owner, is said to make his presence known throughout the house. In addition, some claim to see and hear the ghosts of the owner's daughters, one of whom died at childbirth and another who perished by falling down a staircase at the age of two.

Southern Plantation Phantoms

Bulloch Hall is located in Roswell, Georgia, and was once the home of Theodore Roosevelt's mother, Martha Bulloch Roosevelt. Bulloch Hall, built in 1839, was once a prosperous antebellum plantation with dozens of slaves. Legend has it that one slave girl was found dead in a well behind the mansion. The girl was supposed to light the candles in the main house when it got dark. After her death, people reported seeing flickering lights inside the house, even though it was closed to any visitors. Other sightings include people dressed in Civil War-era clothing looking out from upstairs windows.

Over in Adairsville, Georgia, sits Barnsley Gardens, built in the 1840s by Godfrey Barnsley for his wife, Julia. But, years before, Barnsley had been warned against building at that particular location by a Cherokee elder who lived in the area. The man believed it was sacred ground, and the Cherokee forefathers would be disrespected. Barnsley built anyway, and the result was his beloved wife falling ill and dying soon after. He stopped the construction until he saw her ghost. Julia's ghost begged him to finish what he started, so he did. But that wasn't the end of tragedy; his son died in the Civil War, and his daughter died during childbirth.

Thinking the house and grounds cursed, Barnsley left and moved to New Orleans to start over. What he left behind were ghosts of his wife, Julia, whom many witnesses report in the home, as well as seeing her standing outside at the fountain looking at her beautiful home, the gift of her loving husband.

The Drish House in Tuscaloosa, Alabama, is called the most haunted house in the state. This main house was built in the 1830s by slave owner John Drish, who was an alcoholic and gambler. He died in 1867 by throwing himself off the upstairs balcony, leaving behind a grieving wife, Sarah, who died in 1884. Soon after her death, the home erupted in small fires, but when firemen got there, there were no fires burning, leading some to believe it was the work of Sarah, who was angry over missing candles she had wanted used for her husband's funeral and then for her own. The candles were never found.

In Demopolis, Alabama, another plantation sports its own ghostly activity. Gaineswood is said to be haunted by the ghost of a beloved nanny who worked there caring for the children and got sick, dying in the house during a cold winter. With no means of transporting her body back to her family, the owner of the plantation put the nanny in a box and stuck it down in the cellar until spring, then managed to get it home to her loved ones.

But those who visit the plantation report hearing the notes of a piano, which she loved to play, and a female voice singing.

Ferry Plantation, which is also known as Ferry Farm, is located in Virginia Beach, Virginia. It was built in 1830 in the Federal architectural style, and the main house was once used as a courthouse, school, and even a post office. Today, it hosts history camps for young people interested in the area's rich history. It also hosts ghosts—upward of eleven spirits, witnesses say! The reason may go back to the building site location, said to have been sacred to local Indians, and many of their artifacts dating back to the sixteenth century have been found. The home was built by slaves and is considered a historical landmark. Present-

The main house at Ferry Plantation in Virginia Beach, Virginia, is host to several ghosts, including the Lady in White, the artist Thomas Williamson, and a slave named Sally Rebecca Walke.

day ghost tours reveal many witnesses reporting the ghostly apparitions of those who died in an 1810 shipwreck at the nearby ferry landing as well as the ghost of Sally Rebecca Walke, a former slave grieving over her beloved soldier. There is also an alleged Lady in White, who broke her neck in 1826 falling down a flight of stairs, and the ghost of artist Thomas Williamson, who can often be spotted painting at the top of the stairs.

Also reported is the sound of dragging chains related to the house once operating as a courthouse, where slaves and prisoners were brought before the judge in chains.

Edgewood Plantation in Charles City, Virginia, is said to be haunted by a ghost of a woman who died of a broken heart. Built in 1854, the mansion was used as a Civil War lookout post and is haunted by the ghost of Lizzie Rowland, who waited there for the return of her soldier and lover, who perished in the war. She is reported moving around the upstairs bedroom by those who come to stay at this now lovely bed-and-breakfast, which offers tours and tea parties. Other haunted hot spots include the grounds where misty apparitions of people dressed in Confederate clothes walk and the nearby slave buildings, where several suicides occurred.

Imagine trying to restore an old building and being interrupted by the ghost of a small girl looking for her mother. In West Point, Mississippi, the Waverly Mansion and Gardens underwent restoration after years of neglect. But the ghosts of the little girl stayed as well as a man in military garb who wanders about to appear in mirrors and objects moving on their own.

Built in the 1840s for owner Colonel George Hampton Young, this cotton plantation included a magnificent main house, an ice pit twenty feet deep, a self-sustaining farm, a kiln, a tannery, a gristmill, gardens, and orchards. And slaves. It was a showplace during and after the war, but in the early 1900s, the last of the Young family had passed away, and the location deteriorated before being purchased by a couple in 1962, who lovingly restored it back to life.

Ghosts haunting the house and grounds also include a horse and rider that show up on occasion and a dinner party of ghostly guests who are heard talking and laughing. It is now open to the public for tours.

Drayton Hall Plantation in Charleston, South Carolina, started out as a tract of 750 acres (300 hectares) of land first owned by Edward Mayo in 1678. He sold the land in 1681 to Joseph Harbin, who built the first house, which was later sold to John Drayton in 1738. The Drayton family came from Barbados and had many slaves and indentured servants with them. They occupied the home from the early 1750s and used the land to grow Carolina Gold, a special type of rice. The family also raised cattle and pigs and employed about forty-five slaves.

John Drayton, a member of the Royal Governor's Council, was married to a woman named Margaret Glenn in 1752. She died twenty years later, and he remarried in 1775 to a woman named Rebecca Perry. He had sons educated in the finest schools, and much of the style and furnishings in the house were imported from England. John's son, William Henry, was a revolutionary elected to Congress and a loud and belligerent drinker when he got fired up over his political beliefs, who died at the age of thirty-seven. Drayton and his family fled the plantation during the Revolutionary War in 1779, when British soldiers marched on the land. Drayton died shortly after and left behind his four sons and their families.

Eventually, the family sold the plantation to the National Trust for Historic Preservation due to the high cost of maintaining the property. The remaining acreage was sold to the state of South Carolina. The National Trust for Historic Preservation acquired the home in 1974, and it was opened to the public for tours in 1977. Since then, many people, including docents working on the tours, have reported seeing a man in an upstairs window, in a narrow room upstairs, or walking the grounds. They believe him to be William Henry, the fiery and patriotic activist son of John Drayton, who died so young.

Some of the most notorious and famous hauntings have occurred not on land but at sea. From ghost ships appearing out of nowhere to boats and luxurious liners that are home to spirits, even to the lighthouses onshore that help guide them back to safety, the dead seem as drawn to water as they are to the landbound places they once called home. Because so much tragedy has occurred at sea, it's only natural the ghosts of the dead continue to haunt the treacherous waters eternally seeking the comfort of the safety of shore.

Before today's massive and modern cruise ships and speedboats, traveling by water was a long, arduous, dangerous journey often made more so by the unpredictable weather. There were no luxury liners to take people from one country to another, and even as ships and boats became more modernized and functional, they still suffered accidents, crashes, sinking, and the whims of Mother Nature. The bodies lost at sea were rarely recovered, doomed to roam the ocean depths, although some managed to make it back to land and haunt the places that meant something to them in life.

Ghosts of the *Titanic*

The most famous haunted ship is no doubt the *Titanic*, yet the ghosts associated with this legendary liner don't haunt the underwater home of the wrecked ship. Instead, they appear to visitors of exhibits of artifacts from the RMS *Titanic* that tour the world. Divers recovered these numerous artifacts long after the 1,496 passengers perished on April 14, 1912, and since 1994, the artifacts have been exhibited in museums and halls in many major cities. Volunteers, staff members, and visitors have all reported strange phenomena while viewing the artifacts, including the voices of an elderly woman and man captured on digital recorders and the presence of a young crewmember.

While working at the display in Atlanta, a volunteer felt a hand move through her hair, and a small boy kept asking about a lady he was seeing that the adults around him failed to see. In an Iowa museum, volunteers and staff members often smelled cigar smoke near a cigar holder artifact from the ship. An actor portraying a ship's officer at an exhibit in Orlando, Florida, also reported the smell of cigars nearby and even stated he saw the face of a real-life *Titanic* crewmember when he looked into a display mirror. He asked, "Who's that?", and the mysterious officer smiled and walked away.

Much of the activity associated with the *Titanic* occurs at the massive Titanic Museum in Branson, Missouri, where over four hundred artifacts are on permanent display. The display includes an exact replica of the ship's exterior in half size and even a basin filled with water the same temperature as the water was on the fateful night when the ship sank, giving visitors an idea of the conditions the passengers were exposed to as they struggled to survive before dying of hypothermia.

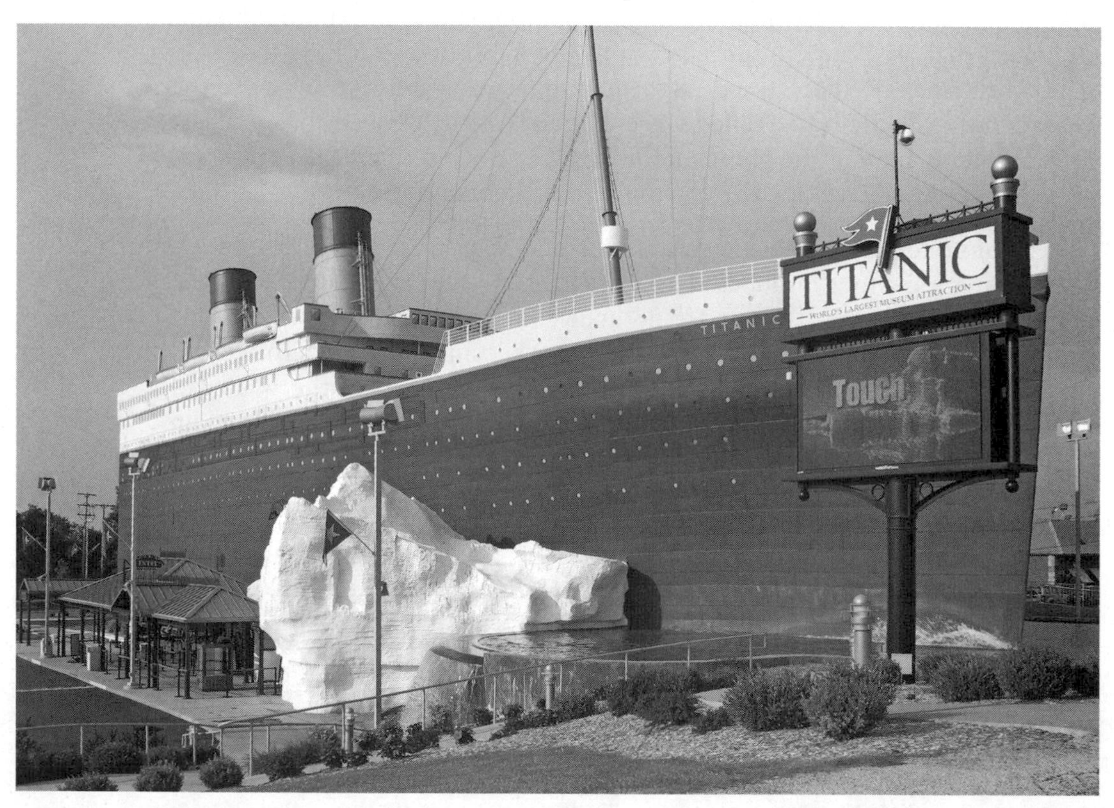

The Titanic Museum in Branson, Missouri, houses a substantial collection of artifacts from the ill-fated ocean liner.

The *Queen Mary*

It's impossible to talk about haunted ships without mentioning one of the most famous and fascinating of all: the RMS *Queen Mary*. Nicole Strickland is a paranormal researcher, author, writer, and public speaker from San Diego, California. She is the founder and director of the San Diego Paranormal Research Society (SDPRS); cohost of the "Spirits of the Adobe" tours at the Rancho Buena Vista Adobe; and writer for various magazines, including *Paranormal Underground Magazine* and *Let's Talk*. In addition to her three books about the RMS *Queen Mary*, Strickland has published *Field Guide to Southern California Hauntings, San Diego's Most Haunted: The Historical Legacy, Paranormal Marvels of America's Finest City,* and *Spirits of Rancho Buena Vista Adobe*. Strickland has appeared in a variety of media outlets regarding her work as a paranormal researcher, including television, film, radio, and print media.

Strickland has encountered many of the resident ghosts and spirits aboard the *Queen Mary*. Known nationally and internationally for her knowledge of the *Queen Mary,* she spent over fifteen years researching the *Mary's* rich history and paranormal phenomena. Over the years, she has developed a solid rapport and bond with many of the liner's ethereal residents, including Jackie, one of its most beloved energies. Strickland discusses the ship's noted ghosts, spirits, and paranormal hot spots in her books *Haunted Queen of the Seas: The Living Legend of the RMS Queen Mary* and *Spirited Queen Mary: Her Haunted Legend*. Some excerpts follow:

> The task of building the RMS *Queen Mary* represented a brave and elusive responsibility, especially in the early 1930s, as she was to be the biggest, quickest and most luxurious liner ever constructed. The RMS *Queen Mary's* design concept began in 1926 and continued for two years. It came at a time when there was fierce competition between ship building companies in Britain, Germany, Italy and the United States. Cunard's elderly trio of express liners, *Mauretania, Aquitania* and *Berengaria,* were eventually replaced by the *Mary* and her running mate, the RMS *Queen Elizabeth*.
>
> History was made at about 3:10 P.M. on September 26, 1934, as Her Majesty Queen Mary echoed, "I am happy to name this ship the *Queen Mary*. I wish success to her and to all who sail in her." As the bottle of Australian wine collided with the port bow, thus, signaling the launch of this almost inevitable liner, these unforgettable words from a woman the world admired were etched into the memory banks of all those who sailed aboard this British Masterpiece. This event was the first time that a reigning Queen of England ever endorsed the naming of a merchant ship.
>
> The RMS *Queen Mary* commenced her maiden voyage on May 27, 1936. Until August 1939 and after World War II, the ship maintained a North Atlantic sailing route from Southampton, Cherbourg to New York City and back. She carried people from all walks of life, including numerous celebrities, business moguls and members of the aristocracy.
>
> Cunard's excellent reputation for personal service is one example of why the *Queen Mary* was, and is, such a treasured ship as it always regarded itself as the epitome of high-ranking luxury and service. The company meticulously selected its stewards and stewardesses, some of whom lengthened their family's tradition. These crewmembers were thoroughly trained to both anticipate and remember traveler's individual likes and dislikes.

Continued...

(Continued from previous page)

With room layouts chosen and accepted, various world-wide artists and craftsmen were recruited, encompassing thirty artists, sculptors, painters and interior designers. As one can imagine, the *Queen Mary* is known as having received some of the finest renditions of Art-Deco-inspired paintings and murals. In fact, there is so much art aboard the vessel that many people have often overlooked some of the minuscule detailing that added to her overall charm and stately ambience.

—From *RMS Queen Mary: Voices from Her Voyages*

August 30, 1939, the *Queen Mary* sailed from Southampton to New York, as war was imminent. In September 1939, war was officially declared between Britain and Germany, ultimately placing the legendary liner in a precarious situation. Both the RMS *Queen Mary* and her sister liner, RMS *Queen Elizabeth*, were therefore requisitioned for service in World War II. In March 1940, the British government informed Cunard that the *Queen Mary* would be outfitted for troopship duties, lasting the length of combat.

—From *Spirited Queen Mary: Her Haunted Legend*

It is very difficult to fathom having several thousand souls on a single voyage for a ship that was merely designed for a holding capacity of just a few thousand. Due to the *Queen Mary*'s sheer size coupled with her immense speed, we can see why her troop volumes amplified from 5,000 to 10,000 to 15,000. With numbers steadily increasing during the war, the RMS *Queen Mary* eventually carried up to 16,683 souls during one of her missions in July of 1943. If you want to take home one fact about her war career, please hold onto the notion that during her five years of war service, having sailed hundreds of thousands of miles in oceans all over the world, she never once encountered an enemy subma-

The RMS *Queen Mary* was used as a troop transport vessel during World War II. Here she is sailing into New York City in 1945.

Continued...

(Continued from previous page)

rine, nor was she ever fired upon from the air, land, or sea. Also accompanying this miraculous 5-year record is that she never came into contact with a bomb nor fired at the enemy with angry intentions.

The RMS *Queen Mary,* alongside her sister ship, the RMS *Queen Elizabeth*, has contributed to the World War II allied forces in so many unimaginable ways. Sir Winston Churchill said, "Built for the arts of peace and to link the old world with the new, the Queens challenged the fury of Hitlerism in the battle of the Atlantic. Without their aid, the day of final victory must have unquestionably been postponed."

The RMS *Queen Mary* was one of the ships instrumentals in carrying numerous war brides and children to the United States and Canada after the dissolution of World War II. Still adorned in her camouflaging war paint colors, the *Queen Mary* commenced her war bride transportation duties on February 3, 1946. Statistics show that she carried 30% of all the America-destined brides, safely conveying 12,886 women, 1,683 children and 2,085 infants in six voyages alone from February to May of the same year. When the end of May approached, the *Mary* carried Canadian brides up until the end of September.

—From *RMS Queen Mary: Voices from Her Voyages*

The City of Long Beach made history on December 9, 1967 by welcoming the RMS *Queen Mary*. "No finer ship ever sailed this ocean. They will never build another like her. I don't want this to be a nostalgic crossing. We will go out in a blaze of glory and then onto Long Beach. California's climate will be good to her," commented Captain John Treasure Jones on the *Mary*'s 1,001 final peacetime voyage.

—From *Spirited Queen Mary: Her Haunted Legend*

There are many theories for why the *Queen Mary* is known as one of the top ten haunted places on our planet. Ghosts and spirits seem to be attracted to places that have experienced a lot of emotion, tragedy, and death. There seems to be a connection between sentimental states and psychokinetic energy. The *Queen Mary* has been witness to both ends of the spectrum. The ship has seen its score of tragedy, sadness, joy, happiness, and euphoria; thus, these left-over emotions from long-lost crewmembers, passengers, and World War II personnel may remain saturated deep within the ship's hull.

Furthermore, just imagine the thousands of people who travel each year to the *Mary* to witness her paranormal events. This energy alone could play into and be the cause of some ghostly events. However, the strong emotional history of the ship can vigorously produce psychokinetic powers robust enough to cause psychokinetic (PK) occurrences throughout the vessel.

Usually, the paranormal events surrounding a location coincide with its past. History and the paranormal are intensely connected. Thus, historical impressions have been retained in the environment and hold imprints from years ago. The *Queen Mary* has an unprecedented historical past, both during its luxury ocean liner days and stint as a troopship. Today, the ship still speaks of its living legend, sharing its time on the oceans.

The *Queen Mary* holds numerous artifacts and original furniture pieces. It is theorized that some energies are attached to a particular object. People who have had an emotional bond to their items want to be near them or make sure that they are kept safe and preserved. This can explain why some homes, museums, antique stores, and libraries become haunted.

Continued...

(Continued from previous page)

Places that contain portals and vortices are also known to house ghostly energy. They are difficult to explain and understand. Generally speaking, a *portal* allows spirits to travel from the living world to the spiritual world. Think of it like a bridge connecting two planes of existence. A vortex assists the entity in being continuously charged with energy. The *Queen Mary* is said to have at least two portals; however, many believe that the entire ship is a bridge from our world to the afterlife.

Many people, crewmembers and passengers alike, have stated that they feel "at home" when aboard the *Mary*. If they feel at home on the liner while alive, you'd think they would also feel the same sentiments toward the ship in spirit as well. Could this be one of the main reasons why the *Queen Mary* is such a spiritual magnet? Are many of the ship's former crew, passengers, and World War II personnel consistently paying their respects to the ship in spirit form?

—From *Spirited Queen Mary: Her Haunted Legend*

Jackie is the ship's most known spirit. Sadly, there are many rumors about her on the Internet that are not entirely true. For one, there is no forensic evidence to suggest that Jackie drowned in either the first or second-class-pool. There are many questions that abound for this little spirit. Was she a stowaway that somehow got lost aboard the ship? Was the name "Jackie" a middle name, which could explain why she does not appear in the passenger manifests? Did she travel the RMS *Queen Mary* with parents and other siblings? Or was her father one of the many servicemen fighting for freedom during World War II? Has she come through one of the alleged portals? Is she somehow the *Queen Mary*'s innocent voice? Has Jackie been chosen to be the *Queen Mary*'s spiritual ambassador? Investigators and researchers have tried to answer these questions—and many others.

Strickland speculates that Jackie comes from the RMS *Titanic*, ethereally boarding the *Queen Mary* as it commemorated the lost souls of the doomed vessel on its maiden voyage in 1936. Actually, it is theorized that many of the spirited souls of the *Titanic* have made their way onto the *Mary*. Personal experiences and captured evidence alike suggest this possibility. There is really no way to prove intuitive inclination and messages as they lie outside the boundaries of logical black-and-white science. However, Strickland does believe that Jackie's origins may lie with the *Titanic*.

Maybe the mortal world is not supposed to understand why Jackie spiritually resides aboard the *Mary*. She appears to be around six years old with a striking resemblance to actress Shirley Temple. Even though her origin is elusive, Jackie intelligently makes her presence known to many people. She seems to be drawn to certain individuals and enjoys singing songs, such as "Twinkle Twinkle Little Star," "London Bridge," "Ring-around-the-Rosy," etc.

Jackie is often heard, seen, or felt in the former first- and third-class pool room and dressing stalls. However, Strickland has sensed her energy in other areas of the ship, including staterooms, aft engine room, boiler rooms and the Observation Bar. Jackie is the loquacious and precocious type, very bright and mature for a young child. Strickland also wonders whether Jackie passed away as an adult but chooses to represent a child in spirit form. She goes on to say, "Indeed, Jackie is a very special spirit on the RMS *Queen Mary*. I, as well as many other people, feel that having an encounter with little Jackie can be a life-changing experience. As for me, my very first spirit encounter on the ship was with Jackie and it is something that I hold very dear to my heart."

The display of the bunks, where the passengers slept, is home to a ghost who leaves an indentation on one of the pillows, and the handprints of a child are often found on the glass window of the display of the captain's bridge.

Some witnesses claim the ghosts of those lost in the wreck haunt homes, hotels, and buildings they once lived in, including the Jane Street Hotel in New York and the South Street Seaport Lighthouse, which is home to a *Titanic* memorial.

But is the place where the *Titanic* sunk into the water haunted? According to "Ghosts of the Sea" at *ghostsofthedead.com*, many witnesses say yes, reporting orbs hovering over the waters where the hull rests. There are even reports of strange radio interference and signals experienced by submarines near the site. One report that sounds more like an urban legend occurred in 1977, when Second Officer Leonard Bishop of the SS *Winterhaven* gave a tour of his ship to a soft-spoken man with a British accent. Bishop thought there was something strange about the man, but he didn't discover what until many years later, when someone showed him a photograph of a Captain Edward J. Smith. Bishop recognized Smith as the man he gave the tour to. Captain Smith, he learned, was the captain of the *Titanic*.

Perhaps the watery depths at the site of the *Titanic* shipwreck are filled with ghostly spirits that never see the light of day. Maybe they have instead chosen to return to land and haunt the places they once lived and loved, such as touring a great ship, like Captain Edward J. Smith does.

The USS *Constellation*

Docked at Baltimore Harbor, the USS *Constellation* is a favorite tourist spot today, but when operational, she was the U.S. Navy's first ship. Over the course of the ship's 175-year history, there has been a lot of bloodshed on her decks during battle. Ghostly apparitions of the ship's captain have been reported by several people in later years, including Lt. Commander Allen Ross Brougham, who in 1955 took a photograph of an apparition in the forecastle believed to be the captain himself. Ghost hunter Hans Holzer, author of *Portals to the Past*, claimed when he was on board that three ghosts haunted the ship. He wrote in his book of a Catholic priest who toured the ship alone in 1964 and was approached by an old sailor, who offered information about the ship's equipment and history.

When the priest went above deck and told others about his encounter, he was told by tour guides that there was no such person belowdecks. They all rushed downstairs to where the priest had talked with the sailor, but there was no one there.

Phantom Ships

Some ships are haunted by ghosts. Other ships are themselves ghosts. A ghost ship, also known as a phantom ship, is a ship with no living crewmembers

USS *Olympia*

By Laurie Hull

Launched in 1892, the USS *Olympia* is the oldest steel warship afloat in the world. The ship was a cruiser in operation from 1895 until 1922 for the U.S. Navy. As such, she has a few stories to tell. During the first gunnery practice on the ship, Coxswain John Johnson was killed when the gun his group was operating jumped off its mooring and smashed him against the bulkhead. From that point on, the ship was believed to be haunted by Johnson, who has manifested as a shadowy figure in the area where he met his end.

During many visits to the *Olympia*, I have encountered unexplained knocking and disembodied footsteps in the section where Johnson died. Although these were eerie experiences, the most haunted area of the ship has to be the engine rooms.

Since the ship is not currently running, one just has to imagine how immensely hot it must have been down in the boiler area. It wasn't unusual for men to collapse from heatstroke. One night, we were sitting quietly in the area of the boilers when we heard footsteps approaching. I went to check to see who was there and found the area was empty! That wasn't the last time we heard footsteps that night or on other occasions we spent time there. In addition to the footsteps, we saw shadowy figures and once heard a loud moan that sounded like someone in absolute agony. The moan was also found on our audio recordings!

The most intense manifestation I experienced in the boiler area had to be the night that I felt two cold hands touch my arm. I was alone in the area at the time, and as I felt the icy touch, I literally froze in place. I had been walking away from the boiler area at the time toward the front of the ship. Others have reported similar experiences in that part of the ship.

The USS *Olympia* was also the ship that brought the body of the Unknown Soldier

The USS *Olympia* is now a floating museum docked at Philadelphia's Penn's Landing. According to psychic Laurie Hull, the spirit of Coxswain John Johnson is still on the ship where he was accidentally killed.

Continued...

(Continued from previous page)

home to America. The body was kept in an area behind the Captain's Quarters. This is where many people have reported sighting a shadowy figure as well as full-bodied apparitions of a man in a naval uniform. Many voices have been recorded in this area as well, including one that said, "Save the ship."

Voices have also been recorded in the sick bay. During the influenza epidemic, the ship was used as a floating hospital off the coast of Italy. Could these voices be the last words of those who suffered and died during the epidemic? Many of the recordings here were whispery and faint, therefore difficult to make out. One of the voices recorded here was speaking in French and said "Merci," which means "Thank you."

It seems as if there are many spirits on the USS *Olympia,* and from the number of recordings and experiences, they clearly desire to be seen and heard by us! The *Olympia* is currently docked in Philadelphia, Pennsylvania and is open to the public for tours.

Laurie Hull is an author, psychic, and paranormal investigator from Springfield, Pennsylvania, and has had a lifelong interest in ghosts and the supernatural that began while she was growing up in a haunted house. She is the founder and director of Tri-County Paranormal Research, which can be found at www.tricountyprs.com.

or passengers on board. The vessels are seen floating on the waters, often looking as though enveloped in a reddish glow or a fog, and may have their origins in folklore and tales of high seas adventure and mystery. Phantom ships are often described as transparent and even shimmering, as if a mirage or projection. They can appear to come close to real ships, and witnesses even say it looks as though they might crash, but upon alleged impact, they vanish into nothingness.

However, there are also real ships such as the *Mary Celeste* that were found without anyone on board floating at sea or drifting onto shore. These derelict ships spawn their own brand of mystery and lore surrounding the fate of the missing crewmen but usually involve missing lifeboats or other signs of the crews having abandoned ship or dying at sea. Often, dead bodies are found on the derelict ships. But they don't become apparitions themselves, just physical pieces of history to be debated and mulled over.

Golden Gate Phantom Ship

Long before the Golden Gate Bridge was built in 1937, and long before over a thousand people jumped to their deaths, a steamship named the SS *Tennessee* got caught in the deadly current near the Golden Gate Strait and smashed into the rocks. The ship was torn apart, but luckily, 550 passengers and fourteen chests of gold got to shore safely before it crumbled into the fog and swirling waters.

The ghost ship has been reported on dark and foggy nights, and once the bridge was completed, dozens of witnesses saw the ship and heard screams coming from on board. Even other ships passing under the bridge have seen the ancient ship on foggy nights, including the USS *Kennison*, a destroyer that passed the *Tennessee* close enough that its crewmembers could tell the decks were unmanned. The ship's name was clearly written on the side and it left a wake as any other ship would, but it never showed up on radar and vanished as quickly as it was seen.

There is now an embankment called the Tennessee Cove in Marin County, part of the Golden Gate National Parks Conservancy, named after the ship.

THE LEGENDARY *FLYING DUTCHMAN*

The most legendary ghost ship is the *Flying Dutchman*. A huge body of legend, myth, and lore has been built around this mysterious ship, considered a dark and terrible omen to anyone at sea who witnessed her in passing. The origins of the *Dutchman* are referenced in a number of writings that date back to the late 1700s of a ship that was in distress off the Cape of Good Hope in 1641, led by Captain Hendrik van der Decken, who tried desperately to get to safe harbor as a terrible tempest arose. The Dutch man-o'-war ship fell to the treacherous weather conditions, and every soul on board perished at sea.

The *Dutchman* may have been a part of the Dutch East India Company, and sightings of her ghostly, apparition have been reported since, usually in the form of a phantom ship that appears to be about to crash or as a ship surrounded by a ghostly, red light. King George V of England wrote in 1881 of an encounter with the *Dutchman* early one morning, when the ghost ship crossed the bow of the ship the king was on. The *Dutchman* was surrounded in a reddish light, and the first sailor who saw her later fell to his death.

The first reference to the *Dutchman* comes from 1790 in *Travels in Various Parts of Europe, Asia and Africa During a Series of Thirty Years* by John MacDonald. The common story of the ship falling to the weather trying to make it into safe harbor was later repeated in numerous writings and became a legend built on superstition. In John Leyden's *Scenes of Infamy*, written in 1803, the appearance of the ghost ship was said to be punishment for the crew having committed some awful, undisclosed crime, and therefore "ordained to traverse the ocean on which they perished, till the period of their penance expires."

In 1812, Sir Walter Scott wrote about the *Dutchman* as a "pirate ship," adding a new layer to an already burgeoning legend. Other written sources point to a seventeenth-century Dutch captain named Bernard Fokke as the model for the *Dutchman*'s own captain, although later writings mention Captain Hendrik van der Decken, a staunch seaman, as the captain of the Amsterdam vessel.

Sightings continued into the twentieth century, with numerous ships coming into near contact with a ship they thought was real, until it vanished before their eyes. Could the *Flying Dutchman* have been nothing more than an optical illusion, such as a mirage? Perhaps those who claim to have seen the ghostly vessel really saw an actual ship sailing below the horizon, reflecting the rays of the sun in a way as to create an image of the ship floating on the water. It might also be a "looming," an atmospheric event that occurs when light rays bend across different refractive indices to create the image of a ship levitating in the air above the waves.

The Walt Disney Company created its version of the *Flying Dutchman* for its *Pirates of the Caribbean* movies as well as being a giant prop at Castaway Cay, an island owned by the company in the Bahamas. Tales of the ghost ship date back to the seventeenth century.

Whether she was a real ship or not, the *Flying Dutchman* has gone down in history as the most widely known ghost vessel. Renditions of the story, and the ship, have appeared in the form of art, operas, movies, television shows, novels, and cartoons, embedding the legend in pop culture and giving new life to a ghost of the past. There is even a popular tobacco blend called the Flying Dutchman!

HAUNTED MARITIME MYSTERIES

The legend and lore of many seafaring peoples often includes the deaths of passengers on board a ship that ran aground or sunk due to treacherous weather conditions. Though there were scientific explanations proposed, it didn't stop rumors from spawning embellished and exaggerated legends that continue to this day. Mysterious, ghostly vessels reported around the world include:

The SS *Bannockburn*—Known as the "*Flying Dutchman* of Lake Superior," this cargo ship ran aground at full speed in April 1897 on the rocks near the Snake Island lighthouse. The ship was badly damaged and sank months later in October, carrying grain to be taken to Kingston, Ontario, from Chicago, Illinois. The *Bannockburn* struck against the wall of the Welland Canal and sprung a leak, sinking to the bottom. Luckily, no lives were lost. The ship was refloated and repaired.

In November 1902, the ship set out from what is now known as Thunder Bay, headed for Georgian Bay. She ran aground and turned around to head back to port, but there was no damage, and she set out again for Georgian Bay. Later that day, the ship was spotted by Captain James McMaugh, who was on the freighter *Algonquin*. The *Bannockburn* was seven miles northeast of his ship. Later that night, strong storms hit the area, and at 11:00 P.M., a passenger steamer saw the *Bannockburn* headed for the Soo Locke.

The *Bannockburn* was never seen again.

Those who awaited the cargo ship thought she had just been set back from the storm, but the *Bannockburn* never showed up to dock. Several nights later, a steamship reported a debris field just off the Stannard Rock Lighthouse. On November 30, 1902, the *Bannockburn* and her crew were officially pronounced lost at sea. A month later, one of the ship's life jackets showed up onshore.

There were many theories attempting to explain the ship's disappearance. Sailors later claimed to see the *Bannockburn* with skeletons on her deck. Other witnesses report seeing the ship just before a storm, fog, or bad weather condition, and the vast majority of ghostly sightings occur in the month of November. Many of these reports made the local newspapers of the times, turning the disappearance of the cargo ship into local legend and lore.

The SS *Valencia*—A Canadian coastal passenger liner carrying 108 people set sail for San Francisco but sank off the coast of Vancouver, British Columbia, in 1906, killing all but thirty-seven passengers. The cause of the sinking was a submerged reef off Vancouver Island. The passengers were said to have clung to the ship's railings for up to a day and a half before a giant wave took the ship down for good. All of the women and children on board died. Rescue attempts were thwarted by storms and deadly rocks. The tragedy resulted in the building of the Pachena Point Lighthouse and a trail for shipwrecked mariners now called the West Coast Trail. For several decades after the sinking, fishermen in the area witnessed a ghost ship with human skeletons on board. Indian fishermen found a lifeboat manned with skeletons. There was a lifeboat found from the ship, Lifeboat No. 5, twenty-seven years after the tragedy occurred, and it is now on display at the Maritime Museum in Victoria, British Columbia. The wreck of the *Valencia* became known as the worst disaster to strike in the "graveyard of the Pacific," a stretch of dangerous coastal waters from Vancouver Island down to Oregon in the United States.

The *Ourang Medan*—This ship sent out a distress call in 1947, which was answered by two American ships that were passing through the Strait of Malacca. The distress call came from a crew member who claimed everyone on board was dead and ended with his final words, "I die." When the American ships found the *Ourang Medan*, it was in good condition, but the crew were all dead with terrified facial expressions. Even the one dog on board was dead. Before the cause of death could be determined, the ship exploded, which may have been due to the illegal nitroglycerin the vessel was carrying!

The *Carroll A. Deering*—In 1921, this ship ran aground near Diamond Shoals off Cape Hatteras in North Carolina. This area was notorious for disabling sea vessels. The Coast Guard investigated after several days had passed and found the ship abandoned of crewmembers as well as equipment, logbook, and two lifeboats, indicating they may have escaped. However, other ships had also vanished in this same area, sparking rumors of pirates or the nearby Bermuda Triangle.

The *Lady Lovibond*—On board this ill-fated schooner, Captain Simon Peel was to be married the day before Valentine's Day in 1748 as his ship sailed toward Portugal. But his friend and first mate was in love with the captain's fiancée, too, and, in a rage, killed the helmsman and steered the ship directly into the Goodwind Sands off southeast England, a sand bar notorious for shipwrecks. The ship sank, and everyone on board drowned. Every fifty years, witnesses living near Kent, England, claimed to see the strangely green, glowing ship, but when rescue craft were sent to investigate, there was no ship to be found. Seafaring legend had it that bringing a woman on board a boat was bad luck. Had the captain listened, his wedding may have been a true celebration and not a tragic disaster.

The *Mary Celeste*—This famous story involves a merchant ship found derelict and adrift in the Atlantic Ocean in 1872 in perfect condition with sails hoisted and the personal belongings of the crew left untouched. There was also a huge cargo of alcohol barrels on board and food in the cargo hold. Missing were one lifeboat, the captain's log, and, of course, the crew. Rumors rose of poisoned food, mutiny, a terrible storm, or some issue with the ship that may have sent the crew overboard in the lifeboat. They presumably died at sea because their bodies were never found. The ship's history since is filled with tales of ghostly sightings and apparitions, even sea monsters and alien abductions of the crew!

The *Baron Falkenberg*—Germany's North Sea is the setting for a legend surrounding the medieval Baron Falkenberg, who was in love with his own brother's fiancée. At the wedding, the baron killed the groom, and the fiancée ran screaming, declaring she would rather die than be with him. The baron stabbed her through the heart, then ran to the beach, where a mysterious man with a boat was waiting for him. The boat took the baron to a larger ship, and witnesses later claimed to see the ghost of this ship always heading north without a helmsman. But the baron could be seen on deck playing dice with the Devil for his soul.

The story of the *Mary Celeste* is truly creepy. Found adrift in the Atlantic Ocean, its lifeboat was missing along with the crew, who were never seen again.

THE *PALATINE* LIGHT

Rhode Island's Block Island is home to a ghost ship of its own, one that appears during the week between Christmas and New Year's. The eighteenth-century ship called the *Palatine* is one of the most famous ghost ship legends in the United States. The ship appears at night, brightly lit against the black sea and sky, but interestingly, there is no record of a shipwreck involving a ship called the *Palatine* and in fact may be the actual borrowed story of the *Princess Augusta*, a ship that ran aground on Block Island in 1738 carrying a group of German "Palatines" who were seeking religious freedom in America. In 1925, a deposition taken from crewmembers referred to a terrible fever that killed most of those on board and a captain that refused to let the sick and starving go ashore. Another version, written about in John Greenleaf Whittier's poem "The Palatine," appeared in the *Atlantic Monthly* in 1867, spreading his story of locals luring the ship to shore, then taking the contents and killing the passengers, burning the ship to hide evidence of their pillaging. Whichever story is true, locals still claim to see the ship glowing at night during that one holiday week each year.

The *Baychimo*—This cargo steamer was abandoned and adrift near Alaska for forty years. Owned by the famous Hudson Bay Company, the *Baychimo* was launched in the early 1920s to trade furs and pelts with the Inuit of Northern Canada. In 1931, the steamer became strapped in pack ice and could not break free. While the crew were airlifted to safety, the badly damaged ship was left behind. The ship stayed afloat for decades off the coast of Alaska and became a legend to the Eskimos, who would watch it float amid the ice drifts. It continued to be seen up until around 1969, when it vanished. Although it most likely sunk, several search expeditions have failed to locate the wreckage.

San Diego's Haunted Ships

San Diego is a harbor city home to some amazing historical ships. All are out of service but are now popular tourist attractions. The USS *Midway* is a massive, decommissioned U.S. Navy aircraft carrier that was the largest tonnage ship in the world up until 1955. She served for forty-seven years and saw action in the Vietnam War before becoming the flagship of the 1991 Operation Desert Storm. She was officially decommissioned in 1992 and is now a museum. Though thousands of people tour the ship yearly, the staff is quiet about the ghosts some claim are on board. Paranormal investigators suggest there are over thirty ghosts on the *Midway*, and it is considered one of the four haunted ships featured in the 2012 Maritime Ghost Conference in San Diego.

Nearby is the famous *Star of India*, built on the Isle of Man in 1863 out of steel rather than the usual wood. She is the world's oldest active iron-hull ship and is alleged to be haunted by the many men who died on her decks. One such man was a young stowaway named John Campbell, who died in 1844 when he fell from the high rigging, crushing his legs when he hit the deck. Three days later, he was buried at sea. Visitors report a ghost that touches them with a cold hand when they stand near the mast where he fell.

Other visitors claim they smell the scent of baking bread coming from the galley, even though it has not functioned for decades. Pots and pans are said to move around on their own, and there are a number of cold spots reported throughout the ship. The ship is now a hugely popular museum and tourist spot and has a lot of foot traffic, which helps continue the legend of the *Star*'s tragic past and haunted present.

The *Caleuche*

Off the Chiloe Island of Chile, terrible storms lurk along with the ghost of a ship called the *Calueche* that witnesses say has blood-red sails and glowing, white sides. There are those who even claim the ship is alive and glides over the water, then dives into it like a giant whale. The ship sunk in the deadly waters, and there were no survivors. Locals claim they can sometimes see survivors on the sands, yet when they set out to rescue them, there is no one there. This ghost ship appears almost nightly and is described as beautiful and filled with the spirits of all those who drowned at sea. There are often sounds of music and celebration on board the empty vessel. This story is a part of Chilota legend, which claims the three water spirits, the Sirena chilota, the Pincoya, and the Pincoy, summon the spirits of the dead to the ship. Once they are back on the ship, they are drowned, and this enables them to resume their lives before they initially died.

Northumberland Ghost Ship—A ghostly, three-masted schooner on fire has been witnessed since the late eighteenth century by those living near Canada's Northumberland Strait, the body of water separating Prince Edward Island from Novia Scotia. Most of the sightings last but a few moments before the ship vanishes, but others have reported sightings over an hour. Rescuers have attempted to sail out to the phantom ship, but the ship vanishes as they close in on it. In 2014, a postage stamp of the ship was launched by Canada Post as part of their "haunted Canada" line.

A ghostly, three-masted schooner on fire has been witnessed since the late eighteenth century by those living near Canada's Northumberland Strait....

Chaleur Bay Fireship

Another Canadian ghost ship, also appearing to witnesses to be on fire, is seen in the Chaleur Bay area of New Brunswick. The ghost ship appears at night and often is stationary for hours, although others report it skimming atop the waters. The ship is associated with a number of shipwrecks that have occurred in the region, but scientists claim the apparition might be the result of an electrical phenomenon known as St. Elmo's Fire, when inflammable gases are released beneath the sea. Another explanation is the presence of phosphorescent marine life where the ship is often sighted.

Gardiner Bay Phantom Fighters

In 1754, a letter in the *New York Gazette* written by fishermen on Plum Island, which is near Long Island's far eastern tip, claimed that three ghost ships sailed in Gardiner's Bay with sailors on deck. The ships were said to engage in gun battle for a few minutes before the ships vanished entirely. The story was repeated in 1882 in the *New York Sun* newspaper about another fisherman who saw a giant schooner emerge from out of nowhere but heading straight for them. As the schooner was about to hit the fisherman's boat, it vanished.

Spectral Submarine

The German UB III Class submarine was a powerful weapon during the First World War. One in particular seemed to be cursed. During the building of this sub, three men suffocated on diesel fumes, and two men were crushed by a falling girder. A crewmember drowned during its first testing, and two more men died after the sub sank and filled with toxic gases from a damaged battery.

But the curse continued, and during an early mission, eight crewmen and one officer died from a freak torpedo explosion. The officer's ghost would later be seen walking the ship in ghostly form. But it doesn't end there because after that, the sub captain was decapitated by flying shrapnel. The captain's ghost was reported standing over his headless body that very night.

Haunted Lighthouses

Just as ghost ships haunt the seas, the shorelines have their share of haunted lighthouses rich in history and regional and local legend and lore. Thought to be the beacons of hope and comfort for ships lost at sea, showing them the way back to the safety of solid ground, many lighthouses carry with them tragic tales of their own and reports of paranormal phenomena from ghosts to strange voices to the appearance of beacons when the buildings have long since been abandoned and lamps disabled and shut down.

Because most lighthouses have a long history attached to them, they abound with ghosts and hauntings. Here is a short list from A to Z of some of the more widely known haunted lighthouses and the stories behind them.

Bakers Island—The Bakers Island Light is located in Salem Harbor, Massachusetts. Built in 1907, locals report hearing the fog bell go on and off by itself. Perhaps it's related to a story of a ferry crash in 1898 that killed one of the keepers during a severe storm during a keepers' reunion on the island.

Barnegat—The Barnegat, New Jersey, lighthouse was built back in 1856 and sports the ghosts of a couple who had been on a ship off the coast during a storm. The ship was evacuated, but the husband stayed aboard, and his wife chose to stay with him. They sent their infant daughter to shore with a shipmate, but the husband and wife went down with the ship. Their ghosts are said to appear on cold days in the months of January and February and approach parents walking their babies in strollers, only to vanish into thin air when they realize the infant is not their daughter.

Nicknamed "Old Barney," Barnegat Lighthouse on the northern tip of Long Beach Island in New Jersey is the site of a sad tale of parents forever separated from their daughter.

Battery Point—This Crescent City, California, lighthouse sits on a little peninsula on a tiny island of its own. The lighthouse survived a major tsunami in 1964 that destroyed much of the town of Crescent City on the mainland. The lighthouse ghost is a playful one who likes to rock a rocking chair, move the keeper's bedroom slippers around, and annoy the cat. Perhaps it is a ghost of a dog that once lived there!

Big Bay Light—The Big Bay Point Lighthouse is located in Big Bay, Michigan, on the Upper Peninsula. It was opened in 1896, and William Prior became the first keeper. Now a bed-and-breakfast, the innkeeper and guests report the ghost of a man who may be William who slams kitchen cabinet doors ... until the innkeeper yelled at him to stop. Since then, William is silent as well as five other ghosts said to haunt the lighthouse.

Bird Island—This Sippican Harbor, Massachusetts, lighthouse, built in 1890, is the home of a ghost named William Moore, the first keeper who may have been a convicted pirate doing time at the lighthouse. He had a terrible temper and took it out on his wife, Sarah, a small woman who may have been beaten by her husband. In 1832, William raised a distress flag. Mainlanders went to the lighthouse and found the dead body of his wife, Sarah. William claimed she succumbed to tuberculosis, but others suspected William murdered her. After he left the island, the new keeper reported the ghost of a small, frail woman who would come to the door, then fade away when the door was open. Fishermen in the area in 1982 reported seeing a weeping ghost that may have been Sarah.

Block Island—Block Island Southeast Lighthouse in Rhode Island was built in 1874. The ornate, Victorian-style lighthouse is said to be haunted as well as the entire seven-thousand-acre island it sits on. In the 1900s, one keeper killed his wife, pushing her down the tower stairs. Her spirit continues to haunt the entire island. Phantom pirate ships are seen off the island as well as the ghosts of those who may have died in shipwrecks along the perilous shoals and ledges off the coastline. The island is open to the public by ferry.

Boston—Built in 1783, the official Boston, Massachusetts, lighthouse sports the ghost of an elderly sailor. Footsteps and cold spots accompany the sightings, and a rocking chair moved on its own. The ghost hates rock music, as discovered by Coast Guard officers who would play a rock station on the radio when nearby, only to have it suddenly jump to a classical music station.

Bug Light—The Long Beach Bar Lighthouse is located in Orient, New York, but got the name "Bug Light" because the rocks where it was located made it look like a bug at high tide. Built in 1870, the original lighthouse helped mariners navigate the dangerous sandbar between Orient Harbor and Gardiner's Bay. Sadly, in 1963, arson destroyed the lighthouse, and a foundation was established to rebuild it. The whole restoration project took only sixty days, thanks to the input of locals who loved their lighthouse and innovative planning and construction designs. The ten-inch, solar-powered light was relit on September 5, 1990, to great fanfare and is a popular tourist spot as part of the East End Seaport Museum. Although there are many haunted locations around Long Island, the Bug Light may or may not have its ghosts, depending on which locals you ask, mainly due to the fact that the new location is not where the original was built.

Gibraltar Point—Built in 1808 on Toronto Island in Canada, this lighthouse was named by the then governor who wanted the lighthouse fortified as strong as the Rock of Gibraltar. The first keeper, who was also a bootlegger, was a man named J. P. Radan Muller and may be the ghost that haunts the lighthouse. It is assumed Muller was murdered when soldiers from Fort York came to him for whiskey, and he refused to give them what they wanted. Remains of a body were discovered in 1904 and since then, workers and visitors have witnessed unexplained lights, shadowy figures, bloodstains on the staircase, and eerie wailing and moaning. The lighthouse is now a historical landmark and no longer in use.

Heceta Head—A ghost named Rue haunts this Yachats, Oregon, lighthouse built in 1894 and overlooking the Pacific Ocean, setting off fire alarms and moving objects around during work hours. The keeper's house is now a bed-and-breakfast and appears to patrons now and then, although in a benign manner.

New London Ledge—Connecticut's New London Ledge Lighthouse sits in the New London Harbor and is home to a ghost named Ernie. Ernie was the keeper, and in 1936, he discovered his wife had run away with the captain of the Block Island Ferry. Despondent, he jumped from the roof to his death and has haunted the lighthouse ever since, opening and closing doors, turning televisions on and off, turning the fog horn on and off, and even untying secured boats on the dock.

Old Point Loma Lighthouse—San Diego, California's Point Loma is home to this two-story lighthouse that first became operational in November

1855. It operated for forty years and also served as a family home. Today, it is a popular tourist spot as well as a historical landmark. Tourists can go inside and see how the family once lived and might even encounter the ghost of Captain Robert Decatur Israel, the last lighthouse keeper before it was shut down.

Old Presque Isle—Presque Isle, Michigan, is home to this well-known, haunted lighthouse on Lake Huron. The ghosts of a screaming woman who may have been a keeper's wife locked away in the tower years ago is often heard as well as the ghosts of George Parris, who, with his wife, moved into the lighthouse keeper's cottage in 1990 to run the museum and give guided tours. Ever since his death, the beacon light comes on at dusk and shuts off at dawn each night, even though the light has been permanently disabled! The light has even been reported by Air National Guardsmen flying over, even after the Coast Guard went in and removed the old light for good. Or so they thought.

Owls Head—The Owls Head Light State Park in Maine is open year-round. With lovely views of Penobscot Bay, the lighthouse and keeper's

Built in 1840, the Old Presque Isle Light in Michigan was the first lighthouse on the island. Former museum caretaker George Parris is said to still haunt the building, turning its beacon light on and off each night.

residence is not open to the public. Locals claim a three-year-old girl, who was the daughter of a former keeper, once told her parents that the fog was rolling in and it was time to put the foghorn on. The parents learned she had an imaginary friend who informed her, an old sea captain who left footprints outside the snow, polished brass in the house, and even turned down the thermostat!

Plymouth—The Plymouth Lighthouse was originally built in 1769 at the mouth of Massachusetts's Plymouth Bay. It was built upon land owned by John and Hannah Thomas, who became the first keepers. John was killed during the Revolutionary War, leaving his wife as the first known female American lighthouse keeper. The lighthouse was rebuilt twice, once in 1843 and again in 1924, when it was automated. Many visitors believe the ghost of Hannah Thomas haunts the tower in the form of a floating apparition, sometimes just the upper portion of a woman's body, dressed in old-fashioned clothes and with long, dark hair.

Point Lookout—Scotland, Maryland, is home to the Point Lookout Light, which paranormal experts call the most haunted lighthouse in America. The lighthouse was built upon land once used for a Civil War hospital, and a prison camp was built next door by the Union Army, creating a literal breeding ground for disease, illness, and death. This may explain the apparitions reported of both males and females and doors that open and close on their own. Voices and footsteps have been reported as well as mysterious snoring, despite there being no one there. One of the first keepers, Ann Davis, is reported to haunt the lighthouse and has been seen standing at the top of the tower stairs. Other figures appear throughout the basement area. The lighthouse went dark in 1966 and is now part of a state park.

Point Sur—The Point Sur Lighthouse sits atop a mound of massive, volcanic rock between California's coastal towns of Big Sur and Carmel. The light, which went operational in 1889, once warned ships of the treacherous coast, but many a shipwreck occurred anyway, and the ghosts that haunt this historic tower are said to be the spirits of those who drowned in the shipwrecks. They now roam about the lighthouse and surrounding buildings, including a ghost of a tall man in dark blue clothing reminiscent of the nineteenth century. The lighthouse is now part of Point Sur Historic State Park and is open to the public for guided tours.

Port Boca Grande—You might hear the sound of a young girl giggling and moving about in the upstairs keeper's area of this Gasparilla, Florida, lighthouse near Fort Myers. There is now a museum inside the lighthouse building, and many a visitor has heard the sounds of what may be the ghost of a former keeper's daughter who died in the building. You might also see a headless apparition of a woman named Josefa walking on the sand near the lighthouse, who was a Spanish princess decapitated by a pirate.

Saginaw River—The full name of this lighthouse is Saginaw River Rear Range. It is located in Bay City, Michigan, on the Great Lakes and may be one of the first two lighthouses to be built on the lakes. The lights of the range helped mariners navigate through the river's shipping channel. Coast Guard officers who have stayed at the house report heavy footsteps on the iron staircase of the tower, which has been closed to the public since the 1970s and remained unoccupied after that.

Seguin Island—Bath, Maine, is home to the Seguin Island Lighthouse, Maine's tallest and second-oldest lighthouse. The now desolate site, on an island accessible only by boat or helicopter, was once the home of a keeper and his wife. When she would get bored in the winter, the keeper got his wife a piano, but it only had sheet music for one song. She had to play the same song over and over since the island was unreachable due to ice. Eventually, the keeper went insane, chopped up the piano with an axe, took it to his wife, and then took his own life. Some say you can hear the sound of piano music on a quiet night and see the keeper moving about the house.

Eventually, the keeper went insane, chopped up the piano with an axe, took it to his wife, and then took his own life.

Seul Choix—Gulliver, Michigan's Seul Choix lighthouse overlooks Lake Michigan. The seventy-eight-foot tower was first put into service in 1892. One of its first keepers, Captain Joseph Townsend, now haunts the tower and museum. He died in the keeper's house in the early 1900s, but his body wasn't discovered for months due to the snow and weather. It was kept in the basement and may be the reason his spirit haunts the tower to this day. Staff and visitors alike have reported the smell of cigars, which Captain Joseph loved to smoke, and even the apparition of a man looking out the windows.

Sherwood Point—The Sherwood Point Lighthouse is located about fourteen miles east of Manistique, Michigan, on Lake Michigan. The last of the Great Lakes lighthouses to be turned over to automation, it ended personnel service in 1983. It is now used as a private Coast Guard retreat and is open to public tours. U.S. Coast Guard reservists have reported hearing noises at night and seeing the spirit of a woman who may have been Minnie Cochems, who operated the lighthouse with her husband and died there in 1928.

St. Augustine—The St. Augustine, Florida, lighthouse has a notorious reputation for being haunted. Built in 1824 and then reconstructed in 1874, the many ghosts that make the lighthouse their home are that of a twelve-year-old girl who was the daughter of one of the lighthouse builders and a dark, male figure in the basement who may be a caretaker who hanged himself in the lighthouse. Many paranormal groups have investigated the lighthouse and found it to be highly active.

St. Simons—St. Simons Island in Georgia is home to a haunted lighthouse of its own. The beautiful and towering St. Simons light overlooks the

Atlantic coast of Georgia and is considered a historical landmark. The tower was built in the 1870s as part of an older structure still in place, Fort St. Simons, built by the founder of the state of Georgia, General James Oglethorpe. During the Spanish attack of 1738, the area was evacuated, and the fort was then used by the Spanish. During one bloody battle, the fort was destroyed. In the early 1800s, James Gould built the lighthouse tower and became its first keeper. It was destroyed by the Confederate Army in 1862, then rebuilt by architect Charles Cluskey in 1872. The 104-foot tower is in use even today. But beware of the resident ghost of Frederick Osborne, one of the past keepers who was shot by his assistant keeper, John Stevens, after Frederick made inappropriate comments about the assistant's wife. His footsteps and the sounds of men arguing can be heard from the vacant tower in the still of the night.

White River—Whitehall, Michigan, is home to this Great Lakes lighthouse, which was sadly deactivated in 1960. There is now a museum on-site, and the staff and visitors say they hear footsteps of someone pacing back and forth in the limestone tower and keeper's house. Perhaps they belong to the lighthouse's very first keeper, Captain William Robinson, who served as the keeper for forty-seven years before he died in the building. His wife, Sarah, may also be haunting White River, as apparently, someone likes to dust museum cases when no one is around!

This is only a sampling of the many haunted lighthouses both here in the United States and in Canada. Sadly, many older lighthouses have fallen to complete disarray, and no money has been available for restoration purposes. One can only imagine the ghosts that walk their grounds, wondering what happened to the homes they so loved and found solace and comfort in.

VEHICLES, TRAINS, TRACKS, AND ROADWAYS

If there are ghost ships that roam the high seas, it makes sense there would also be other haunted vehicles and craft. Airplanes, submarines, cars, trains.... If someone can die in it, or from it, there's a good chance a ghostly legend is attached to it!

Pippo

During World War II, the people in Northern Italy encountered a mysterious and vengeful plane called *Pippo*. No one was able to identify the type of plane, but it would appear out of nowhere and fire its machine guns at anyone who got in its path, making a pip-pip sound, for which it was named.

Pippo only attacked at night, so people would turn off the lights or cover the windows with thick curtains to avoid being hit with everything from poisoned candy to powerful bombs. *Pippo* would sometimes fire upon innocent farmers. The legend took on a mystical aspect, although historians venture that *Pippo* may have been a British reconnaissance plane.

The Lincoln Phantom Train

Imagine the ghost of an actual train appearing to people in 180 cities! Every April, one such train emerges out of a thick, black fog to make its long trip to Springfield, Illinois, carrying the coffin of Abraham Lincoln. The ghost train makes the 1,650-mile (2,655-kilometer) trip each year, starting in Washington, D.C., but no one ever sees Abe's ghost on board. They do report seeing uniformed Union soldiers guarding over the coffin on the long trip that mysteriously vanishes before it ever reaches its destination. People also report that clocks and watches stop when the train is passing through their town.

Canada's St. Louis Ghost Train

The St. Louis Light is visible at night along an abandoned railroad track between Prince Albert and St. Louis, Saskatchewan. However, this ghost train was debunked when two students determined the cause to be a diffraction of the lights of distance vehicles. Not only did they duplicate the ghost train phenomenon, they won an award for it, too.

A Phantom Bus in London

From the 1930s to the 1990s, Londoners have reported seeing a phantom red London double-decker bus with the route marker 7 on it, but this bus was never a good-luck charm. In fact, it always appeared at 1:15 A.M. with no lights on and drove right at oncoming drivers, who would swerve in a panic to dodge the bus, only to find it vanish before it ever hit them. A London driver died when his car exploded after trying to avoid the phantom bus in 1934 while driving near the junction of St. Marks Road and Cambridge Gardens in Ladbroke Grove.

Soviet Death Car

In the Soviet Union during the 1960s and 1970s, people reported a terrifying encounter with a car they swore was right out of hell itself. The Black Volga was a mysterious limousine with white rims and curtains. It would appear out of thin air, with horns instead of rearview mirrors, and some say the Devil was its driver. The frightening phantom car would steal children and kill anyone who got near it. Many would drop dead within one day after encountering the car.

The Black Volga would become the stuff of legends throughout the Soviet Union, Poland, the Ukraine, and Mongolia. Some believed it to be nothing more than a very expensive car driven by a Soviet politician to intimidate the poor and downtrodden.

The Silver Arrow

Stockholm, Sweden, has always been known for being a lovely capital city, but deep in its subway system, a ghostly train called *Silverpilen* makes stops at random stations. Sometimes the train is empty, but other times, people report it is filled with ghosts. If you board the train at one of the random stations, you might not ever be heard from again.

The *Silverpilen* was a real train, an experimental train that was used as a test unit but never made it into production. It was used now and then as a backup train during peak hours. It was retired in 1996, but even today, subway workers report seeing the ghostly train moving through abandoned stations.

Haunted Railroad Tracks and Train Stations

South of San Antonio, Texas, is a stretch of railroad near the San Juan Mission. Sometime in the 1930s or 1940s, a school bus stalled on the railroad tracks. The speeding train smashed into the bus and killed ten of the children on board and the bus driver. Locals say that anytime a car stops near the railroad tracks at this intersection, they will feel unseen hands pushing their car across the tracks to safety. Perhaps it is even the spirits of the dead children and bus driver!

Interestingly, many of the haunted train stations are located in countries outside of the United States. In West Bengal, locals insist the Begunkodor Railway Station is haunted by a lady in a white sari. Located in a very remote village, the station had been shut down for over forty years but was reopened in 2009.

In Delhi, India, the Dwarka Sector 9 Metro Station is haunted by a very angry female ghost who was killed on her way to school by the train. Now she chases cars that go by the station, knocks on the doors and windows, and scares those who dare to travel late at night.

In Kolkata, the Rabindra Sarobar Station is haunted by shadow phantoms who are seen on the platform, the spirits of the many suicides that occur on the metro tracks. The apparitions appear around 10:30 P.M. when the last metro runs.

In Ireland, the Connolly Station in Dublin runs rampant with ghostly sightings of soldiers who died in bombing attacks during World War II, seen in many buildings throughout the station area.

If you ride the Caobao Road Subway in China, you might feel invisible hands pulling you toward the platform or, in the case of one unlucky man, being pushed off the platform or see the spirits of those who may have been embalmed at a nearby mortuary or were the victims of several mysterious deaths at the station. Those near Line 1 of this Shanghai subway system also report the ghost of a girl wearing red, who committed suicide, seen sitting on the platform.

England's Addiscombe Railway Station was home to many ghosts until the year 2001, when it was demolished to make room for a tramline. The figure of a man was often seen roaming the station and may have been a train driver killed in the early 1900s. Trains move here in the nighttime, when nobody is around to move them!

Singapore is home to many haunted stations, but none more so than the Singaporean MRT (Mass Rapid Transit) station in Bishan, central Singapore, which was built on a former cemetery, and the Novena station nearby, which was also built on a cemetery! The ghosts of headless figures, spectral coffin bearers, and phantom passengers roam both stations, according to witnesses.

The Panteones Metro Station in Mexico is a terrifying place after dark, according to witnesses and train engineers who hear screams and knocks and see apparitions all along the track. The name Panteones means "graveyard," and the station is built near two cemeteries, which could explain the paranormal phenomena often reported here. One of the most haunted spots is a tunnel between the Panteones and Tacuba stations, where shadowy lumps appear and disappear and strange knocks are heard in the pitch black.

Canada has its Waterfront Station in Gastown, Vancouver, built back in 1915. It is one of Vancouver's most haunted buildings and sports a female ghost dressed in 1920s flapper attire dancing to music. She, and the music, vanish when approached. The ghost of an elderly woman dressed in white roams the station, and even poltergeist activity has plagued workers there, who say their desks move around by themselves.

In the United States, the most notorious haunted station is Union Station in Phoenix, Arizona. Before the airport was built in the 1950s, Union Station was the transportation hub of the area. Closed by Amtrak in 1995, the station since then has been used now and then for tourist trains and now is the headquarters to company offices. Employees have seen shadow figures running away from the station and moving about in the attic. A ghost named "Fred" has been popularized as one of the main spirits, although he was named by a maintenance worker who said the name just came to him. Maybe it is Fred who opens and closes a heavy door at random times, scaring the workers out of their wits.

Another haunted American train station is the Saginaw, Michigan, train station on Potter Street. It is one of the largest Victorian-era train stations in the country, opened in 1881 and designed by the famed New York architect Bradford Lee Gilbert. The last passenger train left the station in 1984, and the station officially closed in 1986 after being used for freight trains only. Witnesses claim to have seen the ghosts of dead soldiers who were shipped back to Saginaw from the war via the train. A local casket maker would build caskets for the soldiers, and his actual shop was located in the depot itself. Some people report seeing a "lady in white" floating around the station, too. The station is now private property and part of the Saginaw Depot Preservation Corporation.

Spooky Tunnels

You don't have to be claustrophobic to be terrified of entering a long, dark tunnel, for who knows what lies waiting for you in its depths? Ghosts like to hang out in tunnels because there are plenty of haunted ones to go around, perhaps because many accidents occur in the darkness, when drivers are disoriented or distracted. Many tunnels are associated with local urban legends and lore, so if the thought of rats, spiders, and other creepy crawlies don't scare you, buckle up. The spirits will.

The Moonville Tunnel in Vinton County, Ohio, was once part of a railroad track system through a remote, woodsy area. The region was used for coal mining, so no train ran the tracks for over twenty years since it was closed down.

But that doesn't stop locals from seeing an old railway brakeman's ghost standing at the tunnel entrance. He's an old man, dressed in engineer garb, holding his lantern, which he waves at oncoming cars. His appearance has become a common occurrence to the folks in Vinton County.

Niagara Falls, Ontario, is home to the aptly named Screaming Tunnel, a now unused passageway for farmers moving livestock under the railroad tracks. The tunnel is said to be haunted by the ghost of a young girl who died under the limestone bridge, although locals don't exactly agree on how she died. Some say she was a murder victim who was killed at the tunnel, and others suggest she may have escaped a house fire and died under the archway of the bridge.

Legend has it that if you stand in the middle of the tunnel and light a match, it will go out and you will then hear the ghost girl's screams. However, some locals say the sounds are echoes of the cries of coyotes, which are always nearby.

Another Canadian tunnel known as the Blue Ghost Tunnel became so popular with ghost hunters that authorities were forced to board it up! A paranormal investigator stumbled on the Merritton Tunnel in Thorold, Ontario, while looking for a different tunnel. But this longer tunnel also had its own ghosts, including an eerie, blue mist inside the tunnel and the spirits of two engineers who died when their respective steam locomotives crashed in 1903.

Tennessee's famous Sensabaugh Tunnel was built in 1920s and named for the man who owned the land, Edward Sensabaugh. Rumor has it that Ed let a homeless man into his home as an act of charity, and the man tried to steal some jewelry. When Ed confronted him, the homeless man used Ed's little girl as a human shield. The man ran away with the little girl and drowned her in the tunnel. But another rumor states Ed was a madman who killed his entire family and threw their bodies into the tunnel. People today claim to hear the cries of a baby girl and say if you turn off your car engine in the middle of the tunnel, you won't be able to start it up again.

The Screaming Tunnel near Niagara Falls on the Canadian side is where a young girl died. If you enter the tunnel, you can still hear her screaming.

Central Colorado is home to a number of tunnels along a 35-mile (56-kilometer) stretch. Three in particular are said to be haunted and are named "One," "Two," and "Three." Legend has it tunnel "Three" collapsed on top of a school bus filled with children in 1987, killing everyone on board. If you are traveling through the first two tunnels, you may hear the giggles of little children. However, at the entrance of tunnel "Three," you will more likely hear terrifying screams.

However, there is no real proof this bus accident ever happened. Tunnel "Three" did partially collapse back in 1987, and there are those who claim to see the ghosts of dead railway workers, but this is one case where there is no reality to the legend.

The Hoosac Tunnel in Massachusetts opened in 1876 and at the time was the longest tunnel in North America and the second longest in the world. The tunnel soon became known as the "Bloody Pit," thanks to many accidents that occurred during construction in 1867. A leaking gas light caused an explosion and wall of fire down the main shaft. Thirteen people died in the blast, and when the shaft later flooded, the bodies appeared. Overall during the twenty-four-year project, over 195 people lost their lives. Later, workers would hear and see the ghosts of several men in the tunnel at night, and the ghosts of miners would appear on the hillside near the tunnel. However, one tunnel worker named Joe Impoco claimed that in the 1970s, he encountered a disembodied voice that warned him to stay out of the tunnel twice, both times saving his life.

Virginia's Big Bull Tunnel was built in the nineteenth century by rail workers who also built a Little Bull Tunnel. For fun, they named the shorter tunnel Big Bull! The shorter tunnel is now home to some ghostly apparitions, most notable those of a man who was scalped in the tunnel in 1901 and another man who fell from a train in 1904. Workers in the tunnel have reported hearing the voices of men coming from inside the walls and have not been able to find their origins.

Bridges

Collapsed bridges. Burning bridges. Haunted bridges. Add to those suicide bridges, where ghosts filled with despair haunt the very place they took their own lives. Crybaby bridges, where people report the crying of ghostly infants thrown off the bridge by their own mothers. Just as there are haunted railways, tunnels, and stations, there are many bridges with a reputation for being a ghostly stomping ground. There is a word for fear of bridges—gephyrophobia. Being on or even under a bridge brings about anxiety and a sense of helplessness and dread to people with the fear. When the bridge is haunted, that fear is doubled.

Texas Bridges

Texas is home to three creepy bridges with historical connections. The Old Alton Bridge is listed in the National Register of Historical Places. But to locals, it will forever be known as Goatman's Bridge. Situated between Denton and Copper Canyon, this bridge was originally built by a manufacturing company as a means of moving both people and cattle. Named for the abandoned town of Alton, the haunted aspect comes from a local legend of a goat breeder named Oscar Washburn, who called himself the Goatman. Washburn was abducted by members of the KKK after he hung a sign out on his bridge to drum up business that said, "This Way to the Goatman." The Klansmen hanged Washburn from the bridge, but when they checked to make sure he was dead, they didn't see his body hanging below, so in an act of anger, they killed Washburn's family.

Witnesses report strange lights and the apparitions of a man herding his spectral goats over the bridge, and legend has it if you drive across with your lights off, you will see him there. His wife's ghost also haunts the bridge, according to some locals.

The Donkey Lady Bridge near San Antonio, Texas, crosses Elm Creek. Local folklore suggests this otherwise normal little bridge is home to the ghost of a woman who was almost burned to death. The story dates back to the mid-nineteenth century, when a wealthy merchant's son had an altercation with the donkey of a Texas family. The son beat the donkey but was stopped when the family threw rocks at the man. The man vowed revenge and later returned to the Texas family's farm with an armed posse. They burned the family's home and shot the husband dead when he tried to get away.

The wife was badly burned but did escape, and legend has it she hid out at Elm Creek, never to be seen again except as a ghost who appears as a horrific human–donkey hybrid to those who park in the dead of night on the bridge and turn their car lights off.

The Devil's Bridge is also located in San Antonio, Texas, near the San Juan Mission on Ashley Road. This is one of many "devil's bridges" located all over the world that may date back to medieval times. All have a reputation for being places where evil lurks at night, thanks to legends that suggest these bridges were built by the Devil himself or were crossroads where one could make a deal with the Devil. The legends are similar all over the world, but this particular bridge, being located near a holy mission, may have been built to conquer the Devil instead. There were numerous accidents during the construction, which many believe the Devil created to keep the bridge from being completed. But it was completed and is now home to paranormal activity such as the smell of sulfur, the sense of a demonic presence, and a darkness around the bridge that is so thick, light will not penetrate it. Paranormal investigators who have visited the bridge report strange voices that show up on their digital recorders (EVP—electronic voice phenomena).

Suicide Bridges

Many bridges have the sad honor of being places where people end their lives. Often, witnesses report seeing the ghosts of the dead wandering on or near the bridge, as if lamenting their deaths as they did their lives. The higher up the bridge was, whether over land or water, the more it was likely to be used as a suicide bridge. One such bridge is the High Bridge in Chicago, also known as the Lincoln Park Arch. The arch was high enough that sailboats could pass under it and became such a popular death spot, it was given the nickname "The Bridge of Sighs."

Since it was built back in 1892, over eighty people jumped to their deaths from this bridge before it was torn down in 1919, and the ghosts of these poor souls remain. Some died of broken hearts, others of deep depression. They usually jumped, but one man hanged himself from the girders.

Other suicide bridges of note include the New River George Bridge in West Virginia, where three or four people jump off every year; the Coronado Bridge in San Diego, California, which is a favorite place for suicide jumpers and those who attempt but fail; San Francisco's Golden Gate Bridge, from which over 1,600 people have died of suicide; and the Parc des Buttes-Chaumont in Paris, France, which became such a popular suicide choice that mesh was put up to prevent people from making that fatal leap.

The Colorado Street Bridge in Pasadena, California, has long been a favorite jumping-off point for suicides. It now has a suicide prevention rail.

The Colorado Street Bridge in Pasadena, California, has the terrible reputation as a favorite of those who seek to end their lives. More than a hundred people have jumped from this bridge, which sits high about the deeply cut Arroyo Seco. The bridge, built in 1913, connected Pasadena to Los Angeles and was a part of the famed Route 66 until 1940, when the Arroyo Seco Parkway was built. In 1981, the bridge was listed in the National Register of Historic Places but fell into disrepair, especially after the Loma Prieta earthquake in 1989. The bridge reopened in 1993 with suicide prevention rails. However, the locals attest to a host of ghosts that roam the bridge and the Arroyo Seco below.

Creepy Covered Bridges

Not too far from the famous Gettysburg battlefield in Pennsylvania, itself said to be haunted, is Sach's Bridge, which dates back to even before the Civil War. Local legend says it was the place where three Confederate soldiers hanged themselves after deserting the Battle of Gettysburg. The soldiers haunt the creepy covered bridge, and witnesses report screams of the wounded and dying and a shadowy mist that moves across the bridge.

Another spooky covered bridge is Vermont's Gold Brook Bridge, also known as Emily's Bridge, named for a young girl said to have died on the bridge. How she died, though, is open to a range of rumors, including one that claims she was jilted by a lover and hanged herself from the rafters and one that claims she drove her horses and carriage off the bridge in an angry frenzy after the man she loved left her abandoned at the altar. No one really knew who Emily was or how she died, but in later years, people contacted Emily using Ouija boards. One rumor spawned from a Ouija session claimed she was killed by her own mother-in-law.

In any event, she still haunts the covered bridge in the form of footsteps, strange noises, scratch marks on vehicles parked on the bridge, the sound of rope dragging across cars, and a ghostly lady in white who floats around the general area where the bridge is located.

Kentucky's Colville Covered Bridge covers the Hinkston Creek in Bourbon County. Originally built in 1877, the bridge has undergone much renovation over the decades and was dismantled in 1997 and reopened in 2001. This covered bridge was the alleged site of two teenagers who lost control of their car on the way home from prom night and drowned in the creek when their car veered off the bridge. Residents in the area later reported strange lights under the bridge. Other people report the ghosts of the teens accompanied by the ghost of an older woman named Sarah Mitchell who died crossing the bridge as well as vapors and orbs that appear at night.

Bridges from Hell

Hell's Bridge in Michigan's Algoma Township is really a narrow walkway over a River Rouge tributary. But this simple walkway is surrounded by supernatural lore revolving around a fictional mid-nineteenth-century man named Elias Friske. The horrifying story claims Friske was responsible for a host of murdered children. He came across as such a nice man (as many serial killers do); after many children in Kent County went missing, the townspeople asked Friske to watch the remaining children while they went out searching the woods. While they were gone, Friske killed the remaining children and tossed their bodies into the River Rouge.

Visitors to this old structure claim to hear phantom noises and see floating orbs and strange lights in addition to the apparitions.

The parents came back to find the dead bodies of their children under the narrow walkway. Friske was captured and blamed demons for the dead children, but nobody was buying it. He was lynched from the bridge, his body falling into the river below.

South Carolina's Poinsett Bridge is located in Greenville County on Route 107. It is considered one of the state's most haunted sites and the stomping grounds of a ghost of a young man who died there in the 1950s. The stone bridge is also haunted by the spirit of a slave who was lynched on the bridge. Visitors to this old structure claim to hear phantom noises and see floating orbs and strange lights in addition to the apparitions.

Crybaby Bridges

A crybaby bridge, as stated before, is haunted by the ghosts of dead infants and children who are usually murdered by their parents or the victims of horrible accidents. Ohio has its own crybaby bridge, Egypt Road Bridge, which is now closed down and off-limits to trespassers, although ghost hunters visit it often. There are many stories associated with the bridge, all of which involve a baby or toddler who drowned in the waters below. Witnesses report paranormal activity during the day as well as the night, which is a bit unusual, and claim to hear the crying of a baby or child when there is no one around.

Another crybaby bridge exists in the town of Anderson, Indiana. An old bridge on County Road 675 in Madison County is said to be haunted by the ghost of a baby thrown into the water from a car after an accident on the bridge. Another rumor from the 1950s suggests the ghost baby's cries belong to the child of an unwed mother who threw her newborn over the railing after giving birth in the back of a car on the bridge. However, the story states the baby landed on the ground, not in the water, and his haunting cries alarmed drivers on the bridge, none of whom ever bothered to stop.

The baby's body was found by the police, but they couldn't identify it. Shortly after, people heard the cries of a distraught baby as they crossed the bridge late at night. The sad thing about crybaby bridges is that they exist in the first place, suggesting that infants and children often meet their deaths in the most horrific of ways.

Haunted Roadways

It makes sense that so many roadways would be haunted. Accidents on the roads take the lives of thousands each year from infants to the elderly. Sometimes in the case of multiple car crashes, many lives are tragically lost. Still, there are some highways and roads with reputations for being notoriously haunted by the spirits of the victims who lost their lives there. Some haunted roads have given birth to local urban legends and blurred the lines between reality and the imagination. And rather than avoid these roads altogether, many curiosity seekers flock to them in hopes of experiencing the road trip of their lives.

Questhaven Road

One such road was even experienced by the author of this very book! In Northern San Diego County, there is a Christian retreat called Questhaven up in the hills above what is now San Elijo, adjacent to the Elfin Forest. This area is known to be haunted by the Lady in White, a ghostly presence that often appears on the more remote, woodsy roads near the retreat and has been sighted by hundreds of people over the years. The entire Elfin Forest/Questhaven area is a hotbed for all kinds of alleged urban legends, including a huge, white owl that appears out of nowhere. Another legend claims there was once a mental hospital on the land, and many of the patients who died there now haunt the area (although there is no evidence of any mental hospital ever having been located anywhere near the area!).

Rumors abound that the woodsy area was home to devil worshippers, gypsies, witches, and cultists and was once sacred Native American land, which is why many locals claim to have seen the ghosts of slaughtered Native American children. But the Lady in White is the prominent legend and the one whom this author wanted to see proof of existence. She is the ghost of a woman whose husband and son were killed in the area and now floats around scaring people and causing car crashes along the road leading into and out of the Questhaven retreat, although the windy, tree-lined roads could account for the many crashes, as people tend to ignore signs to slow their speed!

Rumors abound that the woodsy area was home to devil worshippers, gypsies, witches, and cultists and was once sacred Native American land, which is why many locals claim to have seen the ghosts of slaughtered Native American children.

While on a drive through this area over twenty years ago, this author noticed the lovely, clear, and sunny skies overhead. Suddenly, the car stalled in the middle of a dirt road. Surrounded by trees, there was no one in sight and no way to call for help, as this was the era before cell phones. Within a few moments, the skies turned dark and rain poured down relentlessly, unusual for an area that gets little rain and the fact that the skies were clear up to that point. In a short time, the dirt road flooded and was impassible, so this author panicked and tried to turn the car around but got caught in the mud.

After a few very frightening moments, the car skidded forward and was able to be turned around. This author sped back to the main road and was shocked to notice that the skies were clear and sunny there, even though it was only about half a mile away. There was no sign of clouds or rain anywhere, and the ground was dry as dust.

What made this experience so chilling was finding out later that dozens of others had had similar experiences in which their cars stalled out and they felt trapped, even panicked. Was it just coincidence? Being on a back road with few homes around? A freak storm? Or the work of the Lady in White, who didn't want this author, or anyone else, trespassing on her domain? No, this author did not see the Lady in White, a giant owl, or the ghosts of Native American children but can attest to a powerful feeling of dread and foreboding and the sense of being watched for the duration of the event.

Which begs the question—are haunted roads haunted because people say they are? Let's take a look at some of the more harrowing highways and byways.

Zombie Road

Lawler Ford Road is a two-mile road that stretches through forest and hills in Glencoe, Missouri, near the Meramec River. Once believed to be a Native

American travel route, the area was also the location of a flint quarry. In the earlier part of the 1800s, a ferry operated along the river to allow settlers to cross the Meramec River. In the 1850s, the Pacific Railroad line stretched parallel to the river. The wife of the local justice of the peace was killed by the train in 1876, one of many deaths in the area's early history. In the 1900s, it became more of a resort community with clubhouses and homes later lost to the major flooding of the 1990s.

The name Zombie Road may have come from the former railroad workers who rose from their graves according to legend, accompanied by phantom, old-time music. Another legend claims that a mental patient escaped from a facility nearby, and only his bloody gown was found on the road. His nickname had been "Zombie," and the road was named in his honor. During the Prohibition, the area was ripe with gangsters and the occasional murder. Bodies were never found.

Today, the area still takes its bodily toll, with children dying along its banks, falling into the river waters, only to be washed up onshore. Ghosts abound as well as shadow figures that run out into the road, then vanish. Those brave enough to come to Zombie Road report phantom voices and the sensation of being touched by unseen hands. Maybe even ... zombie hands....

Riverdale Road

There is an 11-mile (18-kilometer) stretch of road through Thornton, Colorado, that is packed with urban legends and ghostly goings-on. People traveling this long road have reported seeing a phantom runner attacking parked cars on Jogger's Hill and a phantom Camaro that revs its engine as it speeds up and down the winding road. There is even the shell of an old mansion where, rumor has it, a man burned his wife and children alive. A ghostly woman dressed in white wanders the charred grounds. Other ghosts of slaves are often seen on the grounds as well, once hanged from a charred tree. Bizarre paranormal phenomena have been reported on this road since the 1850s, and whenever there is an accident, it is attributed to the demons who are said to roam the area.

Nash Road

This rural stretch of road in Columbus, Missouri, is home to a strange spectral entity known as the "Three-Legged Lady." She is said to chase drivers down the dark road at night, banging on the hood. She has three legs, but one is a rotted limb that is sewn to her body. Generations of locals claim she is real and may come from an urban legend involving musician Robert Johnson selling his soul to the Devil or, in this case, the Yazoo Witch. As with any urban legend, she is often said to be the mother of a girl who was dismembered in an accident, and all she could find was the torn-off leg. Others claim the leg belongs to a dead lover she refuses to give up on. Whatever the truth is, she appears if you turn off your lights while driving down Nash Road. Try it if you dare.

The Notorious Clinton Road

West Milford in Passaic County, New Jersey, is home to one of the creepiest roads on the planet, according to those unlucky enough to have traversed it. Along the 9.3-mile (15-kilometer) stretch of roadway that winds through the thick northeastern woods, witnesses have reported everything from ghostly activity to the presence of the KKK, Satanic cults, and bizarre Druid ceremonies. Along the road, one can encounter such places as the dangerous, old, stone walls at "Dead Man's Curve"; the home of the legendary Ghost Boy Bridge, where legend has it one can toss a coin into the water and the "ghost boy" below in Clinton Brook will toss it back; the ruins of Cross Castle, which many say is a meeting place for the KKK, Druids, and Satanic groups; and some say the area crawls with ghostly animals at night that were once a part of the nearby safari-themed park, Jungle Habitat.

The abandoned animal theme park was shut down in 1976, but West Milford residents and those who visit the area claim to have seen both the ghosts of animals that may have been killed by a hunting party after the park was closed and real animals that may have been let loose when the park was shuttered.

This abandoned, nineteenth-century smelter near Clinton Road has been taken for a Druid temple by those who believe the roadway is a hot spot for pagan and Satanic worshippers.

People driving along Clinton Road, now a popular paranormal hot spot, report strange phantom headlights, eerie, red, glowing eyes staring out from the trees, and even a possessed albino deer roaming the woodlands. The fact that this rural road is a very twisty, windy one with hairpin turns and no streetlights might have something to do with its supernatural reputation, but those who have driven it in the dead quiet of night will say otherwise.

The Phantom Hitchhiker of Highway 87

Montana's Black Horse Lake is home to a phantom hitchhiker who hangs out on a desolate stretch of Highway 87 near Great Falls. Drivers often report the body of a dark-haired Native American man in jeans suddenly slamming into their windshield, bouncing off the front of the car. But when the driver gets out to look for the body, there is nothing there ... and no damage to the windshield. This strange hitchhiker does this repeatedly, as if stuck in some ghostly time loop, but some folklorists say he is part of a "vanishing hitchhiker" phenomenon that dates back to the nineteenth century and seems to show up in all regions of the country. This urban legend likes to play on the fear of picking up a stranger only to have he or she turn out to be some ghost or demonic entity, and when it happens on a rural road with no one in sight to come to one's aid, it's even more frightening.

Shades of Death

Another haunted New Jersey road is the 7-mile (11-kilometer) stretch of woodsy rural roadway in Warren County called Shades of Death Road that parallels the Jenny Jump State Forest, itself a paranormal hot spot. Drivers report everything from an unnatural fog that comes off the nearby Ghost Lake to spirits roaming the mist, possibly the ghosts of murder victims killed in the thick cover of the woods, including a man beheaded by his own wife and a local who was shot and buried in a mud pile beside the road; racial lynchings that once took place nearby; and even those who died in the area during the 1850s malaria outbreak. More ghostly activity in the form of mysterious, white lights that turn red when stared at can be found on Lenape Lane, a paved, dead-end, road off Shades of Death Road.

The biggest local legend revolves around a ghostly woman named Resurrection Mary, who has been seen hitchhiking along the road dressed in a white party frock since the 1930s.

The Jenny Jump Forest itself is the stuff of spooky lore. There is a cabin by Ghost Lake that is haunted, and the nearby Bear Swamp was renamed Cat Swamp by locals because of rumored packs of vicious cats!

Archer Avenue

This 7.2-mile (11.6-kilometer) stretch of road (Illinois Route 171) runs across the southwest side of Chicago and passes by a host of potentially haunted locations. Woodlands, cemeteries, quietly spooky lakes, even old churches dot this road, which has been called one of the city's most haunted sites thanks to a long history of paranormal oddities. Two of those sites are the Resurrection Cemetery at one end, and the St. James at Sag Bridge Church at the other end.

The biggest local legend revolves around a ghostly woman named Resurrection Mary, who has been seen hitchhiking along the road dressed in a white party frock since the 1930s. Be careful if you encounter a blonde, blue-eyed woman in white thumbing for a ride because those who have dared to stop say she vanishes upon entering the car! Other supernatural activity includes phantom horses with riders running across the road at 95th and Kean; the notorious "gray baby" that locals have described as either a rabid human or a werewolf haunting the horse-riding trails and woods near the Sacred Heart Cemetery; and the ghost monks that walk the grounds of the St. James at Sag Bridge Church.

Woodland Death Trap

In the southern section of Aroostook County in Maine, there is a road known to be a death trap not just because during the winter the icy patches along the rural road cause dozens of accidents taking the lives of truck drivers who have to navigate the slippery roads in their rigs. But other ghosts haunt Route 2A through Haynesville, closed in by forest on both sides, including two little girls who were killed in an accident involving a semitruck in August 1967 and the ghost of a woman who was killed with her husband and can be seen along the side of the road, begging drivers to stop and help her. Those who do stop report feeling a cold chill before the ghost vanishes before their eyes.

Route 2A even inspired Dan Fulkerson to write a country song (performed by singer Dick Curless) called "A Tombstone Every Mile," which warns those thinking about taking a ride down one of most haunted roads in the United States.

Over in Wisconsin, another rural, woodsy road boasts its own ghostly apparitions. Boy Scout Lane in Stevens Point is a 3-mile (5-kilometer) stretch of unpaved roadway originally meant to lead to a campground for the Boy Scouts of America, thus the name. But the project was never started. Local legend states that a Boy Scout troop tried to camp in the woods sometime between the 1950s and 1960s and never came back out. Rumors abound, including one that suggests their scoutmaster murdered them. Other rumors suggest a bus crash or forest fire, but there are no records of either on the books.

Shiprock is a rock formation that is on Navajo Nation land in New Mexico and is only accessible via Route 491, the "Devil's Highway."

Drivers who dare to go down Boy Scout Lane report hearing heavy footsteps in the woods and strange, red flashes emanating from within the forest. Some unfortunate travelers even witness the ghosts of the boys themselves covered in blood.

Tulare, California, is known for the headless motorcycle ghost that haunts Bardsley Road. This rural road has been home to such rumors since the 1940s, but the only factual case of a motorcyclist killed on the road comes from the 1960s. Though the exact cause of death is as much the stuff of legends as the ghost itself, many locals report seeing the ghost of a man on his bike riding down the roadway and headlights that appear in the dark out of nowhere.

Route 491 is never to be driven at night. That's according to the drivers who have experienced a plethora of terrifying events along this "highway to hell" that was once called Route 666. Often called "Devil's Highway," it runs north–south through the Four Corners region of New Mexico, Utah, Arizona, and Colorado. The official state route was designated in 2003 and runs through desolate desert land, passing two tribal nations, the Navajo and the Ute Mountain, as well as an extinct volcano named Shiprock and the Mesa Verde National Park.

Road trips along the route may include sightings of UFOs, reports of Skinwalkers that often take the form of humans (more on this later), huge, black dogs with glowing, red eyes known as Hellhounds, an appearance by a strange, brightly lit, black sedan called Satan's Sedan that tries to run drivers off the road, and even a demonic, glowing semitruck that runs drivers off the road before vanishing into thin air! There is a ghostly young woman in white found walking along the highway who vanishes when spoken to and an incredible number of unexplained, single-car accidents, including brand-new cars suddenly breaking down without explanation. Drivers also report feeling a sudden sense of utter doom or dread on the road, but with this kind of haunted reputation, that isn't far-fetched.

The Devil's Backbone

There are a number of scenic roads in Texas Hill Country that are a vortex of crazy, spooky activity day and night. Texas Farm Roads 12, 165, 32, 2325, and U.S. Highway 281 stretch for 122 miles (196 kilometers) and provide some stunningly beautiful scenery, but they are also filled with ghosts. Because of the rich history of the area and the violence between white settlers and Native American tribes, the spirits that roam these roads are restless. Drivers have reported seeing the ghosts of a woman, who was the widow of a miner, and her child, who roam the area. On Purgatory Road, apparitions materialize on the hoods of cars and vanish just as quickly. Shadow people lurk on the sides of the roads, and an area ranch foreman reported waking up to the sights and sounds of twenty mounted Confederate ghost soldiers and their spectral horses running across his land.

A Native American ghost named Drago herds his cattle near ranches along Purgatory Road, according to more than one witness living nearby. Plenty of deadly accidents occur along the more treacherous roads, adding to the spooky atmosphere of the surroundings.

Woods and Trails

The Most Haunted Forest in the World

The home of the most haunted forest is Japan, where hundreds of people have committed suicide in the Aokigahara Forest at the base of Mount Fuji. The mountain is a sacred place to the Japanese, but the forest that spreads out beneath it is a terrifying place that has become, sadly, the most popular suicide destination spot on the planet. In the year 2010, 247 people attempted to take their own lives in the dark, eerie forest.

Aokigahara has a long history of tragedy. It may have been what the Japanese call "ubasute," a place where the elderly and sick were dropped off and abandoned. Obviously, the remoteness of the forest was perfect for leaving someone to die, and now the forest is said to be haunted not only by those who took their lives there by choice but by those who didn't have a choice.

HAUNTED HIKING TRAILS

Hiking is a strenuous enough activity, but when the trail might be haunted, it makes it even more challenging. Nothing like getting out in nature and exercising and encountering all kinds of creepy spirits along the way. Forget coyotes, rattlesnakes, and bears, oh my. These ghostly hiking spots offer a whole new kind of danger.

Bash Bish Falls in Massachusetts is named after a Mohican woman who was sentenced to death for adultery but was rescued by a cloud of butterflies.

The Grand Canyon in Arizona is a popular tourist spot for its magnificent grandeur and immense rock formations dating back millions of years. There are several hiking trails of varying difficulty, but one trail offers a chance to experience paranormal activity while enjoying Mother Nature. The Transept Trail stretches along the North Rim Campground to the Grand Canyon Lodge and passes by the ruins of a pueblo along the way. Hikers might see the ghost of a lady in a white dress with blue flowers, known as the Wailing Woman gliding along the path. They might also hear her wailing moans and sad weeping. She took her own life at the lodge after her son and husband were killed in a hiking accident nearby.

Mount Washington, Massachusetts, boasts the highest waterfall in the state, the Bash Bish Falls. The strange name comes from the legend of a woman named Bash Bish, a Mohican, who was sentenced to death after being accused of committing adultery. The villagers intended for her to die by tying her inside a canoe and dropping it down the 60-foot (18-meter) basin. On the day of the execution, a cloud of butterflies surrounded Bash Bish as the canoe tipped over the edge of the falls, and she was able to escape. Pieces of the canoe were found, but a body was never recovered. Years later, her daughter killed herself by throwing herself over the very same spot. Hikers report a ghostly young woman who can be seen standing just behind the falls.

Ghost House Trail in Big Ridge State Park passes by the old Norton Cemetery and what remains of the Matson Hutchinson Homestead in Tennessee's backcountry. Locals say one of the Hutchinson family daughters died of tuberculosis on the homestead in the late 1800s. Hikers today claim to hear her cries and wails, and some have snapped pictures of the cemetery to find a ghostly presence appearing on film hovering behind the family tombstones.

Hikers in need of a rest often stop at the Punchbowl Shelter along the Bluff Mountain Appalachian Trail in Virginia. Whether they are attempting the entire Appalachian Trail hike or a smaller segment, this is one spot that may stand out on their journey thanks to the ghost of a little boy who wanders the trail. The ghost is attributed to a four-year-old boy, Ottie Cline Powell, who died over a hundred years earlier when he wandered off from school and got lost on the mountain. Hikers have left many stories in the registry at the location of their encounters with the playful spirit of Ottie.

The Lake Morena Campground 63 miles (101 kilometers) east of the city of San Diego offers trails and campsites with ghostly activity to go with them. The campground is located at the foothills of the remote eastern slope of the Laguna Mountains, home to thousands of acres of chaparral-covered hillsides, old oak trees, and huge rock formations. In a grove of woodsy trees across from the campground, a "lady in white" walks back and forth dressed in a long, white gown. The ghostly woman stares at hikers and campers, then vanishes into thin air. She also reportedly laughs and sings, and her footsteps can be heard outside of tents, but when campers unzip their tents and look, there is no one there. No one knows who she is, but she seems to enjoy making this particular spot in nature her haunting grounds.

Iron Goat Trail is located just 60 miles (97 kilometers) northeast of Seattle. Tucked away in the lush Stevens Pass in Washington State, the hiking trail is a 6.7-mile (10.8-kilometer) loop that offers views of lush flowers and scenery. The trail follows the train in the upper and lower sections of the now abandoned Great Northern Railway Grade. In 1910, an avalanche derailed two passenger trains going along the 6-mile (9.7-kilometer) trail, and close to one hundred people were killed when the trains were knocked off their tracks, making it one of the nation's worst rail disasters. Today, hikers won't see the tracks—they've been removed—but they claim to hear the screams of the passengers and the screech of metal as the trains derailed and crashed along the grade. The most haunted spots are the tunnels, where hikers hear the echoes of screams of the dead.

Another ghostly railroad trail, also in Washington, is the Spruce Railroad Trail in Olympic National Park. The eight-mile loop circles Lake Crescent, the home of the "Lady of the Lake." She is said to be the spirit of a waitress, Hallie Illingworth, who was murdered in 1937. Her body was dumped into the lake, and fishermen found her remains three years later. Now she is often seen in her white dress by the lake along the trail.

Empire Mine Road is an isolated path in Antioch, California, with the notorious reputation as the "Gates to Hell." On the side of the path is a metal barricade that prevents cars from going beyond that point, but people on foot ignore the warning. Rumor has it the land beyond was once home to an insane asylum where lobotomies and shock treatments cause agony, even death, for patients. Their spirits now haunt the area around the gate along with the ghosts of animals that lost their lives at a slaughterhouse that was once on the grounds.

The hills around this trail are haunted by an evil ghost called "Spearfinger" by the local Cherokee because of the entity's one long finger in the shape of a sharp blade.

Norton Creek Trail is a part of the Great Smoky Mountains in North Carolina, an area not only known for its amazing natural beauty but its history. The hills around this trail are haunted by an evil ghost called "Spearfinger" by the local Cherokee because of the entity's one long finger in the shape of a sharp blade. Spearfinger is said to be female and roams the mountains of North Carolina and Tennessee disguised as a kindly, old woman. Spearfinger lures children to their deaths, but other ghosts that haunt the trail are much less malevolent, appearing as a friendly, white light or the spectral apparition of a murdered settler who helps lead lost hikers to safety through the thick woods.

Many trails are linked to Native American tribes of the region and often are reflective of their legend and lore. Chilnualna Falls Trail in California's Yosemite National Park is home to some of the country's most naturally stunning, and utterly dangerous, hiking trails. The Mist Trail is home to two famous waterfalls, and the Chilnualna Falls Trail boasts three along the 8.4-mile (13.5-kilometer) loop past Grouse Lake. It was here, according to Awahnechee legend, one can hear the cries of a young boy who drowned in the lake, and legend has it, anyone who jumps into the water to try to save the child will also drown. There is also an evil spirit named Pohono who pushes those who get too close over the 240-foot (73-meter) edge.

Long Path in Thiells, New York, is in the beautiful, woodsy section of Rockland County north of New York City along the western side of the Hudson River. The path goes by the Letchworth Village cemetery, with hundreds of T-shaped markers that served as the final resting place for the residents of Letchworth Village, a mental institution built in 1911. Once the home to epileptics and mentally ill patients, most of whom were children, the institution was overcrowded and notorious for experimenting on the patients with drugs and vaccines to see if they were safe, including the untested polio vaccine. In the 1970s, *ABC News* documented numerous cases of horrible abuse and neglect, and the facility shut down in 1196. Most of it is in ruins, although the hospital wing is intact as well as smaller buildings. Ghost hunters love the site, as do hikers and those eager to see a place where such tragedy occurred. Reports of paranormal activity include shadow figures, phantom voices, and the sense of being pushed, touched, and watched. Letchworth is also home to a converted church and rectory dating back to the 1800s that now houses a charming bed-and-breakfast. It is located at the south end of Letchworth State Park, and the hauntings began after the renovations on the church began. Rumor has it one of the priests, Father Maurice, died in the rectory, and his ghost lingered on to haunt the new Heaven Sent Bed and Breakfast, where guests can feel the sensation of being touched and shaken awake in their beds, and the sounds of footsteps and children running and laughing are heard at all hours of the day and night. Guests also claim they can hear hushed conversations outside the closed doors to their rooms, but when they open the doors … no one is there.

Across the country in California, Warm Springs Canyon Road may sound nice and easy but is in fact an extreme, 16-mile (26-kilometer) hike through Death Valley National Park. Between the scathingly hot temperatures and the spooky, abandoned homes along the trail, it's easy to see why this is considered an unsettling hike. But it may be where the trail leads to that is most unsettling of all, for it goes directly to the infamous Barker Ranch, the former hideout of the Manson family, including cult leader Charles, who lived there with members of his "family" in the late 1960s after the murders of actress Sharon Tate and six others in Los Angeles, California. Eventually, law enforcement caught up with Charlie and family, and they were captured amid gunfire that took several other lives. Barker Ranch was destroyed by fire in 2009, but the shells of buildings remain. Anyone brave enough to walk the ruins, or spend the night camping, may hear the screams of those who died there, the feeling of being watched, and the distinct smell of decomposing bodies.

Altadena, California, has its own haunted forest, a woodsy trail that leads to the Sam Merrill Trail, which in turn leads to Echo Mountain. There is a now vacant estate that was once called the Cobb Estate and was built in 1918 by lumber magnate Charles Cobb. The sign out front states it as a "quiet refuge for people and wildlife forever" and over its history has been home to the Pasadena Freemasons and a group of Catholic nuns. The actual house on the estate grounds was torn down, and the haunted forest was designated public land by the U.S. Forest Service in 1971, although some of the building's foundation remains. There are ghosts around the area, including what might be the ghost of one of the estate's most famous owners, the Marx Brothers, who had the home razed in 1959. Also nearby is the Altadena Haunted Gravity Hill, located at the northeast perimeter of the Rubio Wash Debris Basin. People say if you start at the bottom of the hill with your car in neutral, it will roll uphill! Is it some bizarre natural phenomenon, or is it supernatural? Rumor has it if you put baby powder on the hood of the car, you might see handprints on it, as if the car were being dragged up the hill by ghosts.

Mount Rubidoux

Another creepy California hike goes up a hill called Mount Rubidoux, at the northwest edge of Riverside, paralleling the Santa Ana River. The hill was named for a Mexican land grant settler, Louis Rubidoux, who was also a rancher, miner, and winemaker. It was once private property owned by a man named Frank Miller, who built the road that leads to the top of the hill. Miller put up a cross at the top of the hill to honor Father Junipero Serra, who founded the many famous California missions. The cross is accessed by a winding, paved road that goes past the Peace Bridge and Tower, ending in a stony peak where Easter sunrise services are given. This is where people are rumored to have seen the ghost of Jesus Christ at night as well as other ghostly figures lurking about. The Evergreen Cemetery is adjacent to the hill and dates back to 1872, and Frank Miller was buried there in 1935, so perhaps one of the many ghosts is his, wandering the hill to the cross he loved so much.

Haunted Caves and Mines

Do you have claustrophobia? Going inside a cave system can strike fear in anyone despite the possible presence of ghosts or evil entities. The feeling of walls closing in, lack of fresh air, darkness.... It takes a brave soul to go exploring in the many cave systems available and open to the public. But what about those that offer more than just interesting rock formations, strange drawings on the cave walls, and the possibility of finding gold and buried treasure? What about those that contain within their depths the spirits of the dead unable to find the light in death as they were in life?

Witnesses have claimed to have seen Jesus lingering around the cross erected at the top of Mount Rubidoux in Riverside, California.

Mammoth Cave

Kentucky's Mammoth Cave is one of the longest cave systems in the world. It was once a shelter for tuberculosis patients in the late 1830s, and the bodies of those who died were laid at the adjacent Corpse Rock before they were buried. The patients were kept in the cave by a doctor named Frank Gorin, who believed the fresh air above would kill them and that the cave air would cure them. It didn't work. It's hard to tell what killed them—the harsh cave existence or the tuberculosis itself. Perhaps both, and visitors to the cave today claim they can hear phantom coughing when no one is around. H. P. Lovecraft used the Mammoth Cave setting for his story "The Beast in the Cave," in which a tourist finds himself stalked by a terrifying humanoid creature.

H. P. Lovecraft used the Mammoth Cave setting for his story "The Beast in the Cave," in which a tourist finds himself stalked by a terrifying humanoid creature.

During the 1920s, the cave system was a popular tourist attraction, and some of the individual caves were owned by private individuals who had the money to buy them. One owner, Floyd Collins, called his cave the Crystal Cave, and it was a hot spot until it started waning in popularity. Collins tried to dig a new entrance but was trapped when a boulder was dislodged and fell on top of him. No one was able to move the large boulder, and Collins became quite a media darling as he lay there trapped, with souvenir stands popping up as rescuers tried to dig him out. Locals came to see him, as if he were an animal in a zoo, and another cave-in eventually blocked him off from hope of rescue. He died of exposure. His corpse stayed in the cave for years before the family was able to bury it in a local cemetery.

Collins's father later had his son's body exhumed and put in a glass case on display in the cave until the National Park System purchased the cave in 1961. The ghost of Floyd Collins was said to have haunted the cave since then and still does. People report rocks being thrown at them and the voice of a man calling out of the darkness, begging for help. Today, tours not only take visitors through this cave but the entire Mammoth Cave system, including the abandoned "tuberculosis village."

Swallow Cave

The seaside town of Nahant, Massachusetts, is where tourists find Swallow Cave, only about 24 yards (22 meters) deep but deep, but ripe with history. In 1675, during the King Philips War, around forty Native American warriors attacked the town of Lynn and were driven into Swallow Cave to hide out. Even though the cave was small, the warriors remained unfound, and the people of Lynn turned to a fortune teller from Salem by the name of Witch Wonderful to help the raiding party find them.

The witch told the men exactly where to find the Native American warriors. The men headed to Swallow Cave for a confrontation, but just before any weapons were fired, Witch Wonderful appeared and begged the two sides to come to an agreement. She got her desire, and peace prevailed until her death. She is now reported to float about the entrance to the cave or sit atop a hill overlooking the entrance.

Grand Canyon Caverns

The Grand Canyon is home to a haunted hotel, haunted hiking trail, and haunted caverns! The Cavern Hotel is located at the Grand Canyon Caverns in the northeastern part of Arizona along the famous Route 66. They represent the largest dry caverns in the country and go down to three hundred feet belowground. Within the caverns is the fully functional Cavern Hotel, a full-amenities hotel with very unusual surroundings.

A number of ghosts haunt the caverns and hotel, including two brothers who were found dead in 1927 by a man named Walter Peck. The brothers had died of the flu and now are reported to haunt the area, along with Peck, whose spirit has a special penchant for riding on the elevator. A more tragic ghost guest is that of former hotel manager Gary Ringsby, who sadly hanged himself in the bunkhouse, where his apparition is often seen floating around. Other haunted hot spots include the curio shop, restaurant, and, of course, the elevator.

Moaning Cavern

Enter the Moaning Cavern in Vallecito, California, and chances are good you might hear the phantom moans and mournful cries coming from deep within as well as the distinct sound of a hammer banging against rock. This particular cavern is said to be haunted by the Tommyknockers, mythical, little leprechaun creatures that cause mischief and trouble. Other people believe the spirits encountered in the cavern are of those who died there such as gold miners who perished after falling into the deeper parts of the cave or those who died in the occasional cave-ins. The knocking and hammering sound is believed to be evil spirits trying to cause a cave-in … or the ghosts of the dead trying desperately to hammer their way out.

This is also the site of a huge, cryptozoological, saber-toothed cat that died in the cavern and now appears to visitors with a chipped tooth from its fatal fall.

Strange monster cats, gnomelike figures, hammering and knocking … this is one cave system that seems more the stuff of urban legend, but don't take my word for it if you decide to find out for yourself.

Canyon Diablo

Arizona ghost town Canyon Diablo is found just off Interstate 40 and is a relic of the days when men built railroad tracks to allow settlers to go further west into California. The town was a place of lawlessness and home to many gamblers, outlaws, prostitutes, and crooks, who enjoyed the many brothels, bars, and gambling halls. When the railroad was complete, the town lost its allure and soon became Two Guns, a traveling post for those journeying along Route 66.

Long before, in 1878, a band of Apache Warriors massacred a Navajo camp in the same spot, killing men, women, and children. The Navajo attempted to retaliate and tried to track down the Apache in the desert when they experienced a blast of hot air coming up from the ground. They were standing on a cave system where the Apache were hiding, and the hot air was coming from fires below. The Navajo stuffed the openings with wood and brush and set it all on fire, killing forty-two Apache and their horses. The caves were considered cursed ever since, yet white settlers chose to build Canyon Diablo and Two Guns there anyway, ignoring the warnings.

An 1890 photograph of Canyon Diablo, Arizona, during a time of prosperity when it was a railroad town.

Shadow figures, phantom moans, screams, groans, and apparitions near the cave entrance haunted the townsfolk ever since, and to this day, the cave area is still accessible, but locals warn against going inside, claiming they will not only encounter ghosts but terrible misfortune. In fact, those who go in are told they might never come out again.

Nebraska Caves

Pahuk Bluff in Lincoln, Nebraska, is part of a vast sandstone cave system that visitors and locals claim are haunted by the restless ghosts of Native Americans who died there under tragic conditions. When white settlers arrived, the area's Pawnee tribe was booted off their land. Eventually, Lincoln would become the state's capital, but those who ventured into Pahuk Bluff claimed to hear the chants and drumming of the Natives they cast out. A part of the same cave system called Robber's Cave was a hiding place and rest stop for slaves along the Underground Railroad until it was turned into part of a brewery in 1869.

In 1873, the brewery went out of business, and the cave was later used by a hodgepodge of criminals, thugs, outlaws, and escaped prisoners as a hideout. The infamous outlaw Jesse James once used the cave to dodge law enforcement. Many people must have died there, as those who currently venture into the cave system insist they hear phantom voices, laughing, Pawnee chanting and drumming, screaming, moaning, and creepy chattering in the darkness.

Mines

Haunted Mines

The only thing more claustrophobic than a cave is a mine. The brave souls that go down into the earth often reside deep within tunnels with little air and dim lighting, often only provided by the helmets on their heads. A mine shaft can be a very terrifying place to be if you are not acclimated to closed-in, dark spaces. Abandoned mines are often said to be home to the ghosts of the men who died working there.

Haunted mines have some strange commonalities. Disembodied voices and strange, flickering lights are often reported, even in mines that are still functioning. Miners report sounds of voices from areas that were blocked off from fallen debris or collapsing rock. The mine shafts may be closed off beyond a certain point, but that doesn't seem to stop the phantom activity that goes on there, including the sounds of hammers and chisels meeting hard rock walls. Some of it is blamed on Tommyknockers, which may be the spirits of underground entities that enjoy knocking on walls and walkways.

Mysterious lights and orbs are often reported, especially the dim beacons of miner's hats in places where there aren't any miners around.

Mysterious lights and orbs are often reported, especially the dim beacons of miner's hats in places where there aren't any miners around. Since many men die in mines, ghosts abound, and their eerie whispers can be heard echoing off the walls, along with the swinging of chains; strange, mechanical noises; and screams of those who perished alone in the dark.

The Big Thunder Mine in Keystone, South Dakota, was once a gold mine that now hosts tours as part of the area's tourism, especially at Halloween. The area around Keystone also includes a haunted cemetery that has the honors of being listed as one of the "100 Most Haunted Cemeteries in America" and has been visited by a popular ghost-hunting television show to look into the local paranormal lore, including the activity at a local, historic schoolhouse that was built in 1900.

But it's the mine that draws the most attention from tourists and ghost-hunting groups who point to the mining community's exposure to so much death as a reason why. The Holy Terror Mine, as locals call it, is surrounded by places where people were hanged, murdered, and, of course, killed inside the mine.

The Waldeck Mine in Nevada is said to be filled with ghosts and demons. In 2016, the YouTube Channel's "Exploring Abandoned Mines and Unusual Places" wanted to test out some new flashlight equipment in the mine. But while there, phantom whispers were recorded on tape coming from deep within the mine.

Another Nevada mine, the long-abandoned Horton Mine, is home to not just ghosts but the sounds of swinging chains and mechanical noises that sound like there is still active mining deep inside. Located within the Humboldt-Toiyabe National Forest in the central part of the state, the mine was put into operation in the 1800s as the bigger Victorine Mine. Several deaths occurred inside the mines, and it was given the reputation of being one of the most haunted in the country. It has been abandoned now for a while but continues to earn a dark reputation for the amount of paranormal activity witnessed there, including gusts of cold within the mine shaft, objects moving on their own, phantom voices and noises, shadowy figures moving about, and the strong sense of doom and foreboding upon entering the mine shaft.

Pennsylvania Mines

Pennsylvania's coal mines were the sites of many deaths thanks to a two-hundred-year history of coal mining in the state. In the nineteenth century, the Neshannock Township of Lawrence County, located in the western part of the state, had dozens of mine shafts alone, and the first ghost of a miner was reported as far back as 1898. The ghost entered the mine with his pick and his lantern each night, work for a while, and then come back out at dawn to vanish into thin air. Some miners at the time believed it to be the ghost of Elijah Bowaker, who vanished inside the mine the prior year and never came out again.

In the later part of the nineteenth century, there were on average five deaths recorded per month at the Wyoming Coal Fields in Scranton. The youngest victims were ten-year-old boys, who were allowed in mines at the time, and the oldest were sixty-nine and seventy-two when they lost their lives. The Bellevue Shaft was a particularly hot spot, with a six-foot-tall vapory apparition appearing to miners in 1872.

In Taylor, Pennsylvania, a mine owned by the Delaware and Hudson Company was haunted by a white-robed form with hollow eyes that carried a light. Several miners tried to approach the ghost in November 1906, but it vanished when they got too close. In Kittanning, miners were frightened by the apparition of a man that would appear carrying a lighted dinner pail. It would float from room to room of the mine and ordered the men to stop working. Some men stated it was half-human, half-beast and would set down their tools and run in terror for the entrance, then refuse to work for the next few days.

In the Jeddo Mine in Lancaster, it was common for miners down below to see strange lights with no explanation as well as the ghost of a man whose lips move but speaks no words aloud.

Canada's Atlas Mine

In the Canadian Red Deer River Valley Badlands, there were once 139 coal mines in the Drumheller area of Alberta, providing nearby homes with coal for heat until natural gas took over and the mines and surrounding towns were abandoned for greener pastures. One of the mines was the Alton Mine, which is said to be notoriously haunted, long after it served its functional purpose. This area was rich with coal deposits as discovered back in 1792 by explorer

Red Deer River Valley in Alberta, Canada's Badlands was once home to over a hundred coal mines. Mining was a dangerous and deadly business, so it is not surprising the ghosts of dead miners may linger still.

Peter Fidler. In the following years, ranchers and homesteaders came to dig coal out of riverbanks and coulees to heat their homes, and the first commercial mine followed when Sam Drumheller opened it in the early 1900s.

It was said that hundreds of thousands of people came to find coal, many from European countries who had come to America. By the end of 1912, there were nine operational coal mines. Over the years, as more mines opened, the mining industry had several successes providing safer working conditions for the miners, which included better ventilation and washhouses. In 1911, boys under the age of fourteen were forbidden to work underground.

The mining camps, often called "hell holes," were still dirty, rough places to live, with little in the way of sanitation and few comforts, and many miners turned to gambling and drinking, which often led to violent fights. Eventually, even that improved, as families came to live in the towns and modernizations followed.

By 1979, there were 139 mines total in the Drumheller Valley, and thirty-four of those remained highly productive for many years. The Leduc Oil Strike in 1948 put coal mining on hold and suddenly elevated natural gas to importance, and that was the end of the coal industry's heyday. Communities turned into ghost towns, and the Atlas Mine shipped out its final load of coal in 1979.

Since then, it has become a National Historic Site in Canada and the home to ghosts that appear to many paranormal research groups that have visited the mine. They've reported the paranormal activity isn't just in the mines but in the houses that remain, including the washhouse. One ghost is of a woman in a brown dress who was a miner's wife that appears running into the office as she did when she was alive to warn the mine manager of an explosion. The mine manager went into the mine to investigate and died, possibly of exposure to methane gas. Orbs of light streak across the rooms, especially during thunderstorms, and apparitions are frequently seen, although no one can identify exactly who they are.

However, some people suggest these are nothing more than echoes of noises occurring above and outside the mines or fakery committed by those who hope to make money offering mine tours. But those who venture inside on their own or with research groups have a different story to tell.

BATTLEFIELDS, CEMETERIES, AND CHURCHES

Along the nation's highways and byways are places where the dead are more likely to roam. No matter what state, there are historical places that speak of the past as a time where hundreds, thousands of soldiers perished during the many big and small battles fought or of a graveyard or cemetery where the bodies of the dead lay for all eternity. Even those places of worship where people celebrated life, and mourned death, hold ghosts that will not rest.

Historical places carry with them the spirits of those who lost their lives, whether in accidents, wars, or natural causes, but are said to be especially haunted because often, the deaths were tragic and in larger numbers. Yet, isn't all death tragic, not just to the victim but to those who loved him or her? Even one death can bring with it a ghostly presence that lives on.

Some of the most haunted locations in existence are reminders of those who lived and died in the past, whether two hundred years ago or ten years ago, and how they continue to affect the present and the future.

HAUNTED BATTLEFIELDS

Battlefields bring to mind a vision of brave soldiers fighting for a mighty cause, even freedom or to vanquish a powerful enemy. Because they are places where so many die, it is only natural that those who live near them, or like to visit them, report ghosts of dead soldiers, often dressed in the proper uniform. Some are even said to be going through the motions as if the war they once fought continues on in another dimension of reality. Perhaps these are places where time is caught in a loop and history is doomed to repeat itself over and over for anyone lucky, or unlucky, enough to witness it.

ANTIETAM

On September 17, 1862, the Civil War came to Antietam Creek in western Maryland. Even though this particular battle lasted about four hours, the loss of life was astronomical, with twenty-three thousand men killed or missing in action. In fact, the small road where the battle took place was later called Bloody Lane to commemorate the massive number of dead. Some of the worst bloodshed occurred on a 1.6-mile (2.6-kilometer) stretch called the Cornfield Trail, were as many as eight thousand soldiers where killed or wounded during a barrage of artillery fire, attacks, and counterattacks. In fact, it was at the Cornfield Trail that the Confederate Army had its biggest number of dead and wounded for any of the Civil War battles.

The entire battlefield is said to be haunted by spectral soldiers and the sounds of gunfire, but one of the most haunted areas is the Burnside Bridge, where Union soldiers under the guidance of Ambrose Burnside pushed the Confederate Army back. It was also the unfortunate burial place for the bodies of the dead, left in shallow, unmarked graves. Nearby, the St. Paul Episcopal Church was used as the Confederates' makeshift hospital and is now said to be haunted by those who perished there. A local legend claims the church floors were so stained in blood, not even sandpaper can remove it. An 8-mile (13-kilometer) tour of the area is available to tourists, and a visitor center offers a background to the history of this famous field.

The name of the battle depends on which side you were on. In the Union north, the battle was Antietam, named after the creek. In the Confederate south, it was called Sharpsburg, which was the nearest town. The nearby Antietam National Cemetery is home to over 4,700 Union soldiers who were buried elsewhere initially, then reinterred here, and the entire battlefield became part of the National Park Service in 1933.

CHICKAMAUGA

The Chickamauga Battlefield in northern Georgia was home to a bloody Civil War victory for the Confederate Army, but the losses totaled more than thirty thousand soldiers. The word Chickamauga is Cherokee for "river of death," and Native Americans in the area believed it to be cursed.

During the Civil War, the battlefield saw action on September 19–20, 1863, that resulted in the second-highest body count of the war (second only to Gettysburg Battlefield). The Confederate Army would be victorious but not before over thirty-four thousand soldiers on both sides lost their lives either from the battle itself or from sickness.

Yet, this area's history continued with the Spanish–American War of 1898. The battlefield area was home to over seventy thousand soldiers, and many of them eventually became sick and died from typhoid fever and malaria,

Civil War-era cannons stand like silent sentinels among tombstones and memorials scattered across the Chicamauga Battlefield, where about four thousand Union and Confederate soldiers lost their lives and over twenty thousand were wounded.

according to some reports. Yet, some claim the men died from unsanitary conditions and food or from their battle wounds.

Regardless of how they died, the high body count would no doubt spawn many stories of paranormal phenomena in the area. The local Cherokee believed a Sasquatch roamed the area and may have been the foundation for a popular urban legend: Old Green Eyes. After the end of the battles in September 1863, two women walking the battlefield claimed to have been approached by a tall humanoid creature with fangs, light hair, a protruding jaw, and two green, glowing eyes. As the legend grew, Old Green Eyes became a shape-shifter, as influenced by Native American lore.

Another popular ghost is the Lady in White, who wanders around in her wedding gown searching for her beloved. Add to this the ongoing reports of phantom battle sounds, sights, and even the haunting music of the fife and drum bands that once played their victory songs, and this battlefield is as active today with the spirits of the dead as it was in the past with the armies of the living.

Cold Harbor Battlefield

The spirits of dead soldiers roam this battlefield in Mechanicsville, Virginia. This battlefield is the home of one of the country's bloodiest battles, the Overland Campaign of Union Lieutenant General Ulysses S. Grant. The entire strategic battle included a number of raids and grisly skirmishes and lasted from

May 31 to June 12, 1864. Though Grant's army totaled over 109,000 soldiers to Confederate General Robert E. Lee's fifty-nine thousand, there was massive bloodshed on both sides thanks to clever defensive and offensive moves.

One of the bloodiest days occurred on June 3, when Grant got a little too eager and sent his men into battle unprepared. Seven thousand soldiers died. Eventually, the Confederate Army under Lee was victorious here but not without first losing five thousand men. Grant's losses were close to thirteen thousand. Today, the ghosts of the dead haunt the battlefield, often appearing in a dense mist that comes out of nowhere and is accompanied by the sounds of phantom cannon fire. Local newspapers often report ghostly sights and sounds from the battlefield, such as men screaming, gunfire, and the distinct scent of gunpowder.

The Garthright House, a family home, was used as a makeshift hospital on the grounds, and the young daughter is said to haunt the building along with some of the ninety-seven soldiers who died there and were buried under the front lawn.

Gettysburg—The Most Haunted Battlefield in America

It is known as the most famous battle of the Civil War and certainly one of the bloodiest. From July 1–3, in 1863, the small town in southeastern Pennsylvania was home to the one battle most considered the vital turning point for the Union soldiers during the Civil War. But the price paid in suffering was tremendous for the approximately 163,000 Union and Confederate soldiers. The Battle of Gettysburg took the lives of tens of thousands of men and injured thousands more, so it only makes sense that this location is considered one of the most haunted historical places in the United States. Nothing compares to over 140 years' worth of reports of ghost soldiers moving about on the battlefield that continue even to this day, making Gettysburg one of the hottest paranormal hot spots in the country and favorite tourist destinations for those who love history.

Other witnesses report seeing flags waving across the battlefield at the National Military Park and headless horsemen that ride out from the shadows. In fact, there is even a ghostly legend involving just how the Union succeeded in battle ... involving the ghost of a very famous historical figure himself. Legend has it that members of the 20th Maine Division were guided up the Little Round Top by a uniformed man riding a white horse. The man's uniform looked old-fashioned, and he was believed to have been the ghost of George Washington helping the Union soldiers to flank the Confederate Army and thus win the battle. The strange man was given the nickname the "Phantom on Horseback," and the men who saw him said he emitted an otherworldly "glow."

Other hot spots are the Devil's Den and Plum Run, where ghostly figures interact with witnesses as if the war were still raging. Devil's Den was the spot

A memorial stands on the spot dedicated to the address President Lincoln gave at the Gettysburg battlefield, one of the most costly and horrific battles ever fought in history. Today, it is said to be one of the most haunted places in the United States.

where Confederate sharpshooters hid behind an outcropping of rock, and visitors today often report seeing the "Phantom of Devil's Den," a rag-clothed man who appears out of thin air and says "What you're looking for is over there" before vanishing again.

The sounds of soldiers talking quietly, and even yelling the word "Charge!", have been reported on electronic voice phenomena (EVP) recordings used by paranormal enthusiasts who have visited the site.

It isn't just the battlefield that is filled with ghostly activity but buildings nearby, including the Daniel Lady Farm that once served as the makeshift Confederate hospital. This hospital was where severely injured soldiers came to recover, and many died of their wounds. The suffering here alone was immense, and some witnesses claim the area is haunted by General Isaac Ewell and his corps of ten thousand soldiers.

Stories abound of the hauntings associated with Gettysburg, including ghostly apparitions, objects that move on their own, and strange sounds and lights at the nearby Gettysburg Hotel and the Baladerry Inn. The ghost of a dancing woman haunts the Gettysburg Hotel ballroom, dancing to music only she can hear. Baladerry Inn boasts amazing views of the countryside and also once served as a Union field hospital. The owner and visitors claim to have experienced encounters with the spirits of Confederate soldiers buried beneath a tennis court as well as soldiers who died at the hospital.

One story involves a shop in the historic George House, where the body of Union Major General John F. Reynolds was said to lay in state after he was killed on July 1 during the battle. Two women window shopping late one evening stopped to peer through the window of a craft shop and saw a woman in mourning black keeping vigil over a man on a cot. The room itself was empty except for the cot and the rocking chair the woman sat in. When the two women returned the next day, the shop was back to normal, filled with crafts. There was no woman in black or man on a cot, not even mannequins or statues. But the shopkeeper did confirm that a door they saw in the empty room existed, now covered by a large pegboard.

Despite there never being any cannon fire in this battle, those who visit the historic location today report hearing the sound of cannon fire!

The Cashtown Inn, eight miles west of Gettysburg, is said to be the spot where the first soldier died during the battle, and the owners claim to have experienced a host of bizarre activity, including knocking on doors, lights going on and off, orbs and skeletons appearing and vanishing, doors opening and closing, and spirits walking the premises, some of which they claim were caught on camera.

There are numerous tours of the entire area, including the Ghost Train, which takes visitors on a ninety-minute ride across the actual Gettysburg Battlefield. Often tourists experience a variety of sights, sounds, and even smells, such as cigar smoke, that can only be attributed to those who came before us, the ghosts of the past who continue to remind us of the costs of war.

MANASSAS NATIONAL BATTLEFIELD

Manassas National Battlefield Park is a popular hiking spot in Prince William County, Virginia. Just forty-five minutes from Washington, D.C., this battlefield was the home of two major Civil War battles between 1861 and 1862: the First Battle of Bull Run in July 1861 and the Second Battle of Bull Run in August 1862.

Today, park rangers and visitors alike report seeing the lights of houses where there aren't any and smelling black powder. Cold spots are common around the battlefield. But the spookiest activity is the appearance around dusk of soldiers wearing red pantaloons, white leggings, and sleeping caps. The phantom men move near the woods on the park's western end and are attributed by locals as the 5th New York Zouave regiment that fought in the Second Battle of Bull Run.

STONY POINT BATTLEFIELD

In Rockland County, New York, about forty-five minutes north of Manhattan, the Stony Point Battlefield is the location of a surprise attack during the Revolutionary War that was incredibly successful for our side. In July 1770,

General Anthony Wayne, also known as General "Mad Anthony" Wayne, led the American Corps of Light Infantry into a surprise, thirty-three-minute, midnight attack that had the British forces so unprepared, they couldn't get their cannons loaded in time to fire them. The British were captured on-site, and the Continental Army was later able to cross the Hudson River without resistance to achieve victory over the British.

Despite there never being any cannon fire in this battle, those who visit the historic location today report hearing the sound of cannon fire! Nearby is another haunted location—the Stony Point Lighthouse, which is the oldest extant lighthouse on the Hudson River. It was built in 1926 and continued to operate for ninety-nine years before the light was replaced by an automated beacon. To this day, people roaming around by the lighthouse report hearing the moans of someone in pain nearby as well as the echo of gunfire and the boom of a cannon.

International Battlefields

War happens all over the world. Here are some of the notorious haunted battlefields in other countries.

Culloden Moor

The Battle of Culloden in Scotland was fought on April 16, 1746. The bloody rebellion of Jacobite soldiers was motivated by the desire to return the Stuarts to the throne, but they were vastly outnumbered. Within forty minutes, the entire Bonnie Prince Charlie's army was dead, either exhausted from the long days of marching back to England or by the government forces that charged them at their weakest.

Those lucky enough to escape the initial artillery fire from government forces fell on the enemy frontlines, especially when the government army utilized a new type of attack called the "highland charge." Enemy soldiers stabbed the Highlanders with swords and bayonets in a manner that pierced the Scottish Army's sword arms, which were unprotected. Anyone who survived that was subsequently slaughtered. Bonnie Prince Charlie was able to evade death and escape to Italy, never to return to his homeland.

Those who visit the site hear the cries of the wounded, the clank and crash of steel weapons, and visually witness the ghosts of the dead soldiers rise and fight, then vanish. Locals say birds living in trees near the battlefield refuse to sing during the times the soldiers appear.

Passchendaele

The Battle of Passchendaele in Belgium was fought during World War I. Through heavy rains and thick mud, the Germans fought the British and their allies from Canada, New Zealand, South Africa, and Australia. The Ger-

Carnations lay at a memorial dedicated to the Battle of Stalingrad in what is now the city of Volgograd, Russia. The successful resistance against the Nazis by the Russians turned the tide of World War II, though at a huge cost of human life.

mans were hit from all sides with thousands of guns and shells, and a one-mile area was riddled with a million shell holes. Approximately four hundred thousand soldiers died on both sides during the difficult and physically brutal battle. To get over the mud, wooden slats were placed on the ground, but they often became death traps themselves due to the slippery wood. Many soldiers fell to their deaths through the slats.

Those who visit the battlefield claim to hear the sounds of gunfire and men shouting and screaming.

The Battle of Stalingrad

The city once known as Stalingrad is now Volgograd in Russia. Those who live there understand the magnitude of what happened on the battlefield there during World War II and, in fact, refer to it as the "mother of all battles." From August 1942 to February 1943, battle raged on and resulted in the deaths of one million Soviet soldiers, eight hundred thousand German, Romanian, and Italian Axis troops, and over five hundred thousand civilians. This battle was considered a watershed event in the war because it was the final major defeat of Nazi Germany. Many of the dead still rest on the same ground where they were slain, and bodies are still being dug up to this day.

The entire city is a memorial to the past and the massive numbers of dead, many of whom roam the city as ghostly figures. In fact, locals say some entire neighborhoods are considered haunted by the soldiers and civilians who laid down their lives there so long ago.

Stoney Creek

During the War of 1812, Ontario, Canada, was home to the Battle of Stoney Creek and a woman by the name of Mary Jones Gage, who lived with her family in town. Her husband died during the American Revolution. In 1813, an invading American army invaded her town, and troops entered her home to demand it as their new headquarters. The family hid in their basement as the Battle of Stoney Creek broke out the very next day. Though Mary died later in 1841, her ghost is said to haunt Stoney Creek even today along with the spirits of dead soldiers.

Towton, England

Known as the "Wars of the Roses," the battlefield at Towton in 1461 resulted in over thirty thousand dead, perhaps because of a massive snowstorm that made it even more difficult to survive and hide from enemy fire. Every seven years, Towton experiences a similar blizzard, and those who dare to walk onto the battlefield during the storm can witness the two sides in battle for several hours. Then, for the next seven years, there is no activity, as if the soldiers who died are caught in a loop doomed to repeat history for eternity.

Forts and Barracks

Forts were used during wartime as outposts, observation points, and to secure an area from outside invaders or at least deter them. Just as many battlefields are said to be haunted by the suffering and death of the past, there are forts that make the same claims.

Fort Meigs

During the War of 1812, General William Henry Harrison established this fort south of Toledo, Ohio, to defend against British attack. The fort provided secure protection for about a year before it was eventually burned down. Harrison would go on to be president of the United States (though only briefly because he died of pneumonia), and the ghosts of the dead would live on in the sound of cannon and musket fire, fife and drums, and mysterious footsteps, sometimes accompanied by apparitions. Perhaps the ghosts of the over five hundred soldiers buried nearby and beneath the fort now roam around the grounds, trying to find their way to the light. The fort was rebuilt and opened to the public for tours in 1974.

Fort Warren

Located on George's Island outside of Boston, Massachusetts, this massive fort was built to withstand just about any force of man or nature. It has a long history and was once used to imprison Confederate soldiers in the Civil War. It is most known for the ghost of Melanie Lanier, known as the "Lady in Black," who was captured and denounced as a spy after she accidentally killed her husband, a Confederate soldier imprisoned there during a rescue attempt. She was hanged within the fortress, and her ghost is seen to this day dressed in a black mourning cloak, roaming the grounds or leaving footsteps in the snow outside the fort. Sometimes, her sad cries are heard echoing through the hallways.

Fort Fisher

By December 1864, the Civil War had raged on for three years, and thousands of soldiers died or were wounded in battle. Fort Fisher was just south of Wilmington, North Carolina, and was considered the only remaining strong-

Confederate soldiers stand guard at a damaged gun. The Civil War was almost over when this photo was taken in 1865.

hold keeping the Confederate Army equipped by protecting the only open port allowing seafaring trade from Britain and Europe. Eventually, the fort would fall to the U.S. Navy under Admiral David Porter, who led a twenty-day bombardment of the fort, resulting in two thousand men dead inside trying to defend themselves. Today, there is little left of the fort, but you can walk through the remains, and some say if you stand on the parapets, you can see the skeletons of the dead blockade runners under the surface of the ocean. Visitors also report the ghost of a Confederate officer looking out to sea and hear footsteps along the wooden walkway when no one is around.

Fort Concho

This San Angelo, Texas, outpost was built in 1867 to protect early settlers. For over twenty years, it was served by historical names such as Pecos Bill and William Shafter and is now a historical landmark as both a location for a number of important battles and as the place where soldiers stopped the illegal profiteering between Mexican and American traders known as the Comanchero Movement.

Among the ghosts said to haunt this fort are James Cunningham, George Dunbar, and Ranald MacKenzie, who was considered the fort's most well-known commander. His ghost is said to haunt the fort's Officers Row, where he lived. Other spirits include a twelve-year-old girl named Edith Grierson.

Fort William Henry

New York's Lake George area was home to Fort William Henry, used during the French and Indian War. It was here that a massacre occurred between Indian and British soldiers, and the grounds are now said to be haunted by their restless spirits. Visitors to the site also report the sound of footsteps, and wind chimes, even when the air is still.

Drum Barracks

Many people have no idea that the state of California was involved in the Civil War. The Drum Barracks, a five-company post established in 1862 at Wilmington and originally called Camp San Pedro, was later named Camp Drum in honor of Lieutenant Colonel Richard Drum, an adjutant general of the Department of California. The barracks were situated on 60 acres (24 hectares) of land, with another 37 acres (15 hectares) near the harbor, and was built to house over five hundred soldiers and three hundred horses. It became the main post for staging, supplies, and training for the Southwest's military operations, and over seventeen thousand soldiers came through the barracks on their way to fight in the Civil War for the Union.

The actual post was decommissioned in 1871, but the hospital on-site stayed open another two years to tend to the wounded soldiers. After it closed, the land was auctioned off, and only a few of the original buildings remained. The post was open to the public in 1987 as the Drum Barracks Civil War Museum, and many visitors report paranormal activity in the old building, such as the sound of chains being dragged, phantom noises, and footsteps when no one is there. Some visitors and staff claim to have seen the ghost of a woman known as "Maria" who wears a hoop skirt and smells strongly of lavender and violet perfume. Others report the apparition of a man in an 1800s soldier's uniform smoking a pipe, the smell of which fills the museum.

Cemeteries

The sheer number of cemeteries reported to be haunted in this country alone could fill several books. The places we bury our dead are no doubt ripe with spirits who refuse to stay buried, at least in nonphysical form. While some people wonder why a ghost would want to haunt the place its body is buried and not somewhere fun and happy, others suggest that a graveyard is the natural portal between the dead and the living because it is the final resting place form that spirit took in life. If you want your spirit to stay settled, you might consider cremation.

Anaheim Cemetery

California's Anaheim Cemetery boasts being the oldest public cemetery in Orange County, located between San Diego County to the south and Los Angeles County to the north. Established in 1866 and called "God's Acre," the original settlers to the area are buried there along with their many descendants. In 2002, the Orange County Historical Commission officially recognized the cemetery as a historical site. The first mausoleum in the state was erected here in 1914. Today, the cemetery is said to be haunted by its own "Lady in White" and other ghostly apparitions that appear at night and vanish at the first sign of dawn.

The places we bury our dead are no doubt ripe with spirits who refuse to stay buried, at least in non-physical form.

Not too far away, the Yorba Cemetery in Yorba Linda, California, is home to a ghost called the "Pink Lady," described as a seventeen-year-old girl dressed in a pretty, pink gown. She is usually crying and may be the ghost of a girl who died in 1910 in a horse and buggy accident. Other locals believe she is the ghost of Alvina de Los Reyes, who died of pneumonia. The cemetery was opened back in 1834 and boasts other ghosts thanks to its long history. The gates were officially closed in 1939, but today, there are public tours available through the grounds.

Bachelor's Grove

In Midlothian, Illinois, there is a small, abandoned, and desolate cemetery that is strangely named for the number of single men in the Chicago suburb. Though no one has been buried there since the early 1960s, the site now serves as a meeting place for people practicing voodoo and Satanism. But nothing rivals the ghosts, including those of murder victims dumped by gangsters on-site in the 1920s. Other ghostly presences include a farmer with his horse and plow; a White Lady, who may have been buried at the gravesite; and even a phantom farmhouse that appears out of nowhere with swinging lights on the front porch. The farmhouse disappears if anyone approaches it. Phantom cars can be seen and heard on the roads around the cemetery, and the ghost of a woman is often reported sitting on the tombstones.

Bonaventure Cemetery

Savannah, Georgia, is a city with a reputation for being haunted, so it's only natural they have a cemetery of their own with the strange and eerie ghost of a little girl named Gracie Watson, who died of pneumonia and was buried on the grounds. Not only is little Gracie's ghost seen walking among the tombstones, but a statue by her own grave is said to cry tears of blood. The lush cemetery is filled with eye-catching monuments, and Gracie's statue sits behind

With its dense tree and ground cover, historic Bonaventure Cemetery in Savannah, Georgia, conveys the perfect spooky atmosphere for ghosts.

an iron fence. She is carved beautifully, with her right hand placed upon a tree stump marker.

Gracie's story is a creepy one indeed. She was the daughter of Wales and Margaret Frances Watson, who managed the lavish Pulaski Hotel in the 1880s. They threw huge parties for society folks, and Gracie would charm the guests with her presence, acting as a little hostess. She would often steal away from the parties to play beneath a back stairwell, and guests would delight in asking "Where's Gracie?" when the hour was getting late.

Just before Easter of 1889, little Gracie died of pneumonia. Her distraught parents claimed they could still hear her playing behind the stairwell. The couple eventually moved to another hotel to manage and to escape their sorrowful memories, but those working at the Pulaski Hotel continued to hear Gracie playing, and some reported the sounds of moaning and metal clanging in the basement. To honor his daughter, Wales hired a sculptor named John Walz to carve out her likeness, which became her grave marker. Her ghost not only haunts her gravesite and the Pulaski Hotel but also the new building where the hotel was before being demolished in 1957. Gracie is seen peering out the windows and even playing in the nearby public Johnson Square.

El Campo Santo Cemetery

Known as "America's Finest City," San Diego is home to many haunted locations, including the El Campo Santo Cemetery in the famed Old Town historical district. Built in 1849, it was in use until 1880 and was originally a Catholic cemetery. As the city grew, the living decided the graves could be moved or built over to make room for progress, and a horse-drawn streetcar later drove right over eighteen graves. Today, only a little over four hundred of the original graves that were not moved or paved over remain, and the cemetery is a quick few blocks' walk away from another major San Diego haunted locale—The Whaley House.

Those who walk near the old cemetery report cold spots and cars refusing to start from the adjoining parking lot. The ghosts of a former gravedigger and a young boy who appears to be confused show up to some lucky—or unlucky—witnesses.

Howard Street Cemetery

Located in the spooky, historical city of Salem, Massachusetts, this cemetery is the oldest in the area and home to the famous ghost of Giles Corey, a victim of the Salem Witch Trials, who was tortured and killed in the late 1600s, when he refused to admit guilt or innocence when asked if he was a warlock. The method of death, called "pressing," was especially gruesome. Corey was forced to lie in a hole with a board across his chest. Stones were placed upon the board, crushing Corey to death over the course of two days. Now his ghost is said to seek vengeance and appears right before something terrible is to occur, like an omen or portent of doom.

Many of the early Puritan settlers were buried at King's Chapel Burying Ground in Boston, Massachusetts.

King's Chapel Burying Ground

Boston, Massachusetts's King's Chapel Burying Ground dates back to 1610. This is the final resting place of many of the nation's Puritan settlers, including Governor John Winthrop and Reverend John Cotton. Because of its rich history, the cemetery is said to be haunted by a host of ghostly types, including the pirate Captain Kidd, whose voice can be heard spooking people. Strange lights appear and disappear, and the restless spirits of the dead whose graves were later moved by the city roam the grounds, including a woman decapitated by a carpenter, who holds her head in her hands. Visitors report that pictures and video vanish from their cameras the moment they leave the graveyard.

A Theme Park and a Burial Ground

Imagine building a theme park on top of an ancient Indian burial ground. Sounds like something right out of a horror movie, but it happened at Lake Shawnee Amusement Park in Rock, West Virginia, in the 1920s. Owned by businessman Conley T. Snidow, the theme park consisted of a swing set, a Ferris wheel, and a large pond turned into an open-air swimming pool. The park was cursed from the start, though. A little boy would drown in the pool, and five other people would die there before it was closed down, including a little girl in a pink dress who was killed while on the swing set. A truck accidentally hit and crushed her when it reversed down the path directly to the swing set. In 1966, the park was shut down. Later, in 1988, an archaeological excavation turned up the bodies of over a dozen children. The amusement park has been built on top of a Native American burial ground.

After the park was shut down, people reported the sounds of children crying and laughing near the Ferris wheel, and the new owner of the property, Gaylord White, claimed in an episode of the Travel Channel's "Most Terrifying Places in America" that his own son saw the ghost of a little girl dressed in pink, covered in blood. It is now a favorite hot spot for paranormal investigators.

Maple Hills Cemetery

In this cemetery, located in Huntsville, Alabama, there is an adjacent playground, Maple Hills Park, where the spirits of dead children buried in the cemetery are reported to play. The area has been given the appropriate name "Dead Children's Playground" by locals who can hear the sounds of laughter and giggling late at night when no one is around.

Resurrection Cemetery

A young girl named Mary died after a hit-and-run in the 1930s and has become something of a local urban legend at this Justice, Illinois, cemetery. Known as "Resurrection Mary," she is said to stand roadside and hitch rides from young men, only to vanish from their car as they approach the cemetery gates.

Silver Cliff Cemetery

Located in the town of Silver Cliff, Colorado, this cemetery is not known for ghostly apparitions. At Silver Cliff Cemetery, it's phantom blue lantern lights and bright, white orbs that roam the grounds, appearing at night and bouncing over tombstones. This cemetery is still in use today, and no one has come forth with a natural explanation for the phenomenon, so the locals consider the Silver Cliff Lights paranormal activity.

St. Louis Cemetery

Not located in Missouri but in the haunted city of New Orleans, Louisiana, this graveyard is the alleged home of the Voodoo Queen herself,

Marie Laveau. People come to her grave and mark it with an X, believing she will grant them a wish from beyond the grave. Visitors who dare walk among the graves report hearing crying beneath the ground, moans and groans of suffering and pain, and a ghostly face of a man that appears on one tomb. Other ghosts include a man who delivers flowers to his wife's grave marker, then vanishes into thin air. However, it may be the living who are more dangerous in this cemetery, as it has been the location of robberies and acts of violence, encouraging tourists to go on a tour and not walk the grounds alone.

Stull Cemetery

One of the most notorious haunted cemeteries also happens to serve as a gate to hell itself. That's right. A gate to hell. Located in the tiny, rural town of Stull, Kansas, about 10 miles (16 kilometers) to the west of Lawrence, the Stull Cemetery grounds contain the rubble of an old church. Rumor has it that if you knock on one of the rocks in the rubble, the Devil will answer. Legends abound at this overgrown place atop Emmanuel Hill, including ghostly activity, the presence of witches, and even strange winds that whip up out of nowhere.

But the most fascinating aspect of Stull is its longtime association with the Devil dating back to the 1850s, when locals claim the town was named "Skull" because of the rampant black magic that went on there. Though rumors abound as to why Stull's little cemetery and abandoned church became known as one of the "seven gates to hell" and a beloved stomping ground of the Devil himself, those very rumors continued to spread and morph well into the 1980s and beyond, including one that stated the Pope refused to allow his plane to fly over the cemetery!

The old, stone church was torn down in March 2002, and the three property owners came forth to state they did not authorize the destruction. There was even a spooky "hanging tree" on the site with a horrible reputation of its own, cut down in 1998 by locals who hoped to deter tourists and looky-loos. Even today, there are those that claim a stairway to hell exists on the property, used by the Devil to come and go amid the world of the living at will. This stone staircase appears on Halloween night and on the night of the spring equinox at the stroke of midnight and leads into the dark underworld.

Visitors claim that during rainstorms, rain never falls within the grounds, so should you go visit in the rain, don't be surprised if you stay bone dry during a downpour.

Westminster Hall and Burying Grounds

Home to the ghost of Edgar Allan Poe, who makes an appearance on occasion, this cemetery in Baltimore, Maryland, next to the Westminster Presbyterian Church is also where visitors might hear the muffled cries of the

The Mystery of the Black Angels

When the topic turns to strange cemetery markers and haunted artwork, nothing rivals the story of the mysterious Black Angels, cursed graveyard statues that have shown up at two different cemeteries in two different cities.

In Iowa City, Iowa, the Oakland Cemetery is home to one of the Black Angel statues. This one is over eight feet tall and is a burial monument for the Feldevert family. It was erected in 1912, rested upon a granite pedestal, and has become the source of many legends of haunted activity, including the claim that it turned from its original golden bronze to the black, stone look it has today. After several of the family members were buried here or their ashes buried beneath the angel, it changed color. Some locals claim it happened after a freak storm the night of one family member's funeral, when the statue was struck by lightning. Others say it is nothing more than the effects of oxidation. But all point to the strange angel and its association with one family member, Teresa Feldevert, said to be an evil woman or possibly a witch. She and her husband Nicholas are buried beneath the looming statue, and one legend states it was upon her death that the statue went from bronze to black. The Black Angel, unlike other angel statues found in cemeteries as grave markers, is looking downward as if sorrowful or sad, and the arms are outstretched with the right wing pointing upward and the left one slanted downward. Is this a sign of the presence of evil that lurks underneath in the spirit of Teresa Feldevert?

The Black Angel statue at Oakland Cemetery in Iowa City is one of two such cursed statues in Iowa. The other one is in Council Bluffs.

Another Black Angel statue is found in Council Bluffs, all the way across Iowa, at the Fairview Cemetery. This particular angel stands as part of the Ruth Ann Dodge Memorial and marks the burial site of the famous wife of General Grenville M. Dodge, a Civil War veteran. This Black Angel is beautiful compared to its sister statue, holding a vessel of water that formed a lovely fountain in working order until 1960. It was then restored in 1985 and is still operational today.

Visitors to both cemeteries report spectral visions, balls of light near the statues, and a feeling of foreboding if they get too close. The legend of the Black Angel in Iowa City has even made it into motion picture history, where it was part of the Iowa City folklore incorporated in the movie *Field of Dreams.* But don't kiss a woman in front of the statue, for legend has it she will be dead within seven years (unless she is a virgin).

Cambridge Skull, which is the ghost of a minister murdered nearby. Once dead, he never stopped screaming, so the killers dug up his body, stuffed his skull, and buried it inside a concrete slab that now serves as the gravestone. Not that cement can ever stop a ghost, as he is still active, and those who hear him long enough are said to be driven insane.

Union Cemetery

This Easton, Connecticut, cemetery is quite old, dating back to the 1600s. Locals call it the "White Lady Cemetery" in honor of the lady in white who roams the graves at night. Sometimes, she appears on the adjacent road, and drivers claim to have hit her with their cars! She vanishes at the moment of impact, thankfully. Other reports mention glowing, red eyes that peer from the dark shadows of the cemetery at night.

Churches

Haunted cemeteries and churches often go hand in hand since many churches have their own burial grounds on the same property. All over the country, there are churches big and small that host their own ghosts. While we think of these places as sacred and holy, they are also places where the spirits of the dead might seek solace and peace, especially if in life they were the victims of trauma, suffering, and a tragic death.

New York's Haunted Churches

The state of New York is rich with history, and no doubt its many churches reflect that. One of the most famous churches in the world is located in New York City and has an adjoining cemetery. St. Paul's Chapel is said to be haunted by a headless man who roams the cemetery at night looking for his head.

In Tuxedo, New York, the St. Mary's-in-Tuxedo church is home to ghostly activity dating back to the 1940s, one of which may be a former member of the clergy.

The Most Holy Trinity Church in Brooklyn, New York City, was built back in the 1880s. The school building was built upon cemetery grounds and is said to be one of the most haunted locations in the Big Apple. Spirits abound, including the benevolent ghost of a pastor who built the rectory in 1872. Visitors report ghostly bells ringing, lights switching on and off, voices in the empty hallways, disembodied feet, and the bloody handprints of a bell ringer named George Stelz, who was butchered in the church by burglars!

On the borough of Staten Island in New York City, St. Andrew's Episcopal Church is a common destination for ghost hunters, who claim it is filled with spirits, disembodied voices, chimes, strange noises, and even organ music that comes from nowhere. This Anglican/Episcopalian church was built in the eighteenth century and has its own spooky cemetery on the grounds.

Other Ghostly Churches

Washington, D.C.'s National Cathedral is a huge, spooky building said to be haunted by the ghost of former president Woodrow Wilson, who is the only president interred in the cathedral. He walks the halls at night, along with the ghost of a church employee. The cathedral sports a creepy crypt and numerous gargoyles, enough to terrify visitors who don't believe in ghosts. Some visitors to the cathedral report feeling as if they were being watched by unseen eyes coming from the shadowy basement. Another Washington, D.C., church is St. John's Lafayette Square, known as the "Church of the Presidents." Visitors report hearing bells toll when someone famous dies, and six ghosts appear in the president's pew every night at midnight before disappearing.

Grace Episcopal Church in Alexandria, Virginia, has its resident ghost of a man who appears in the church library. Loud footsteps can be heard on the third-floor hallway at night, well after the building is closed for the day.

The Civil War church, Aquia Episcopal, in Stafford, Virginia, is home to a ghost of a former soldier who was killed near the church as well as a young woman who was murdered in the church tower. Visitors claim to hear her cries and see strange lights throughout the building. Another Civil War church is St. George's Episcopal in Fredericksburg, Virginia, where a ghostly lady in white roams the building.

Egg Hill Church in Potter Township, Pennsylvania has its own horrifying legend of a minister who killed his entire congregation during a Halloween service in the late nineteenth century. The minister passed around poisoned bread and wine, and while the congregation began choking to death, their children ran up from the rooms below to watch their parents die before their eyes. The minister hanged himself at the altar, and his ghost is said to haunt the abandoned church, although others have claimed the ghosts of his innocent victims walk the grounds as well. Though there is no historical or factual basis for this legend, it persists to this day.

Washington, D.C.'s National Cathedral is said to host the ghost of President Woodrow Wilson.

In Mississippi, the Chapel of the Cross sits close to a cemetery. This stone church lies on the grounds of the estate of a wealthy family, the Johnstones, who also owned the church grounds in the 1850s. One of the Johnstones, Helen, was going to marry a young man who later died in a duel before the wedding. His body was buried in the cemetery and Helen visited his grave every day until she died in 1916. The ghost of Helen Johnstone haunts the cemetery, at night, and visitors hear church bells and strange noises during the early morning. The ghosts of children are said to pass through the iron gates and vanish outside the church grounds.

Few people realize ... the darker side of these missions, for many of them represent a much deadlier past to the Native Americans who once lived on the lands.

St. Paul's Episcopal Church in Key West, Florida, was built in 1828 but was later destroyed during a hurricane. The church would be rebuilt, only to be destroyed again and again from the forces of Mother Nature well into the 1900s. The adjoining St. Paul's Cemetery is where the ghosts are most active, including that of the church's benefactor, John Fleming, which is often seen in a thin, white vapor. Other ghosts that haunt the cemetery may be those whose bodies were buried there until a massive hurricane in 1928 devastated the area and sent bones flying into the nearby trees. Legend also has it the church was built on an old Seminole burial ground, too, and the ghosts of the Native Americans joined up with the ghosts of those buried there afterward to now haunt the church, cemetery, and surrounding grounds.

California's Haunted Missions

Like churches, missions are rich with history and often have cemeteries or small burial grounds on-site. California is known for its uniquely beautiful missions with their lovely gardens, which are always popular tourist spots for those traveling throughout the state. Few people, though, realize the darker side of these missions, for many of them represent a much deadlier past to the Native Americans who once lived on the lands. Some are even said to be visited by the Devil himself, who rebelled against their holy presence.

Mission San Diego de Alcala

During the Spanish Mission Period of 1769 to 1833, twenty-one missions and mission/forts were established up and down the coast of California. The first of these was Mission San Diego de Alcala, founded by Father Junipero Serra in 1769. The San Diego area was full of Native Indians, and the mission served to Christianize them. All along the El Camino Real, starting in San Diego, these missions continued to thrive until they were secularized in 1836. But the lives of Native Indians were changed forever with the arrival of Spanish settlers seeking to spread the Catholic religion into the region and influence the Natives, often by force. The Spanish also brought with them diseases and violence against the Indians, and death reigned.

This San Diego mission was moved inland and located closer to the Indian villages near the San Diego River. It would later serve as a school for Indian children and eventually was abandoned. In 1931, the mission was rebuilt and is now an active church with a museum. Those who visit it and work there claim it is haunted, including the parkland trails on the grounds. Strange lights are often reported, and some claim the ghosts of Indians used as labor for a nearby mine also haunt the area.

Mission San Juan Capistrano

Up the coast a bit from San Diego is a beautiful mission located on 10 acres (4 hectares), home to the famous swallows that return annually to San Juan Capistrano. A popular tourist spot, this mission was founded in 1775 at the encouragement of Father Junipero Serra. The mission was under attack, partially destroyed by Indians, and was refounded in 1776. Local Indians were friendly and helped build the new mission and church in 1777. A bell tower was added later, and the mission grew so fast, a larger church was later built to accommodate it. Today, tourists talk of the ghost of a faceless monk who roams the back halls at night, and a headless soldier standing guard at the garrison. People also hear bells ring at night hear the crack of a whip that may have belonged to a malicious flagellant, and see the spirit of a young girl named Magdalena who died on the grounds during a huge earthquake in 1812.

Mission San Miguel

Located in central California's coastal community of San Luis Obispo, this mission was set up at one point as a bed-and-breakfast, where visitors could only pay in gold. The owner, William Reed, became rich over the deal and buried over $200,000 in gold somewhere on the mission grounds. After boasting about it, Reed was killed along with many other mission occupants by British pirates who sought the gold but never found it. To this day, the mission is open, and there are regular services there. The bell tower, rose garden, and fountains are all favorite spots for tourists as well as a vinery and cemetery on the grounds. Ghosts include Mr. Reed, who can be heard whispering his name. There is a resident Lady in White, too, who will threaten you with damnation if you aren't a true believer. Other people report seeing a red-horned demon that appears now and then, perhaps the Devil himself.

Mission San Gabriel

The mission at San Gabriel boasts well-kept gardens and landscaped lawns, a gift shop, a lovely fountain, and a baptistry. This favorite tourist spot is devoted to the worship of Mary and has a shrine and statues in her honor. The

Never Build Anything on Top of Ancient Indian Burial Grounds

Anyone who has ever been to the movies knows that the haunted Indian burial ground is a favorite trope in horror films. It might be a family home, a courthouse, a cemetery, a church, or even an amusement park, as we've seen. It doesn't matter what the building is, it only matters where it is built, and in the case of an ancient Indian burial ground, considered sacred to the Native Americans, it's not a good idea. In fact, chances are pretty good that building will be cursed. Many such burial grounds were unmarked by gravestones or markers and therefore prime for building upon by those who didn't know the history or even that the graves existed just below the ground. But it didn't matter to the spirits, who made sure to exact revenge on the disrespectful.

Some of Hollywood's favorite "haunted burial ground" movies include the classic Steven Spielberg horror movie *Poltergeist* (1982), in which a family experienced the horrors that often accompany new suburban tract homes built on sacred Indian land. In *Pet Sematary*, based on the Stephen King novel of the same name, a man is driven mad when his son is killed and learns he can resurrect him from the Mic Mac burial ground he is buried in. Other people and animals buried in the same place also come back from death, but they are not the same as they were in life.

The Amityville Horror (1979; remake, 2005) tells the story of a family suffering the same murderous fate as those who lived there before them, thanks to a possessed father who may be influenced by the spirits of the insane. It seems the Native Americans would send their crazy people there to die on the same land the New York suburban house was built upon. In the movie *Identity* (2003) with John Cusack, a group of people in a motel are picked off one by one, and only later do we learn the motel was built up on an Indian burial ground. Same goes for the famous hotel portrayed in Stephen King's novel *The Shining* (1977), in which a writer named Jack goes mad from "all work and no play" and attempts to kill his wife and little boy, Danny, who is warned of his father's unraveling when he sees the word "redrum," or "murder" backward.

spirit of this mission is more benevolent and peaceful than some of the others, and the ghosts that haunt it are far less frightening. Visitors report the scent of roses where there are none, the sound of a woman weeping in the shrine (perhaps Mary herself weeping over the tragic fate of her son Jesus?), and statues that cry tears of blood when someone evil comes close to them.

Mission San Buenaventura

Ventura is a beautiful coastal city in central California and the location of a mission that once survived a devastating fire, which may explain the specific types of ghosts that haunt the grounds. Among the peaceful gardens are statues of saints and historical artifacts tourists can enjoy on self-guided tours. But there are ghosts lurking, from a young boy to a man with a disfigured face to a red-haired prostitute, all of whom are said to have perished in the fire. Visitors to the mission report the peaceful tranquility is shattered now and then by phantom screams and the distinct smell of burning flesh. Some of the statues have faces that change and distort when stared at, as if reacting to the pain and suffering of being burned, and crosses that fall off the walls for no apparent reason. Not too far from here is a huge cemetery that became a controversial battle between locals and historians and the city council, who were accused of digging up graves and tossing headstones into the ocean so they could build a more modern dog park. Many of the graves belonged to the very founders of the city of Buenaventura, and the residents were barely warned that their loved ones and descendants would be covered over with a blacktop parking lot and greenbelt.

Mission San Buenaventura was once nearly destroyed by fire. Several victims of the conflagration still visit the grounds.

MUSEUMS, LANDMARKS, SPORTS, AND THEATER

From museums to brothels, courthouses to jailhouses, amusement parks to corner bars, if a place is old, abandoned, or steeped in history, chances are it may be haunted. And if someone died there under preferably tragic or horrific circumstances—or more than a few "someones"—then it takes on a whole new level of paranormal possibility. We tend to forget that ghosts can haunt a new building, too, if the person who died there refuses to depart this world for the next. Yet, the lure of history's mysteries is a strong one, and we'd be hard-pressed to drive by an old, broken-down motel or asylum or enter a restaurant that was once the site of a mass murder and not wonder what spectral spookiness roams among the living.

What if every inch of ground we stand upon is teeming with ghosts just beyond our visual reach? Yet, some places are truly notorious for the strange and supernatural activity that exists within their walls. Some cities are more haunted than others, as if ghosts, like humans, gravitate to specific areas that hold a deeper meaning for them.

Tourists and visitors to such locations may not be aware of the ghostly goings-on. Many of these locations bustle with crowds during the day, so the ghosts only come out at night when all is still and quiet. Other landmarks are said to be haunted 24/7, desolate and abandoned places where there is little life to speak of yet plenty of deathly action for those lucky, or unlucky, enough to be at the right place at the right time.

Spooky Museums

Sometimes it's the building that is haunted. Sometimes it's what's inside the building, as in the case of haunted museums. Whether they display ancient artifacts or modern paranormal objects, ghostly and ghastly attachments seem to come with the territory. Is it possible for ghosts and demons to attach to objects at all? It is, according to the many reports of haunted dolls, toys, paintings, furnishings, weapons, articles of clothing, personal items, torture devices—the list goes on. This makes many museums ripe locations for apparitions and paranormal activity.

Some spirits refuse to give up the material objects they so loved, or were most associated with, in life, or they use these items as vessels and channels to manifest long after their physical death—like little wormholes in space and time connecting the living and the dead. There are many creepy museums all over the world housing all kinds of objects one might associate with ghosts, demons, and paranormal phenomena, but not every museum has been reported to be haunted. Here are a few that have:

The Smithsonian Institution Museum Complex

So, we start with the biggest of the biggest. The Smithsonian Institution is the largest museum, education, and research complex in the world. Most of the complex's museums are located in Washington, D.C., but others are spread out in Arizona, Maryland, Texas, Virginia, New York City, Pittsburgh, and even as far away as Panama and Puerto Rico. In fact, there are over two hundred affiliated institutions in forty-five states, Puerto Rico, and Panama that are visited by over thirty million tourists every year!

Founded as a result of a large sum of wealth left by British scientist James Smithson to his son, who had no heirs, the money went to the state with orders to use it to create an establishment for the "increase and diffusion of knowledge," according to the estate decree. Today, this major historical complex is called "The Nation's Attic" for the sheer volume of items on display—upward of 154 million items! There are nineteen different museums, nine research centers, and a zoo. Such a huge and sprawling complex no doubt has its many haunted sites, but the most often reported ghosts are the curators themselves!

The [Museum of Shadows] ... once housed a saloon and brothel but now contains over one thousand bizarre and haunted items from all over the world.

Reports in the early twentieth century from various night watchmen tell of ghostly apparitions and eerie footsteps that were attributed to noted members of the Smithsonian Institution, including Emil Bessels, an arctic explorer; Fielding Meek, a paleontologist working on-site; Joseph Henry, the institution's first official secretary; Spencer Baird, the first official curator; and even the founder of the institution, James Smithson, who passed away long before the first museum was ever erected. Smithson's remains were kept at the main museum from 1904 to 1973, when his body was disinterred on the orders of the current curator at the time, James Good, after numerous sightings of Smithson's ghost, but his skeleton was right where it should have been in the casket!

Museum of Shadows

Plattsmouth, Nebraska, is home to the Museum of Shadows, considered one of the most haunted museums in the country. The three-story building once housed a saloon and brothel but now contains over one thousand bizarre and haunted items from all over the world. There are public ghost hunts held after hours at the museum, and visitors have reported everything from phantom hands touching them, apparitions roaming around, and even the sound of laughter coming from thin air.

Edgar Allan Poe Museums

Over in Richmond, Virginia, the Poe Museum was built in 1754 in honor of Edgar Allan Poe. It sits just a few blocks away from Poe's childhood home and boasts several ghosts that are in some way attached to the building. The museum

The Poe Museum in Richmond, Virginia, and the Poe House in Baltimore, Maryland (inset) are both haunted, the former by the spirit of Poe and the latter by his grandmother Elizabeth.

itself holds exhibits devoted to the master of horror, and he is particularly active, according to visitors. His ghost appears to be attached to several items in the museum and may even be responsible for strange goings-on such as a shipment of Poe bobbleheads that were unpacked and put on shelves all by themselves! The other two ghosts are believed to be two blond children who were part of the family who built the house that the museum is located in. Visitors report these children showing up in photographs taken during museum events but are never seen in the museum otherwise.

The actual Edgar Allan Poe House is on Amity Street in Baltimore and is said to be haunted not by Poe himself but by Poe's grandmother, Elizabeth Poe, who died there in 1835. She is said to haunt the room she stayed in, and current visitors might be lucky enough to feel her tap on their shoulders. She also shows up in the form of an old woman with gray hair and a heavy build, dressed in clothing of the era. There was one sighting of the ghost of Poe by a man in 1999 who said he looked up from the street to see Poe sitting in the attic writing. The Poe House is open to the public along with the Poe Museum.

New Orleans, Louisiana, has a reputation for being a haunted city, with ghosts and spirits occupying every corner and roaming every historical home, building, or graveyard. The Bloody Mary Haunted Museum is a haunted locale in the famous French Quarter and home to displays, ghost hunts, tours, and séances to contact the spirits of the dead, many of which are said to exist on the premises. The two-hundred-year-old museum is run by television celebrity, psychic medium, and Voodoo queen Bloody Mary and contains items such as voodoo dolls, a shrine to Voodoo queen Marie Laveau, haunted dolls, authentic, turn-of-the-century occult artifacts, and a "ghost photo gallery." The museum even offers classes on communicating with the spirit world.

Connecticut Museums

Coventry, Connecticut's Nathan Hale Homestead is both a historical site and a haunted museum. Nathan Hale was a soldier and spy during the American Revolutionary War, who was eventually captured by the British and executed in 1776. The home is part of the National Register of Historic Places and also goes by the name "The Deacon Richard Hale House." Visitors can see how life in Colonial times was lived in the house but may also run into the ghost of Nathan Hale's father, Deacon, who died there in 1802. His ghost is said to appear wearing colonial clothing as well as the ghost of Nathan's brother, Joseph, who rattles chains in the basement, and the ghost of a "lady in white" that may have been a household servant. Ironically, no one has ever reported seeing the ghost of Nathan Hale on the premises.

Another haunted museum in Connecticut has a more recent history. The Warrens' Occult Museum is the oldest occult museum of its kind, according to the website. It attracts hundreds of thousands of visitors who flock to see famous haunted objects that have appeared on many television reality shows devoted to ghosts and demonic activity as well as a number of movies such as *The Conjuring* and *Annabelle*. The late Ed and Lorraine Warren were well known for their paranormal investigations and ghostly interventions, and it's only natural they put their many artifacts and objects on display. The museum is home to the largest collection of obscure, haunted artifacts, many of which were said to be used in dangerous occult practices and demonic activities. Touch them at your will, although some of these deadly, cursed objects are under glass lock and key. Visitors report seeing the Annabelle doll moving her head up and down as if watching them. The museum is now seeking a new location.

Zak Bagans' Haunted Museum

Another famous occult museum is located in Las Vegas, Nevada. Television ghost-hunting star Zak Bagans opened Zak Bagans' Haunted Museum to showcase many of the unusual objects and artifacts he has come across in his years investigating the paranormal. The eleven-thousand-square-foot museum was built in 1938 by Cyril S. Wengert and was alleged to be haunted from the start by ghosts that terrorized family members and guests over the years. Today, the building boasts creepy, winding hallways and even secret passages leading into and out of the thirty rooms of displays. Malicious spirits abound, and Bagans and guests have reported seeing a black-cloaked figure pass through an exhibit's closed door during a tour. Other guests and staff have also reported spectral activity, including a dark corner where the original staircase from a famous demonic house in Indiana sits, so spooky that during its installation, a construction crew walked off the job. Children under sixteen are not allowed on the premises, and guests are asked to sign a waiver before entering the museum and experiencing what paranormal phenomena awaits.

Ohio Museums

The Cleveland Museum of Art in Cleveland, Ohio, may not be the first place that comes to mind when asking which museums include their own resident ghosts, but to the staff and many visitors, the ghost of famed artist Claude Monet likes making appearances here. The ghost of Monet has been reported surveying the museum site and standing on a balcony above his own art displays. But Monet isn't the only spectral spectator, for the museum also boasts a number of paranormal events that have occurred there, including the ghost of former museum director William Mathewson Milliken wandering about in the 1916 building and a host of strange electrical, light, and mechanical issues that staff cannot ascribe to any error … of the human kind.

I suddenly felt an energy like I have never felt before. It was not the chills, or anything caused by nervousness, because I was very comfortable in the room.

The Zak Bagans Haunted Museum

Gregory Ludwig

Even as a young boy, I have had paranormal experiences, so it should be no wonder that I am a fan of shows like *Ghost Adventures*. Furthermore, the thought of Zak Bagans opening a haunted museum in my favorite place, Las Vegas, could not have been any sweeter. Now, after filming the "Annabelle's Curse" Halloween episode for *Ghost Adventures*, perhaps it is a little more bittersweet thanks to several paranormal experiences that followed that night. It all started the afternoon of June 23, 2017. I stopped by the museum with family just to check the place out. I knew it was not open to the public yet, but I just could not resist stopping by. The museum itself was just an ordinary house. There were a few odd things on display outside, like gargoyle lawn statues, a circus train cage, and a palm tree at the front of the property with clown dolls stuffed on it. Still, even though I call it an "ordinary house," there was a mystique about the place. To me, it seemed alive in a way, or at least I could sense energy radiating from within it. I took a few pictures from outside the perimeter fence, and we went on our way. It was fun stopping by, and I found it difficult to leave, to be honest. Late that night, 1:00 A.M. the next morning to be exact, I received an odd notification that friends liked the picture "I" posted on Facebook. The only problem was, I did not post anything on my Facebook. When I opened the site, I was shocked to see the picture I took of the clown doll tree with the caption, "You can call it." What the heck! I am conservative on Facebook and would not have posted this picture. Furthermore, the picture posted at 3:10 P.M. while I was still driving back from the museum to our hotel. Puzzled and a little freaked out, I tossed my phone to the end of the hotel bed. Then, literally five seconds after doing so, the door to our room shook violently, so much so that we were certain someone was trying to break into the room. But then there was nothing. Not a sound. No voices in the hallway or footsteps. No doors opening or closing. Just a silence that assured a sleepless night. I tried reaching out to Zak Bagans to tell him about this bizarre experience but did not connect, so I entered the Travel Channel/*Ghost Adventures* contest, where I explained my experience on a short video. Amazingly, I was selected as a winning contestant to assist Zak and his team with investigating the Haunted Museum. It was a mind-boggling night, to say the least. The museum is a warm, cozy, yet eerie place filled with creepy objects. Zak told me that night that they did not select me to be on

The Zak Bagans Haunted Museum offers tourists the chance to see such creepy items as the haunted Dybbuk Box, a possessed wine cabinet, and the Volkswagen in which Dr. Jack Kevorkian ended the lives of terminally ill patients.

Continued...

(Continued from previous page)

the show; the spirits within the museum did. I can say, with the experiences I have had during and since that night, that Zak was exactly right! During our investigation, Zak gave me the great privilege of spending about twenty minutes alone in the pitch dark of night with the infamous Dybbuk Box—perhaps the most haunted item in the world. Even though they did not use this experience in the "Annabelle's Curse" episode, I am sure that Zak Bagans himself would agree that it was nothing short of extraordinary. There is so much to this story, but let me at least tell you this. As I stood in that room with the Dybbuk Box, asking whatever questions came to mind, I suddenly felt an energy like I have never felt before. It was not the chills, or anything caused by nervousness, because I was very comfortable in the room. It was more like a low-voltage electricity that surrounded my entire body. It felt exhilarating! I felt this energy twice from head to toe for several seconds each time. It was apparent to me that I was being examined by something, and it was something massive. Several people have had experiences within the room that houses the Dybbuk Box, but I might be the only person that has stood face-to-face with the entity who dwells within it. Whatever was in that room with me that night can only be described in one way: *It's a monster!*

Gregory (Ghost) Ludwig is the author of Night at the Haunted Museum.

The Mad River & NKP Railroad Society Museum in Bellevue, Ohio, is a museum founded in 1972. However, the building was once a mansion, then a YMCA, and may have more history than first meets the eye. An Ohio paranormal group investigated the site in 2010 and found that the spirit of the original founder was haunting the grounds as well as the ghost of a hobo named Steam Train Maury Graham, whose apparition has appeared on the back of a train caboose.

Fort Worth, Texas

Fort Worth, Texas, is home to the Fort Worth Museum of Science and History, but it may also be the home of a goblin! This strange creature has been seen near the play area of the museum. Although a former employee named Jim Miller went on record to debunk the sightings after they appeared on the social forum Reddit, the same man admitted to hearing a host of reports of paranormal shenanigans associated with their Titanic exhibit, including shadowy figures moving across security camera footage. Another Reddit user posted a photo of a spectral, old hag that appeared to be stalking children in the museum's mock grocery store.

England's Haunted Museums

England is home to a particularly spooky museum where books fly off the shelves in the shop (duck!) and a strange, Victorian-era-dressed lady roams around in a blue dress, according to Carl Smith, the museum's manager. The

Torquay Museum was founded in Devon in 1844. Its rich history and collection of antiques and artifacts may be fertile ground for the rise of paranormal activity reported by staff and visitors.

Another terrifying museum in England is the Thackray Medical Museum. Located in Leeds, West Yorkshire, this massive, Victorian building was used in 1861 as the Union Workhorse, where the homeless and poor were sent when they had nowhere else to go. The original on-site infirmary became St. James Hospital in 1925, then closed and reopened in the 1990s as the Medical Museum, housing a collection of supplies, instruments, and equipment. Along with the material objects come a number of ghosts of former inhabitants who provide ample poltergeist activity, shadow figures, phantom hands, and spooky voices.

The British Museum stands out because of its association with a real curse, at least according to those unlucky enough to have experienced it. Located in the Bloomsbury area of London, the museum is dedicated to human history, culture, and art. One of its collections involves ancient, Egyptian artifacts, including an unusually painted mummy board made of plaster and wood. The board was originally the lid of a coffin and has a painted image on it of a priestess. It is said to date back to 900 B.C.E. and was acquired by the museum in 1889. Ever since then, it has been associated with an array of bad luck, enough to eventually label it the "unlucky mummy."

One photographer who took shots of the coffin lid claimed when he developed the photo plates, the mummy's face had changed. It was not the calm, serene face depicted on the board but instead was the face of a living Egyptian woman with a malevolent stare. A few weeks later, that photographer died under mysterious circumstances. Other photo plates show a tormented, anguished face or a furiously angry face. Sometimes, staff reported strange noises near the exhibit and the sound of a woman crying.

Writer Bertram Fletcher Robinson investigated the mummy board's history and found a long list of accidents and deaths associated with it. The most noteworthy cursed incident occurred after it was sold to an American buyer and shipped on board a large vessel known as the *Titanic*. The rest, as they say, is history.

Western Spooky Places

The O.K. Corral

A haunted corral? OK! As in the O.K. Corral in Tombstone, Arizona, considered one of the spookiest places in the state. This Wild West town was founded back in 1877 by a silver prospector and has kept its historic appearance and a few ghosts as well. Residents and visitors report seeing apparitions of dark, shadowy figures at the corral, even apparitions of cowboys in their traditional gun-fighting stance, as well as a tall, dark man who rises from a park bench. The

Tombstone, Arizona, circa 1880, around the time of the shootout between the Clanton gang and the Earps.

nearby Boothill Graveyard, named because many of the men buried their dead with their boots on, is a favorite stomping ground for ghosts, including the spirit of Billy Clanton, a notorious cowboy shot dead by Wyatt Earp in the famous gunfight at the O.K. Corral. He is seen regularly walking about the cemetery and into town.

Tombstone was also home to a theater, saloon, and gambling hall called the Bird Cage Theater, and during the eight short years it was open, it also became a brothel and the scene of twenty-six murders. This may explain the sounds of phantom music and voices that come from inside the building, even though it has been closed for years. It is not a popular tourist spot and a favorite site for ghost hunters.

Arizona is also home to the Red Garter Inn in the city of Williams. This inn is over a hundred years old and was once a bordello, saloon, rooming house, general store, and opium den! It was built in 1897 by a German tailor with hopes of cashing in on the local copper boom in the nearby Grand Canyon. Because of its reputation as a bordello, drug den, and saloon, the local sheriff was often called there to investigate murders or brawls courtesy of the many visiting cowboys, loggers, miners, and railroad workers coming through town.

A murder allegedly took place on the stairs of the inn and led to a crackdown on bordellos throughout the city and the closure of both the saloon and brothel on-site. Later, the building became a rooming house and a general store. Once it became the Red Garter Bed and Bakery, staff and guests began report-

My Experiences in Haunted Arizona Landmarks

Katie Mullaly

Arizona is the heart of the Wild West, and it has the ghosts to prove it. People like the idea of popping in to a town like Tombstone for a few selfies or an old mining town like Bisbee or Jerome, all of which are very impressively haunted, but in my experience, the best places for ghosts are the ones you may have never known about.

Globe, Arizona, is about two hours north of Tucson and not directly accessible by the interstate. It's a sleepy, little town with lots of old buildings and antique stores. One such building, and my personal favorite, is the Noftsger Hill Inn Bed and Breakfast. "The Noftsger," as we ghost aficionados call it, is named for the original owner of the land on which it is built. It was built as a high school in the early 1900s, but when Globe built a newer high school, the building was lovingly repurposed into a space that could be appreciated by everyone who visits Globe for a night or two.

It's also *crazy* haunted.

I was accompanied by my husband, Mikal, and my friend Patrick (who happens to have coauthored a few books with me about haunted places). Now, I love ghosts and haunted houses, and I have had some pretty compelling experiences in my life, but up until staying at the Noftsger, I never really felt like I had that one awesome experience that gave me goose bumps and made the hair stand up on the back of my neck. We had the run of the place the very first night we stayed there, and it was awesome just to get to explore the space unfettered. Rosalie, the owner, has an apartment upstairs and makes it very clear that she is available for any urgent matter, at any time, except for anything at all having to do with the building being haunted. Seriously, when it gets dark outside, she packs it in for the night.

Being the intrepid investigators that we are, we put a voice recorder on the dresser and left the room. We were out of the room (but still in the building) for about an hour. When we returned, we got ready for bed and made our first attempt at falling asleep. It should be noted that Mikal is a skeptic from Jump Street and won't even entertain anyone's scary stories without a hearty scoff and an almost audible eye roll, so when he was the first one saying "Something just sat on my foot" after lights-out, it absolutely gave me pause. He took a few flash photos before turning on the light, and damned if there wasn't an odd light streak through the photo.

Sleeping in an unfamiliar and haunted place is difficult. The bed is uncomfortable, there is no muscle memory, and you can't even find the lamp on the nightstand quickly in the event of a panicked freak-out. Sleep paralysis is a hazard of the trade, and if you are prone to shedding your body for an unsolicited bit of astral projection, it makes the line between awake and asleep very blurry. I woke in the night to Patrick pacing the room, and he woke to a filmy mist floating over me while I slept. The punchline is that he wasn't pacing, and I wasn't sleeping. He was *dreaming* that he was pacing, and somehow, I saw this for several seconds before I felt that sense of being jarred awake to a dark and eerily quiet room, everyone else sound asleep, awash in a sense of isolated dread as though I had been somewhere I never should have gone. The rest of the night was spent trying to fall asleep, being technically unconscious but certainly not resting. Drifting in and out to the sounds of children giggling, the sound of something being dragged across the cement floor outside our room, and of a wooden ball rolling underneath the bed made for a long night. A long, terrifying night that I wouldn't trade for anything.

Continued...

(Continued from previous page)

We spent one night and returned home the next day. Mikal looked over the photos while I listened to the recording we'd made. It was about the same time that he found the image of the woman in the upstairs window as I was startled by the sound of a woman gasping followed by the slam of a door on the recording, a door inside an *empty room*.

That *seriously* creeped me out.

Let me also tell you about the old Bisbee Courthouse. It is absolutely one of my very favorite haunted places I have ever had the opportunity to investigate. The building is sublime and gorgeous, with its straight-up Gatsby-esque Art Deco design. As a devotee of vintage style, this building definitely had me at "hello."

We were invited to investigate, which is amazing given that it is a federal building. We were chaperoned but given free reign. We must have been there at about two in the morning. The place is big, beautiful, and freaky. One of my favorite parts of the courthouse was the evidence room. If I recall correctly, our chaperone said that they are required to keep certain evidence for like ninety-nine years or some other such lengthy time frame. The room had boxes full of stuff that made it look like college kids were getting ready to move for the summer, except the boxes were full of murder weapons and blood-soaked clothing. There was a safe that had a hole blown through the bottom of it. There was a big, rolled-up carpet standing in a corner, and a bullet-ridden door that had been taken from its hinges and tucked away. It was like a big locker chock full of felony. When you consider that Tombstone, Arizona, is in the same county and just a few miles down the road, it just punctuates that sense of gritty cowboy crime that makes this neck of the woods pretty notorious.

The top two floors of the building are solid steel capsules of prison cells that are now used for storage. The lights are few, dim, and flickering. Their buzz was the only sound that broke the thick, intense silence. Of course, the buddy system failed me as I immediately got lost in a dark labyrinth of long, skinny, mostly dark, metal corridors. With no cell reception and completely disoriented, I had to just meander for what felt like an eternity until I saw the flash of Mikal's camera and followed that. When I finally caught up with him, I was so incredibly relieved. So much so that I didn't soil myself when we both heard the distinct and deliberate, heavy footsteps walking toward us from the hallway in which I had just been. We stood and drank in the moment, making sure that the other heard it, too, and neither of us could find any other source for the footsteps. We were the only two people on that floor.

We weren't the only two people who had some crazy phenomena on that particular investigation. Other folks reportedly saw an apparition and heard whispers coming from one particular cell that, as we found out later, was the site of a particularly heart-wrenching suicide of a young, teenage boy.

While I fully acknowledge that science has still yet to prove the existence of ghosts, I would gladly suggest to any skeptic to spend a night there if they ever had the chance. This place is hands down one of my favorite haunted places in Arizona.

Katie Mullaly is the author of Scare-Izona: A Travel Guide to Arizona's Spookiest Spots and Finding Ghosts in Phoenix.

Formerly the Navajo County courthouse, where infamous murderer Goerge Smiley was tried and hanged, the building is now a historical museum.

ing ghostly activity such as doors slamming shut, footsteps, and clunking noises throughout the building, beds in the inn shaking for no reason, and the feeling of someone touching people's arms. There are numerous reports of the apparition of a young, Hispanic girl with long, dark hair who no one seems to be able to identify but who has told psychic mediums during séances that her name is "Eve" or "Eva."

Navajo County, Arizona, is home to a courthouse dating back to 1898 that would become the location of notorious trials over the years. The basement housed jail cells, and the courthouse boasted no escapees from the small, dark rooms. One of the more notorious prisoners held there was George Smiley, a murderer who was scheduled to hang in front of invited Arizona officials in 1899. But his execution was stayed for thirty days and then rescheduled, and eventually, Smiley was executed by hanging in January 1900. The courthouse served the Navajo County public until 1976 and since then has become the Holbrook Chamber of Commerce, the Visitor Center, and the Navajo County Historical Museum. Those who visit and work there claim the ghost of George Smiley lurks about the building, pacing up and down halls and stairs, closing doors, and making all kinds of strange noises. Staff members also report objects moving around on their own, no doubt at the hands of the man who died there, or could it be the work of another ghost on the premises? A former prisoner named Mary is often seen looking out the windows of the building. She died in one of the small, dark prison cells while looking out the window and dreaming of being free.

La Llorona of the Southwest

Throughout the Southwest, the legend of La Llorona, which is Spanish for "weeping woman," is a pervasive part of Hispanic culture and lore. The ghost appears as a tall, thin woman with long, black hair and a beautiful face. She wears a white gown and walks along rivers and creeks, wailing loudly at night as she searches for child victims to drag into the river. Such a cruel legend has many origins, one involving a mother who drowned her children and now eternally searches for them in the rivers, creeks, and lakes of the region. She may have been a peasant, but her beauty caught the eyes of many male admirers.

Legend has it her name was Maria, and she left her children home alone while she went out with men. Perhaps the children drowned on their own, but many say she killed them. Yet another legend claims Maria was a sweet, good woman who was the victim of an abusive, cheating husband who turned against her own children in a rage, only to deeply regret it when she tried to save them but couldn't.

No matter the origin of this story, many people claim to witness La Llorona walking and weeping in her white gown along the banks of the Santa Fe River but also along creek beds near Mora and Guadalupita....

No matter the origin of this story, many people claim to witness La Llorona walking and weeping in her white gown along the banks of the Santa Fe River but also along creek beds near Mora and Guadalupita, New Mexico, where she often is seen floating on the water itself. As with most legends, this one has grown, and La Llorona has been reported across the region at a variety of lakes, rivers, and creeks, although most of the sightings occur at night. She has been seen as far north as Montana, walking the banks of the Yellowstone River, sadly searching for her dead children.

Sports Ghosts

From the desert Southwest to Chicago's Wrigley Field, ghosts are everywhere. According to Mickey Bradley and Dan Gordon in their book *Haunted Baseball*, Wrigley Field is an actual haunted ballpark complete with the ghosts of those who once loved the Chicago Cubs baseball team. Security guards report hearing the bullpen telephone ring in the middle of the night. They believe the caller is former Cubs manager Charlie Grimes, who worked with the team in the 1930s and 1940s and whose ashes are buried out in left field. There have been reports of Grimes's ghost walking the hallways, disappearing when he's spoken to.

Other staff and fans report seeing the ghost of famous broadcaster Harry Caray in the press box and in the outfield bleachers as well as the ghost of Steve Goodman, who wrote the popular Cubs anthem "Go, Cubs, Go." He is often seen sitting behind the batter's box, and it is rumored his own ashes are buried beneath home plate.

Alabama's Haunted Field

After the Civil War battle of Shiloh, the Montgomery Military Prison was established in the spring of 1862 and housed over seven hundred prisoner soldiers. Historic records show the prisoners were kept under harsh conditions, and many went without much food or water. One hundred ninety-eight men died of disease and starvation, and many were buried in the Oakwood Cemetery nearby. Some of the soldiers were buried in nearby National Cemetery in Marietta, but some remained behind. The Montgomery Biscuits sports stadium now sits where the filthy prison once existed, and many attending baseball games there have seen ghosts of dirty soldiers wearing torn, filthy clothing. One in particular is seen every summer huddling near the fence trying to stay warm in the sun. Those who dare to approach him find that he vanishes before they can reach out a hand to him.

In the early hours of the morning, people have heard phantom screams and moans from within the stadium, and a dark, skeleton-like figure often appears during the seventh-inning stretch.

The Ghost of Eddie Plank

Eddie Plank had the honor of being Major League Baseball's first left-handed pitcher to win three hundred games. His career ended in 1917 with 326 victories. After his death in 1926, his ghost has been haunting his former house in Gettysburg, Pennsylvania, where the current owner has heard and seen Plank trying to pitch to a phantom catcher. The owner stated that the series of sounds exactly fit the process of Plank winding up and pitching the ball at a length of sixty feet and six inches, the distance from the pitcher's mound to home plate. After about a month, the sounds ceased. Maybe Plank went off to play in the majors in heaven.

Pitcher Eddie Plank played for the Philadelphia Athletics from 1901 to 1914. He passed away twelve years later, apparently lingering by his Gettysburg house after his death.

Frontier Field

Rochester, New York's Frontier Baseball Field was built in 1996 and currently is home to the International League's Rochester Red Wings. According to an ESPN report in 2005, the stadium construction crew turned up some human bones and believed the grounds may have been haunted, possibly an ancient burial site. A Rochester paranormal group came in to investigate and found a number of ghosts on-site, and photos taken by their director, J. Burkhart, show apparitions, floating heads, and ghostly figures.

Football Ghosts

A number of haunted football stadiums exist around the country. Though the sport isn't usually associated with the paranormal, ghosts like to hang out where the pigskin flies downfield.

Indiana University was attended by a student named Michael Plume in 1960. He was an active Air Force member and suffered a mysterious death. He was found hanging from the rafters of the west side of the stadium stands, still under construction. He was only nineteen years old. His shoes were clean, which added to the mystery of his suicide. Some locals believed he might have been involved in spying or a murder, but his death was ruled a suicide. His ghost lingers at Memorial Stadium on the campus and is often seen dangling from the same spot he was hanged from.

Lee Williams High School in Kingman, Arizona, was built upon the Old Pioneer Cemetery that was once filled with hundreds of coffins of the original Kingman settlers and members of the local Hualapi Native American tribe. The football field and bleachers are on sacred ground, and when renovations in 2010 turned up dozens of coffins and artifacts, the ghosts may have been freed to begin roaming the site. Nowadays, the stadium is haunted by a man in a bowler hat, a little girl who always wants to play, and a host of disembodied voices and orbs of light.

Attend a football game at Kansas State University, and you might run across a spirit named Nick, a player who was injured during a game and was taken to the campus cafeteria to be attended to. He died later. The place he died is now home to the Purple Masque Theater, and Nick is always around moving chairs and playing music, making wooden crates levitate in the air, and spinning fire extinguishers on the wall.

Hockey Ghosts

The Hockey Hall of Fame in Toronto, Canada, is filled with hockey history and a few spirits to boot. The hall is haunted by a gal named Dorothy, who was a Bank of Montréal teller who used to be in the same building. Dorothy showed up for work one day in 1953 and out of the blue decided to shoot herself. Nobody knows why, but employees of the bank began hearing strange noises shortly afterward, and items on their desks would move around. Dorothy continues to haunt the building, usually accompanied by cold spots and strange sensations of being watched.

Bobby Mackey's Music World

Bobby Mackey's Music World used to be a slaughterhouse, which gives it a built-in sense of horror. Known to be a "gateway to hell," according to many ghost hunters, this Wilder, Kentucky, nightclub has quite the notorious haunted

A Theater of Ghosts

By Jason Roberts

My passion for the world of the paranormal has always been the history and the people behind the stories. I have always said you cannot have the paranormal without the history. When I joined Everyday-Legacy Paranormal in 2009, I could not wait to dive into the possible locations that were coming our way. The one city in Kansas that I always wanted to explore and study was Dodge City because from what I had heard, the city still embraced its Old West roots. So it was on my bucket list for investigating.

It was in 2011 when the team finally got in touch with a good contact that helped us set up an investigation for a historical building there in Dodge City. It is a little over two-hour drive from Wichita, where we are based out of, to Dodge. The building we were heading to sounded amazing, and we were told it was a pretty huge location, so we needed to bring everything we had to investigate. It was called The Depot Theater, an old Santa Fe train depot built in 1898, and was also the site of a Fred Harvey Hotel and dining area. It has gone through renovations and is now a wonderful dinner theater, several city offices, an event location for Dodge, and Amtrak makes a daily stop as well. The Depot Theater building was very much alive and working; we just didn't know how alive it would be for us.

Karl, who is the one employee who knows the building inside and out, gave us a tour of the depot and shared some of the stories he had of the hauntings inside. The one spirit he said that he interacted with the most was who he thought was a little girl on the second floor by his office. Karl claimed she could be heard at times on the stairs leading up to the third floor either talking, giggling, or walking around but sometimes crying. He felt that she followed him around wherever he went in the building except for the basement. So, we set up our gear and went to work.

We split up to tackle this giant of a building, in which I went with Leo to the second floor by the stairs to try our luck with talking to the little girl. It started off quiet as we stared upward to the third-floor landing, which was unfinished at the time, and it was the location of part of the old Fred Harvey Hotel. Trying to talk with her, we weren't having much luck besides some taps or feet shuffling. Then I spoke up, asking, "Is there anything I can do for you, help you in any way?" At that moment from above us, we heard a girl's voice say "No." Startled, I looked up just in time to see what I thought was the tail of a long dress round the top corner of the stairs and disappear from view. We ran upstairs but found no one there, and this landing went in a circle and there was only one door up there that was shut and never opened. I was so excited that I had heard her that it was hard for me to concentrate after that.

Since that night, we have investigated the depot countless times and hold public ghost hunts there with all donations going back to the Depot Theater. While investigating this building, we have encountered multiple spirits throughout and may have gotten names for them after listening to recordings. There are two male spirits down in the basement in which one likes to mess with you, while the other seems a little annoyed we are all there. We have discovered more spirits in the theater area itself around the stage and catwalk, yet this is a newer area than the rest of the building.

So, if you ever find yourself wanting to head back to the Old West, I suggest heading to the Depot Theater and take a tour, hear the history, and stay for a show in the dinner the-

Continued...

(Continued from previous page)

ater, because you never know who may be walking the halls with you or watching a show next you.

Jason Roberts has been a member of Every-day-Legacy Paranormal (www.everyday-legacy.com) and a tour guide for the Wichita Ghost Tour, which is owned by Ghost Tours of Kansas, since 2009. He took ownership of Road Trip Paranormal (www.roadtripparanormal.com) in 2013 and provides public events all over Kansas.

reputation. In the 1850s, it was indeed home to a large slaughterhouse and meat-packing plant. A well beneath the building captured the blood, guts, and waste from the slaughtered animals above. Though the slaughterhouse closed way back in the 1890s, it then became, according to legend, a meeting spot for Satanic groups who not only sacrificed animals near the blood-filled well but other humans, too.

In 1896, a horrific murder of a twenty-two-year-old woman made head-lines and added to the area's already creepy reputation. Pearl Bryan was a young, pregnant woman from Greencastle, Indiana. Her boyfriend, Scott Jackson, was a college student at the Indianapolis Dental College and tried to get her to go to Cincinnati, where he would help her get an abortion. Unfortunately, he and his roommate, Alonzo Walling, tried to do the abortion themselves and ended up killing Pearl's. They wanted to cover their tracks, so they surgically cut off her head and left her body in an empty field near the former slaughterhouse. Stupidly, they left Pearl's shoes on, which helped identify her and lead the police back to the two young men along with testimony from one of Scott Jackson's friends, a pastor named William Wood, who confessed later that Scott had come to him to ask what to do about Pearl's unwanted pregnancy (unwanted by him, that is).

Upon arrest, Jackson and Walling both accused each other of the murder. They were both charged with the crime. On the gallows, Alonzo Walling vowed to haunt the area after his death. Both he and Scott Jackson were hanged to death on March 20, 1897, but they took a long time to finally die because their necks were not broken right away. It was later revealed they administered massive doses of cocaine to Pearl, then causing her death by the back-alley-style abortion.

Interestingly, Wood admitted he, too, had intercourse with Pearl, which put into question whose baby she was carrying.

During Prohibition, a new building was built with a casino, nightclub, and speakeasy. After Prohibition, the building became known as the "Primrose" and eventually drew the attention of mobsters who wanted to control the casino operations. After much violence and attempted murder, the building later became the "Latin Quarter" dance club in the 1950s, where a young, pregnant dance hall girl named Johanna fell in love with a singer. Her father had the singer killed by a hit man, and Johanna then poisoned her father and committed suicide in the basement of the building. Later, in the late 1970s, a number of fatal shootings shut down the club.

It wasn't until 1978 that a country singer named Bobby Mackey bought the building and made it a music hall and tavern, which stands today. With its rich paranormal history, it's only natural that staff members and patrons report a host of ghostly activity, including phantom footsteps, a demonically possessed former caretaker (his actual exorcism was performed by a minister on the premises), flying trash cans, the overwhelming smell of roses in the basement, poltergeist activity, physical attacks by phantom spirits in the basement where the portal to hell still exists, lights turning on and off, hot and cold spots with no definable sources, and a headless ghost dressed in clothing Pearl Bryan may have worn before she was beheaded by the man she loved.

Jackson and Walling both accused each other of the murder. They were both charged with the crime. On the gallows, Alonzo Walling vowed to haunt the area after his death.

The location is a favorite spot for ghost hunters and paranormal tours, as apparitions and demonic activity is said to be pretty consistent there on any given day … or night.

Looking for another haunted watering hole? Captain Tony's Saloon in Key West, Florida, has a history of being a speakeasy, a cigar factory, a city morgue, and a wireless telegraph station. The site of many tragedies over the years, it's no wonder many visitors report ghosts in the bar. Perhaps they are the ghosts of people whose bodies were washed out into the street during a hurricane when the building housed the morgue. Maybe they are the spirits of the people who were killed and buried between walls during major renovations. Rumor has it a woman even murdered her own child in one of the bathrooms, and a tree that grows up through the roof of the building was said to be the place where several townspeople were hanged, including a woman who was said to be wearing a blue dress covered in the blood of family members she murdered. Today, patrons of this pub report seeing the ghost of a lady in blue, hearing sounds and sensations they cannot explain, and hearing bathroom stall doors slam shut when no one is in the room.

HOTELS, MOTELS, INNS, HOUSES, AND CASTLES

In October 1974, best-selling horror novelist Stephen King and his wife, Tabitha, decided to spend a night at the Stanley Hotel in Estes Park, Colorado. The hotel first opened back in 1909 and catered to the upper class. It was built by Stanley Steemer founder F. O. Stanley and consisted of 142 rooms in the Colonial Revival style with amazing, panoramic views of the Rockies and Lake Estes. For the King couple, it was a place to stay during a road trip.

The facility was closed for the brutal winter, so they were the only two guests staying there. They stayed in room 217, where King had a vivid dream of his young son running through the hallways terrified of something chasing him. That incident served as the inspiration for his classic book *The Shining,* which was also made into a movie. People have been flocking to the Stanley Hotel ever since, and many insist room 401 is haunted. Visitors report hearing children running up and down the halls at night, when no children are around or awake. They've experienced blankets being pulled tightly across their legs or the bed shaking as they slept. The bar and billiards areas of the sprawling hotel are home to the ghosts of F. O. Stanley and his wife, Flora. Often, her piano can be heard playing itself in the music room.

Strangely translucent apparitions also roam the Stanley, and it's no wonder this location is a favorite among ghost-hunting groups. There is a maze out front reminiscent of the one little Danny tries to navigate in *The Shining* movie as well as nightly ghost tours and an on-site psychic. A television in the hotel plays the movie in a continuous loop. Imagine hearing Jack Nicholson's voice over and over again saying, "HEEEERE'S JOHNNY!". Many of the rooms are reported to be haunted, so call ahead to book and spend a weekend with a ghost … or two. Of note, the hotel staff and historians both admit the Stanley was never reported as haunted until Stephen King made it famous. Today, it is a notorious paranormal hot spot; in fact, if you visit, be sure to go to the second floor and listen for the phantom cry of a young boy calling out to his nanny.

Queen Anne Hotel

San Francisco's Queen Anne Hotel is located on Sutter Street. It was finished in 1890 and is built in the atmospheric "Painted Lady" Queen Anne architectural style. Originally, it was the site of a girls' boarding school, sitting among other lovely Victorian and Edwardian mansions in the Pacific Heights area. It barely survived the famous 1906 San Francisco Quake and Firestorm and is now a popular ghost-hunting spot as well as a luxurious hotel with antiques throughout. Witnesses report the headmistress of the girls' boarding school haunts room 410, where she had her office. She wanders about and looks after guests much like she once looked after her wards. The third floor of this lavish hotel is said to be the most haunted, with visitors feeling the hairs on their arms stand on end, cold spots throughout the floor, and the strong sense of being watched.

The beautiful Queen Anne Hotel in San Francisco is a mecca for ghost hunters searching for the ghost of a little girl in room 410.

The Crescent Hotel

The Crescent Hotel in Eureka Springs, Arkansas, is considered the nation's most haunted hotel. It has a long history of over 135 years as a women's college and, before that, a notorious hospital run by Norman Baker, said to be a crackpot doctor. Ghosts human and animal (a cat named Morris) haunt the atmospherically eerie building, which was restored in the late 1990s when Marty and Elise Roenigk purchased it and its long-associated haunted history.

Constructed in 1886, the hotel is a historical landmark that has stood the test of time. Today, it is a resort and spa, but visitors can attest to the host of ghosts that roam the many rooms and hallways. The new owners asked two psychic mediums to read the building and were told the hotel contained a portal to the "other side." Nightly ghost tours are in their seventeenth year at the site, which continues to deliver plenty of paranormal activity to those brave enough to take the tour or stay at the hotel itself. Many visitors faint around the tour shop area without any explanation (although there are perfectly scientific reasons why this might be in an older building). Another portal is said to be over the morgue a few floors up. The morgue is said to be haunted by victims, mostly women, of Norman Baker, a con man who claimed he had a cure for cancer, for the right price, of course, and subjected his many patients to a number of bizarre procedures that resulted often in the patients dying. His treatments were found to be fraudulent, and he was eventually indicted on fraud charges by a federal grand jury in Little Rock, Arkansas. Those visiting the morgue, including many television shows, report apparitions wandering about that are often captured on video footage.

If you dare visit the Crescent, you might encounter apparitions, orbs, anomalous photograph images, and all kinds of activity that helped get this hotel into the Historic Hotels of America membership. The media has featured the hotel and spa many times, locally and nationally, and it continues to attract those seeking a different kind of destination experience.

The Bourbon Orleans Hotel

Ghosts are as popular walking the halls and rooms of the Bourbon Orleans as living guests. The former site of the famed Orleans Ballroom and Theater, the building was converted to a convent in the late 1800s and, later in the 1960s, a hotel and is considered one of the most haunted hotels in New Orleans, Louisiana. The two-century-old building was also an orphanage once and has a variety of ghosts now calling it home, including children and women from its days as a convent and home for orphans; a Confederate soldier who roams on the third and sixth floors; and a dancer who once performed at the Orleans Ballroom and Theater when it hosted the biggest social events of the nineteenth century.

While the hotel served as the Sisters of the Holy Family's convent and orphanage, many women and children died of an epidemic of yellow fever sweeping the city. One ghost of a little girl chasing after her ball haunts the sixth floor. The hotel functions today and offers public ghost walks and tours.

The Red Castle Inn

Nevada City in California is the location of one of the few remaining official historical lodging landmarks in the state. The Red Castle Inn is a four-story, brick mansion built in 1860 atop Prospect Hill, which overlooks Nevada City from its high perch. It was built during the heyday of the Gold Rush era, despite its distinct gothic appearance. The one ghost who haunts the inn is said to be so realistic, guests believe they are seeing an actual living human being until she walks through a door or wall. She may be the spirit of the governess of the original builder's family and is always seen wearing gray.

Seelbach Hilton Hotel

As the premier hotel of the state of Kentucky, the Seelbach Hilton opened in 1905 with the distinction of being the city's only fireproof hotel. It was owned by two Bavarian brothers, Otto and Louis Seelbach, who came to America to learn the hotel business. It also boasts being included in the National Register of Historic Places and the home to a famous ghost: the Lady in Blue. She was a guest named Patricia Wilson who had moved to Louisville from Oklahoma. She had been separated for four years from her husband, but they were trying to work things out. He was on his way to talk to her at the hotel in 1936, only to be tragically killed in a car crash as he was on his way to join his beloved. Patricia was so distraught, she threw herself down the elevator shaft. Her body was laid to rest in the Evergreen Cemetery. In 1987, several guests reported seeing a lady with long, black hair wearing a blue, chiffon dress, roaming about on the eighth floor.

This is a photo of the Seelbach Hotel taken five years after its 1905 opening. Here, a woman wearing blue chiffon—possibly the ghost of Patricia Wilson—has been seen on the eighth floor.

The ghost of an elderly woman haunts a mirror in the Otto Café. An employee claimed to try to speak with her once, but she vanished before his eyes. In 2004, a couple staying on the eighth floor awakened to find a man standing at the window. When they turned on the lights, he disappeared. Other guests report footsteps, lights going on and off, and the smell of a woman's perfume. The hotel is now owned by Hilton Hotels and Resorts.

Menger Hotel

San Antonio, Texas, is the home of the Alamo, but right next door to that historical site is a haunted, Victorian-era hotel built in 1859. One of the oldest hotels in the state, the Menger Hotel has over thirty ghosts according to unlucky guests, including the spirit of President Teddy Roosevelt, who is the most famous of the creepy crew. Roosevelt is known to have at this very hotel encouraged patrons to join his Rough Riders in battle during the Spanish–American War.

His ghost hangs out mostly at the hotel bar along with another notable ghost: the spirit of Captain Richard King, owner of the King Ranch, who would stay at the Menger Hotel in his own personal suite for months at a time and was there when he died. He enters and exits his favorite suite, which is now named the "King Ranch Room," but doesn't bother anyone. The ghost of a maid named Sallie White also appears now and then, strolling up on the third floor in uniform, sometimes carrying a load of towels as if she is still cleaning rooms in death as she was in life.

The World-Famous Clown Motel and Cemetery

Black shapes roaming about with eerie, phantom carnival music playing in the background. Items moving around and being placed in different locations. Restless spirits from an adjoining graveyard coming into and out of the motel. Killer *clowns*? Well, maybe not killer clowns, but the notoriously famous Clown Motel in Tonopah, Nevada, is a place unlike any other. A long, desert drive two hours away from the bustling city of Las Vegas, the Clown Motel and Tonopah Cemetery are favorites to tourists, paranormal enthusiasts, clown lovers, and kitschy types everywhere.

The motel, which was founded by Leona and LeRoy David in 1985, welcomes visitors with a giant, grinning, colorful clown face and glowing, neon sign. Its intent was to give truckers, bikers, and motorists a place to stay before heading into the desolate desert on the way to other Nevada destinations. Like a little oasis in the desert, the place caught on, and those who visit delighted in the abundant clown figures, dolls, and merchandise that can be found in the adjoining offices and even the rooms themselves. From stuffed clown dolls to wall hangings, porcelain figurines to puppets, all kinds of clowns are on hand for those who stop by.

The Tonopah Cemetery next door is a century-old graveyard where miners were buried and is abundant with weeds and makeshift grave markers.

Not only a popular tourist attraction for its kitschy theme, the Clown Motel in Tonopah, Nevada, has the added bonus of being haunted. It also sits next to a haunted cemetery!

The abandoned look makes it a favorite for ghost hunters and legend trippers thanks to its history from its founding in 1901. It is alleged that many of the town's pioneer residents are buried there along with victims of a mysterious plague in 1902.

Nearby are other haunted locations such as the Mitzpah Hotel and the Silver Rim Elementary School, suggesting the entire little oasis in the desert stands upon shaky supernatural ground. The Clown Motel and surrounding sites are popular with film crews looking to make cheap horror films. Who doesn't hate clowns? Except for those who love them ... odd creatures they may be.

Hotel Del Coronado

The Nevada desert has its Clown Motel, while the gorgeous city of Coronado in San Diego County, California, has its lavish and famous paranormal hot spot favored by movie stars and normal folks alike for decades. The Hotel Del Coronado is a stunning resort built on beachfront property in Coronado, just south of the city of San Diego. The Victorian hotel was built in 1888 by Elisha Babcock and H. L. Story, who wanted to create a fairy-tale-like seaside resort that would be the talk of the Western world. They succeeded, but the hotel was only open four years when tragedy struck. A woman named Kate Morgan checked in on November 24, 1892. She stayed only five days, waiting for her lover to come and join her. She was very sick, and her death occurred five days later; her body was found on the steps leading to the beach. She had shot herself in the head, depressed over being abandoned by her lover but also possibly in despair over a pregnancy she was trying to end. Since then, paranormal phenomena has been reported such as lights flickering on and off, disembodied voices, objects moving of their own volition, strange lights on the beach at night, unexplained noises, cold spots, and the apparition of a woman wearing Victorian clothing roaming the halls.

Still a popular vacation spot in San Diego, the Hotel Del Coronado was once a place where movie stars such as Marilyn Monroe stayed.

To this day, the Hotel Del, as locals call it, is a huge tourist attraction, a destination for the wealthy (movie stars such as Marilyn Monroe once stayed there) and the general public alike, and those who desire to see the ghost of Kate Morgan floating down the hallway, or in or near the room she favored—Room 3227—at night. The ghost of a maid who hanged herself in Room 3519 also has been sighted as well. And although it has undergone some modern renovations and upgrades, it can't shake its ghostly past.

Not too far from the Hotel Del, in downtown San Diego, two other haunted hotels stand. The Horton Grand Hotel is in the heart of the famous Gaslamp Quarter, which takes up sixteen blocks. The hotel opened back in 1886 as two separate hotels—The Grand Horton and the Brooklyn Kahle Saddlery Hotel. Both were part of the city's former red-light district. They are now the Horton Grand Hotel and a popular tourist spot since it is close to everything. It is also teeming with ghosts, including the restless spirit of a gambler that was caught cheating and later shot by other gamblers in Room 309. Guests report his spirit lurking in the stairway near the room as well as other weird activity like lights turning on and off, doors opening and closing, mysterious hands shaking beds, and even the sound of cards being shuffled.

A few blocks away is the U.S. Grant Hotel, a luxurious hotel that opened in 1910 and cost two million dollars to build, which was quite a huge amount in those days! Today, it hosts many a spirit that walk the hallways, turn lights on and off, and make strange noises to bother guests at all hours of the night.

Ellis Hotel

Atlanta, Georgia's Ellis Hotel is located in the bustling downtown area of Peachtree Street. One of the city's worst fires occurred here back in December 1946 and was even nicknamed the "Titanic on Peachtree." Over 115 people died in the tragic fire when firefighters could only reach the eighth floor of the fifteen-story building. The hotel was completely rebuilt in 1950, and guests began reporting paranormal phenomena such as objects moving around, items vanishing from rooms, phantom voices and women's screams, and the sound of children running up and down the halls. For a period of two weeks, the fire alarm would go off every single night at exactly 2:48 A.M., the same time the 1946 fire broke out.

Hawthorne Hotel

Salem, Massachusetts, is home to historically haunted places. It is a city with a rich background that includes some of the darkest days of our nation's history—the Salem Witch Trials of 1692. The Hawthorne Hotel is located upon land that was once an apple orchard owned by a woman named Bridget Bishop, one of the first women to be accused and executed during the witch trials. Guests who visit the hotel today often report the smell of apples clear as day. Other guest ghosts include some of the original sea captains involved in the construction of buildings near the hotel. The Salem Marine Society was razed to make room for the hotel, so maybe the sea captain ghosts are coming back to their original "haunt." Pun intended.

Room 612 is where a female ghost can be seen wandering just outside the room, stopping at the door. Guests often complain of a sense of a presence in the room with them, the feeling of being touched, the cry of a baby, and lights and sink faucets being turned on and off. Ghosts on the lower deck seem to like moving furniture and items around, and a large nautical ship wheel in the restaurant likes to turn itself as if being turned by a seafarer on the open waters.

The ninety-three-room hotel has hosted quite a few famous living people over its history, including Walter Cronkite, George H. W. and Barbara Bush, Bette Davis, and Colin Powell. The famous television sitcom *Bewitched* filmed nearby, and the cast and crew stayed in the hotel during shooting. Other actors have stayed there, including Jennifer Lawrence and Robert De Niro during the filming of *Joy*.

Fairmont Empress Hotel

Victoria, British Columbia, Canada, is home to the Fairmont Empress Hotel, one of the nation's oldest and most famous hotels as well as its most haunted, proving that America doesn't have a lock on haunted locations. The massive building is an official National Historic Site of Canada and was built

Ghosts of Death Valley

The big, golden state of California is rich with history and known for its haunted missions and Hollywood landmarks. But few people know of the vast number of haunted hotels to be found from San Diego to San Francisco. They would never associate the vast and desolate Death Valley with the location of a couple of haunted hotels.

Death Valley is a foreboding place. Located in eastern California at the northern edge of the Mojave Desert, it is one of the hottest and harshest places on Earth, measuring 3,000 square miles (7,770 square kilometers). The isolated location and extreme temperatures make it a very unattractive place to stay. But the Amargosa Opera House and Hotel was built in 1923 by the Pacific Coast Borax Company to serve their employees and families. The U-shaped complex was built in the Spanish Colonial style. Sadly, little of the original town remains but for the opera house and hotel, both of which are said to be haunted by the ghost of a crying child who drowned in a bathtub, an evil presence who was hanged in the hotel, and a ghostly cat that roams the buildings.

Nearby is the Furnace Creek Inn and Ranch Resort, built on the salt flats of Death Valley back in the 1920s. The mission-style inn was built with thick, adobe walls and is haunted by a friendly ghost named Chef James Márquez, who served in the kitchen from 1959 to 1973 before he became ill and died several years later. Visitors report hearing strange noises in the kitchen and dining room at all hours of the night, tools and equipment moving around from place to place by themselves, and doors opening and closing. Maybe Chef Márquez is cooking up great ghostly meals in the kitchen he once loved.

The Amargosa Opera House and Hotel is an oasis in the middle of Death Valley, which offers beautiful architecture, cultural events, and a bit of the paranormal.

between 1904 and 1908. Both British and American royalty and leaders have stayed or visited there, and it is still open to guests. It has a rich paranormal history, too. Visitors over the years have witnessed the ghost of a thin man with a moustache and cane, who might be the hotel architect, Francis Rattenbury. There is a ghostly maid who cleans on the sixth floor just as she did in life. An elderly, female ghost knocks on doors and asks for help finding her room, only to vanish after she leads witnesses to the elevator. The spookiest ghost is that of a man who hanged himself in one of the elevator shafts. His ghost can be seen swinging from above by guests inside the elevator.

There is a ghostly maid who cleans on the sixth floor just as she did in life. An elderly female ghost knocks on doors and asks for help finding her room, only to vanish after she leads witnesses to the elevator.

THE GOLDEN LAMB INN

The Golden Lamb Inn is the oldest operating business in the state of Ohio, dating back to 1803 in the city of Lebanon, when a man named Jonas Seaman spent $4 on a license to open a "house of public entertainment." The inn boasted prominent visitors over its history, including luminaries in the literary world and a handful of presidents, and eventually, a man named Robert H. Jones took over the place and turned it into a great restaurant and attraction that still stands today. The hotel kept its original name but added on a gift shop, fourth floor, and the Black Horse Tavern.

The inn also took on a haunted reputation. There are two main ghosts that guests interact with: Sarah and Charles. Sarah is the ghost of the former niece of one of the inn's managers. She lived in the inn and had her own room, and although she died elsewhere, her ghost is said to haunt the place she loved by moving pictures and furniture around.

The second ghost may belong to a man named Charles R. Sherman, an Ohio Supreme Court justice who died at the inn in 1928. Guests report seeing him walking the hallways and can smell the scent of his favorite cigars wafting through the air.

NIAGARA FALLS INN

People normally go to New York's stunning Niagara Falls for honeymoons and vacations. The Red Coach Inn is a historic bed-and-breakfast that first opened in August 1923. It served many couples coming to the Honeymoon Capital of the World and was lucky to be located in the center of town overlooking the Upper Rapids. The inn, was built in the old English Tudor style and boasted three stories. The owners, William Schoellkopf and Charles Peabody, put a lot of money and attention into the inn and tried to recreate the style of the Bell Inn in Finedon, England. The Red Coach Inn has its share of ghostly visitors, including a honeymooning bride and groom who committed suicide at the falls on their wedding day and the sound of phantom people walking, laughing, and dancing on the top floor to music played by ghostly musicians in the middle of the night, when no one is there. Objects are also reported to move on their own, including jewelry, according to inn staff.

Omni Parker House

Boston's most haunted hotel might just be the Omni Parker House, which was built in the 1800s by Harvey D. Parker, who also ran the place until his death in 1884. The swanky hotel was a favorite of famous literary figures who attended the long-running Saturday Club, including Oliver Wendell Holmes Sr., Charles Dickens, Ralph Waldo Emerson, and Henry Wadsworth Longfellow. One infamous guest was John Wilkes Booth, the actor who would later shoot President Abraham Lincoln in 1865 at the Ford's Theatre in Washington, D.C. John F. Kennedy announced his candidacy for Congress at the Omni Parker House and even had his bachelor party there.

But there is a truly dark connection, for it was room 303 of the hotel, which is walled off now, that inspired horror master Stephen King to write his creepy story "1408," which was later made into a movie starring John Cusack as a tormented writer staying in a horror-filled hotel room. As for ghosts, though, it is mainly Harvey Parker who now roams the halls and rooms, sometimes as a full apparition with his noted moustache, sometimes as just a misty presence. On the third floor, visitors report an elevator that goes up and down on its own, a young girl ghost that appears at the foot of beds, strange flashes of light and ghostly orbs that float down the hallways, and the creaky sound of a rocking chair rocking back and forth.

Battery Carriage House Inn

This bed-and-breakfast inn is part of a large, five-story 1845 Greek Revival style antebellum mansion in the historical city of Charleston, South Carolina. Located in the garden area of the huge property, the Battery Carriage House Inn is open to visitors, while the main mansion is now privately owned. The inn has a history of hosting ghosts in several of the rooms most favored by guests looking for a unique experience. The entire estate was in a war zone during the Civil War and underwent several renovations and

Battery Carriage House Inn is the home of spirits who were the victims of Hurricane Hugo in 1989.

family owners. In 1989, Hurricane Hugo took quite a toll on the buildings until the current owners moved in and renovated them.

Guests believe the ghosts they've encountered in rooms 3, 8, and 10 in particular might be victims of Hugo or the spirits of pirates that were hanged from trees on nearby land. Whoever the ghosts are, they favor these rooms.

The ghost of a tall man likes to goof around with male guests in room 8. He wears an overcoat and only appears from the torso up, sometimes haunting other rooms as well. Room 8 visitors report seeing the apparition beside their bed, sometimes breathing heavily or wearing a rough cape. Chairs crash against the wall, and the toilet seat has been heard slamming down. Meanwhile, in room 10, a host of activity centers around the "Gentleman Ghost," a presence many describe as a wispy apparition, slender built, around 5 feet, 8 inches tall, with no facial features. Others describe the ghost as a young man who floats through closed doors.

In room 3, one might encounter figures of light that take on various shapes and forms in the sitting room or footsteps that follow you around the room. The bathroom faucet drips all night, but when guests check on it, the sink is dry. Guests also report a host of ghosts hanging out in the basement sitting room and that many apparitions, including the ghostly torso, have been captured on photographs.

Moon River Brewery

Savannah, Georgia, is filled with old, historical buildings, and one of the oldest is the Moon River Brewery, which opened for business in 1999. The building itself dates to 1821, when it was the City Hotel, a high-end hotel that saw its fair share of violence during the Civil War. Heated fights often led to murders and included a Yankee soldier who was beaten to death in 1860. Those who visit the brewery today often report bottles flying through the air and the apparition of a man in the billiards room. Guests are often pushed, tugged, and even slapped by invisible forces.

Houses

The Whaley House

San Diego is also home to one of the most famous haunted buildings on the planet and a place that has become the one tourist spot you must visit if you go to America's Finest City. Located on a quiet street in the Old Town District, this beautiful house has been called the most haunted house in America by *Time* magazine and the Travel Channel. Yes, it has quite a reputation, but why? The long history of this house includes time as a granary, a commercial theater, and even a courthouse as well as the on-again, off-again home to the Whaley family.

The family patriarch, Thomas Whaley, built the house from bricks he had in his own brickyard, and the house was San Diego's first two-story brick build-

The Whaley House in Old Town San Diego has a fascinating history, including periods when it served as a courthouse and a theater. Today, it is open to tours.

ing. The mid-tenth-century Greek Revival style is eye-catching to tourists coming to the Old Town area, and the house became a registered historical landmark in 1960. Today, it is open to public tours as a museum.

Why does it have such a haunted reputation? According to Orrin Grey of The Lineup in his October 2017 article "The Whaley House: The Most Haunted Home in America," the land the house was built on was once the site of gallows, where a man named James Robinson was hanged in 1852. "Yankee Jim," as he was known, took a long time to finally die, swinging back and forth until he was strangled. Thomas Whaley was one of the witnesses to the hanging, and he bought the property in 1857. Once the family moved into the house, the paranormal activity began with the sound of phantom boots moving around the house. Later, the infant son of Thomas Whaley would die in the house, and years after that, the Whaley daughter, Violet, would commit suicide there after being jilted by a lover on her honeymoon.

Thomas's ghost is often seen on the upper landing of the home, while the ghost of his wife Anna haunts the downstairs and the garden in the form of a wispy lady in white apparition. Some people even report seeing the ghost of the family dog, Dolly!

Today, there are nighttime ghost-hunting tours one weekend a month, and, of course, on Halloween.

Robinson-Rose House

Not too far from the Whaley House in the historic Old Town district of San Diego is a two-story building that currently serves as the Old Town Visitor Center. But the Robinson-Rose House was built back in 1853 by a successful lawyer named James W. Robinson, who was also a judge in the city of San Diego. Over the course of many decades, this family home also served as the headquarters of the *San Diego Herald* and a number of other private offices.

Over time, the original home was destroyed by the elements and disuse, and in 1987, it was rebuilt using old photos to try to closely replicate the original. Those who visit the house now to learn more about Old Town's historical background are apt to be visited by ghosts and misty apparitions, phantom footsteps, lights flashing and turning on and off, an elevator that operates itself, and, if you're female, having your hair pulled and yanked. No one is quite sure who the ghosts are, but it appears they don't like women!

Russ House

Marianna, Florida, offers many historical sites but none with the reputation of the Russ House. Currently home to the Jackson County Tourism Office, this building is the city's most photographed historic house, and if you are lucky, you might manage to get a ghostly apparition staring out of an upper window on film.

The original house was built by Joseph Russ Jr. in 1895. Russ was a successful man, and his house showed it. The Victorian-style home was a showpiece to be sure, especially when two-story porches and columns were added in 1910. The land the house was built upon was the 1864 site of the Battle of Marianna, where many men were wounded and killed on the grounds. This might account for the ghostly activity people report as well as the suicide of Mr. Russ in 1930 after an economic crash almost cost him his home.

His family was able to stay in the house after his death, but they were soon plagued with strange sounds and apparitions, the smell of perfume, elevator doors opening and closing, and the figure of a person standing at the second-story window. This activity continues today as the Visitor Center, and public tours are available. The Russ House has become a favorite ghost-hunting destination, with visits by several paranormal groups that claim it is as haunted as ever.

The Winchester House

You may be familiar with Winchester rifles, but did you know they are linked to one of the most notorious and bizarre haunted houses in the world? The Winchester Mystery House is in San Jose, California, and has quite a story

The Winchester Mystery House in San Jose, California, is an architecturally quirky place that makes it more interesting than even, perhaps, the fact that it plays host to paranormal events.

behind it, a story that for a long, long time was built upon nothing but allegations and urban legends. The true story surrounds a woman named Sarah Winchester, who bought a farmhouse in San Jose to be near family after the death of her husband, William Wirt Winchester, from tuberculosis in 1881.With the money she inherited upon his death from his Winchester Repeating Arms Company, she had the means to build a giant mansion if she wanted to. She renovated the property herself, working with various architects to try to complete her vision. Her infant daughter also died, adding to the tragic backstory of this unusual woman.

Eventually, she wrote up the plans for the house herself and ran into many issues that forced her to make changes in her building ideas. The result was a labyrinth of a huge house, and outsiders began spreading rumors about the quiet and introverted woman of wealth who lived within its walls. As for ghosts, they were not even a part of Sarah's experience and were only attached to her story much later. She was attacked for the lavishness of the home and the grounds and criticized for building something many of her poorer neighbors deemed an extravagant display of wealth. Sarah also planned to build a castle and moat, but it never got underway.

But soon, the myth of the house being haunted and the location of late-night séances spread like the flu and, to this day, the Winchester House is said to be a notoriously active site rampant with paranormal goings-on. Sarah did build into the house a séance room, which showed her strong belief in the spirit world. After her death, the supernatural label was slapped upon the house mainly because she was not around to deny it. But to those who witnessed the actual building of the house, which took thirty-eight years from the time she bought the original farmhouse to her death in 1922, resulting in between 500 and 600 rooms, of which now only 160 remain, with forty staircases that lead nowhere, doors that open to eight-foot drops, and the repetition of the number 13 throughout the home, the Winchester House is itself just as much of an enigma as the woman who built it.

Today, it is open to the public as a tourist attraction, and yes, people often report paranormal activity such as breathing and the sense of being breathed on when workers are alone in the house; hammers tapping and screws turning; cold spots throughout; the phantom music of a piano; and even the fleeting apparition of a woman sitting in the dining room or standing by an upstairs window.

Tour guides have reported seeing the ghost of a mustached man in white coveralls in the basement pushing a wheelbarrow who, strangely, shows up in a photograph hanging in the toolshed of workers from eighty years before.

So, despite researchers pointing out a sheer lack of supernatural history behind the home before Sarah died, there are plenty of ghostly goings-on today to challenge their assumption that the Winchester Mystery House is not haunted. Not at all. Tell that to the ghosts.

LaLaurie House

New Orleans high society during the eighteenth century was a sight to behold. One of the grand dames of the social scene was Delphine LaLaurie, who looked the part of the gracious and wealthy lady on the outside but behind closed doors was as evil as they come. She owned slaves and subjected them to horrific treatment, sexually assaulting them, even butchering and performing gruesome experiments on her victims. No one knew of the terrible things she did to the slaves she kept locked in her attack. But one young slave girl, afraid for her life, started a fire that instigated an outside investigation of the home. Locals came to the rescue of slaves trapped in the attic, and soon, the whole of society knew of the LaLaurie torture house. She was eventually run out of town, her home was sacked by a mob of outraged New Orleans citizens, and she died in 1849. But her ghost, along with the ghosts of the slaves she butchered, remain behind.

Ghost-hunting groups investigating the LaLaurie House claim to have seen the shadow people throughout, peering from rooms in the house. Disembodied voices are captured on EVP, moaning and begging for help, and ghost photographs have revealed a woman in eighteenth-century dress looking out a window or walking about the house that could be Delphine. People who boarded at the house were tugged, pushed, and subjected to tugs on their clothing or hair, as if someone wanted to alert them to trouble nearby. Today, the house is open to public walking tours.

Savannah Spookiness

Savannah, Georgia, is home to plenty of reputable haunted locales. But the Gribble House boasts a triple murder that occurred within its walls in 1909, a gruesome crime that kept the city on edge for months, if not years. Also known as the "Savannah Axe Murders," the victims were two women, Eliza Gribble and her daughter, Carrie Ohlander, who were beaten to death inside the home. A third woman, Maggie Hunter, was found barely alive and lived just long enough to identify the murderer, J. C. Hunter, her own husband. She died, and her husband was convicted to die by hanging, but his sentence was reduced, and he was granted eventual pardon by Governor Clifford Walker.

His victims got no pardon, though, and many people believe they have been haunting the house ever since that travesty of justice. Supernatural activity includes lights going on and off, disembodied voices, glowing orbs and flashing lights, the feeling of being pushed or watched, and ghostly apparitions.

Another haunted Savannah home is the William Kehoe House, built in 1892 for the family of twelve. Unfortunately, several of the ten children died young within the home, including twin boys who got trapped while playing in the chimney and died there. The chimney was boarded up with their bodies still inside.

Visitors to the house, now a lovely bed-and-breakfast, claim to hear phantom children laughing and playing, the sound of running and playing in the empty hallways, and plenty of strange activity associated with room 203, where a ghost child appears at the foot of the bed and can be felt kissing guests on the cheek or touching their hands. Other guests report seeing the ghost of the wife, Anne Kehoe, wandering around rooms 201 and 203, searching for her dead twin boys.

ST EDITION. TUESDAY AFTERNOON LAST EDITIO

THREE MEN HELD AS SUSPECTS IN THE TRIPLE MURDER CASE

Photos by Girard.

W. H. WALLS. J. C. HUNTER. W. H. COLEMAN, Col.

David Taylor, alias Charles J. Hunter, was the husband of Mrs. Maggie Hunter and a suspect held by the police in connection with the triple murder. W. H. Walls, another of the suspects held, was known to be friendly with Mrs. Hunter. W. H. Coleman, colored has been identified by a street car conductor as a man who got on an E. & W. Car at Perry and West Broad streets just after the murders were probably committed. He rode around to Bay and Houston streets. He has been in jail with Hunter and was known to be with him upon several occasions.

Three suspects were arrested in the 1909 Savannah, Georgia, murder case, but in the end, the guilty partner turned out to be J. C. Hunter, husband and father of two of the victims.

The Pirate's House

The Pirate's House in Savannah, Georgia, is one of the oldest structures in the state. Built in 1753, it was a place where sailors would go to find rest, relaxation, and a good meal, only to be dragged through a tunnel below the building to the Savannah River, where they were forced to be slaves to pirates. Now a restaurant, those brave enough to come have a meal here report hearing screaming and moaning coming from the basement and seeing ghostly sailors walking the hallways.

The House of the Moving Mannequins

New Hamburg, New York, boasts one of the downright creepiest haunted locations ever. Located near the New Hamburg train station is the John Lawson House, one of six properties that make up the Main Street Historic District. Though no living person or persons have ever been seen on the property or in the house, it is indeed occupied by mannequins, including female mannequins on the porch wearing nineteenth-century clothing. If that in itself isn't twisted enough, the mannequins are dressed and positioned differently each day, as if some unseen person, or persons, is attending to them. Many of them appear to be pointing toward something.

Some locals believe the ghosts are pointing toward an unsolved riddle. Others believe they may be trying to send a message about something inside the house. And others suggest the ghosts of twenty-two people who died tragically in a train crash right in front of the house in 1871 may be what the dolls seem to be pointing toward.

The house was built in 1845 and somehow managed to survive a huge fire that wiped out the rest of the block. Now and then, the dolls point to the only other historical house that withstood the fire. In addition to pointing a lot, the dolls hold strange things in their plastic hands, including books, birdcages, towels, brushes, and items placed on their laps. When it rains, the dolls are not on the porch, yet no one sees anyone bringing them inside. A faint light from the kitchen area has been reported at night, but there doesn't seem to be any movement inside.

Farnam Mansion's Ghost Cat

Yes, there are ghosts of animals everywhere, but not all achieve the fame of the white phantom cat that haunts the stairs of the Farnam Mansion in Oneida, New York. This paranormal hot spot is where several people died, and it has a long history of séances, one of which, in August 2011, conjured up the ghost kitty who has been a permanent fixture ever since. The Renaissance-style home was built in 1862 by Stephen Head Farnam, a wealthy businessman who owned an axe factory and hardware store. Farnam was active in the community and died of a stroke in the house in 1897. Three other Farnam family members also died in the home. After the property changed owners, four more people died in the house.

Most of the bodies were found in the bedroom, although one man died in the basement, where he had some kind of laboratory. The spirits of the dead roam about the home, sometimes as shadow figures in the attic, where one of the newer owners found a slate with the name of a Farnam granddaughter written on it. Disembodied voices and footsteps are heard throughout the house, lights turn on and off, and strange mists form near people standing outside of the bedrooms. The home has become such a popular spot for séances and ghost hunters, there are weekly séances that some researchers believe keep the paranormal activity going.

The Lizzie Borden House

Lizzie Borden took an axe and gave her mother forty whacks.
When she saw what she had done, she gave her father forty-one.

That delightful little ditty refers to one of the most gruesome double murder cases in the history of America. It began in a town called Fall River, Massachusetts, nestled against the eastern shore of Mount Hope Bay. This town thrived in the nineteenth century as a center of the nation's textile industry. Sadly, it is far more often remembered for what happened there on the morning of August 4, 1892.

Before noon, Andrew Borden and his wife, Abby, would be dead, and not just dead, but brutally butchered: Andrew while napping in the sitting room and Abby while in their family home's guest room. Outside the lovely Greek Revival-style home, the maid, Bridget Sullivan, washed windows. Inside, one of two daughters, Lizzie, was alone, the other daughter having been out of town that day. It would be Lizzie who was charged with the murders of her stepmother and father, done with a hatchet. The motive may have been her hatred for her stepmother and anger at her father, but despite no other evidence of anyone else being in the house at the time, the fact that Lizzie maintained her innocence mattered little.

The Lizzie Borden House is still standing in Fall River, Massachusetts, where you can book a room or take a tour.

The crime is still considered unsolved, but the guilt had already been assigned. Lizzie Borden took an axe, and, well, you know the rest. Some people claim the father, Andrew Borden, was quite rich and had many enemies, but the initial investigation showed no sign of entry or exit from the house. Again, this threw the bulk of suspicion on Lizzie and the maid as an accomplice, but no evidence of that was presented during the trial. Lizzie was eventually acquitted for the murders, and she never returned to the family home again.

Over the next 120-odd years, professional detectives and amateur investigators alike have looked into the crimes, hoping to find an overlooked clue and solve the notorious case. No doubt, paranormal investigators and psychics desire to speak to the ghosts of the murder victims and see if they will reveal the identity of their killer. No one has come forward yet with compelling evidence.

The house is open to the public now as a bed-and-breakfast with its own museum. The Fall River Historical Society promotes the Lizzie Borden House as a tourist hot spot, and those who believe in the paranormal insist it is haunted, especially the guest room where the stepmother Abby was killed. Visitors claim to hear screams in the dead of night, see apparitions, hear phantom footsteps, and sense the presence of something that cannot be seen. Yet others claim they experienced nothing more than the terror that comes from spending time in a house where two people were chopped up with an axe. This is one of those true stories that has taken on an urban legend status to the point where most people automatically assume the house is rampant with supernatural activity just because of the horrific tragedy that occurred there.

If you visit the site today, you won't see the original furnishings, but great care has been taken to display furniture and photos that are replicas of those appearing in the crime-scene photos, including a portrait of Lizzie on the piano in the parlor and the settee where Andrew napped before he was hacked to death. You can even stay overnight in Lizzie's old bedroom, if you dare.

Villisca Axe Murder House

On the night of June 9, 1912, deep into the early hours of the morning of June 10, the tiny town of Villisca, Iowa (the Native American word "wallisca" means evil spirit) had no idea what horrors awaited when they woke up. Eight people were being bludgeoned to death during those hours: six members of the Moore family and two houseguests, who were staying at the Moore family home, which is now called the notorious Villisca Axe Murder House. Of the eight victims, six were children. All eight victims died of head wounds. Several men would be tracked down and tried for the crimes. None would be found guilty. Like the Borden axe murders, the Villisca murder spree has remained unsolved.

The Moores were affluent and very well liked in their community. Josiah Moore, the patriarch, was a prominent businessman. On that fateful night, two guests, friends of the Moore daughters, ten-year-old Mary Katherine, were invited to stay the night, only to become part of the horrific murders. A neighbor named Mary Peckham thought it quite strange the next morning when none of the Moore family members came out to do their chores. She tried the door, but it was locked, so she fetched Ross Moore, the brother of the family patriarch, Josiah, and when he couldn't get the door open, he used a house key. He was the first one to see the bloodbath and told Mary to contact local police officer Hank Horton.

Once Hank was on scene, the house was searched, and the bodies were found all bludgeoned and with their bedclothes covering their faces. The murder weapon was found in the guest room. Investigators later stated that they felt all the victims but one were asleep when they were killed. Lena Stillinger, one of the family guests, looked as though she had attempted to fight her attacker/s. She was found wearing no undergarments and may have been sexually assaulted. The ceilings of the bedrooms had gouge marks that were made by the back-swing of the bludgeon, and a pan of bloodied water was found on the kitchen table next to a plate of uneaten food.

The doors were found all locked by police, and a two-pound slab of bacon was found in the downstairs bedroom wrapped in a towel. A second slab was found in the icebox.

The victims of the massacre were:

- Josiah Moore—father—age 43
- Sarah Moore—mother—age 29
- Lena Stillinger—friend—age 12
- Herman Moore—son—age 11
- Mary Katherine Moore—daughter—age 9
- Boyd Moore—son—age 7
- Ina Stillinger—friend—age 7
- Paul Moore—son—age 5

LAST VICTIMS OF MAD MURDERER OF WEST

J. W. Moore, wife and 3 of 4 children who were murdered in bed at Villisca, Ia. Star shows room in which Misses Stillinger, visiting Moores, were killed.

During the last two years, a madman murderer has killed four whole families in the West. In each case he used an axe. The murders have been at Colorado Springs, Ellsworth, Kan., Guilford, Mo., and Villisca, Ia. The last, that of the Moores at Villisca, occurred this week. The slayer shows a terrible ingenuity in making good his escape. Villisca police arrested Sam Moyer, relative of Moore family. Produced alibi. Released.

Irishman: "Give me three cigars."
Shopman: "Strong or mild?"
Irishman: "Give me the strong ones. The weak ones break in my pocket!"

An article in the June 14, 1912, issue of *The Day Book* showing the victims of the axe murderer.

Among the many men who became suspects was Reverend George Kelly, who was tried twice but acquitted both times. Kelly was in the area at the time and was at the children's program the Moore children were to be involved in. He left town around the same time the eight bodies were found. Suspicion fell upon Josiah's business connections, who may have held a grudge or been a part of a bad business deal, as well as a serial killer named Henry Lee Moore, who was not a relative of the family. Because there was no central fingerprint database, it was impossible to use prints found on the crime scene without having access to the killers to compare them to. Unfortunately, the crime scene was compromised in the hours after the bodies were found by curiosity seekers who took items from the house for mementos of the horrific crime.

With little evidence that was helpful, the investigation by Sheriff Oren Jackson and federal agent M. W. McClaughry looked at many different motives for the crime. Because the father, Josiah, was the most brutally bludgeoned, they suspected he was the main target of the killers. By looking into his past, the investigators found links to politicians and businessmen who may have had a falling-out with Josiah, including a man named Frank Jones, who lost a very lucrative contract to Moore and who knew of a sexual affair between Moore and his daughter-in-law. Another suspect was a mentally ill vagrant named William Mansfield. But in the end, there wasn't enough evidence to convict anyone.

In 1994, Darwin and Martha Linn of Corning, Iowa, bought the house and returned it to its original condition using old photographs. They opened it for tours to the public, and it was listed in the National Register of Historic Places. Ghost-hunting groups and paranormal investigations abound there, and some claim to have experienced spectral images; phantom voices of children and adults, mostly male; the sounds of footsteps and people running down the stairs; cold spots in the bedrooms; the presence of someone in many parts of the house; and ghostly voices showing up on EVP recordings. Other overnight guests report strange banging sounds, objects moving about of their own accord, and creepy images that show up on photographs of the rooms in which the bodies were found.

Haunted Houses of Salem, Massachusetts

Salem, Massachusetts, is filled with haunted locations thanks to its history, and one of these is called the House of Seven Gables. Locals also know it as the Turner-Ingersoll Mansion, named after the two families that made the building their homes. In 1668, the Turner family patriarch, merchant ship-owner John Turner, built the home, a gorgeous Colonial mansion with seven gables. It is the oldest surviving timber-framed mansion in North America. It boasted seventeen rooms spanning 8,000 square feet (743 square meters) and large cellars beneath the home. Unfortunately, financial difficulties caused them to have to sell it to Captain Samuel Ingersoll in 1782.

His wife, Susan Ingersoll, was the cousin of the famous author Nathaniel Hawthorne, and he wrote a novel about the home in 1851 called *The House of the Seven Gables*. Susan lived there until she died at the age of seventy-two. Her spirit is said to be the most active ghost, often seen peering from an upper-story window. The ghost of a young man plays in the attic and strange sounds are commonplace, as are faucets and lights that turn on and off. Today, it is considered a National Historic Landmark and open to tours.

The Joshua Ward House was built in 1784 and is haunted by the ghosts of Sheriff George "The Strangler" Corwin and a man named Giles Corey. The house was built after the Salem witch trials, in which both men were heavily involved, and is built upon land the sheriff owned. He was considered a sadistic man who enjoyed torturing suspected witches up until his death in 1697. His body was originally buried in the house's basement but was later moved to the nearby Broad Street Cemetery. His ghost is said to hang around the cemetery and choke visitors who get too close.

One of the men who was tortured by Corwin was Giles Corey, who was accused of being a warlock. His ghost is often seen in the house and is said to enjoy pulling items off shelves and knocking over trash cans. Another female spirit also haunts the house, possibly one of the alleged witches tortured and executed by Corwin.

Not too far away sits the Witch House, which is owned by another witch torturer named Jonathan Corwin, who was a key player in the Salem witch trials. Corwin was a judge, and he was responsible for investigating claims of witchcraft. During his tenure as a judge, he condemned nineteen people to execution. His house is open as a museum now, but visitors claim it is highly active with cold spots, people being touched by unseen hands, and the voice of a ghost child, who may have been a victim or the child of a woman Judge Corwin executed.

The Grove

The riverport city of Jefferson, Texas, is home to many historical properties, but the most haunted is The Grove, a private residence open to tours located in the old Stephen Smith Land Grant section. The original house, much of which still stands, was built in 1861 by Frank and Minerva Stilley and has been structurally changed a couple of times, mainly with the additions of another room, indoor bathroom, and a porch, so most of the home remains intact, and apparently, that goes for the ghosts, too. The home was originally called the Stilley–Young House because of the land the home was built upon. It was given in a land grant to Lucy and Daniel Alley, who were the cofounders of the city of Jefferson. Before the Stilleys built their home on the land and named it The Grove, there was a log cabin there that went through various owners dating back to 1847. The Stilleys lived there while their cotton-brokering business was bankrupted, and after Minerva's death, Frank sold the house and moved away.

Ghostly tales about the house have been told for over a century and began in 1882 when T. C. Burke purchased the home for his family and left within a month, stating only that they could not live there. Another resident of the home, Louise Young, who lived there in the early 1900s, told many friends that she lived with "haunts," the ghosts that haunted the home. Apparently, they weren't unfriendly because Louise stayed in the home until her death in the 1980s.

One lady of the house brought her Bible to bed with her every night so she and her husband could pray, and one night, she was awakened by a black

Built in 1861, the Stilley–Young House in Jefferson, Texas, is on the National Register of Historic Places. It has been called the most haunted house in Texas.

mass going on in the bedroom along with disembodied voices. Another former owner, Patrick Hopkins, reportedly saw a ghost of a woman dressed in white going into the powder room and never coming out. There were also reports of a woman's perfume and also the smell of someone with very bad body odor as well as mysterious, wet footprints in the hallway, even though there was no rain at the time or leaks in the home.

Maybe that had to do with the other residents onsite, including a Lady in White who walks the same exact path through the house every time she is seen; the Garden Guy—a man walking quickly through the gardens; and an entity that teases women in the home's den and could be the ghost of Charlie Young, a barber who lived there in 1885.

The Grove is now listed on the National Register of Historic Places and is also a Recorded Texas Landmark, and yes, it is open to public tours.

Haunted Places in the United Kingdom

Over across the pond in Norfolk, England, is Raynham Hall, a haunted site that may have produced the most famous ghost photograph of all time. The

Brown Lady was captured on film in a 1936 photograph originally published in *Country Life Magazine*. It depicts the ghostly figure of what appears to be a woman descending a wooden staircase. The ghost may be that of Lady Dorothy Walpole Townshend, the wife of the second viscount of the Raynham estate. They resided at the hall until her death in 1726.

The first time the Brown Lady appeared was in 1835 when a holiday guest at the hall saw her standing on the main staircase. She was described as having a face that glowed and having dark sockets where her eyes should have been. She carried a lantern and looked exactly like the woman in the portrait on the wall of Lady Dorothy. The ghost even appeared to King George IV, who woke in the middle of the night and saw her standing beside his bed with her hair a mess and her face ashy and pale. He never spent another night at the hall.

Baskerville Hall is the central location featured in the Sherlock Holmes novels, but its haunted reputation comes from the history behind it.

Lady Dorothy may be gone, but her ghost lives on and, to this day, the famous photograph is still the subject of debate between those who believe it caught a ghost on film and those who believe it is a hoax or film anomaly.

Powys, Wales, is home to another very famous haunted hall-turned-hotel. Baskerville Hall is the central location featured in the Sherlock Holmes novels, but its haunted reputation comes from the history behind it. The enormous edifice was built in 1839 and immediately, visitors were reporting banging noises in the hallways, phantom footsteps, a ghostly White Lady who hangs out in the rose garden, and as the notorious hellhounds that were later made famous in the Holmes novel franchise. Arthur Conan Doyle indeed must have gotten his inspiration inside this amazing mansion, for there are also other spirits said to haunt the hall, inside and out, including a male ghost who stands upon the grand staircase as if to welcome guests.

Castles

Just the thought of an old castle standing against a gray sky evokes intrigue, even fear. The buildings themselves run the range from glorious and majestic to terrifying and foreboding. Though Europe is most known for their ancient and medieval castles, they exist in the United States, too. Like lighthouses, many have fallen into disrepair and were abandoned eons ago, but some remain open to the public as hotels, tourist attractions, and popular ghost-hunting destinations.

Spending the night in a castle, whether haunted or not, is usually not permitted by law due to the dangers of the ruins and lack of running water, bathrooms, and potential for injury. But then, who would want to spend a night in an old, cold, dark, and creepy castle where the living roam the halls and towers lament their fates? Probably the same kind of people who would spend the night in a haunted hotel, motel, inn, house, lighthouse, cemetery.... You get the picture.

Preston Castle

One castle you can visit is Preston Castle in Ione, California. The striking, massive, red-brick building is in the Romanesque Revival architectural style and looks like a castle but is the current home to the Preston School of Industry, yet it has quite a history of murder and mystery. It was originally a reform school in 1894 to seven minor children who were under California's guardianship. They were transfers from the San Quentin Prison, and later residents would include hundreds of other troubled kids, including Merle Haggard, writer Edward Bunker, and a poet named Neal Cassady.

Eventually, the building was vacated, and a new building was constructed in its place. The institution closed officially in 2011. Over its long history, paranormal phenomena have been reported within and outside of Preston Castle. From the cold spots, strange sensations, and ghostly sounds to apparitions of the wards who died there, the building also may be home to the ghost of a housekeeper, Anna Corbin, who was bludgeoned to death there in 1950. News media claimed she was beaten to death in her locked room in the castle, and all 637 wards there at the time were questioned, but there was never a conviction. To this day, her murder remains unsolved.

The building is now a registered historical landmark, and The Preston Castle Foundation maintains the building, which is open to the public for events and ghost hunting.

Castle Mont Rouge

Artist/architect Robert Mihaly loved the style of Russia's castles, so he built one in 2005 just like them on Red Mountain in Rougemont, North Carolina, out of cinder block and marble, with spires and copper domes. He intended to use the fantasy castle as his art studio, but his wife died before the castle was completed. He was so depressed, he never finished the interior. The castle is now abandoned, but those who have peeked inside claim there is a first-floor room with a bed, small kitchen, and books. Mihaly attempted to raise funds to finish the castle but was unsuccessful, even after the popular website *Abandoned Homes of North Carolina* published a photo. The wife, Anna, is said to haunt the castle now.

Bannerman's Castle

Pollepel Island sits on the Hudson River just north of New York City. In 1900, a Scottish immigrant built a gorgeous, Scottish-style castle to use for his military surplus goods business. It was said to contain a huge arsenal of weapons.

The castle experienced several fires and explosions and was eventually abandoned, but a smaller version was constructed near the warehouse castle. The Bannerman family lived there until 1940. Unfortunately, they didn't know that they were living on cursed Iroquois land, and all kinds of bad things began to happen. A tugboat captain died when he crashed into the island, and after New York City bought the castle in 1967, visitors have reported seeing his ghost walking near the castle calling out for help. It is now an official historical site.

Hearthstone Castle

Imagine a medieval-style castle right in Danbury, Connecticut. The Hearthstone Castle is a massive building originally with four smaller structures named for the many stone fireplaces within the imposing main house. It sits upon 7 acres (3 hectares) of beautiful forest land and was built by E. Starr Sanford in 1897 as the family's summer home. They only lived there for five years. The castle changed hands several times before it was abandoned. The city of Danbury has built a chain-link fence around the now abandoned building to keep people out, but those who walk or drive near the castle claim to see a ghost dog on the grounds and a ghostly man running across the lawn. Perhaps it is the ghost of E. Starr Sanford himself, who died under bizarre circumstances in 1914, when the ship he was on was struck by lightning. The castle is now a registered historical site and part of Tarrywile Park under ownership of the city of Danbury.

Although it is in Connecticut, Hearthstone Castle looks like something out of medieval Europe. Sometimes called Parks' Castle, it and its four nearby buildings are on the National Register of Historic Places.

Gillette Castle

In East Haddam, Connecticut, the ghost of William Hooker Gillette roams the medieval-style castle looming above a river valley. Gillette was an actor and playwright best known for first bringing Sir Arthur Conan Doyle's Sherlock Holmes the stage and giving the character his iconic cape, deerstalker hat, pipe, and the catchphrase "Oh, this is elementary, my dear fellow." Gillette performed the role over a thousand times and built a nice fortune, nice enough to build the castle he would retire in and call home. The castle was built from local fieldstone and took five years, completed in 1919. There are forty-seven doors in the castle, each with a unique, wooden puzzle lock that must be solved to open the door. There is a disappearing bar, a small-scale working railroad set up with tunnels and bridges that goes around the property, and mirrors that he could use to spy on guests. The 128-acre estate was quirky, as was Gillette, and when he died in 1937, having no wife or offspring, the state of Connecticut took over the property. Since then, some renovations have been done and improvements made on the grounds as well as the addition of a café and visitor's center. The castle is open for tours year-round, and if you are lucky, you might get to see unexplained flickering lights and the fluttering apparition of the man himself at the place he loved so much.

Wyckoff Castle

Carleton Island near Cape Vincent, New York, was the spot William O. Wyckoff chose to build his gorgeous estate upon. Once the grandest estate in the Thousand Islands region, it seemed cursed from the beginning. Wyckoff, who invented the Remington typewriter, was a very wealthy man, but he died in his sleep from a heart attack on the first night he spent in his new castle home. His wife had died a month earlier from cancer.

Their son, Clarence, wasn't interested in the castle, so it fell abandoned for over sixty years. The last known owner was the corporation General Electric. The castle was on the market recently for only $495,000, although it would cost millions to restore the home and the grounds. And only the bravest of souls would want to live in a castle said to be haunted by the ghost of William and his wife. Visitors have reported the words "help me" scrawled on a high ceiling in one of the upper-story bedrooms.

There are dozens, if not hundreds, of creepy castles all over the world, many abandoned, many haunted, some open to the public as hotels or museums. Just too many to list here. Some of the spookiest include:

Arundel Castle

England's Arundel Castle, located in West Sussex, is home to ghosts who have resided there for hundreds of years. The medieval structure is terrifying and looks like something from an old, black-and-white horror movie, and it's filled with paranormal history. Founded on Christmas Day in 1067, the castle has undergone several renovations since, and it once hosted such luminaries as Empress Matilda, Henry II, and Edward I. Most of the castle that still stands today is open to public viewing along with the grounds. But people are warned they might meet up with a colony of white, owl-like birds that have been living in the castle since its restoration in the fifteenth century. Yes, ghost owls, and seeing one is an omen of bad things to come. They are often seen peering out a window or on the grounds outside, but legend has it that anyone who saw the owls in the past would meet with an untimely death.

Having existed for nearly a thousand years, Arundel Castle has had plenty of time to wrack up an all-star cast of ghosts ranging from an earl to even a parliament of white spirit owls.

Other ghosts that haunt Arundel include a young servant boy who was beaten and abused there; a ghost that appears as the top half of a man with long hair; a young woman who took her life leaping from the Hiornes Tower after the end of a tragic love affair; the Blue Man, who may have been a cavalier from the King Charles I period and favors haunting the castle's library; and the ghost of the first Earl of Arundel, who oversaw the original construction of the castle and roams the keep as if watching over the place he once called home.

Moosham Castle

Known as the "Witches' Castle," Moosham Castle in Unternberg, Austria, has quite a bloody history dating back to the twelfth century. Between 1675 and 1690, the castle was at the center of the Zaubererjackl Salzburg witch trials. Over the course of fifteen years, over 130 people were tortured, condemned to death, abused, and executed on the grounds. Most of the accused were men. It appeared the accusers weren't too concerned who they accused, as they executed children as young as ten up to adults as old as eighty in their religious frenzy. Those who weren't immediately killed were the unlucky ones. They were subjected to horrific torture and branded with hot pokers to mark them as witches.

Some of the accused had their hands chopped off, and others were burned at the stake, hanged, or decapitated while alive or dead. The majority of the victims were homeless, beggars, paupers, the poor. One twenty-year-old named Paul Jacob Koller became a local legend when he vanished after his mother was executed for sorcery and theft. Known as Wizard Jackl or Magician Jackl, he was

British Isles Castles

There are many abandoned castles all over the world where you can, if permitted, walk among the ruins. But some castles have become actual hotels and tourist attractions, giving guests a taste of modern amenities in an ancient or medieval setting. An added bonus, the potential encounter with resident ghosts and entities that are as much a part of the castles as the doors and windows.

Scotland boasts many amazing castles, and Tulloch Castle in Ross-shire comes with visits from the Green Lady, a ghostly apparition in a long, green, silk dress who walks the grounds. She is the spirit of Elizabeth Davidson, the daughter of a former castle owner. She appears to be very sad, and when approached by guests, they claim to feel a sense of overwhelming sorrow. Sometimes, they hear her whispering "Why?" over and over, and yet, no one knows why. She may be an attachment spirit because the castle is filled with antiques and a museum. The castle itself dates back to the sixteenth century—a lot of time for various deaths and tragedies to occur.

Ackergill Tower in Caithness, Scotland, was the site of a feud between the resident Keith family and the local Gunn family. Helen Gunn, known as the "beauty of Braemore," was to be married one night, but before the nuptials, she was kidnapped by the Keiths and either fell or jumped from the tower trying to escape. Her ghost is seen wearing a long, red ball gown.

Edinburgh Castle in Scotland is perhaps the most famous haunted location in the United Kingdom and is said to be haunted by numerous spirits, one of which is the Lone Piper, a young boy who was trapped in the secret tunnels underneath the huge castle, who now can be heard playing his pipes, perhaps in hopes of being discovered. This massive, hilltop, twelfth-century castle is on land that was inhabited long before, in 850 B.C.E., by various settlements as a defensive fortress during the Stone Age. After the castle was built there, it was home to royalty between the twelfth and eighteenth centuries, and it later served as a prison and an army garrison. The underground dungeons served as a prison to many men who were forgotten about and starved to death. Now many of them appear as ghosts roaming about the castle, moving objects, creating cold spots, and, in the case of a headless drummer boy first reported in 1650, appearing to warn of pending danger.

In England, the Lumley Castle is in County Durham and haunted by a fourteenth-century lady of the manor, Lily Lumley. She was reportedly murdered by local priests when she refused to convert to Catholicism. She now haunts the castle. In 2005, members of the Australian cricket team staying at the castle refused to stay in their rooms because of the paranormal activity.

Walworth Castle, also in County Durham, is a rustic, twelfth-century building with a modern hotel experience that belies its age-old exterior. It comes with a ghost of a maid who once had an affair with the lord of the house. She fell while she was pregnant, and the evil lord walled her up inside the wall of the castle's spiral staircase. Current guests claim to hear footsteps near the stairs and see an apparition that comes out from the wall. The desperate cries of a woman can be heard inside the staircase stone wall.

Ireland's Ballyseede Castle is in County Kerry and is a sprawling, eighteenth-century building that once served as the family home to the Blennerhassett family. It is haunted by a ghost of a World War I nurse, Hilda, who was a member of the family and can be seen most often in her former bedroom, now called the Crosby Room, staring out the window. She even

Continued...

(Continued from previous page)

talks to visitors and makes predictions about their futures, many of which have come true!

Castle Leslie in Ireland's County Monaghan looks like a large estate and was home to the Leslie family. Built in 1870 in the Scots Baronial style, it boasts an equestrian center and a restored stone-stable lodge on its lavish grounds. The Leslie family patriarch, Norman Leslie, was killed during World War I, and his mother, Lady Marjory, was the first to see his ghost at her bedside reading through a stack of letters. Norman most often appears in the Red Room, and guests say he often is seen shuffling papers or telling other invisible spirits to "Shhhh...."

One castle to avoid in Ireland is the terrifying Leap Castle, built in the thirteenth century by the Clan O'Bannon as a family home. However, two of the brothers were contesting who was to be chieftain of the clan. To solve the problem, the brothers jumped into a gorge, and the survivor was the winner. Two hundred years later, the Earl of Kildare tried to seize the castle and ended up destroying part of it. Then the O'Carroll clan took over, but their sibling feuding resulted in one brother killing the other, and now, the ghost of the murdered, who was a priest, haunts the chapel. The ghosts of two young girls also appear playing together, and one of them is often reported falling from one of the battlements. They may be sisters Emily and Charlotte, who lived there during the 1600s. The scariest ghost is a demon the size of a sheep with a human face that stinks of rotting flesh. It is seen roaming the grounds but doesn't appear unless you first provoke it. Some locals say the castle is located on the crossroads of two ley lines and was once the site of druid initiations. No, you cannot stay there. Nor should you want to, as the current owner has reported numerous freak accidents while trying to renovate the castle.

Constructed in the mid-sixteenth century, Tulloch Castle has served as a family home and, during World War II, a hospital.

believed to have made a pact with the Devil according to a confession his mother, Barbara Kollerin, and her partner, Paul Kalthenpacher, gave. He was hunted down by the executioners, but they never found him. A twelve-year-old beggar known as "Dirty Animal" was captured and claimed he had been in contact with Wizard Jackl and that Jackl had amazing powers as a result of black magic. He was rumored to have died two years later, when his friends were rounded up and tortured until they confessed of his powers. If that wasn't bad enough, Moosham Castle experienced an even creepier mass death when, in the 1800s, hundreds of deer and cattle inexplicably died around the castle, resulting in even more deaths of innocent citizens who were believed to be werewolves.

Today, the castle is haunted by a number of apparitions, phantom footsteps, noises, bangs, and knocks, and people claim to be touched by invisible hands or feel someone breathing on them when they are alone.

The Castle of Frankenstein

The Castle of Frankenstein in Darmstadt, Germany, sits atop a hill that overlooks the town. The castle was built back in 948 B.C.E. as a family home,

Yes, there really was a Frankenstein Castle as well as a man named Dipple von Frankenstein, whose activities as a grave robber helped inspire Mary Shelley's classic horror novel.

and in the 1600s, the last of the Frankenstein family died in an accident on the way to see his beloved, Anne Marie. He never showed up, and she died of a broken heart. Her ghost, along with that of her lover, Knight Frankenstein, haunt the castle to this day, but they are never seen together. Years later, Konrad Dipple von Frankenstein made the castle his home. He was an alchemist and grave robber, and rumors soon spread of his experiments with various dead body parts of humans and animals and his attempts to resurrect the dead. His laboratory castle took on an ominous cast, as people in the town believed he was creating a monster. They stormed the castle, but he barricaded himself in and drank a poisonous potion before they could kill him.

Visitors to the castle claim they see his ghost in the laboratory he once loved, hunched over his equipment in his search for immortality. The Brothers Grimm told this story to Mary Shelley's stepmother, and years later, Mary visited the castle and used the story of Konrad Dipple von Frankenstein for her own masterpiece horror novel *Frankenstein*.

Zvikov Castle

Of the hundreds of castles scattered about the region, Zvikov Castle in what is now the Czech Republic has the reputation of being the "King of Castles" for its difficult-to-reach fortress on the grounds, where the Vitava and Otava Rivers come together. This ancient castle was built during the time of Marcomanni rule over Bohemia in the first and second centuries B.C.E., and the huge tower called Markomanka was integrated hundreds of years later. According to Slavic folklore, the tower is where imps or tricksters haunt, but the entire castle is said to be filled with spirits thanks to the many bloody battles that occurred on the grounds and surrounding areas for centuries. Fire hounds from hell have been sighted on the grounds, guarding an underground tunnel. The castle is open today for tours, and visitors report technical issues (tricksters love to mess with technology), ghostly visions, cold spots, phantom noises, and weird images that show up on photographs.

Houska Castle

In Blatce, Czech Republic, an isolated castle sits in the middle of nowhere. Built in the fourteenth century by Bohemian ruler Ottokar II, the castle seems to serve no purpose in terms of defense against invaders, as many castles do, serving as both family homes and fortresses. It is not close to any trade routes, water sources, or strategic battle zones. Yet, it may have been built to cover something on the inside rather than defend against outsiders. Over the centuries, it changed ownership and fell into disarray but went through a Renaissance redesign in the sixteenth century. It then fell under the radar of a very sinister presence—Nazis.

Legend has it the castle was built over the gateway to hell, and there was a bottomless pit beneath the castle that allowed demons to come into our world from hell itself. The chapel stood above the pit and was dedicated to the archangel Michael with gory frescoes adorning the walls showing demons clawing their way out of the pit. Because of Hitler's obsession with the occult, the Nazis performed many occult experiments at the castle between 1939 and 1945. The skeletons of those who conducted the sinister experiments were found later during excavations, but the actual records of the experiments were destroyed.

Visitors today report multiple ghosts, including a woman who stalks the corridors of the castle, bizarre animal entities, and cold spots, phantom voices, and the sense of being touched or having hair tugged. One might imagine how haunted the castle could have been had the hole to hell not been closed by building a chapel over it!

Castle Reszel

Poland's Castel Reszel is a hotel today, but the huge, red-brick structure has a dark history dating back to the 1800s. In 1806, the entire town of Reszel was burned to the ground by an arsonist. She was identified as Barbara Zdunk a year later, and her accusers attached claims from witchcraft to arsonist. The true story of her persecution may have been related to her breaking social boundaries by having a boyfriend half her age (she was thirty-eight to his nineteen), but she was sent to the castle dungeon to await her execution. She was kept there for three years or more, repeatedly raped and tortured by her captors. She ended up giving birth twice, but no one knows what happened to the babies. She was eventually burned at the stake on the castle grounds. Today, hotel visitors believe she and her children haunt the building and grounds and profess to hearing screams from below in the dungeon as well as the smell of strange perfumes, objects moving on their own, doors opening and closing, and phantom hands that touch people when no one is there.

Dragsholm Castle

Denmark boasts a castle with over one hundred active ghosts. Dragsholm Castle is the oldest in the country, dating back to 1215. It was built by the Bishop of Rosilde and was fortified during the Middle Ages to make it the strongest castle in the country at the time, which was proven when the armies of Christoffer, Count of Oldenburg, failed to destroy it during a three-year battle. After the Reformation, it became property of the government and was turned into a prison for noble prisoners with individual cells that had toilets and windows, something lower-ranking inmates were not given. One prisoner was James Hepburn, the third husband of Mary, Queen of Scots. He was captured in Norway in 1573 and sent to the castle, where he supposedly was tied to a pillar and given barely any food or water. He went insane and died, but his ghost is said to ride his phantom horse throughout the courtyard. Dozens of other ghosts are seen and heard on the grounds, including "The Mad Squire," a Danish prisoner who died at the castle and now moans and rattles his dungeon cell. Phantom ladies walk the corridors, including "The Gray Lady," who died from medicine she was given for a toothache. "The White Lady" also roams the grounds. She died after being locked in a room by her own father for disgracing him when she took a commoner as a lover and became pregnant. Her skeleton, still wearing a white dress, was found during renovations in the twentieth century.

PRISONS, HOSPITALS, AND ASYLUMS

So many ghost stories are associated with places where great suffering and death took place. Places where men, women, and children were subject to pain, isolation, abuse, and even torture. It is in the halls of prisons, hospitals, asylums, and institutions for the insane or infirmed that the agony of the past survives as the ghosts of today, seeking respite from their pain even in death. In many cases, people died under heinous circumstances simply because they were exposed to the crudest attempts of science and psychiatry to save their lives and minds. In other cases, people who were cast out of society because of deformities, disabilities, debilitating illnesses, or committing crimes became subject to daily abuses that must have made them cry out for a quick death.

Overnight ghost hunts at these locations often produce the most activity, according to paranormal investigators who visit often and brave the dark in places that would terrify even during daylight hours. The pain of the past seems to be trapped within the walls of these buildings, manifesting in spirits and entities that carry with them the anguish and agony of their own pasts to be experienced over and over again for all eternity.

HAUNTED PRISONS AND PENITENTIARIES

Criminals are often treated like animals, even those who commit minor infractions. Society is cruel to those behind bars, and in many cases, such as killers and rapists, that cruelty is well deserved, at least according to those on the outside of the cells. Haunted prisons exist the world over, but none has the reputation of the place called "The Rock," now a legend thanks to motion pictures and television shows set on the island prison off the coast of San Francisco, California.

Alcatraz

The infamous criminals who have stayed in the cells of this most infamous prison include some of the most notorious mobsters and murderers such as Al Capone, George "Machine Gun" Kelly, and Arthur "Doc" Barker. So many of the men confined in this maximum-security island facility have gone down in history themselves until the prison was shut down in 1963; it was later reopened to the public for tours by the U.S. Park Service.

Alcatraz was said to have been designed specifically for hard-case criminals. This prison was where the most defiant, rebellious criminals broke, given only the very basics of food, clothing, shelter, and medical aid. Anything else was not given. No bribes. It had to be earned, and earning it meant being able to withstand the brutality of guards and staff. Each cell had only a toilet, sink, and one light bulb. At night, a mattress would be placed in the cells. This was a federal penitentiary, not a spa, and the prisoners were treated as such. Over its long history, thousands of inmates spent time there, and a number of men committed suicide, were driven insane, or were murdered by fellow inmates.

No longer a prison, Alcatraz was possibly the harshest, least escapable incarceration center in the United States for over a century. The horrors that occurred within its walls have left a dark, sinister impression that can still give tourists a sense of dread.

One of the most notorious locations was D-Block, which was composed of forty-two cells with different restrictions for those incarcerated there. They had no contact with the general population and were restricted to one visit to the yard and two showers per week. Meals were taken only in the cells. A handful of cells were called "Strip Cells" or the "Hole," and only the most serious offenders spend time in these cold, dark, isolated rooms. There was often only a toilet, sink, and a dim bulb, and the prisoners were not allowed outside for exercise or to shower. They had no reading materials and were left alone for up to nineteen days. The most severe punishments happened in the "Oriental" cell, a dark, steel-encased cell with only a small hole in the floor for waste.

Inmates were thrown into the totally dark, cold cell naked and given little food, although usually for only a night or two. That was usually enough to cause their minds to snap, and many men came out with permanent psychological damage.

Alcatraz was often called "Hellcatraz" by inmates, and it's easy to see why. It's also easy to see why after the prison was turned over to the public, it became a hot spot of paranormal activity. Cell 14-D, one of the notorious "hole" cells, is one of the most active in the prison, with visitors and employees reporting cold spots, overwhelming feelings of dread and foreboding, and the sound of sobbing and crying from within the empty cell. One story often told is of a prisoner who was locked inside the cell in the 1940s. He began screaming one night, claiming a creature with glowing eyes was killing him. The next day, guards found him strangled to death. Yet, guards the next day counted one extra prisoner in their head count, as if the dead man's ghost was in line with the living inmates.

Another story is told of "Warden Johnston," who experienced someone sobbing inside the prison walls while he was showing a group around the prison. A cold wind blew past the group, although no doors or windows were around. In cellblocks A and B, visitors have heard crying and moaning from inside empty cells, the smell of smoke, unexplained cold spots throughout, and the ghosts of prisoners and military personnel inside and on the grounds. Before it was a federal penitentiary, Alcatraz was a military barracks and before that, it was believed by Native Americans to be the stomping ground of evil spirits.

Sometimes, when the island is shrouded in fog, people report screams, clanging metal doors, whistles, shouts of men's voices, and cries of pain coming from the prison, especially near the dungeon area. Guards and their families who lived on the island when it was a prison claimed to constantly experience apparitions of phantom soldiers and prisoners as well as a strange entity with glowing eyes they dubbed "The Thing." They also heard phantom cannon fire, gunshots, and screams so real the guards believed prisoners had escaped and were firing at them. But there was never anyone there. Now that the island is a national park, park rangers are often on scene, and some have reported hearing the sound of a banjo coming from the shower room inside after all the tourists have gone home for the day.

Many men died, prisoners and guards alike, during several escape attempts, including one in May 1946 that resulted in the deaths of three inmates and two guards, with eighteen other men wounded. Two more prisoners were executed after a trial was held, and they were found guilty.

Some psychics and paranormal researchers suggest Alcatraz may be a portal to another dimension, known to the Native Americans who once lived on the island. That could explain the decades of terrifying events, or it could just be haunted by the ghosts of those humans who suffered there.

West Virginia Moundsville Penitentiary

From 1867 to 1995, the West Virginia Penitentiary operated in Moundsville. Over its century of operation, it would gain the reputation as being one of the most notorious prisons and even made the Department of Justice's Top Ten Violent Correctional Facilities. It was considered the final stop for over one thousand criminals. One location in the prison was a recreation room labeled "The Sugar Shack," a hotbed of raping, fighting, and gambling. Thirty-six murders occurred in the prison before it was closed, and in 1983, Charles Manson asked to be transferred there but was denied.

One of the most notable dates associated with the prison is January 1, 1986, when one of the most infamous riots in history took place at the prison caused by a combination of lax prison security with declining conditions, overcrowding (often there were three men in one cell), and the rapid spread of diseases. The fact that it was also a holiday meant fewer employees and guards on staff. Knife-wielding inmates took over a dozen hostages, and in the end, two prisoners were killed.

But even prior to the riot, death was everywhere. From 1899 to 1959, ninety-four men were executed there, often by hanging. Up until 1931, the public was invited to view the hangings. Around 1951, execution by electrocution was the order of the day, and an electric chair named "Old Sparky" was built by a prison inmate named Paul Glenn. In 1965, the state outlawed execution.

Ghost-hunting groups visit the prison often and report a host of paranormal activity, including apparitions, ghostly screams, voices from empty cells, cold spots, and an overwhelming sense of heaviness and foreboding. Some of the more notable ghosts on-site include the spirit of an inmate who posed as the maintenance man to spy on other prisoners and report them to the staff. He was attacked in the bathroom and brutally murdered. His ghost now lurks about the bathroom where he was killed. Another ghost, Robert, was an inmate killed by guards who enjoyed beating the prisoners close to death. In Robert's case, he died, and his body was buried inside the wall. His ghost now walks the prison and terrifies visitors who try to communicate with him.

Another inmate, Avril Adkins, was hanged to death, but his execution was botched when he fell through the gallows trap doors and bled from a head injury. The guards took him back up and hanged him again, this time killing him for sure. His ghost is reportedly seen walking around the gallows.

PHILADELPHIA EASTERN STATE PENITENTIARY

Opened in 1829, Eastern State Penitentiary served as a prison until it was closed in 1970 and was eventually abandoned. It was once the most famous and most expensive prison in the world, but today, it is a National Historic Site that relies on fundraising efforts and notoriety from ghost hunters to preserve the building, now home to the "Terror Behind the Walls" haunted attraction and tour. The great, grand architecture looks like a gothic castle and once housed an experimental prison that sought to reform prisoners through strict isolation for twenty-three hours of the day, with only a daily visit from the guards or warden. The prison had running water, heat, and flush toilets before the White House did and became the model for prisoners worldwide both for its wagon-wheel floor plan and the use of solitary confinement.

Former inmates include gangster Al Capone and bank robber "Slick Willie" Sutton, and although the prison doesn't have the violent reputation of Alcatraz, visitors today report phantom shouts, whispers, laughter, and weeping from inside the empty cellblocks as well as mysterious images captured on cameras.

THE OLD JAIL

In St. Augustine, Florida, a city itself steeped in history, the Old Jail was built in 1891 by a man named Henry Flagler. It served as a prison until 1953. There were about sixty prisoners, and the sheriff and his family lived inside the same building, adjacent to the prison. Visitors to the jail today can tour and see the actual cells, weapons of the time, and even the execution gallows that took the lives of many prisoners who didn't die of disease and pestilence. Many tourists report strange odors, the sound of footsteps, disembodied moaning, jangling chains, and the barking of phantom dogs. The building has since been listed in the National Register of Historic Places and the National Directory of Haunted Places.

Once one of the most expensive and secure prisons in America, the Philadelphia Eastern State Penitentiary now hosts haunted tours.

The Notorious Andersonville Civil War Prison

No doubt the most notorious prison ever built on American soil, the Civil War prison in Andersonville, Georgia, was a horrific place. Home to over forty-five thousand Union Soldiers from 1863 to 1865 and hundreds of guards and prison staff, the horrendous conditions led to the deaths of at least thirteen thousand men before it was shut down. In fact, historians and researchers alike have said the war was the easy part. Andersonville was living hell. No wonder its front gates became known as "the gates to hell." The stockade fence was made of fifteen- to twenty-foot-tall pine logs, and twenty feet within the perimeter was a light fence known as the "deadline." Prisoners who attempted crossing the deadline were immediately shot by guards.

The Confederate prison camp was built about sixty miles southwest of Macon, Georgia, and took its name from a village in Sumter County, as it was originally named Fort Sumter. It was built upon swampland and bisected by a stream, which no doubt led to some of the thirty thousand prisoners being exposed to deadly typhoid and typhus. Along with starvation, lack of water, infections and injuries left untreated, scurvy, fevers, and other illnesses, the men held in the hellhole known as Andersonville died at a rate of three thousand per month from March to August 1864.

The horrific treatment caused outrage in the outside world, but it didn't save the lives of the thirteen thousand who died there. When the war ended, Captain Henry Wirz, the stockade commander at the prison, was convicted of murder and sent to the scaffold on November 10, 1865. The prison has gone down in history as an "American Auschwitz." There are numerous ghosts to attest to the suffering experienced on the grounds.

The ghost of Captain Wirz is often seen near the old stockade grounds, and the sounds of large groups of men talking can be heard by visitors, including shouts and yells from inside the camp. At night, it is not unusual to hear phantom cannon and gunfire and the moans of men pleading for mercy. People also report apparitions of Civil War soldiers in Confederate and Union uniforms in and around the old prison grounds and the Andersonville National Cemetery, including a man with one leg and a crutch who floats just above the ground.

The cemetery contains 13,714 graves, 921 of which are unmarked. When fog surrounds the area, the sound of invisible horses can be heard as well as men talking and crying and the smell of food cooking over a fire. Strange lights dance within the fog, but upon further inspection, there is nothing and no one there.

Ohio State Reformatory and Ohio State Penitentiary

The state of Ohio is home to two notoriously haunted prisons. The Ohio State Reformatory is in Mansfield (often referred to as Mansfield Reformatory) and was made famous in the popular movies *Air Force One* and *The Shawshank*

Redemption, the latter of which was based upon the novel by Stephen King. Opened in 1896, it specialized in reforming prisoners who were too old for a juvenile facility but not violent enough to be sent to the Ohio State Penitentiary in Columbus. Those sent to the Mansfield facility were first exposed to humane conditions before the prison, which saw thousands pass through its walls during its operational years, deteriorated into a place where abuse, torture, and death were commonplace. By 1930, the prison was drastically overcrowded, and inhumane treatment was the norm until it closed in 1986. In fact, a number of inmates filed a federal lawsuit against the prison for abusive practices.

Now that it has been closed, the only residents are ghosts of former inmates, guards, and staff in the form of apparitions, phantom footsteps, and overwhelming feelings of dread upon entering the cells. Ghost hunters love the site for its rich activity and even claim the ghost of Helen Glattke, the wife of a former warden, wanders about the apartment they lived in. She was killed in a rather bizarre way, when a loaded gun fell from a closet shelf and shot her.

Ghost hunters love the site for its rich activity and even claim the ghost of Helen Glattke, the wife of a former warden, wanders about the apartment they lived in.

Ohio State Penitentiary opened in the city of Columbus in 1834, when 189 prisoners were moved there under guard from the small frontier jail. It stayed open until 1983 and over its history, hundreds of thousands of prisoners were sent there, thousands of whom died. It was condemned as a place of great abuse to the more violent hard-case criminals incarcerated there, and in 1885, the outdoor gallows were moved inside the prison and the first of twenty-eight men were hanged there before death by electrocution took over in 1897. Over 315 men and women died in that electric chair over the years.

It was not unusual to die from outbreaks of cholera and other diseases related to the awful sanitary conditions if prisoners didn't die first from fire, executions by electric chair, torture at a whipping post, hot ash and coals rubbed into wounds, starvation, or beatings from guards. Those who were sent into the underground "hole" suffered unthinkable agony. Often, prisoners murdered other prisoners, adding to the facility's death count. In April 1930, a massive fire in the prison killed 322 inmates in the west block. It was the worst fire in state history and the worst prison fire ever in the country. After that, inmates reported sightings of apparitions until the entire building was destroyed and replaced with a modern sports arena, which is also said to be haunted! In 1968, a horrible series of riots broke out, which led to the eventual closing of the facility. In 1972, most of the prisoners had been transferred to the Ohio Correctional Facility. Those who remained were the most violent, the psychotic, and the infirm until 1983, when everything was closed for good.

Before its closure, inmates claimed many of the cells were haunted by the ghosts of those who died there. The roar of phantom flames has been reported, as have the screams of men who were burned alive trapped in their cells. Even today, as the sports arena and home to the Columbus national hockey team, people claim to see ghostly apparitions and hear screams and moans inside the facility with no apparent origin as well as in the parking lot late at night.

Lake County Jail

Notorious gangster John Dillinger put Crown Point, Indiana's Lake County Jail on the map of infamy when he escaped from this "unescapable" jail in March 1934. Lake County Jail was built in 1908 and consisted of residences for the local county sheriffs and jail cells as well as police station processing facilities. There were 150 maximum security cells, living areas for the warden and law-enforcement families, a kitchen, barber shop, and garage. Thought to be the finest of its kind in the state, it stayed in operation until the 1970s and is now a historic site. It had the reputation of being unescapable, but Dillinger took away that title.

Though the facilities have undergone restorations, it hasn't stopped stories of people seeing apparitions in the cells and walking the corridors, doors opening and closing by themselves, lights that turn on and off, phantom foot-

This photo of a cellblock at Missouri State Penitentiary illustrates what an absolutely grim, soul-killing prison it was for its inmates.

steps and voices, and spooky images appearing in photographs by volunteer staff and visitors. Don't look for Dillinger's ghost, though, as he did successfully escape!

Missouri State Penitentiary

Also known as "The Walls," this state prison system in Jefferson City was built in the 1830s by the soon-to-be inmates themselves, who made the bricks that the walls were built with. It was originally a small prison with only fifteen inmates, a guard, a warden, and a foreman to oversee the brick making but was expanded upon over the years until it was closed in 2004. The prison was home to some infamous criminals like gangster Charles "Pretty Boy" Floyd, Martin Luther King Jr. assassin James Earl Ray, and notorious kidnappers Carl Austin Hall and Bonnie Heady. All were executed within the prison. A riot in 1954 resulted in the deaths of several inmates, dozens of prisoners and guards suffered injuries, and several buildings were burned.

Forty inmates were executed by gas chamber over the history of the prison, and *Time* labeled it "The Bloodiest 47 Acres in America" due to the rampant violence inside the walls. Nowadays, it is a favorite paranormal hot spot thanks to staff and visitors reporting seeing and interacting with apparitions and ghosts.

Yuma Territorial Prison

Arizona's Yuma Territorial Prison opened on July 1, 1876, when seven inmates were locked inside cells they had built themselves. Over the next thirty-three years, more than three thousand prisoners, including twenty-nine women, would live at the prison. One hundred and eleven of them would die there, mostly from tuberculosis, and although the prison had a reputation for humane treatment, one terrifying place was called the "dark cell," in which misbehaving prisoners were put into isolation and kept on a ball and chain. The prison gave well-behaved inmates regular medical attention and the chance to learn to read and write in the library, where they could check out books for a fee. They also had well-lit and well-ventilated cells compared to others of the time, thanks to a nearby electric generating plant.

Overcrowding forced a new facility to be opened, and the last prisoner left Yuma in September 1909. Yuma High School occupied some of the former prison buildings from 1910 to 1914, and afterward, the prison was overrun with the homeless and drifters, including poor families who lived there during the Great Depression.

Today, there are many ghosts that haunt the prison, offices, and a museum on the Yuma Territorial Prison State Historic Park, including apparitions and prankster ghosts that state historian Marshall Trimble says like the color red and are attracted to children. Objects in the museum move about. At one time, the coins in the cash register drawer of the gift shop lifted out and threw themselves across the room before going back into the register on their own, and people are poked, pinched, and touched with ice-cold fingers. One ghost is claimed to be inmate John Ryan, who was imprisoned around 1900 and wasn't liked among the prison community; he committed suicide in cell 14. Visitors who dare enter the "dark cell" report feeling a dark presence and a strong sense of someone being inside the cell with them. A writer from *Arizona Highways* magazine attempted staying in the dark cell for two days and nights and was given food, water, and a blanket but couldn't survive one day. Within just hours, she was calling out for help and claiming she was not alone in the cell.

Old Charleston Jail

Once called the Old City Jail, the Old Charleston Jail sits upon 4 acres (1.6 hectares) in Charleston, South Carolina. Operational from 1802 to 1939, the prison saw upward of ten thousand deaths from illness, execution, or injuries. It was originally built to house just 130 prisoners, but the usual head count was often double that or more, causing overcrowding and violence. Diseases spread like wildfire among the inmates, many of whom had gained notoriety. Among the most noted inmates were Lavinia Fisher, the first serial killer in the country, along with her husband and gang members; high seas pirates; Denmark Vesey, who attempted a slave revolt and was executed in 1822; and a number of Civil War prisoners of war.

Visitors who dare enter the "dark cell" report feeling a dark presence and a strong sense of someone being inside the cell with them.

In 2003, the facility was opened to tours and ghost hunters and has been featured on several ghost-hunting television shows that claim paranormal activity, including doors that open and close, shadow figures roaming the corridors, strange, white orbs floating throughout the building, phantom footsteps, and the sounds of chains dragging across the floor. A few visitors report seeing a female ghost they believe is that of Lavinia Fisher.

Maxwell Street Police Station and Jail

Imagine a police station located in the heart of a neighborhood so violent, it's been given the nickname "Bloody Maxwell." The Maxwell Street Police Station was built in Chicago, Illinois, in 1889, when the city was made up of Italian immigrants, including the Genna Brothers, who worked with gangster Al Capone making bootleg liquor during Prohibition. When the prison opened its doors, it quickly got a bad reputation not just because of the criminal inmates but because of the crooked police department, who enjoyed mistreating, even torturing, the prisoners. The basement of the prison served as a torture chamber, where inmates were kept in horrific conditions. These prisoners were often poor and incarcerated on minor offenses but subject to brutal treatment because they didn't have the money to bribe the guards or police. Another nickname soon given to the facility was "The Wickedest Police District in the World." Those who visit the imposing corner building today report hearing phantom moaning, crying, and chains rattling as well as shadowy figures moving about the premises.

Haunted Hospitals, Asylums, and Sanatoriums

Today, we think of hospitals as places we go to in an emergency. The goal is to be treated, healed, and hopefully sent home to recover. But there are many older hospitals and institutions where patients didn't fare very well either because of lack of proper treatment or falling victim to strange experimentation. Some hospitals shut down long ago, but the ghosts remain. This is especially true for asylums and institutions for the mentally ill and criminally insane, for often, these people are institutionalized against their will or volition by family members or the courts, and while the end goal may begin as a means to see them get well and become functioning members of society, it rarely ever ends up that way.

These facilities are notorious for the emotional and physical suffering endured within their walls. Whether at the hands of cruel staff or due to a lack of knowledge of correct psychotherapeutic practices, it mattered not because the patients suffered regardless, and their cries and moans of pain and fear can still be heard today.

Linda Vista Community Hospital

Ghost hunters talk about California's Linda Vista Community Hospital as a truly paranormal hot spot filled with ghastly, ghostly activity. The hospital was built in 1904 as the Santa Fe Coastlines Hospital in East Los Angeles, and for a time, it was a great facility that mainly serviced employees of the Santa Fe Railroad. In the early twentieth century, it became the hospital for the growing family neighborhoods of Los Angeles—namely, Boyle Heights—and in 1924, the hospital underwent an expansion, allowing it to increase staff and serve more patients. It officially became the Linda Vista Community Hospital in 1937.

Both the Great Depression and World War II took a toll on the hospital and the neighborhood around it, both becoming less and less affluent. Eventually, gangs came in, and violent crimes escalated. The hospital lost a lot of its funding and staff, and in the 1970s and 1980s, the death toll rose, often consisting of gunshot victims and gang stabbings. In 1988, the hospital was no longer able to accept ambulances, and the level of care declined until the very last patient was released and the hospital closed in 1991. Rumors would persist for years that the high death rate was not about gangs or gunshots but because of abuse and mistreatment of patients by hospital staff.

One hospital that paranormal researchers have considered a hot spot for ghosts for many years is Linda Vista Community Hospital in East Los Angeles.

Even after it closed as a hospital, the site was often used in movies and television series, and soon, security guards and production crews were talking about the ghostly activity. Some were being pushed and touched by unseen hands. Others saw apparitions and shadow figures and heard strange humming from inside the building when no one was there. Three spirits reported most often include a young girl in the surgical room who died in the middle of a surgery, an orderly making his daily rounds, and a nurse or young woman pacing a third-floor hallway. The now abandoned and empty rooms are a favorite spot of overnight ghost-hunting groups, tourists, and vandals. Ghosts and demons seem to prefer room 323, according to those brave enough to have stayed in the hospital overnight. This was where a patient died, and his angry spirit is said to have stayed behind, growling and howling at night. The boiler room is also a hot spot where doctors burned the bodies of the dead patients to make room for new ones. Here, people claim to hear moans and wails of pain.

Part of the hospital was converted to the Linda Vista Senior Apartments, but the ghostly activity remains despite attempts to remodel and remove them.

The Old Tooele Hospital

The Old Tooele Hospital in Utah was once the Lee family home back in 1897. In 1913, it became the Country Poor House, where elderly and special-needs patients were sent to be attended to. By 1953, the building became the official Old Tooele Hospital and boasted improved patient care and accommodations, including bathrooms in each room and an on-site morgue. It closed down in 2001 and is famous for being featured in the television miniseries *The Stand* based on the Stephen King novel.

The site now is haunted by a former Alzheimer's patient called Wes, who likes to visit the room he stayed in before his death. A young child ghost roams the halls as well as Samuel F. Lee, the man who originally built the house in 1897. One of the creepiest reports claims that the child can be heard saying "Daddy, shot, sorry," and the Utah Ghost Organization later researched and learned there had indeed been a child patient in the hospital who had been shot by his father!

Spanish Military Hospital

This hospital operated in St. Augustine, Florida, from 1784 to 1821. During those years, patients and staff often reported a powerful sense of dread or evil, hanging like a dark cloud over the hospital. In 1921, the original building housing the Spanish Military Hospital was torn down to be rebuilt. Part of the restoration involved replacing water lines, and when the city dug up the old ones, they made a horrific discovery. Thousands of human bones had been buried below the hospital, and it was then learned that the original land was once a sacred Indian burial ground. Now, the spirits of the dead had been awakened and soon joined the ghosts of the many patients who came into the hospital sick, horribly disfigured, or wounded. Some patients had to undergo amputations, and their screams of agonizing pain can still be heard echoing against the walls.

Thousands of human bones had been buried below the hospital, and it was then learned that the original land was once a sacred Indian burial ground.

Today, the Spanish Military Hospital Museum stands in its place. Every room of the hospital is said to be haunted, and hospital beds often move by themselves, doors open and close on their own, and apparitions appear and disappear throughout. Visitors also experience strange cold spots and thick fogs and claim they can feel the heaviness of despair that hangs over them like a blanket when they enter the hospital, just as the patients and staff did so long ago.

Taunton State Hospital

Massachusetts's Taunton State Hospital carries the notorious reputation of having housed some of the most notoriously evil people on Earth, including the infamous Jane Toppan, a serial-killer nurse who took the lives of thirty-one people while at Cambridge Hospital. Axe murderess Lizzie Borden claimed she stayed there, but records show she was never admitted to the hospital, only to the jail nearby during her trial. Originally called the State Lunatic Hospital, the facility opened in 1854 on a sprawling piece of land and was later expanded in the 1870s. In the 1930s, juvenile facilities, sick wards, and group homes were added to the 154-acre location. The original main Kirkbride Building stood for over 150 years. The hospital closed in 1975 and was added to the National Register of Historic Places. In later years, the buildings fell to disrepair, the main dome collapsed, and a large fire in 2006 destroyed a large part of the complex. It was later restored in part, enough to stay open to house at least forty-eight beds, and today, the site is also home to a women's addiction recovery program, a residential program for youth offenders, and a greenhouse that provides produce to the staff and public.

During its early years, the hospital was known for mistreating patients, nothing new for many older institutions, but the true evil that occurred there involved satanic rituals and sacrifices in the basement, where doctors and nurses used patients to torture and kill. The building today is haunted by shadow figures who creep about the basement and crawl up the walls.

Athens Mental Hospital

Athens Mental Hospital opened in the town of Athens, Ohio, in 1874 and specialized in the treatment of mentally and criminally insane patients who were admitted by their families through the court system. Before closing in 1993, over 1,900 patients died there and were buried on hospital grounds with headstones marked only with a number. Though the hospital was home to violent criminals, many were just mentally ill and were subjected to horrendous treatment, including electric shocks, ice pick lobotomies, and being immersed in ice-cold water for extended periods of time.

In December 1978, a woman named Margaret Schilling was a patient at the hospital. She was playing hide and seek with the nurses. The nurses were distracted and forgot about Margaret. One year later, a maintenance worker found her body, and today, visitors say you can see the imprint of her form on the floor, even after years of cleaning.

The burial site is known to be haunted by a number of ghostly entities that appear at night beside the grave markers along with the sounds of tortured screams.

People visiting the Kennedy Museum of Art on the Ohio University campus in Athens might not realize that it was once a mental hospital that closed in 1993.

Alton Mental Health Hospital

This mental hospital in Alton, Illinois, still operates today and had the nice and politically correct sense to not call itself a "lunatic asylum." Built in the early 1900s, it had a reputation for patient abuse and even torture, including ice pick lobotomies, electric shock therapy, and ice-cold water immersion, all of which were "normal, standard practices" in mental institutions of the time quite simply because they lacked the scientific knowledge of more modern times.

Today, staff, patients, and guests all report doors slamming shut, disembodied voices, unusual noises at night, and even a voice that asks, "Who's that?" when no one is around. The hospital is not open to tours, as it is still a functioning facility, but visitors of sick patients report seeing strange orbs with painted human faces on them.

Byberry Mental Hospital

This Pennsylvania mental institution opened its doors in 1907 and was originally a working farm for the mentally ill. It became an actual hospital in the 1920s and soon, the population was overflowing and conditions deteriorated. Patients suffered from neglect and, in some cases, horrific abuse, and many had no clothing, little food, and slept in sewage-filled hallways. Money was tight, and the hospital operated on such a low budget, it often took it out on the most vulnerable, the patients, who soon became subjected to regular beatings, padded cells, restraining devices, and lobotomies to control their behavior.

The state shut down the hospital in 1990 after the horrific living conditions were exposed in an investigation, and it soon became the home of Satan worshippers, vagrants, drug users, gangs, and criminals. There were claims of huge catacombs beneath the hospital where a violent patient was said to hide out and slit the throats of anyone who crossed his path. Today, visitors and ghost hunters alike experience a host of strange sounds, apparitions, humanlike growls, and scratches on their bodies.

Arkansas Tuberculosis Sanitorium

Known to locals as "Booneville," the now abandoned sanitorium was built in 1863 on a rural hill just outside of Booneville, Arkansas. The eight-hundred-acre property is off the beaten path and once housed over a thousand patients and three hundred staff members. The main hospital was named after state senator Leo Nyberg, who himself was a tuberculosis (TB) patient. The disease ran out of control for thousands but in the 1800s and early 1900s, there was little known about the causes and proper treatments. Sanitoriums were built all over the country to accommodate and quarantine the sick away from the general public, and often, patients were kept in horribly inadequate conditions until they died. Young people suffered the most from TB as well as the poor.

Booneville consisted at one point of seventy-six different buildings and became its own city with telephone lines, a chapel, lodge, water treatment plant, and fire department. Patients paid ten dollars a week to stay. The sanatorium closed in 1973 and is now owned by the state. Some of the buildings still serve patients as the Booneville Human Development program, and the first floor of the main Nyberg Building was completely renovated. The basement and additional floors are vacant. The sanatorium has been added to the National Register of Historic Places as of 2006. It is not open to the public, but some ghost-hunting groups have been allowed on-site to do investigations and have come away with tales of being touched, having pebbles tossed at them, and seeing apparitions, including one of a little girl and another of a man wearing a top hat. Maintenance crewmembers report encounters with apparitions, cold spots, and a foreboding heaviness and sense of dread on the upper floors and basement.

Danvers Lunatic Asylum

The Danvers, Massachusetts, asylum was a prison and an asylum in one. The gothic building was built in 1878 as a prison for the criminally insane but soon added mentally ill people, the handicapped, alcoholics, and regular felons into the mix. In the early 1930s, the facility had become so understaffed that patients would die and days would pass before their bodies were even discovered. Designed to house only six hundred patients, there were often over one thousand waiting in complete isolation for days, even weeks, to be attended to. As with most asylums, shock therapy and lobotomies were standard practice in those days, and this facility is considered one of the first to use prefrontal lobotomies.

To take care of the large number of deaths, a large cemetery is located on the grounds. The asylum was officially closed in 1992, demolished, and replaced with apartment buildings. But what makes this particular place so spooky, and allegedly haunted, is the fact that it was built upon the original "Salem Village" of the Salem witch trials fame, and it is even referred to as "The Witch's Castle on the Hill," which explains the vast array of paranormal activity on the grounds from full-body apparitions to flickering lights moving about the halls to unexplained noises, phantom footsteps, doors opening and closing, and shadowy figures in and around the cemetery.

Pennhurst Asylum

Spring City, Pennsylvania's Pennhurst Asylum is considered one of the most haunted places in the state. Its actual name is Pennhurst State School and Hospital and was originally intended as a school and hospital but not a mental hospital. Yet, when it opened its doors, it was under the name Eastern Pennsylvania State Institution for the Feeble-Minded and Epileptic. It was supposed to offer rehab services for mentally challenged and disabled individuals, all good intentions, of course, and in 1908, the first patient was admitted to the complex of buildings.

Below the buildings, fireproof tunnels had been built that connected one to the other, and there were dormitories and cottages throughout the grounds.

An aerial view of the Pennhurst State School and Hospital taken in 1934 shows an extensive complex of buildings. The hospital was under investigation a couple of times for poor conditions and staff abuse of patients.

Though it was described as a school, very few patients got any education services there. Instead, patients were taught basic hygiene and self-care, and soon, there were reports of patient abuse and humiliation by staff. Other patients were drugged through their IVs to be kept sedated, and some were chained to their beds to keep them from getting out of control.

Like so many other mental hospitals, overcrowding became an issue, and lack of funds meant there was a shortage of clean diapers, food, and even water. The building would stink of urine, mold, and feces, and residents were filthy and miserable, but they couldn't speak out because of their mental illnesses. Over ten thousand adults and children passed through the asylum doors over its history, including many who were autistic, an illness no one at the time knew how to treat or even deal with. Child patients would be found trapped inside metal cribs, smeared in their own waste, injured from trying to pry their way out.

Cruel treatment and punishments were common, and many patients simply lost their will to live. Often, they would bite as their only way to show anger only to have their teeth removed in a disgusting, rusty dentist chair with old, rusted tools. Visitors were appalled at the conditions, and in 1968, a television news station did an exposé and uncovered the many atrocities there. The asylum closed its doors for good in 1987, and the buildings and tunnels were left to neglect.

Caretakers on the property today, as well as visitors and ghost-hunting groups who love to explore the site, report slamming doors, angry spirits of past patients, phantom footsteps, and the sound of vomiting from inside empty rooms. The spirit of a little girl is said to roam the main building, and it is normal to experience sudden drops in temperature in different places in the building. Items move about on their own and sometimes are hurled across the room at visitors. People are also pushed by unseen hands, and chilling EVP has recorded disembodied voices saying things like "Get out!", "Why won't you leave?", and even "I'll kill you!"

Full-body apparitions are seen in the school areas of the building, and ghost hunters report feeling something brushing past them. Doors slam and open and close, and in the mental hospital section, where a great deal of suffering occurred, children can be heard crying and screaming in pain.

Sierra Sky Ranch and Resort

Apparently, it's never a good idea to turn a cattle ranch into a sanatorium for tuberculosis patients, then turn that into a guest ranch. All those changes tend to stir up spirits. The Sierra Sky Ranch was once a working cattle ranch in Oakhurst, California, near Yosemite National Park back in 1875. By 1898, it was the largest cattle ranch in the state. It was sold in the late 1920s and turned into a tuberculosis sanatorium. In World War II, it was also used to treat wounded and sick soldiers after the U.S. Army purchased the land. Today, it is a popular guest ranch for tourists heading to Yosemite National Park nearby and is haunted by a number of ghosts, including a cowboy who committed suicide during its ranching days, two children and a nurse who died at the sanatorium, and a piano-playing spirit that can be heard at random times. Spooky mists float through the air on the grounds, possibly apparitions of other ghosts that died on the property under one of its many incarnations.

Norwich State Hospital

The doors to the Norwich State Hospital in Preston, Connecticut, opened for business in October 1904. The grounds took up almost one hundred scenic acres of land along the Thames River that was once a Native American village. At the time, there were only ninety-five patients, but with the advent of tuberculosis, the hospital was expanded to 470 acres (190 hectares) with over thirty buildings housing over two thousand mentally ill and sick patients as well as those who were chemically dependent or alcoholics. There were also approximately seven hundred patients labeled criminally insane. The first death was recorded the year it opened when a patient hanged himself. In 1919, a hot water

Open from 1904 to 1996, Norwich State Hospital in Connecticut grew from one to thirty buildings treating the mentally ill, drug addicts, geriatric patients, and people with tuberculosis.

heater exploded, killing two hospital staff members. Other deaths occurred over the years, both patients and staff, before the hospital closed its doors in 1996. A hospital employee was killed crossing the road outside the grounds. A nurse committed suicide in her home, and many patients died at the facility while undergoing treatments that no doubt bordered on barbaric. In fact, published reports and investigations into abuse allegations revealed the staff members were starving, beating, sexually abusing, and exposing patients to solitary confinement and harsh restraining methods. They were even accused of packing living patients in ice!

Underground tunnels connected the main buildings, including the most actively haunted according to ghost hunters, the Salmon and the Earle buildings. The town of Preston purchased the property in 2009, and it has been abandoned since. The buildings have been vacant for years partially due to the cost of clean-up of the original site.

Paranormal activity has been reported by ghost hunters who visit the site, including apparitions, disembodied voices, unexplained mists and shapes, objects moving about the hospital on their own, doors opening and slamming shut, the phantom cries of a woman sobbing, strange beeping sounds coming from the former lobotomy room, and sudden blasts of cold air during the hot summer months with no visible source.

Essex Mountain Sanatorium

In 1873, the Newark City Home was opened as an orphanage in Essex County, New Jersey. The building, often called Overbrook because it overlooked the Peckham River, also served as a place to reform children with behavioral problems, but a fire forced the reconstruction of two buildings, and the decline of female patients resulted in the female "dorm" becoming the new Essex Mountain Sanatorium in 1906. This would be a place specifically devoted to tuberculosis patients. It was known by locals as the Hilltop, and in 1917, the county took control of the facility and added eleven new buildings.

When medical treatments for TB caused a decrease in patient numbers, the buildings at the top of the hill eventually became abandoned; however, rumors spread of activity at the asylum involving torture using medieval restraint devices and surgical tools. By the 1970s, the vacant wards took in an overflow of mental patients from the nearby asylum, and soon, stories were spreading of lunatics running loose in the hills around the facility.

Only the really brave dare to explore the tunnel complex underneath the facility or the lower-level morgue, where shadow figures are commonly seen.

The sanatorium closed its doors officially in 1977. Since then, it has become a popular ghost-hunting spot, and some people love to drive up the sanatorium road to the top of the hill and explore the vacant buildings that stand amid the forest, often encountering ghost faces looking at them through windows, wheelchairs moving down the halls on their own, phantom footsteps and the sound of running, and eerie, disembodied voices shouting, "Get out!" Only the really brave dare to explore the tunnel complex underneath the facility or the lower-level morgue, where shadow figures are commonly seen. Apparitions are sometimes attributed to the twenty-four patients who died over the course of twenty days at the facility when the boilers failed and a spate of cold weather caused frostbite and eventual death from exposure.

Rolling Hills Asylum

Rolling Hills Asylum began in 1827 as the Genesee County Poor Farm in the small town of East Bethany, New York, near Lake Ontario and Lake Erie, between the cities of Buffalo and Rochester. It was basically an immense almshouse where the poor, infirm, orphaned, and widowed were sent to live alongside the severely mentally handicapped, criminally insane, and alcoholic. Over 1,700 undocumented deaths occurred on the site, and hundreds of unidentified bodies are buried beneath the asylum, making this one of the most haunted places on Earth. Over the years, it also served as a tuberculosis sanatorium and as an orphanage and in 1964 became a nursing home until it was closed in 1974 because of building code issues. Many of the outbuildings were torn down, as were the dorms, to keep out vagrants and criminals.

The 53,000-square-foot (4,925-square-meter) main building is haunted by shadow figures that creep out from rooms and shuffle or crawl down the hallways. Phantom screams are commonplace, as are doors slamming, ghostly touches, full-body apparitions, and weird voices heard on EVP. The apparition of Roy Crouse, a 7.5-foot (2.3-meter) giant who died as a patient there in 1942, walks the building. He was fifty-two and had spent most of his life at the asylum. One hot spot is "Hattie's Room," a room on the first floor in the East Wing, where an elderly woman's voice was captured on a digital EVP recording saying "hello." Former employees who heard the tape identified the voice as being Hattie's. On the second floor of the East Wing, people report shadowy figures moving down the hall toward the infirmary, sometimes human-shaped and other times more amorphous.

Ghostly voices are common down in the morgue, and people have been shoved and pushed in the room. There was once a cemetery on the property, with tall grass now covering crumbled stone markings. Many asylums did have on-site burial grounds for the horrendous number of deaths that occurred within their walls. Rolling Hills appears to be no different.

Trans-Allegheny Asylum

TALA, the Trans-Allegheny Lunatic Asylum in Weston, West Virginia, is hugely popular with ghost-hunting groups and has been featured on numerous television reality shows. The building itself is incredibly impressive and is the world's second-biggest, hand-cut stone masonry building in the world after the Kremlin. Even before entering, the building looks imposing and the stuff of horror and thriller movies. It was built during the Civil War and began taking patients in 1861 even before construction was completed. It officially opened in 1864 to house about 250 patients but, as with other asylums written about here, ended up overcrowded. At one point, over 2,400 people were patients there, including cult leader Charles Manson.

The Trans-Allegheny Lunatic Asylum is a treasure trove of history and stories about the Civil War, a gold robbery, ghosts, and more. Tours are available, and the facility has been featured on ghost-hunting TV shows.

Formerly known as Weston State Hospital, it sat upon, eerily, 666 acres (270 hectares) of land, and the first floor was called the Civil War Wing, the oldest, and many claim the most haunted, part of the building. Many of the patients in the asylum were thought to be possessed by demons, and many others were sent there for ridiculous reasons such as "female troubles," falling off a horse, and laziness. Women who were deserted by their spouses often were committed alongside murderers and the truly insane. Soon, the abuse and barbaric treatment of these individuals, who often had no family to look in on them, marked this facility as a place of great suffering and horror. As overcrowding spread, so, too, did the abuse and poor living conditions. It officially closed in 1994 and was reopened in 2007 for historic and ghost-hunting tours. It soon became a favorite ghost-hunting destination and favorite spot for paranormal events and guided tours with popular television stars, charging hundreds of dollars to attend and get a firsthand look at the asylum and its resident spirits.

Ghostly activity has been reported for decades since the closure of the asylum in 1994, including apparitions roaming the hallways, disembodied voices, doors opening and slamming shut, strange smells, phantom screams from the electroshock room, and the sounds of gurneys squeaking down the corridors. A ghost boy is often spotted in the corner of one room, and a former staff member claims she saw forty doors slam shut at the same time. The ghost of a woman named Jane Harvey, who committed suicide in 1884, roams the second floor of Ward B. Her voice shows up on EVP recordings, and visitors claim someone is strangling them when near her room.

Another ghost of a man named Jesse Albright, who died in 1949 after spending seven years at TALA, is often heard whispering to guests, and he answers when his name is called.

Waverly Hills

Anyone interested in ghost hunting and paranormal research is sure to react to the name Waverly Hills. This two-story facility located in southwestern Louisville has been a hugely popular destination for those interested in seeking out the spirits of the dead, and it is considered a highly active site, if not one of the most active in the country hands down. In the late 1800s, Waverly School opened in Kentucky and in 1910 was converted into a hospital intended to accommodate up to fifty tubercular patients. But no one knew just how badly the disease would spread, and as the epidemic grew, so did the asylum's capacity, taking in over four hundred patients at one time. The facility had a great reputation for cleanliness and care and stayed open until 1961, when antibiotics were introduced to fight TB.

But that's not the whole story behind Waverly Hills. During the fifty years it was functional, over 64,000 patients died there, mostly from TB, but others from mistreatment, outright abuse, and, rumor has it, human experimentation, including illegal syphilis studies. Deaths became so frequent that a "death tunnel" was created—a type of chute to send dead patients underground via a motorized rail and cable system that took the bodies to trains waiting on the tracks at the bottom of the hill.

Today, it is open to tours and ghost hunts, and one of the most haunted rooms is Room 502, where a distraught nurse who was pregnant by the owner of the sanatorium hanged herself in 1928. A second nurse fell to her death from the same room; she has been caught on EVP and may be the ghost of a nurse in her white uniform that roams the floor. The death tunnel is actively haunted with apparitions and disembodied voices. A little boy ghost named Timmy can be seen and heard playing with rubber balls. The ghost of a man dressed in a white coat and pants lurks around the cafeteria and kitchen and visitors report smelling cooking food, despite the kitchen, having been closed to the public for over forty years.

Children are seen and heard running through a third-floor solarium, slamming doors, and walking in many of the rooms. Perhaps the eeriest spectral spook is that of a phantom, old-fashioned hearse that is seen delivering coffins to the back of the facility. Waverly Hills is now closed to the public except for arranged tours and special paranormal events.

CREEPY SCHOOLS, COLLEGES, AND UNIVERSITIES

Education is the foundation of a successful life as long as the presence of ghosts doesn't interfere with the learning process. All over the country, there are schools, colleges, and universities with their own amazing ghost stories. It's hard enough to get students to focus on their work. Imagine taking an important test while apparitions walk past the classroom door, waving hello.

Ohio University

Ohio University is a large public research university in Athens, Ohio. Founded in 1804, it is home to approximately twenty-four thousand students on the 1,800-acre campus. It is considered one of the most student-friendly universities in the country. It is also considered one of the most haunted campuses in the country. It was built upon a former burial ground. It was also the site of a former insane asylum. Talk about a double curse. It is located in the center of a pentagram shape of nearby cemeteries, too. All bets are off here, where a number of rooms and buildings are said to be home to spirits, including the infamous haunted dorm room 428 of Wilson Hall. In the 1970s, a woman attending classes began shouting in a strange language and acting as though she were possessed. She fell to her death from a window and haunts the school so much that the actual room 428 in Wilson Hall was shut off to students to this day.

Smith College's Spirits

Smith College in Northampton, Massachusetts, is the largest women's college in the United States. Since 1871, it has given the world some notable alumnae including Gloria Steinem, Betty Friedan, and Sylvia Plath as well as a host of other influential leaders, writers, artists, and scholars. The buildings date back to the Colonial Era and sport a rich history filled with murders, epidemic outbreaks, and accidents, thus giving it another title: one of the most haunted colleges in New England. In fact, the college website continually updates reported ghost activity on campus. One of the most tragic centers is the Sessions House, which was built in 1751. The building was once an old boardinghouse. An American young woman and a British soldier were lovers who met under a hidden staircase, and their spirits are said to be quite active along with the ghost of a senior citizen who died from a gas oven left on, a little boy who died in the attic, and a mother who walks the floors with the baby she murdered in real life. The baby can be heard crying at night.

University of Notre Dame

This legendary university doesn't need ghost stories to have become famous. It has the Fighting Irish football team, the legendary alumnus Knute Rockne, and a top-rated marching band to boot. Founded in 1842, the University of Notre Dame du Lac is a private research university located in the community of Notre Dame, Indiana. One of the few universities to regularly rank in the top twenty-five in the *U.S. News & World Report* survey of best American colleges, it is both a legendary "football campus" and one of the most prominent Catholic universities in the country. It is also alleged to be widely haunted, thanks to its rich history, with activity thick around the Washington Hall theater. Built in 1881, a construction worker fell off the roof to his death and now haunts the building along with a music student who likes to play the French horn at night when there is no one around. The most famous Notre Dame spirit, though, is football hero George Gipp, who died in 1920 of pneumonia after having won the biggest victory of his playing career. Gipp played several positions, including quarterback, halfback, and punter, and was named the university's first Walter Camp All-American player. He had incredible spirit in life and sometimes played with injuries that would have benched any other player. After his death, Coach Knute Rockne went on to give his memorable "Win One for the Gipper" halftime speech. Students and staff on campus report seeing the Gipper's ghost riding a white horse up the stairs and through Washington Hall.

Gettysburg Has a Haunted College, Too!

Located near the haunted battlefield where some of the bloodiest Civil War skirmishes and attacks played out with ultimate casualties reaching as high as fifty thousand soldiers, the Gettysburg College also has some ghost stories of its own. The four-year liberal arts college was built in 1832 on 225 acres (91 hectares) just adjacent to the battlefield. The college's Penn Hall, the oldest building on the campus, was used during the war as a hospital and morgue, so it's only natural much of the paranormal activity centers there. Campus administrators report being in the elevator when it malfunctioned. The elevator took them down to the building's basement, where they were shocked to see a ghostly field hospital in operation when the doors opened complete with doctors and wounded soldiers covered in blood.

Ghosts also wander the halls of two residence halls, Stevens Hall and Huber Hall, dressed in soldier's uniforms. One particular ghost, the Lone Sentinel, is a soldier carrying a gun that marches on top of Penn Hall and takes aim at passing students, who sometimes don't realize they are looking at a spectral shooter.

Wells College

Originally founded in 1868 as a women's private liberal arts college, Wells College bears the name of its founder, Henry Wells, who also founded Wells Fargo Bank and American Express. The sister college to Cornell University is smaller in size, located in the rural town of Aurora, New York. There are approximately 125 staff members and five hundred students on campus of both genders. In October 2004, after 136 years as a women-only institution, Wells announced it was opening its doors to male students as well. There were protests on campus over the decision, and a lawsuit was filed opposing the decision on behalf of female residents but was rejected in court. In 2005, Wells College officially became coeducational.

It has consistently been at the top of the *U.S. News & World Report*'s College Rankings list and boasts a strong educational learning system. It also boasts ghosts! During a particularly harsh winter, the campus was hit with a bad flu breakout, and the fourth floor of the main building on campus was used as a quarantine area. Several students died, and because there was no place to bring the bodies, another room was turned into a makeshift morgue, with its door painted red to warn anyone against accidentally entering the room.

The elevator took them down to the building's basement, where they were shocked to see a ghostly field hospital in operation when the doors opened....

Years later, the door was repainted on several occasions, but the red kept coming back through. Even though the building has undergone some changes, students allegedly search for the mysterious red door. The ghosts that haunt the campus include Max the security guard, who lost his wife while getting students to safety during a fire on campus. His hands are reported to push students in a stairwell as if trying to get them out safely. A former female science student haunts Zabriskie Hall. The story goes that she was stabbed to death by her professor after accusing him of stealing her work and putting his own name on it. Students studying late at night say her ghost will approach them and ask to have the knife pulled from her back only to have her then try to stab them with it!

Kenyon College

Ransom Hall at Kenyon College serves currently as the admissions building. The Ohio college is haunted by several spirits, including a student who died in a fraternity hazing and nine others killed in a fire.

Kenyon College is another private liberal arts institution, located in Gambier, Ohio, on a rural, 1,000-acre (400-hectare) campus that includes a nature preserve, the Brown Family Environment Center, which boasts over 382 acres (155 hectares) and seven different ecosystems. Founded in 1824 by Ohio's first Episcopal bishop, Philander Chase, it has under two thousand undergraduates on campus and is officially credited by the Higher Learning Commission. It is one of the oldest and most prestigious learning institutions in the Midwest.

Despite its tranquil setting (it is nicknamed "Hidden Ivy" for its remote setting), the entrance to the South Campus is known as the "Gates of Hell." The south entrance is avoided by students anytime close to midnight, when church bells chime. Legend has it if you cross the stone pillars while the bells are ringing, your soul will go straight to hell. The oldest known ghost on campus is Stuart Preston, who died back in 1905 in a fraternity hazing. He was left on a trestle by his frat brothers, who then forgot to come and take him down. He was struck and killed by a train. Even today, as his spirit haunts the Old Kenyon Residence Hall, the DKE fraternity members have a ritual of carrying a coffin to the trestle and reading the coroner's report aloud.

Other ghosts are said to be those of the nine students tragically killed in a fire in Old Kenyon in 1949. Students report waking up to bloodcurdling screams, flickering lights, and shouted warnings to get out of the building. The Greenhouse Ghost was a diver who was killed when he dove through a glass ceiling into the Shaffer Pool below. The Caples Residence Hall is home to a young, male ghost who died falling down an elevator shaft in 1979. Students in Caples report waking up to the smell of alcohol and the sense of an invisible person sitting on their beds.

A professor named Tim Shutt had led ghost tours of the college, and security guards claim the security office is a part of one of the most haunted buildings on the campus.

Boston University

Boston University is a private, nonprofit, research university located in Boston, Massachusetts. The university has been historically affiliated with the

United Methodist Church but is a nonsectarian learning institution. The university has more than 3,900 faculty members and nearly thirty-three thousand students and is one of the city of Boston's largest employers. There are two very famous ghosts that haunt the campus.

Famed dramatist and Nobel laureate in literature Eugene O'Neill died in 1953 in what is now Kilachand Hall. Before becoming a college building, it was a hotel frequented by the writer, known for *Long Day's Journey into Night* among other masterpieces, whose ghost is said to continue to haunt the hall. Flickering lights, an elevator that halts randomly on the fourth floor, and bizarre knocks on doors have been reported by students who reside there.

The second ghost of note is that of the notorious Boston Strangler serial killer, whose spirit now lurks around Myers Standish Hall. The Boston Strangler, who was later revealed to be a man named Albert DeSalvo, murdered thirteen women in the Boston area during the early 1960s. He later confessed, and DNA evidence confirmed his link to the final murder victim.

Rumor has it that students come back to their dorm rooms in Myers Hall to find their rooms being rummaged through, despite the doors being locked. As a creepy aside, the building code to Myers Hall is 666. Perhaps he is seeking new victims in death among the college students returning late at night to the safety of their rooms.

Penn State

Pennsylvania State University is a multicampus institution with campuses and affiliate facilities located throughout the state. The main campus was established in 1855 in the rural University Park area and boasts approximately fifty thousand students with an additional fifty thousand at satellite campuses. It is considered one of the most prestigious learning institutions in the country, if not the world, and it is riddled with ghosts.

The main campus alone is notoriously haunted, spawning the university's own paranormal research group on the site, the Paranormal Research Society, which has over forty members. The paranormal activity at Penn is so common and commonly known, there are tours on campus, especially at Halloween, and the hauntings have become a fixed part of the college culture.

Undoubtedly, the most widely known spirit is that of the school's first mascot, a mule named Old Coaly, born in 1855, the same year that Penn State traditionally observes the date it was founded, who continues to wander the halls. Students report the sounds of his hooves clip-clopping across the campus and hear his distinct brays. The Schwab Auditorium is particularly active, with students reporting chairs that move up and down with no one touching them, flickering lights, and the frequent apparition of three different ghosts, including the former janitor. In fact, Charles Schwab, the former industrialist after

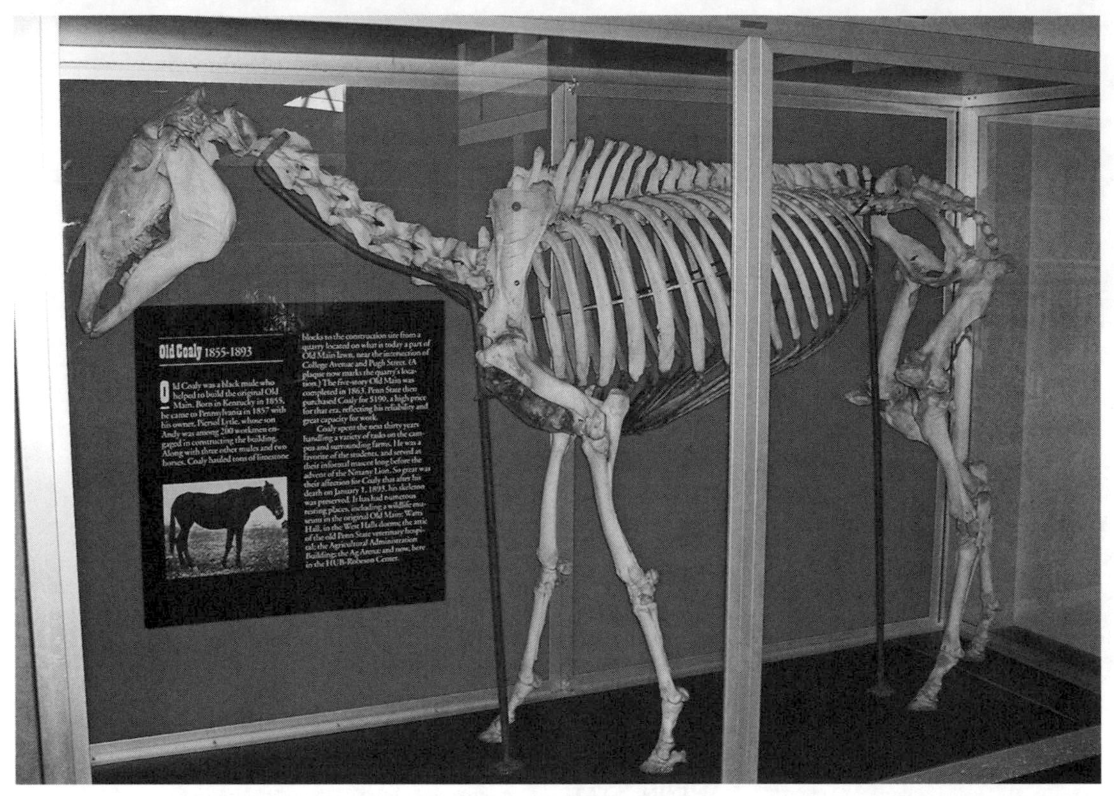

The skeleton of Old Coaly is preserved at Penn State's Hetzel Union Building. The mule, the first mascot of the university, is said to still wander campus halls, and students have reported hearing the clip-clop of hooves.

whom the auditorium was named, is said to be one of the ghosts. He was a former Penn State trustee and funded construction of the auditorium, as he was a huge supporter of the arts. Apparently, he likes to stick around and watch the performances in the small, nine-hundred-seat auditorium. There is also a female spirit, objects that move across the floor on their own, and the sound of noises echoing from upper floors. When students go to investigate, there is no one there.

Another famously haunted site on campus is the Old Botany Building situated along Pollack Road. It is a simple building but houses quite a bit of ghostly activity, according to students and researchers who've visited the red-brick cottage. The ghost of Frances Atherton, the wife of former university president George Atherton, is said to haunt the structure, and she is often spotted looking out an upper-floor window across the street to the cemetery where George is buried. Because the walkway past the building is so busy, there have been numerous reports of Frances standing, looking anxiously out, not even noticing the parade of students below.

Luckily, the many ghosts of Penn State are generally said to be friendly, or at least neutral, but they make for great late-night conversations on dark and stormy nights around the campus. The campus Ghost Walk allows new students to see and hear the legendary stories of the Penn State's paranormal reputation while locating the hot spots they may wish to visit later or avoid altogether.

Mont Alto's Wiestling Hall is the oldest building in the Penn State complex, built in 1807. It has functioned over the years as a dorm, a dining hall, classrooms, administrative offices, and home to at least two different ghosts. The ghosts are said to be those of Colonel George Wiestling himself, who built the manor with money he earned from the iron trade, and that of a woman named Sarah Matheny, who was murdered nearby in 1911. Students who have roomed or dined there over the years reported phantom footsteps and rapping on doors, and those who had the courage to investigate the building claim their batteries would quickly drain and die.

Penn State Abington sports the ghost of Amelia Earhart, who was a student there and would often climb out of the Sutherland Building's roof at night to look at the stars when the building was known as the Ogontz School for Young Ladies. Students today often claim to hear loud footsteps above on the roof, and when they investigate, there is no one there. They believe it is Amelia's ghost going up to see the stars she loved.

Penn State Wilkes-Barre was founded in 1916 to train engineers for the bustling coal industry. A family of coal barons, the Conynghams, donated their majestic home, Hayfield Farms, to Penn State University for its new campus. The father, John Conyngham, is said to have died falling down the home's elevator shaft and now haunts the campus building, slamming doors and making all kinds of noises when no one is around. Others say the ghost of his wife, Bertha, also roams about making sure students respect the building and keep it clean.

Penn State Hazleton is a 125-acre (51-hectare) former estate called Highacres in the small town of Hazelton. It was once the home of a wealthy family, the Markles, who many now believe haunt Schiavo Hall, where night staff and late-studying students hear a host of strange, unexplained noises.

Other Spooky Campuses

There are so many haunted colleges in the country, but some of the most intriguing follow. Chances are whatever college or university one might attend comes fully equipped with its own history as well as its own ghostly tales to tell. This is not a complete list by any means, which suggests that our nation's students are learning their reading, writing, and arithmetic alongside the spirits of the dead. Wonder how their grades are compared to the living?

Flagler College in St. Augustine, Florida, was once the Ponce de León Hotel. The private liberal arts college was founded in 1968 with an additional campus in Tallahassee and is considered the second-best regional college in the South. The college is an example of turn-of-the-century architecture and was built originally as the hotel in the late 1800s by eccentric railroad tycoon Henry Flagler, after whom it is now named. Flagler is known for bringing tourism to the area. His ghost is now said to haunt the Ponce de León Hall. Rumor has it, his last request was that the windows and doors of the building remain open during his funeral, and students claim a janitor closed several, thus resulting in Flagler's spirit being trapped in the building. Students claim that if you speak his name, lights will flicker on and off. A ghost of a small boy who fell from the balcony to his death also haunts the building with ghostly stomping into the wee hours of the night. Students also report waking up to the presence of a ghostly woman dressed in black standing at the foot of their beds and a handyman who likes to whistle as he works in the rooms.

The University of Montevallo is the only public liberal arts college in Alabama. Founded in 1896, it was originally a technical school for women, but many of its buildings are some of the oldest in the state, including King House and Reynolds Hall. It is considered one of the top regional colleges in the South as well as one of the best colleges for veterans. It has a haunted history as well and its own Montevallo Ghost Walk. Reynolds Hall is one of the most active buildings, with the ghost of Captain Henry Reynolds lurking about. The ghost of Dr. William Trumbauer haunts the theater located in Palmer Hall, and the ghost of Edmund King, who built the King House in 1923, is often seen wandering around inside and outside in the orchards carrying a shovel and lantern as he searches for the fortune he buried there during the Civil War. One of the most terrifying ghosts is of a woman who can be heard screaming as she runs down the hall in flames. She is called the Ghost of Main Hall, and in life, she was a student named Condie Cunningham, who tragically died in a fire there in 1909.

Another creepy Alabama college is Huntingdon College, which is in Montgomery. It was originally founded in 1854 as a women's college in Tuskegee. Its two oldest residents are the Red Ladies. The first Red Lady is said to be the ghost of a young woman who wore a red dress and carried a red parasol. She roamed the hallways and the stairs of Sky Alley, the original residence hall. When the college moved in 1909 to the state capital of Montgomery to be able to take in more students, she was never seen again, although some blame her for the fire in one of the new campus's original buildings. The second Red Lady is alleged to be the spirit of a young woman named Margaret or Martha, who took her own life in Pratt Hall by slitting her wrists in the bathtub. She always wore red, and shortly after her death, residents of Pratt Hall began seeing a ghostly female in red. The college today even has an annual Red Lady Run with sorority sisters painting their faces red and running all over campus in black clothing to honor the ghost.

Huntingdon College used to be the Woman's College of Alabama. Today, it is home to not one but *two* "Red Ladies," who are the spirits of students who met tragic ends on the campus.

The University of Illinois at Urbana-Champaign claims a few haunted buildings. The public research university is considered a flagship of the entire University of Illinois system and is home to a female ghost who roams the English Building, which used to be a women's dorm and had its own pool. She allegedly drowned there and now walks the halls and stares out windows. Doors open and close, and phantom footsteps are heard at all hours as well as disembodied voices. The Lincoln Building, Psychology Building, and library are also paranormal hot spots. There is an urban legend on campus about a group of students who got so lost in the maze of the library's main stacks that they died there, and late-night studiers often see a ghost walking among the rows of books. Students who have attempted the maze that is known as a college library can strongly relate to that nightmarish story!

Texas State University opened in San Marcos, Texas, in 1899 as a public research institution. It started out with a little over three hundred students and today has over thirty-nine thousand. Incoming freshmen are given a ghost tour of the many haunted sites on the campus, including the Old Main, which is haunted by a female ghost carrying her books and looking for her classes. Students and staff alike have reported apparitions, disembodied voices, and strange footsteps in the middle of the night.

Saint Mary of the Woods College near Terre Haute, Indiana, is the oldest Catholic college in the state, founded in 1840 by a group of French nuns. It started as a college for women and was one of the first national colleges to offer business and professional courses for women students. Two of the campus buildings, Le Fer and Foley, seem to be the hot spots for ghostly activity, with stories of entities that grab the feet of students who reside there and phantom piano music inside the conservatory, which was demolished in 1989. A special mass took place on campus to cleanse the building. The most popular ghost is the Faceless Nun, who taught art and painted portraits of students for fun. She died before finishing her own self-portrait and, rumor has it, she haunts the art room of Foley Building looking for the unfinished canvas. There is no real record of such a nun ever existing, but she is now reported to have made the campus church her new stomping, or haunting, grounds.

Haunted High Schools

Though college and university campuses are usually far older and richer in history, including paranormal history, there are indeed haunted high schools and grade schools with their own spooky tales to tell. Take Pocatello High School in Pocatello, Idaho, also known as "Poky High." This school became a viral sensation when raw security surveillance video captured a ghostly figure in the hall of the school during a holiday break. The *Idaho State Journal* reported on the story and the video, which also showed lights flickering on and off in a strange pattern. The entity seen on the screen was sitting against a wall, then rose and went into a bathroom, re-emerged, and walked down the hall away from the video camera. Paranormal investigators visiting the school report there are over six ghosts on-site, including one girl who hanged herself as part of a suicide pact in the late 1940s (the second girl never went through with the pact).

Even a former principal, Don Cotent, claimed to have encountered several paranormal events while working late at night at the school. He would hear someone banging beneath the floor, and sometimes, he even yelled at the intruder to stop, but the noises would continue. When students came back to class after the holiday break, they met with a ghostly apparition in the gym bleachers, strange noises throughout the school, disembodied voices, and the sound of someone playing a piano as well as shadow figures hanging out in the school auditorium.

Another haunted high school is Tennessee High School in Bristol. Built in 1939, it originally went by the name Fifth Street School. Over the years, the campus has been expanded and is now haunted by a student named Agnes, who allegedly was killed when her car was struck by a train at a railroad crossing. She was on her way to the school for a formal event and now roams the halls, witnessed by both staff and students, and even showed up once in the auditorium broadcast booth. Some people have reported seeing a phantom train roaring through the gym and down the hallway. It is so loud, it shakes the rooms as it passes by. Another ghost, of a former athlete hit by a car on his way home from a big game, also haunts the school and is often seen hanging out during football games.

El Paso High School in Texas is filled with ghostly tales of strange goop dripping from classroom ceilings, hallways filled with unexplained mists, and hidden classrooms beneath the main building. Ghostly photos exist, including one of the graduating class of 1985 in which a woman in the center of the picture looks as though she might be a ghost. She was never identified, and rumor has it she is the spirit of a student who took her life years before by jumping from a balcony just off a mist-filled hallway. That same ghost is seen by students to this day, jumping off the balcony but vanishing just before her body hits the ground.

The lovely neoclassical architecture of El Paso High School is sullied by strange goop that drips from ceilings in the classrooms.

Arizona's Lee Williams High School sits above a frontier town called Kingman, that was once actively involved in mining cattle driving, and railroading. Students report the ghost of a man wearing a bowler hat walking the halls along with the spirit of a young girl who calls out at night asking to go outside to play. There are flickering lights and motion detectors that go off at random and, thanks to the football field being situated atop a former cemetery, plenty of spectral apparitions in old-fashioned garb seen during graduation events on the field.

Cathedral High School in Los Angeles, California, was built on top of Old Cavalry Cemetery, and during renovations of the school, many old headstones were dug up and are prominently displayed on the football field. The school mascot is called the Phantom to honor the ghostly heritage. Maintenance workers have reported a host of spirits that accompany cold spots in various school locations late at night.

Like Cathedral High, Topeka High School in Kansas was also built upon a former cemetery in the late 1890s. Though the cemetery was relocated nearby, the disturbed spirits are said to still haunt the school, perhaps angry for being awakened from their peaceful eternal slumber. Students and teachers witness apparitions, disembodied voices, and hushed conversations that seem to take place between two invisible entities. Rumors abound of underground tunnels that lead from the school to the hidden cemetery below. Two other city landmarks nearby are allegedly haunted, too.

Lincoln High School in Sioux Falls, South Dakota, opened in 1965. It claims to be filled with paranormal activity, even though no known deaths have occurred on-site. Staff members and students report disembodied voices and footsteps in the halls, keys jiggling on some phantom ghostly body, a ten-foot-tall man in a trench coat who floats six feet above the ground of the school's stage, doors that open and close on their own, and chairs that move around in the basement.

Meanwhile, at Roy High School in Roy, Utah, three ghosts have made their presence known time and time again. They even have names! Backstage

Mabel shows up in the backstage area of the school's auditorium, turning stage lights on and off and moving props around. The Lady in the Purple Hat likes to coax people to follow her but few do thanks to the negative energy she gives off. Last but not least is the Roaming Ghost, an apparition that likes to hang out in the school hallways and who may be the ghost of a student killed by a train. Sometimes, teachers hear pounding on the doors after school hours only to find there is no one at the doors.

Urbana High School in Urbana, Illinois, has its own haunted tower, where a secret door in the school allegedly leads up to the tower, although no one has ever found it. Legend has it a female teacher fell in love with a male student and she hanged herself in the tower. Another ghost is said to be part of a love triangle gone bad, and a third is an alleged suicide victim. Late at night, witnesses have seen strange lights up in the abandoned tower and heard loud tapping noises with no explanation.

C. E. Byrd High School in Shreveport, Louisiana, is home to the ghost of an ROTC sergeant who committed suicide there in the 1960s. Students investigating a rumor of another ghost, which proved to be fake, found out about the suicide of Sergeant Will Stubblefield, who killed himself in October 1962, although it was reported it may have been an accident. His presence continues to be felt throughout the school, usually accompanied by cold spots.

Both a high school and an elementary school back in the 1930s, the Elizabeth V. Edwards School in Barnegat, New Jersey, has been vacant since 2004. It was said to be haunted by the ghost of a student named Lizzy, who liked to slam locker doors shut, turn lights on and off, and play 1940s music. There are other ghosts on the site as well, including a translucent woman in a floral print dress, along with strange activity such as unplugged phones ringing, lights being turned on where there are no light bulbs in the sockets, and objects that move on their own.

Creepy Elementary Schools

Just the thought of sending little children to a haunted school is enough to send chills up and down the spine. Matthew Whaley Elementary School in Williamsburg, Virginia, which was founded in 1699, was named after a boy named Matthew Whaley who was born in 1698 and died only nine years later. The cause of death is unknown, but his grieving mother honored his death by adding on to the existing school. It was first known as Mattey's School, then the Matthew Whaley School. Though the school has been relocated three times throughout the city, his ghost is said to continue to haunt the school along with two other boy ghosts and a host of phenomena, including phantom footsteps. Though Matthew's ghost seems to frequent the bathrooms and playground, the spirits of the two boys, who are said to be the victims of lynchings, seem to favor wandering about the school as well as the nearby city streets.

California's city of Redlands is home to Mariposa Elementary School, home to an urban legend that seems to change according to those telling the tale. The story goes something like this: Billy was a boy hit by a school bus while riding his bike near the school. He may have died in the 1950s or the 1960s, depending on who you ask. The school was built in 1964, and his spirit allegedly swings on the playground swings, knocks on the attendance office door, and has been seen by a number of students … or not. In fact, kids would often take to knocking three times on a door at the school, hoping Billy would respond. But for those who work there, the greater concern is high school-age vandals, not stories of a boy who likes nothing more than to swing and knock about.

Summit Elementary School in Amarillo, Texas, also sounds more like an urban legend but got its start somewhere. As the story goes, in the heat of the civil rights movement, this was one of the segregated elementary schools for African American children. No whites were allowed to attend. The school janitor was rumored to have been a member of the Ku Klux Klan and an avid white supremacist, and he abducted four boys one afternoon and murdered them in the boiler room. Out of guilt for what he had done, or maybe fear of being caught and punished, he went to the roof, climbed the large smokestack, and jumped to his death. Legend has it that if you are there at night, you can hear the screams of the four boys and see a red ball bouncing down the hall leading to the boiler room. Cars in the area report that their radios turn on and off by themselves and the ghost of the janitor himself is sometimes seen leaping from the smokestack only to vanish before he hits the ground. The area is patrolled regularly by police to keep out people who want to see if the ghost stories are real.

Legend has it that if you are there at night, you can hear the screams of the four boys and see a red ball bouncing down the hall leading to the boiler room.

Old Milton School in Alton, Illinois, was built in 1904 and abandoned in 1984. It was later turned into a decorative glass manufacturing company warehouse, and those who work there still claim ghosts abound. During the 1930s, a janitor raped and killed a young, female student named Mary. He later hanged himself in the school hallway. After those two events, students and teachers began seeing Mary's ghost in the office area and experiencing a hostile ghost that may have been the janitor. Also reported were shadow figures and phantom noises. The glass company employees also report a number of phenomena, including objects that appear and disappear, an apparition that sits on the stairs just outside the office, Xs and Os tapped out by invisible hands on computer screens, the apparition of a small girl, and footsteps at night when no one is around.

Our last haunted school is in Forest Falls, California. Fallsvale Elementary School is located amid a forest setting and is home to the "Ghost Children" according to teachers and students who have witnessed them. These are ghostly apparitions that would come out from the forest to play and interact with the children, and many of the students even call the ghosts by names. They aren't hostile, so the children welcomed the playmates. The school is now abandoned, and paranormal investigators visit often, trying to get the children to come out and play and to determine whether it's the forest that is haunted or the school.

Poasttown Elementary School

Poasttown Elementary School in Cincinnati, Ohio, is a legend unto itself. This haunted grade school has probably been investigated by more paranormal and ghost-hunting groups than any other thanks to its rich haunted history. Though the school itself closed its doors in 2000, the new owners have found this historic building is still home to the ghosts of former students who may still believe class is in session. They purchased the building and made it their main home, but it wasn't long before they realized they had permanent houseguests.

The school is in the Middletown section and was originally opened in 1937. It served only as a school until its closing, unlike so many older historic buildings, and many locals remember attending there. Many also remember experiencing strange sensations on the premises, most likely the result of the events that occurred within its fifty-four rooms. The many ghosts seen there may have been victims of two train accidents—one in 1895 and one in 1910—both of which happened, strangely, on July 4. The 1910 crash is considered the worst railroad crash in Butler County's history and involved the head-on collision of a passenger train and a freight train. Twenty-four people died and another thirty-five or so were injured according to Middletown Historical Society records. The land the school was later built upon was used as an emergency triage area for the many crash victims.

Tours are commonplace today and you can pay to stay overnight in one of the rooms, and it is perfectly normal to see people walking about the school with all kinds of strange ghost-hunting equipment or just feeding their own curiosity. Many of the rooms are used for multipurpose community needs as well. Some of the phenomena reported include apparitions and ghosts, people being touched by invisible hands, laughter and the sounds of children playing, footsteps and doors opening and closing after hours, and shadow figures moving down the hallways. The school even has its own motto: "When you leave, you believe."

Traveling by air is one of the safest ways to get where you need to go and sometimes the only way. Every year, there are millions of flights in the world that take off and land safely without incident. Despite Hollywood's big-budget depictions of deadly plane crashes, flying is the safest mode of transportation. The odds of a plane crash are one for every 1.2 million flights with odds of dying being one in eleven million. The chances of dying in a car or other traffic accident are one in five thousand. Yet, because of their terrifying, and tragic, nature, plane crashes would seem like a natural setting for ghosts—in some cases, even angels.

In July 2012, the *Daily Mail* website reported a former FBI employee who claims she saw angels guarding the site of the deadly terrorist crash of United Airlines Flight 93 on September 11, 2001. Lillie Leonardi was a liaison between the authorities and the families of Flight 93 victims and was at the crash site near Shanksville, Pennsylvania. When she arrived, she was assaulted by the strong smell of burning pine trees and jet fuel, and amid the otherwise eerie silence of the scene, she saw angels floating in the mist over the crash site. Others witnessed apparitions and heard phantom cries at the site afterward, and in some of the locations where security services operated nearby, chairs and other objects began to move on their own. The ghost of a woman was reported wandering about the site only to vanish when approached.

Airplane Mysteries

Flight 191

Other crash sites are home only to the mourning ghosts of the dead such as the site of American Flight 191. It was May 25, 1979, when Flight 191 lost parts of an engine upon takeoff. It flipped over on the runway and burst into a

Flight 191 out of Chicago's O'Hare International Airport lost its left engine, crashing next to a mobile home park and killing 273 people, including two on the ground.

fireball, killing the crew and passengers on board and two ground crewmen who worked at the Courtney-Velo Excavating Company, located in one of the old hangars. The captain, Walter Lee, was experienced with DC-10s and had been flying them for over eight years. His first officer, James Dillard, and flight engineer, Alfred Udovich, were also experienced. But they couldn't keep the plane upright.

Afterward, people reported seeing white balls of light dodging about the crash site, and many who lived in a mobile home park near the site claimed that someone was knocking repeatedly on their doors and windows, yet when they went to look, no one was there. A few residents who opened their doors upon hearing the knocking claimed they were met with a distraught person asking for help to get to a connecting flight or find his or her luggage, and a man walking his dog in the area met a young man who smelled of jet fuel who claimed he needed to make an emergency phone call but then vanished into thin air. Motorists driving along roads past the crash site often reported floating lights and shadowy figures and at certain times the temperature will suddenly drop, and they can hear screams echoing in the empty field.

Paranormal research groups flocked to the site with various equipment to measure activity and reported the crash site as highly active with EVP coming through that when asked about the flight engineer, a voice came back with "almost made it" and "need power."

Flight 401

Perhaps the most famous crashed plane site is that of Eastern Air Lines Flight 401, which crashed in December 1972 into the swamps of the Florida Everglades. Of the passengers, 191 died on board, many drowning in just eighteen inches of water, unable to move, and seventy-five people survived. During the long search and recovery mission, people in johnboats on the swamp water claimed they heard the cries and moans of the survivors, except when they got closer, there was no one in the water. The ghosts of Captain Robert Loft and flight engineer Donald Repo haunt other Eastern Air Lines flights. They were seen sitting in the cockpit of other L-1011 flights by several crewmembers.

In the months following the crash, dozens of reports came in of ghostly sightings by colleagues who once knew the pilots. Many of these sightings had more than one witness. The captain and crewmembers of another plane saw

Captain Loft in the cabin and tried to initiate a conversation with his ghost, but he vanished. One flight attendant reported seeing the face of Don Repo staring at her from inside an oven door in the galley kitchen. The oven had been salvaged from the wreckage of Flight 401. Other members of the flight crew came to see, and they all heard Don Repo's voice say, "Watch out for fire on this airplane." A fire broke out the following day in the galley.

First class passengers on a number of flights would witness Don Repo standing before them still in uniform before vanishing into thin air before their eyes. Another documented report had three crewpeople try to communicate with an apparition of Don Repo that appeared in the lower deck. He was clearly identifiable but vanished without speaking.

Eventually, the CEO of Eastern Air Lines, Frank Borman, issued a letter to all crewmembers demanding they stop telling ghost stories for fear it would hurt business. But the stories continued out to local reporters, book authors, and even Hollywood came calling, producing a television movie called *The Ghost of Flight 401*. Ironically, it was the vice president of Eastern Air Lines who later reported having a conversation with a captain who he thought was in command of the aircraft he was on. He was able to identify that man as Captain Robert Loft.

On an even creepier note, ValuJet Flight 592 crashed just two miles north of the Flight 401 site in May 1996, killing all 110 people on board.

B-29 Ghosts

Castle Air Museum in Atwater, California, is reportedly haunted by the former crewmember of one of the B-29 donors used to build the one now on display in the museum. Workers locking up late at night would see lights coming from inside the plane and someone sitting in the cockpit dressed up like a crewmember. The museum is part of Castle Air Force Base, and the B-29 in question is known as *Raz'n Hell*. According to a 2003 story for the November 2003 Merced *Sun Star*, Castle Air Museum executive assistant Karen Machen claimed the haunted museum's B-29 bomber might be home to the ghost of a man named Arthur.

His ghost is said to show up in pictures of the thirty-two-foot-tall, illuminated sculpture, which is of a cobalt blue, red-eyed mustang horse nicknamed "Blucifer."

Airports

Denver International Airport

Usually we associate plane crash sites with ghostly activity, but there are airports with their fair share as well. Denver International is the biggest international airport in the United States, and dozens of employees and flyers have reported paranormal activity in the expansive facility. There is a rumor, of course, that the airport was built upon Native

American burial grounds and that this might account for the numerous hauntings, which allegedly began after the airport staff played Native American chants on the loop bridge that connected Concourse A and the Jeppesen Terminal Building. In 1995, tribal leaders were brought in to do a special ceremony to put the spirits at rest. Visitors continue to report cold spots, the feeling of hands pushing or touching them, and having their luggage moved and knocked over when no one was nearby.

One specific ghost is that of Luis Jiminez, who haunts a sculpture on a hill just south of the airport that he died while creating in 1992. His ghost is said to show up in pictures of the thirty-two-foot-tall, illuminated sculpture, which is of a cobalt blue, red-eyed mustang horse nicknamed "Blucifer." The sculpture project was plagued with issues from the start, culminating with the horrific way Jimenez died, trapped beneath the 9,000-pound (4,082-kilogram) sculpture when it fell from the hoist, landing on top of the artist. Jimenez bled to death on the spot before help could arrive.

The airport is also home to a number of apocalyptic conspiracy theories thanks to the presence of underground tunnels that some claim are meant to house people during the end of the world and the strange artwork found on the walls of the buildings depicting unusual scenes of war and the fight between good and evil. Some visitors have complained about the dark, sinister Nazi and Masonic symbols they claim are hidden within the artwork and the airport's connection to the New World Order.

Mr. Tibble

Sacramento Airport in California is said to be haunted by the ghost of Mr. Tibble, a man who died in October 1982 while awaiting his flight in the gate area. Because he had died sitting, the plane boarded and left with him still waiting until a flight attendant discovered him and tried to wake him up. He may have been Derek Tibble, who indeed died there while waiting for a flight to New York City, so at least this story has some truth to it. His ghost is now said to haunt the same gate, often found sitting in the same chair he died in.

Heathrow's Resident Ghost

London, England's Heathrow Airport is one of the busiest in the world and the third largest in terms of passengers (73.5 million annually) who pass through. Many of those have been lucky enough, or unlucky enough, to witness the ghost of Dick Turpin, a legendary highwayman who went on a robbing, killing, and raping spree in the 1730s. He was known to be narcissistic and was always bragging about his horrific crimes. Even when he was captured and was about to be publicly hanged, he bowed to the audience and grinned. He was clearly a psychopath and became a legend, even a folk hero or a Robin Hood-type hero, despite the awful things he did (which seemed to have been forgotten as his legend grew).

Turpin's ghost is seen all over London at various locations but mainly at Heathrow, where passengers and airport employees claim he lurks about wearing a black overcoat and tricornered hat. He is mostly seen at night and can be heard shouting and screaming, even barking and howling like an animal. Employees claim he breathes down their necks while they work, and he has been accused of phantom pinching, scratching, and shoving. In 2004, an airport employee was dragged by her hair across the ticket counter in front of witnesses, according to one report.

Yet, no one knows for sure why Turpin chooses to continually haunt Heathrow. Maybe he just likes annoying and terrorizing large crowds of weary travelers.

Notorious eighteen-century highwayman Dick Turpin seems reluctant to leave his beloved England, even in death, and apparently favors being around Heathrow Airport.

Another Heathrow ghost is the "Man with the Briefcase," a spirit who appeared after the 1948 crash of a DC3 Dakota from Belgian Airlines while it was approaching the runway. As emergency personnel were dealing with the casualties and injured passengers, a man suddenly appeared asking for his briefcase. He then vanished into thin air, but his body was later recognized by rescue crewmembers. He is often seen around the airport now carrying his briefcase, but some witnesses report they can only see the lower part of his body! Perhaps the most frightening sighting of the man with the briefcase occurred in 1970 when air traffic controllers contacted the authorities to complain about a mysterious man carrying a briefcase out on the runway. When approached by police, the man, who was detected on radar, was not there. The air traffic controllers insisted they could see him, but the police on the ground never found him.

Archerfield Airport

Australia's Archerfield Airport is located south of Brisbane in Queensland and was once the primary airport for the bustling city of Brisbane. It was used as a Royal Australian Air Force station during World War II. On March 27, 1943, an airman was asked to fly to Sydney on a C47 Douglas Dakota. The

The ghost of a teenager on a horse seen around the airport is attributed to the son, Volney Grenier, who died in a horse-riding accident in 1859.

airport was shrouded in a thick fog, but the crew knew they needed to get their bounty to Sydney and attempted take-off anyway. The airman was piloting the plane filled with radio equipment and components when it took off and promptly veered off course from the fog, then rolled and crashed into some trees, ending up in nearby swampland. All thirty-two on board were killed. Afterward, a man in a RAAG uniform and cap, holding a deployed parachute, was witnessed by several people at the airport. He would smile and wave as they passed by. The general manager of the airport revealed that the ghostly sightings could be related to the fact that the airport was built upon a small cemetery called "God's Acre" where the original landowners, the Grenier family, are buried. The cemetery still exists and is maintained by airport employees. The ghost of a teenager on a horse seen around the airport is attributed to the son, Volney Grenier, who died in a horse-riding accident in 1859.

Other reports out of Archerfield tell of phantom aircraft seen at the airfield, unexplained lights, objects moving about on their own, and groups of ghostly figures wandering in the hangars at night.

Asian Airports

The Philippines was once home to the bustling Sasa Airport in Davao City, which is now a refuge for the homeless and for a nearby engineering project. Witnesses hear the moans and cries of people throughout the night, possibly the ghosts of those who died in a deadly bombing in March 2003 that took the lives of twenty-one people. Apparitions are a regular appearance inside the airport.

Thailand is no stranger to haunted airports. Suvarnabhumi Airport has several shrines on-site to protect the area from the presence of evil spirits. It was built upon the site of a sacred burial ground that was known as Nong Nguhao, or Cobra Swamp, and one security expert allegedly was possessed by a demon while searching for explosives at the airport, and the demon commanded a shrine be built. Many of the airlines that use the airport have their own rituals to drive away evil spirits. The Airport Authority of Thailand organized prayer sessions by bringing in ninety-nine Buddhist monks to chant and perform rituals to protect passengers and crewmembers. Crewmembers and passengers have seen spirits all over the airport and hear phantom coughing, choking, and chanting. The ghosts are blamed for a number of strange accidents and are said to be malicious.

Haunted Hangar

On Thursday, May 6, 1937, the *Hindenburg* German passenger airship caught fire and crashed as it attempted to dock with a mooring mast at Lakehurst Naval Air Station in New Jersey. Thirty-five people on board and one man on the ground died. The disaster made the nightly news with radio reporters giving live, eyewitness accounts of the disaster as it happened. Though the tragedy occurred over eighty years ago, ghosts at Hangar 1, which was used as a morgue during the disaster, continue to lurk, and people report the strong sensations of negative energies present.

Phantom footsteps come from the rafters above, and shadowy figures can be seen in the building. Locals won't go there after dark because of the negative juju.

Tarmac Ghosts

A frightening story is told by a pilot of a horde of ghosts that would appear on the runway at Tenerife Airport in the Canary Islands. In March 1977, a KLM plane collided on the runway with a Pan Am 747, killing 583 passengers and crewmembers. Pilots and air traffic controllers at Tenerife would often later see large numbers of figures on the runway, waving as if to try to stop the planes from taking off. Are they the ghosts of the victims of the deadly crash?

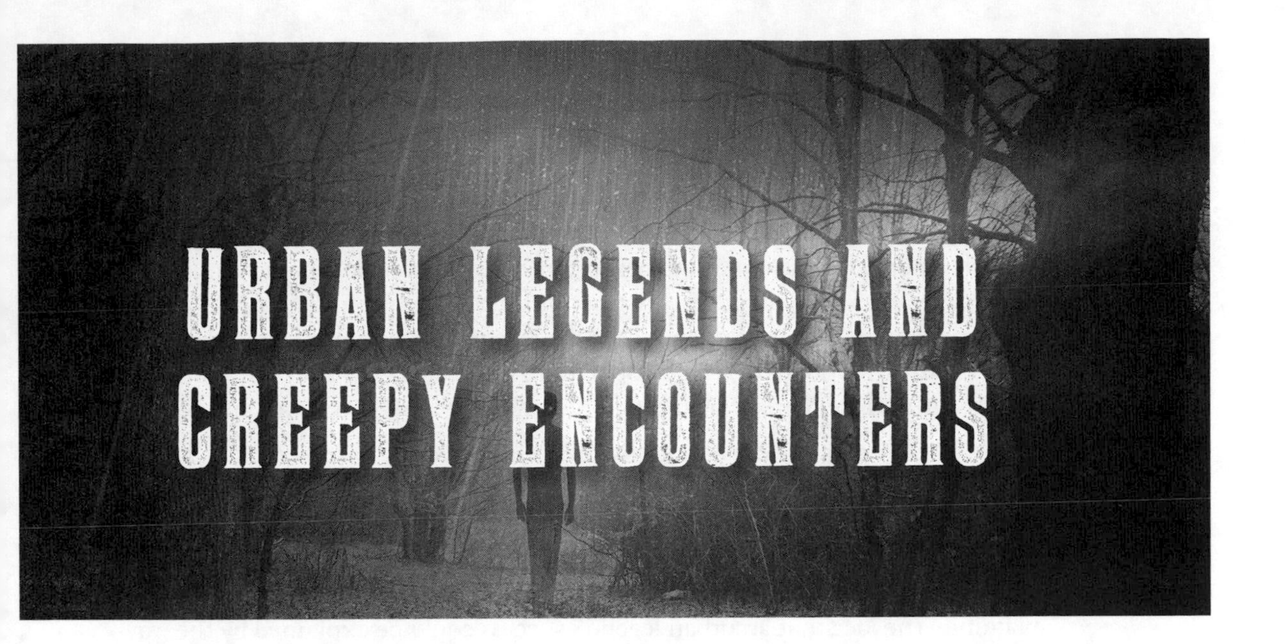

URBAN LEGENDS AND CREEPY ENCOUNTERS

What makes an urban legend different from a typical ghostly encounter or notorious haunting? Sometimes, the lines between the two are blurred, and an urban legend is a ghost or monster story that has, at its core, a nugget of truth or reality. But when stacked with embellishment upon embellishment, many true stories turn into fantastical tales that are often hard to believe, and yet, many people swear they do believe.

The term "urban legend" is a type of folklore that was first brought into the public eye in 1981 courtesy of Professor Jan Harold Brunvand, who used it in his popular books that collect legends from various cultures and examine their origins and key compelling features. Today, with the ability of the Internet and social networks to turn a story viral in a matter of seconds, urban legends (and yes, they include rural stories, too) spread like wildfire and in the process take on new story characteristics and adjustments that were nowhere close to the original. Folklorists love to examine urban legends to try to find that original nugget of truth, describing these outlandish stories as modern myths, yet even ancient myths had truths to tell. They just veiled them in story symbolism.

Urban legends are the darlings of the entertainment industry because of their shock value and sensationalism. And they're just plain scary as hell. Think of the many movies and television shows based on urban legends from Bloody Mary to the "fakelore" of the Rake and Slender Man—entities that, though purely fictional and a part of "creepypasta" (the term means "copy and pasted") horror-related legends created by the public and made viral via the Internet, took on a reality in terrifying ways and were reported by people claiming they really existed. Slender Man, a child-targeting entity created in 2009 as a purely fictional entry in the Something Awful's Photoshop Phriday competition, took on such a life that in 2014, a young girl was stabbed in Waukesha, Wisconsin, by two other female friends who claimed Slender Man, was responsible.

Urban legends are said to take on many of the cultural and societal aspects of their times such as the many stories of vanishing hitchhikers and motorcyclists that pervaded the twentieth century, the stories of people being kidnapped and having a vital organ stolen that permeate our culture today in the age of modern medicine, and the even more recent fears of masked home invaders or faceless entities who may or may not be human. In this way, they are similar to mythology and are more of a cultural phenomenon than people might believe.

There are specific reasons why urban legends go viral so quickly. Today, with texting, email, and social networking on the Internet, our modern folklore gets spread faster than ever and almost behaves like a virus. There is a scientific basis for this, as reported in the *British Journal of Psychology*. A Durham University study conducted by Joe Stubbersfield, Jamie Tehrani, and Emma Flynn examined the idea that an urban legend's success could be explained by the way human brains evolved to learn, remember, and transmit specific types of information more readily than others. Our brains evolved to notice and remember information important to our survival (remember the Reticular Activating System discussed in the first chapter of this book?), and we then evolved a greater level of intelligence to keep track of our social interactions and relationships. Their hypothesis suggested that we evolved to be disposed to social and survival-based information—both very important to us—which left us susceptible to notice, remember, and then pass on stories that contain this information, even if they are not based in reality.

Folklorist Jan Harold Brunvand, a professor emeritus of English at the University of Utah, popularized the term "urban legend" in his books on American culture.

The study involved giving participants an urban legend with both social and survival information and had them read and then write down the stories from their memory. Their stories, written from recall, were then handed to the next participant, who then read them and wrote them down on another sheet of paper from their memory, and so on and so on. This is a process similar to the game "Operator," in which a line of people pass a sentence down until the last person, who then repeats it to find it has somewhat changed from the original. These studies and others showed that people were attracted to stories with survival threats or social relationships and were likely to pass those stories on to another person. If the story contained both survival threats and social information or just survival information, it was not passed as quickly or with as much memory retention as those stories that only had social information, proving that although both are important to humans, those legends with strong social information are remembered longer and with more detail. This seems to apply to folklore, myth, and even novels. Those that focus on social interactions stick with us longer!

Every country on Earth has its urban legends. This book will focus on the United States, but not every urban legend will be presented here because for every state, every city, and every small town, there is one or several (check around because surely your town does, too!). There are far too many to mention in one book, let alone six or seven. In fact, the author of this book grew up with an urban legend that she later found out was *true*: the tale of Shotgun Annie.

Growing up in Garnerville, New York, back in the late '60s and early '70s, the tiny town along the Hudson River, just north of Nyack in Rockland County, had an urban legend called "The Old Lady's Field," which was also known to locals as "Shotgun Annie's Field." Kids who lived on Captain Shankey Drive and Barnes Drive used to cut across the field to get to Red's, the local candy store where you could buy five pieces of sugary, cavity-causing goodness for a quarter. Not cutting across the field meant a long walk down, then back up, Captain Shankey Drive, so it was only natural to seek out a great shortcut.

Well, legend had it that the field was owned by a wicked, old witch named Annie, who had a shotgun and huge killer dogs (Dobermans come to mind), and she would shoot at kids trying to cross her field! She lived in a huge, white house that bordered the main road across the field. No one dared go trick or treating there for Halloween. Yes, we crossed that field a few times, but we ran like we had fire on our heels, stayed close to the side opposite her house and never tried this at night (although one particularly horrific Halloween night does come vaguely to mind when long-standing rules were broken). Rest assured, it was terrifying, despite never being shot at or having huge dogs race across the grass to rip our throats out!

In 1974, my family moved across the country to California, and the Old Lady's Field became one of those fun things we told new friends and family. Decades later, in a Facebook group for people who grew up in the town of Garnerville, other residents who lived there around the same time confirmed the legend of Shotgun Annie was, indeed, true because several locals reported having had encounters with the old gal herself, along with her shotgun! Sadly, that field was later turned into condominiums and Annie, well, who knows what happened to her? The legend persists to this day, and those of us who lived it pass it on to our children and grandchildren.

Urban legends are so popular today that they've spawned a new kind of travel/tourist phenomenon called legend tripping, where people travel to sites known for their urban legends, monsters, ghosts, and other supernatural shenanigans. This can include everything from abandoned buildings; deserted train stations; haunted roadways, waterways, and tunnels; creepy caves; and anywhere else that is surrounded in paranormal mystique. Legend-tripping pilgrimages are usually made in groups, but some brave souls dare go alone only to return with even more far-out tales of supernatural circumstances that then get added on to the original legend they were chasing in the first place.

That's how urban legends work. There is a seed of truth, upon which leaves, buds, and flowers are attached and embellished into a most incredulous story that is hard to swallow. Just don't tell that to Shotgun Annie, wherever her ghost may roam today. So, as you read the following urban legends, keep in the back of your mind that there is embedded within a grain of truth—a real story of a real person, place, or event and, like mythology, folk stories, tall tales, and parables, it is up to us today to attempt to figure out what that is.

The Murdered Peddler

We begin with an urban legend that spawned an entire spiritual field of study. In the 1840s, Mr. and Mrs. Bell of Hydesville, New York, had a visitor, a young peddler who came to shop his wares. The Bells' housekeeper invited the young man in, and he stayed in the house for several days. During that time, the housekeeper was dismissed, but then a week later, she was rehired. The young peddler was no longer at the Bells' home, but many of the items he was peddling were being used in the Bells' kitchen.

She imagined the Bell family bought the items from the man, then he must have left and moved on, only she began experiencing visions of a ghost—namely, the peddler's ghost, who informed her that while she had been no longer working at the home, the Bells murdered him! His body was found in the home, though no record of his identity was ever found. This story was originally told by two sisters, Maggie and Katie Fox, who claimed in March 1848 they communicated with the dead peddler through rapping

The Fox sisters (left to right are Margaret, Kate, and Leah) became the first celebrity mediums in America back in the 1840s.

noises in front of many witnesses, only to later admit the whole thing had been faked. They recanted their story immediately afterward. The Fox sisters became the first celebrity mediums, setting the stage for the founding of a new religion called Spiritualism, which grew in size and popularity from the 1840s to the 1920s. The Fox sisters gained notoriety and were introduced to others interested in contacting the dead.

Local Urban Legends

Indiana is home to the Blue River, the site of a local urban legend involving a headless ghost. According to the legend, a teenage girl was beheaded years ago when she was on the river paddling in her canoe. She was paddling so fast, she never saw the fishing line someone had tied across the expanse of the river and off went her head, severed by the fishing line at the neck. Locals say you can sometimes see her ghost body at night wandering the river banks seeking her head by the light of the full moon.

In Bowie, Maryland, locals swear that a creature called the Goat Man wanders the backroads attacking cars with an axe. Fletchertown Road seems to be the favorite spot of this half-goat/half-human monstrosity many believe is really a former scientist who worked at the nearby Beltsville Agricultural Research Center. He was experimenting with goats when it backfired, and he was exposed to mutations that caused him to form goatlike features. With an axe as his weapon of choice, he began roaming the rural roads near the facility when he wasn't living in the woods alone as a hermit. Another theory states the Goat Man is the Devil himself and that the urban legend was kept alive by bored teenagers who kept repeating the story and making up attacks against lovers locked in an embrace at the local Lover's Lane. Whatever the origins, in 1971, a dog was killed, and some attributed the death to the Goat Man, proving that urban legends can become real in the minds and imaginations of people just as easily as factual reports.

California's Ojai Valley is home to an urban legend surrounding the Camp Comfort Country Park. This is the home of the mysterious Char-Man, the spirit of a horribly disfigured man who was burned in a wildfire back in 1948. The legend states the man and his son were trapped by the fire and when rescue workers found them, the son was alive and fled into the forest. It was revealed the son had strapped his father to a tree and pulled off his skin, leaving him to burn alive. Yet another story claims the Char-Man was a married man who went insane when he was trapped by the fire and unable to help his screaming wife. Regardless of who he is, if you drive onto the bridge in the park at night and get out of your car, the Char-Man will charge at you and attack you to try to rip off your skin.

Out in the California desert is the famous Salton Sea, the largest lake in the state, which attracts many annual visitors to see the shallow, saline, endorheic rift lake that sits directly above the notorious San Andreas Fault line. It is situated in the Sonoran Desert in the southeastern corner of California and includes the Salton Sea State Recreation Area and the Sonny Bono Salton Sea National Wildlife Refuge. It may also include some ghosts. Visitors report all kinds of bizarre activity around this mysterious, isolated locale, including strange humanoid creatures that roam about, victims of radiation poisoning from years of top-secret nuclear testing in the area decades ago. This same theory posits that all wildlife in the area was poisoned as well and that the ghosts of many humans and animals who died there haunt the area. There are many reports of UFOs and strange lights in the sky at night hovering over the lake, and these extraterrestrials may have even had a hand in creating the lake! This was once a thriving resort area in the 1950s and 1960s when Bombay Beach was filled with hotels, homes, schools, and yacht clubs. Now it looks more like a great place to film a movie about the apocalypse. Green sludge and fish skeletons cover beaches once filled with suntanned vacationers. Whatever the truth may be, locals insist visitors should not go there at night.

Jump across the Atlantic to Scotland's infamous Ghost Road, a stretch of rural road marked A75 Kinmount Straight, where drivers are said to encounter

Built in the thirteenth century, Houska Castle near Prague, Czech Republic, is, according to legend, literally harboring a gateway to hell.

everything from strange animals, people running into the road only to vanish before your eyes, a man on crutches who has no eyes, and all sorts of other bizarre activity that serves to terrify those who dare to drive the tree-lined road.

Another haunted forest is in Romania. The Hoia Baciu Forest is the site of many a legend of bizarre creatures, ghosts, phantom laughter and voices, UFO sightings, red balls of light, and people being scratched by unseen hands. Considered one of the most haunted forests in the world, hundreds of people have gone missing here, never to be heard from again. There is even a clearing in the forest where any life refuses to grow, prompting the locals to suggest it may be a portal to another dimension or even hell itself.

Speaking of gateways to hell, Prague's Houska Castle is said to have been built for that purpose or, at least, according to urban legend, to close the gates of hell. Located deep in the forest, the castle was alleged to have been built upon a bottomless pit from which demons entered this world. In the 1930s, Nazis conducted occult experiments at the castle, only they didn't go so well. Years later, during an excavation, the skeletons of many Nazi officers turned up. They had been killed execution style. The castle has been haunted over the years by strange hordes of frogs, a headless, black horse, the ghost of a bulldog, and the usual human apparitions.

Avoid the woodsy backroads of Holland, Michigan, where deformed feral children are said to roam, running out into the street and terrifying drivers. Locals believe these children may be former patients of a local asylum that was shut down in the 1970s and was home to children suffering from a disease called hydrocephalus, which enlarges the forehead.

Some urban legends are more bittersweet, including the legend of the Man in Gray. The residents of Pawley Island in South Carolina talk of a man in gray that goes around warning people of a coming storm or hurricane. He is said to be the ghost of a young man who was coming to town from Charleston to see his beloved when his horse was caught in pluff mud in the marshes. The horse and the young man drowned in the quicksand-like mud, and now, his spirit haunts the shore nearby, warning others of the dangers of the area and oncoming storms and seeking his beloved. The Man in Gray, also known as the Gray Man, became even more famous after Hurricane Hugo when the television show *Unsolved Mysteries* interviewed island residents who claimed they had encountered the Gray Man on the beach before a major storm. He was dressed in a long, gray coat and looked a bit like a pirate. After the storm had passed, they noticed that those who had not seen the Gray Man had had their houses destroyed, but the homes of those who saw him had been spared by Mother Nature.

Speaking of water, in Devil's Hopyard State Park in East Haddam, Connecticut, locals report seeing the Devil himself sitting atop Chapman Falls, a 60-foot (18-meter), cascading waterfall. The Devil likes to sit on the largest boulder at the top of the falls playing a violin while his demon army makes poisonous brews down below in the potholes at the bottom of the falls. Some locals even say you can see burn marks on the rocks around the potholes made by the Devil's hooves.

Many urban legends, such as the Devil playing the violin above, sound like they have ancient pagan influences. The nature god Pan was often portrayed as playing a violin. Another pagan-influenced urban legend is that of the Green Man, said to be a former employee of a local power company near Piney Fork, outside of Pittsburgh, Pennsylvania. Legend has it the Green Man was horribly disfigured in an accident at the power plant. His face melted, and his skin took on a deep green hue. Those unlucky enough to see his ghost report his skin appears to glow as he walks down rural roadways and disappears in the Piney Fork Tunnel. The tunnel, which was built in 1924, became known as the Green Man Tunnel after teenagers reported driving into the tunnel at night, turning off their car headlights, and calling out the Green Man's name, at which time he would appear out of the darkness. If he touched anyone, they would feel a strong electrical charge, and if he touched a vehicle, the engine would stall and fail to restart. The Green Man is also called Charlie No-Face by locals who claim he is merely a horribly disfigured, mortal man who happens to be able to blow cigarette smoke out of holes in his cheeks. Getting closer to the truth behind the legend, the Green Man (aka Charlie No-Face) may indeed be a real person—one Raymond Robertson, who died in June 1985. As a child, Robertson was horribly disfigured in an electrical accident on the Morado Bridge electrical lines. Unable to go to public school, he could be seen walking the roads at night alone using a walking stick to help guide him. He was struck many times by cars, and those who stopped to talk to him described him as friendly, although that didn't stop the urban legend of the Green Man from growing and spreading to future generations.

Famous author Ambrose Bierce based his story "The Difficulty of Crossing a Field" on an Alabama urban legend.

Miltonsburg, Ohio, is home to a man whom locals don't quite know if he is alive or dead or somewhere in between. This urban legend goes back to the late 1700s when a local farmer named Mr. Kaiser was murdered when someone broke into his farmhouse. The local sheriff of the small town banded together with sheriffs in other nearby towns to try to find the cold-blooded

Cropsey, the Child Hunter of Staten Island

The borough of Staten Island in New York City is considered the least urban of the five boroughs. Woodlands abound, and the whole island is more rural and suburban than its proximity to the largest city in the United States might suggest. There is an urban legend here of a homicidal maniac who had a hook for a hand and liked to hunt down children. He was an escapee of the Seaview Hospital, a now abandoned tuberculosis sanatorium for children. The legend of Cropsey began, many locals say, as a way for parents to scare their children into submission, telling them they had to be good or Cropsey would get them. But the urban legend became reality when a janitor at the notoriously horrific Willowbrook State School, an institution for mentally disabled children, began hunting real children. His name was Andre Rand, and he was eventually arrested for the disappearance of a girl with Down Syndrome named Jennifer Schweiger. Her body was later found in a shallow grave on the school grounds. Rand lived on a makeshift campsite on the school, which had been closed down in 1987.

Rand had a long criminal record that included an attempted rape of a child. In 1983, he attempted to kidnap a bus filled with children, but police got to them in time, and no one was harmed. But there were four other mentally disabled children who had vanished around the same time as Jennifer, and none of the bodies were ever found, pointing suspicion at Rand, especially when one of those children was seen with him in a diner in 1984. Rand was eventually charged and imprisoned for another girl's kidnapping and was given two twenty-five-year sentences.

Cropsey wasn't meant to be real; he was just a way to frighten children into good behavior, proving that sometimes truth is as strange as, or stranger than, fiction.

killer but to no avail. On the one-year anniversary of Mr. Kaiser's still unsolved murder, a stranger walked into the town's saloon, shocking the bartender, who said the man looked exactly like Mr. Kaiser. He asked the man if he was Mr. Kaiser's brother or father, but the man just stood there and in front of the bar patrons said he was Mr. Kaiser and that he had never been gone! The man then vanished before their eyes, but locals have since then reported seeing his ghost roaming around, seeking the murderer who took his life.

Another "missing person" urban legend comes from Alabama. In July 1854, a farmer named Orion Williamson (as one version of the legend has it) was walking on his farm near Selma, Alabama. His wife and kids were sitting on the porch, and neighbors saw him walking and made sure to wave hello. Williamson waved back, but then he vanished into thin air! His family and neighbors rushed to where he last stood, but there was no sign of him. A huge search party was formed, and they combed the fields deep into the night but to no avail. The search continued for days with people coming in to help or be looky-loos, having heard about the story via word of mouth. One visitor was a journalist named Ambrose Bierce, who ended up writing about the spooky case in "The Difficulty of Crossing a Field." The legend claims Williamson's wife and son could hear his voice calling to them for help but that as the weeks went by, the voice grew fainter and fainter until it ceased altogether. Was he trapped in an alternate universe? He fell through a wormhole into another world right on his own land!

Urban legends often involve strange animals called cryptids. These are cryptozoological beasts such as the Loch Ness Monster, Bigfoot, and the Dogmen—yes, Dogmen. Some researchers believe these are actual animals, and others suggest they may be interdimensional beings that cross over their world into ours. The Dogmen have been reported for hundreds of years. In the small town of Norton, Ohio, hunters have reported spotting these bipedal dog beasts at night. They are said to stand between seven and nine feet tall when on their hind legs, and they often have red, glowing eyes that pierce the night. They usually travel in groups of two or three and live deep within the forest. Because they don't seek out human contact, they are usually only spotted by humans who happen to be traveling along rural roads or in the backwoods. One such encounter occurred in the Silver Creek Metro Park along the woodsy Chippewa Loop Trail. Two hunters spotted deer running across Johnson Road but then saw what the deer were frantically running from.

Sometimes the creatures are just walking about the backyards or on driveways, but other witnesses report a sense of dread when they are nearby.

Dogmen are muscular, fast, and usually dark in color. Unlike Bigfoot, which has also been spotted in the same area of Ohio, these beasts did not swing their arms when they ran and had doglike heads. The Dogmen occasionally are white in color or black with silver or white markings; they are like wolves, only those who have encountered them know for a fact they are *not* wolves. There have been so many sightings all over the country of Dogmen, and this urban legend has spawned a number of horror movies of attacks by giant, doglike creatures that tower over humans.

Witnesses often hear the Dogmen's awful howls before they see them. Sometimes the creatures are just walking about the backyards or on driveways, but other witnesses report a sense of dread when they are nearby. Writer/researcher Linda Godfrey documented Dogmen sightings, including one near Norton, Ohio, in her book *Real Wolfmen*. Could they be wolves? If you ask those who have seen them, they are liable to ask if you've ever seen a seven-foot-tall wolf running on its hind legs!

Another howler of an urban legend is found in the Ozark Mountains and surrounding areas in Arkansas, Missouri, Oklahoma, and Texas. The aptly named Ozark Howler is another dogbeast that witnesses claim is the size of a bear with horns, a muscular build, stocky legs, shaggy hair, and a howl that sounds like a cross between a wolf and the bugle of an elk. The creature may have been a misidentified large cat, according to some anthropologists, and it may be a hoax perpetrated by a local college student who made a bet with friends that he could fool cryptozoologists who study strange creatures.

Down near Newport, Arkansas, another cryptid roams the White River named, appropriately, the White River Monster. Since 1915, people have reported seeing this beast in the river, nicknaming it "Whitey" and turning it into a local urban legend. Whitey is said to be gray in color and the length of three cars. There have been numerous attempts to catch Whitey but to no avail. In the 1970s, people reported seeing a gray creature with a horn on its head and a spiny back twenty feet long. Locals claimed to have seen three-toed, fourteen-inch footprints near the river bed as well as crushed brush and broken tree branches that looked as though something large moved through the area.

The area became the White River Monster Refuge in 1973 thanks to a bill signed into law by state senator Robert Harvey making it illegal to harm the creature. Though sightings tapered off recently, the locals still wonder if Whitey exists or is just a normal giant fish that unwittingly became a legend.

Common Urban Legends

Some mysterious sightings involve the same type of urban legend seen in a variety of areas. One example is the mysterious vanishing hitchhiker, which has been reported all over the country as a strange man, or woman, seen hitchhiking on the side of a road—sometimes a rural road, sometimes not. When the hitchhiker is picked up, he or she either vanishes upon entering the car or rides along for a while, still and silent, until let out of the car. Then, he or she vanishes. In some cases, the hitchhiker might be a child claiming to be lost and asking to be taken home, but when the driver arrives to the house, they ring the doorbell to find that the child that was standing next to them has vanished into thin air, and they are informed the child died years earlier.

A common urban legend is that of the mysterious hitchhiker who is picked up by a kind driver only to disappear once they enter the car.

Another hugely popular urban legend involves some type of ghostly Lady in White seen floating in the woods near a waterway or across a lonely road. She is usually crying and does not speak or acknowledge your presence. Caught in some kind of time loop, she repeats her tragic walk night after night, never seeming to quite find what she is looking for. She appears all over the world and sometimes dons a blood-soaked dress or gown, always white, suggesting murder or some other tragedy. Other times, she stands at the shore's edge, looking out to the water as if waiting for a loved one to come back to her. The Lady in White has become nothing short of a ghostly icon!

Then there is Bloody Mary, another iconic ghost woman who appears in mirrors to people all over the world who dare repeat her name three times. Children love to invoke Bloody Mary, standing in front of the mirror with their eyes closed as they chant her name. Sometimes, she appears as a woman with long, stringy, black hair, covered in blood. Other times, she is the image of Queen Mary I, who was said to be a bloody ruler and child murderer. Others report seeing one of the queen's innocent, young victims in the mirror. This enduring urban legend is a favorite for sleepovers and spooky séances, yet again shows how a global legend can have the same roots but different accoutrements depending on the location and culture. Yet, one thing remains the same no matter where you are—her name must be said three times with eyes closed, and when you open them, who knows which version of Bloody Mary you will see!

These types of entities appear everywhere and are usually tied to a local place or event, yet because of their universal nature, one has to wonder if there is more to the story behind these urban legends. Are they a part of our collective consciousness, manifesting all over the globe but with a few minor cultural differences? And if so, what do they mean?

One urban legend that does have a home is the Bell Witch, which refers to the Bell family in 1817. The John Bell family experienced a host of ghostly phenomena at their Adams, Tennessee, farm, including objects moving around, flying furniture, mysterious noises, and terrified animals, which they claimed was because of an alleged witch named Kate Batts. Kate was a neighbor to the Bell family who swore she would haunt Bell and his descendants after he cheated her in a land purchase. She made good on her promise and tormented the family after her death, after which she became known as the Bell Witch, although, ironically, the Bell family home activity was later ascribed to the young daughter, Betsy. But who cares about fact when creating an urban legend, and the Bell Witch story took off and became the inspiration for a number of popular modern movies, including *The Blair Witch Project*. After her death, it seemed that any bad luck that occurred to any member of the family was attributed to the Bell Witch. As her legend grew, she became more witch than human in origin and took on a decidedly evil, violent nature, which is the main reason for her popularity today in movies and paranormal television shows.

The Bell Witch even had her own cave on the property, and in 1817, there was a smattering of reports of bizarre animals near the cave and outside the house. The youngest Bell daughter, Betsy, was attacked by unseen forces, resulting in scratches, hair tugging, even physical beatings. The activity stopped when John Bell died in 1820 and Betsy called off her engagement. Today, those who take advantage of the tours of the home and the cave claim they can hear an old woman whispering in the dark, phantom hands that pull hair and even choke, and the sounds of laughing and moaning.

An artist's drawing of Betsy Bell, the youngest Bell daughter who was attacked by the Bell Witch back in the early 1800s.

If the Bell Witch cursing a family of farmers doesn't make you believe in the power of spells, the story of Rehmeyer's Hollow will. Locals call this Stewartstown, Pennsylvania, home the "Hex House," as it was once the home of a man named Nelson Rehmeyer, who was a Pennsylvania Dutch Powwow doctor or medicine man. He performed faith healings and witchcraft learned from his German roots, and he also may have practiced curses. Rehmeyer was the victim of another local witch, John H. Blymire, who believed Rehmeyer cursed him with bad health. Two teenager intruders who were friends of Blymire's beat Rehmeyer to death and set his house on fire to hide the body and other evidence of their crimes, but the house did not burn down. All three men were put on trial and charged with the arson and murder. The house became a favorite haunted hot spot for legend trippers and still stands today on Rehmeyer's Hollow Road.

Fresno's Famous Nightcrawlers

Back in the 1990s, the *Odyssey Online* reported sightings of a strange type of creature that was captured on an anonymous homeowner's outdoor surveillance video in southern Fresno, California. The man and his family were trying to get video of neighborhood dogs that were always trespassing on their property. Instead, they got video of two pale, extremely long-legged things with small heads striding across their lawn. In 2011, the same creatures showed up on security video at Yosemite National Park. The park had set up cameras to identify vandals and thieves who were destroying public property.

A local Native American tribe knew of the entities, claiming they've been walking around for centuries, and other tribes even had wood carvings of similar creatures. Theories include aliens, interdimensional entities, and cryptids, and some people claim the nightcrawlers were nothing but a hoax, except that sightings keep popping up. The SyFy Channel did an analysis of the original Fresno video for their *Fact or Faked* show and deemed it genuine and unaltered. Neither the family nor the police who investigated the initial sighting could figure out what they were seeing except that they were certainly not seeing humans. The family chose to remain anonymous, but the case made the news and took off like wildfire.

Because the entities are so strangely shaped and move so awkwardly, many people believe they are not of this world but have no fear of the creatures. They seem benign, never bother anyone, and for some reason like the areas around Fresno and Yosemite but could be more numerous than we think and exist in places they have not yet been spotted in. There have been no recent video captures of the entities. They caught on and avoid cameras, or they did their tourist thing here on earthly soil and vanished back into the place they came from … wherever that may be.

Walking Sam

South Dakota saw a wave of 103 suicide attempts up to December 2014 on the Pine Ridge Indian Reservation, all of which were attributed to the influence of a shadowy entity called Walking Sam. Teenagers on the reservation claimed to see a slender, shadowy man appear out of nowhere and command them to take their own lives. The first wave occurred in 2013 and resulted in five Oglala Sioux killing themselves. The situation got so bad, Tribal Vice President Thomas Poor Bear found photos on Facebook showing nooses hanging from trees and the plans behind a mass teenage suicide. The entity has been around a long time among Lakota Sioux and Dakota Native American tribes. Known as Stovepipe Hat Bigfoot or Taku-he, he has appeared to tribes as far back as 1974. Walking Sam may have its roots in the same origins as the Slender Man phenomenon from folklore and modern retellings of old legends that include a regional boogeyman.

Dudleytown's Dark Vortex

This Connecticut town is cursed according to many residents, who place the origin of the curse on the ill-fated Dudley family in England. Edmund Dudley suffered beheading for conspiring against King Henry VII. The curse was directed at the Dudley descendants who emigrated from England to Cornwall, Connecticut, in 1748 and helped establish a thriving iron industry. But when some untimely disasters and accidents befell the family, including strange deaths, insanity, and even suicide (some family members ran off into the woods never to be seen again), it was suggested they had brought a curse with them across the ocean. The residents then left the town, and it was abandoned except for the unusual phenomena reported in the area, including sinister wolfen creatures, floating balls of light, disembodied voices, and a bizarre lack of birds and other wildlife in the heavily forested area. There is even a rumor that the ghostly town is guarded by a mysterious, policelike group called The Dark Forest Association, and they are not too kind to trespassers.

A financial minister, speaker of the House of Commons, and president of the King's Council during the reign of England's King Henry VII, Edmund Dudley (at right, shown with King Henry VII [center] and minister Sir Richard Empson) was executed for treason, initiating a curse passed on to his descendants even as they fled to Connecticut.

Black-Eyed Girl

In 1967, seven-year-old Christine Darby was kidnapped from her home in Cannock Chase, England. The kidnapper was a man named Raymond Morris, who repeatedly raped the girl and then killed her, burying her body in a ditch. A year later, authorities discovered the body and arrested Morris, who was convicted of her murder and became suspect number one for other disappearances in the area involving girls Christine's age.

Years later, people in the town began reporting a black-eyed girl wandering the Cannock Chase countryside. Locals believe it is Christine, claiming she was blindfolded during her captivity and it caused her eyes to turn black.

The Berkley Square Horror

Another spooky tale from England happened at the location of 50 Berkeley Square in London and involves monsters. In the 1840s, twenty-year-old Sir Robert Warboys accepted a dare and spent the night in a haunted house with only a gun and candle inside. A guard was stationed outside the house. Late at night, the guard heard shouting and a gunshot. He rushed to Warboys's room on the second floor and found the young man dead. Warboys had allegedly died of fright.

In 1887, two sailors named Edward Blunden and Robert Martin needed a place to stay on Christmas Eve. They stayed in the house at 50 Berkeley Square, which was empty at the time. During the night, Martin heard the sound of Blunden being attacked by something and saw a horrifying, brown form strangling Blunden to death. It had tentacle-like arms and legs and looked as though it came up from the London sewer system. It was clearly *not* a ghost or human.

Martin ran and got a local police officer to return with him. Blunden's body had been thrown out of the second-story window and lay on the ground, crushed.

Today, the house is empty on the second floor, but the first floor is home to an antiquarian bookstore. On police orders, no one is permitted to go to the second floor. Bookstore employees and guests report hearing a host of strange noises above them.

Dog Boy

On Mulberry Street in tiny Quitman, Arkansas, there is a massive half-human, half-beast that chases people down the street biting at their heels like a dog. Only this "dog" looks like he weighs in at over three hundred pounds. This dog boy was a real person, namely Gerald Bettis, the son of the Bettis family, who lived on the street. Rumor has it, Gerald, a budding psychopath, would torture animals for fun, and eventually, he began torturing his elderly parents, locking them inside the home and possibly even murdering his own father. Gerald was later sent to jail for growing pot before it was legal and died in 1988 of a drug overdose. Either he is still haunting the street he called home or the Dog Boy is indeed some modern mutant animal living in the forest. Either possibility is quite horrifying to imagine and another example of an urban legend with a nugget of truth at its core.

Many urban legends start out happening in one or two locations, then go viral like bad memes on social networking. It then becomes hard to separate the fact from the fiction. One such example is the "Dead Body under the Bed" urban legend of a couple checking into a motel or hotel only to find a foul odor coming from under the bed at night. They get up and look and, lo and behold, find a dead body of some murder victim that was, for some strange reason, never spotted by the maid service before. Yet, there are actual claims of this very thing from people who have stayed in hotels in Las Vegas, Kansas City, Atlantic City, and California. It only makes sense that killing someone and leaving their body under the bed of a hotel or motel room would be a great way to get away with murder, so long as the killer didn't check in under their real name.

Another legend tells of a Halloween decoration of a hanged woman that turned out to be a real suicide. The truth in this case is spot-on. In Frederica, Delaware, a woman reportedly hanged herself in a tree near a busy road. The body remained there for over twenty-four hours and was witnessed by a number of drivers before someone reported it to the authorities. Then there are the numerous stories of people being buried alive and witnesses finding coffin lids with scratch marks in them, most likely the buried victims desperate to claw their way out before they perished from lack of air. But, in fact, live burials happened often back in the nineteenth century, so much so that one man, William Tebb, compiled a list of over two hundred cases of near-premature burial, 149 cases of actual premature burial, and a dozen cases where dissection or embalming had begun on a not-yet-deceased body. Granted, this was at a time when medical procedures were not as astute as they are today, especially in identifying a truly dead body from a still living one. The stuff of horror stories indeed, yet based on nuggets of truth.

NOTORIOUS GHOSTS, POLTERGEISTS, AND PARANORMAL HOT SPOTS

Some ghost stories and haunted locations truly stand out for their intensity and the terror they cause, whether to a family living on a farm or the hundreds of drivers who dare travel down a lonely road. Some become so notorious, they end up being made into movies or best-selling novels. In fact, most people don't know these situations even happened until they see it on the big screen or read about it.

Here are a few to ponder....

Famous Ghosts

Amityville Horror House

In 1977, Prentice Hall published a book by author Jay Anson called *The Amityville Horror: A True Story*. Up until then, most people were totally unaware of the horrors occurring in the small town of Amityville on the south shore of Long Island, particularly in a five-bedroom Dutch Colonial home. The story began on the night of November 13, 1974, when a twenty-three-year-old man named Ronald DeFeo Jr. shot his parents and four siblings to death with a .35 caliber Marlin 336C rifle at 3:00 A.M. while they slept peacefully in their beds. Two of the victims may have been awake during the time of the murder. All six were pronounced dead when they were found by Suffolk County police.

The family had lived there since 1965, and they were all buried together in the nearby Saint Charles Cemetery. DeFeo, the eldest son of the family, was taken into custody. He told police he thought the killings were the result of a mob hit. The next day, when his alibi proved false, he confessed to the murders and went to trial on October 14, 1975. He then claimed he killed his family because they were plotting against him. He was convicted of six counts of second-degree murder and was given six back-to-back, twenty-five-year-to-life sentences.

Thirteen months after the murders, the Lutz family took advantage of the home's reduced price and purchased it. They moved in but stayed only twenty-eight days before leaving. What happened to George and Kathy Lutz and their three children during that time has become the stuff of legends, spawning a blockbuster movie in 1979 starring James Brolin and Margot Kidder as George and Kathy Lutz and Oscar winner Rod Steiger as the priest that comes in to help and bless the house. Sequels and remakes soon followed.

But as truth is often stranger than fiction, the Lutz family experienced less than a month of pure terror before they left one night in a hurry. The level of paranormal activity that occurred in the house was through the roof, including:

- George woke up every night at 3:15 A.M., the exact same time as the DeFeo murders.
- Swarms of flies plagued the house, even in the cold winter.
- Apparitions appeared everywhere, and the family members reported cold spots, strange odors, and the sensations of being touched or, in Kathy's case, embraced by unseen arms.
- The image of a demon was burned into the back of the fireplace. The demon had half its head blown off.
- George found a small, hidden room in the basement with red walls, which the family dog refused to go near.
- Kathy had recurring nightmares of the murders and "saw" the order in which the DeFeo family was killed.
- The five-year-old daughter, Missy, claimed to have an imaginary friend named Jodie, a pig with red, glowing eyes, which was witnessed by George on Christmas Day.
- George, who closely resembled DeFeo, began going to the same local bar DeFeo often patronized.
- Kathy developed strange, red welts on her chest while in bed.
- Constant doors and windows opening and closing, strange bite marks, disembodied voices, and even green, oozing slime dripping from the walls.

The Lutzes tried their own home blessing in January 1976, but the paranormal phenomena continued. They eventually left the house with a few possessions to go to stay with Kathy's mother in Deer Park, but the phenomena followed them. With the help of their local priest, who came out to attempt to bless the house and cleanse it but heard a voice tell them to "Get out!", they apparently freed the house of demons, according to some reports, and left permanently on January 14. The priest also claimed he suffered blistering and was slapped by unseen hands in the house before he left.

Interestingly, the mover who came in to load up the rest of their things reported nothing at all wrong with the house.

On the night of March 6, 1976, famed demonologist couple Ed and Lorraine Warren, who founded the New England Society for Psychic Research in 1952, visited the home with a news crew and claimed to have captured a "demonic boy" on camera, which was made public in 1979, when the first film was about to be released. Publicity stunt or just good timing? Noted parapsychologist and author Hans Holzer also visited the house and claimed, along with the Warrens, that the house was indeed filled with evil spirits. Holzer went on to write several books about the Amityville events.

The address of the Amityville horror house (shown here in 2012) had to be changed by the owners in an attempt to confuse and reduce the number of unwanted gawkers and tourists.

Over the years, there has been a lot of controversy about the Amityville case and how much of the story was true and how much was fabricated. Add to that the differences made to the story for the sake of Hollywood's need to sell movie tickets (there were, at last count, sixteen Amityville Horror movies and sequels), and no one will really know exactly what happened in that house except the families who lived there and experienced what happened behind closed doors. The Lutzes took a lie-detector test and were found to be truthful, but the family's former lawyer, William Weber, who had a falling-out over financial issues with the couple, claimed they made the whole thing up to make money. Weber, interestingly, was DeFeo's defense attorney.

The son, Daniel, claims the house indeed ruined his life and continues to have nightmares to this day. He was featured in a documentary called *My Amityville Horror,* which was released in March 2013. Daniel confirmed the original story as told by his mother and stepfather in the documentary. He also makes additional claims that both he and George were possessed, that George demonstrated telekinetic abilities, and strongly suggests that George's interest in the occult, which was not portrayed in the original movie, might have initiated the demonic events.

The Lutzes stood by their story up until their deaths (George died in 2006 of heart disease and Kathy died in 2004 of emphysema). And they never

The Lutzes have stood by their story up until their deaths.... And they never got rich off of books and movies, struggling financially afterward.

got rich off of books and movies, struggling financially afterward. Contrary to many rumors, the Amityville house was not built upon ancient Indian burial ground, as confirmed by the Amityville Historical Society. Whatever happened in that house within the two years between the DeFeo murders and the Lutzes' terrifying encounters, only they know for sure.

The house was home to a number of families afterward, and its street address has been changed as a way to keep tourists and looky-loos away, although the style of the house is hard to miss.

Marion Parker's Ghost

In 1927, a violent psychopath named Edward Hickman kidnapped a twelve-year-old girl named Marion Parker from her childhood home in Los Angeles, California, with the intention of getting a nice ransom from her wealthy father, banker Perry Parker. Hickman caught Marion writing a letter to her parents about her kidnapping, and Hickman went crazy, choking the girl, then cutting off her arms and legs with a razor blade. He still wanted the ransom and told Parker she was still alive. He then powdered up her dead face, fixed up her hair, and sewed her eyelids open before putting her torso in the back of his car covered with a blanket. He drove to the site where the ransom would be waiting and delivered the girl bundled in the blanket to her father. By the time her father discovered she was dead, Hickman was gone. He was eventually caught, convicted of murder, and hanged in 1928. Marion's ghost is said to haunt her childhood home to this day.

The Sultan Prince

New Orleans is a city haunted by ghosts, demons, voodoo, and all sorts of paranormal activity. The large home at 716 Dauphine Street was one such place. It was known as "The Palace" in the 1860s, when the owner hosted loud parties almost every night. His name was Prince Suleyman, a Turkish sultan of a nonspecific Middle Eastern country, or so he told people, and he loved to have lavish parties, orgies, and harems of women and young boys at his whim. He had many wives and a large number of slaves, servants, and family members living at the palace.

Legend has it that a neighbor noticed the palace was unusually quiet one morning and called the police, who arrived to discover a horrifying scene. Bloodied bodies were strewn about the house, soaking the floors and ceilings with blood. The slaughtered victims included men, women, and children, yet the sultan was not among them. He was discovered buried alive in the yard, his hand reaching above the ground.

Police initially blamed pirates, who were active in the area at that time, but some people believed it was a revenge killing because the sultan had stolen his brother's money and fled to America to avoid execution. Whatever the reason, today people report seeing the ghost of the sultan himself and hearing the loud, raucous sounds of phantom partiers inside the palace.

The Connecticut Haunting

In 1986, the Snedeker family decided to rent an old house in Southington, Connecticut. The family consisted of Allen and Carmen Snedeker and their four kids: three sons and one daughter. In the basement, Carmen discovered a stash of old mortician tools, and they learned the house had once been a funeral parlor.

It wasn't long before the oldest son was experiencing terrifying visions and seeing ghosts, and soon, the rest of the family was as well. Allen and Carmen both reported they were sexually assaulted by demonic entities, and one day, while Carmen mopped the kitchen floor, the water turned to blood.

Ed and Lorraine Warren, the same demonologist couple who once investigated the Amityville house (above), were called in, and they claimed the house was infested with demonic spirits. The Snedekers even went on television to tell their horrific story, appearing on national talk shows. The story, of course, became a movie, *The Haunting in Connecticut* (2009), which was based on a book horror novelist Ray Garton wrote in 1992. Garton was hired by the Warrens to write the Snedeker family's story and later admitted he found holes in the story the couple told him.

The Snedekers stood by their story, but the family's maid, who was there at the time of the alleged hauntings, reported to *Skeptical Inquirer* she never heard or saw anything unusual in the two years the family lived there. Rumors swirled that the family, seeing how much publicity the Lutz family got, made up the haunting to financially benefit from the book deal. This theory still plagues the Amityville story to this day. Was it real, or was it made up? Again, only the families involved know for sure.

Paranormal researcher Lorraine Warren is shown here at a 2013 speech she gave at Wondercon. She and her husband, Ed, investigated the doings at Amityville and at the Perron house in Rhode Island.

The Conjuring—The Perron Family Story

Another blockbuster movie, *The Conjuring* (2013), starred Patrick Wilson and

Vera Farmiga as Ed and Lorraine Warren. The film told the story of Roger and Carolyn Perron, who moved into a haunted, eighteenth-century Burrillville, Rhode Island, farmhouse with their five daughters. The family soon realized they weren't alone and experienced a host of frightening paranormal activity, even possession by demonic spirits. Lorraine Warren was a consultant on the film and insisted the movie depicted what she and her husband found when they began investigating the house and the family's claims.

The Perron family lived in the fourteen-room farmhouse for nine years, from January 1971 to 1980, during which time they experienced both harmless and malevolent spirits, including one they called Bathsheba, who acted as though she were the matriarch of the house and resented the mother, Carolyn. According to family members, including Andrea Perron, one of the five daughters, spirits would arrive around 5:00 A.M. and lift the beds up. They stunk of rotting flesh, but the family continued to stay. They never would enter the basement, though, believing it to be a center of activity. Sometimes, Roger would have to go down to fix broken heating equipment and reportedly felt the presence of something cold and awful.

The Warrens visited the farmhouse repeatedly in 1974, but they did not attempt an exorcism, which was the domain of a Catholic priest. Andrea Perron recalled seeing her mother being possessed during a séance and speak in a strange language as her chair was lifted and thrown across the room.

Perron has published a series of books documenting the events from the eyes of someone who experienced them.

Roland Doe, or the Boy with Many Names

Exorcisms of possessed humans are not common, but they have happened over the course of history and continue to do so. One such case served as the foundation for one of the most successful horror movies ever to be released, *The Exorcist*. Released in 1979, the movie was based on the 1971 novel of the same name by William Peter Blatty, which was inspired by the Doe case. Many people who flocked to the theater to see the movie had no idea there was some truth to the horrific story of possession.

Roland Doe, who was also known as Ronnie Doe, Ronald Hunkeler, and Robbie Mannheim, was born in 1935 in Cottage City, Maryland. His mother was Lutheran, and his father was Catholic. His Aunt Tillie (Aunt Harriet) was a spiritualist who introduced him to the wonders of the Ouija board when he was fourteen years old, and after his aunt died, she supposedly possessed him via the Ouija board. The family began noticing the sounds of angry voices and furniture moving across the rooms at night. Roland's body would break out in strange, inexplicable claw marks, and he would feel sharp pains in his stomach, so the family decided to leave for St. Louis, Missouri, to escape the creepy activity, especially when the boy's behavior began turning dark.

While in St. Louis, the family met with Father Raymond Bishop and Father William Bowdern from the Xavier College Church. The two priests entered Roland's room and were immediately assaulted by invisible demons that threw holy water across the room and moved bookcases around in front of their eyes. The men got permission a few days later to perform an exorcism and returned, working over the next few days to free the boy of a host of evil demons. Because the family was so stressed, they carried out the rest of the exorcism rites on Roland at the psychiatric ward of the Alexian Brothers Hospital in South St. Louis, Missouri. The exorcism was considered complete and successful on Monday, April 18, when the final evil demon was banished from the boy.

Author William Peter Blatty wrote *The Exorcist,* which is about the Roland Doe case and was made into a successful horror film in 1979.

From that point on, the Doe boy never experienced another event and lived a peaceful life.

Though Blatty admitted his novel changed a few elements from the original story of Roland Doe, including the child's gender and the location of the home, much of it was indeed based on the Doe story. As with all of these notorious hauntings, skeptics claimed the boy was not possessed at all but perhaps mentally ill or just deeply disturbed. The theory of poltergeist phenomena was also raised, which could have resulted in the moving objects and items flying across the room. Others believed it was just plain trickery and fraud and that all of the alleged behaviors could have easily been faked by the boy (except for the stuff they claimed was poltergeist activity!).

POLTERGEISTS

The problem with ghosts, poltergeists, and demonic activity is that it often looks the same on the surface or occurs in tandem. Poltergeist activity is a whole specific field of paranormal phenomena that involves a specific person—called the human host or human agent—and not a location such as a house or cemetery. The human agent is often young, female, and going through hormonal and behavioral changes that may cause brain activity associated with psychokinesis, the ability to move objects without touching them.

The word poltergeist means "noisy ghost" or "noisy spirit" and comes from the German *poltern* or "to make sound, to rumble," and *geist*, or "ghost, spirit." The characteristics of a true poltergeist involve physical disturbances and loud noises such as objects flying across the room, doors banging closed, knocks on walls, and even large pieces of furniture moving about but also include biting, kicking, slapping, pinching, and hitting. The spirits are described as mischievous and a bit malevolent, if not downright violent, but often don't appear unless prompted or provoked by the proximity of the human agent, who seems to serve as a type of channel. Poltergeist phenomena occur in almost every country of the world but under different names, and accounts date back as far as the first century C.E.

While spiritualists believe these are the lowest of the low spirits on the hierarchy of spirits (that's not very nice!), scientists claim they are nothing but ball lightning.

So, are these ghosts or demons? Or are they some kind of physical manifestation of teenage angst? Are they trickster spirits, or are they natural phenomena, such as the presence of water beneath a house that causes all kinds of creaks and groans, or nearby seismic activity?

While spiritualists believe these are the lowest of the low spirits on the hierarchy of spirits (that's not very nice!), scientists claim they are nothing but ball lightning, although one is hard-pressed to explain how ball lightning can move a couch across the room on its own.

If the cause is indeed psychokinesis and the human agents are usually adolescent girls, or even boys, who somehow are unconsciously manipulating energy to move objects, it would make sense to do more research into the potential of the human brain and the parts of the brain that are active during a poltergeist event. In fact, Dr. Barry Taff, a noted parapsychologist with a Ph.D. in psychophysiology, has studied poltergeist phenomena at length for years, including over four thousand cases, many sharing common characteristics.

His studies began with one of the most notorious cases ever, which served as the basis for a 1982 horror movie called *The Entity*, starring Barbara Hershey as a single mother who claimed she was being raped by spirits. In 1974, Doris Bither and her four children experienced pure terror at the hands of unseen forces in their small Culver City, California, home. Dr. Taff and his colleague Kerry Gaynor visited with Doris and listened to her talk of ghostly activity at the home, then she told them about the rapes. She claimed three spirits were involved, two of which held her down while the third raped her. She was referred to a clinical psychologist at UCLA, but when Taff and Gaynor went back to the house two weeks later, they witnessed a number of things that made them believe Doris wasn't making it all up.

The overpowering smell of rotting flesh, cold spots, and a frying pan that flew out of a cabinet and across the room were enough for the two. Weeks of investigating followed using all types of equipment, ending with the appearance of a full-body apparition that was witnessed by over two dozen people at the house. Even before then, the children reported seeing shadow figures moving across the living room, and soon, even neighbors could see the humanoid shapes that appeared like dark fog moving around or standing in corners of the house watching.

Doris left the house with her family, but the activity followed her wherever she went. However, each time she moved her family, the entities seemed to get weaker and weaker. Eventually, Dr. Taff lost contact with her. But it was from that research Dr. Taff came up with three strong points he felt were responsible for poltergeist manifestation:

1. The location of the activity contains EMF anomalies.
2. The human agent is prone to seizures or is an epileptic.
3. The human agent is neurologically "wired" to not cope well with stress, which enables a hyperactive nervous system response.

These three things may work in concert to produce just the right internal and external environment for a poltergeist event to occur. Taff added that the poltergeist behavior acts like a virus and can follow the human agent from location to location until it just stops on its own. The psychokinesis that accompanies the presence of a poltergeist might be the result of energy fields from the brain acting on the external environment coupled with the anger and angst of the host or human agent. The same parts of the brain that are activated during an epileptic grand mal seizure are the same parts of the brain that seem to be active in a human agent during poltergeist activity. Studies by parapsychologists into temporal lobe epilepsy and its association with raised levels of psi abilities and how bursts of electrical activity in the brain responsible for seizures might also be responsible for PK are ongoing.

His conclusion was the family was indeed under demonic attack and suggested the adopted eleven-year-old daughter, Dinah, was the channel for the sinister activity.

No matter whether poltergeists are purely natural, the stuff of demons, trickster spirits, human agents with PK abilities, or maybe some combination of causes, they are terrifying.

The Dagg Haunting

A quiet farm in Clarendon, Quebec, Canada, was turned upside down in 1899 when a poltergeist attacked the family living there. Mrs. Dagg awoke on a fine, spring day to do her chores, but when she entered the farmhouse living room, she was accosted by a strange smell and the sight of animal feces smeared across the floor. The young farmhand, Dean, was accused of the foul deed since he worked outside with the hogs and often entered the house with his filthy shoes on. He had been warned before about doing so and was told he would be fired. He denied ever even being in the house that morning, but he was fired anyway.

As the days went by, more bizarre activity occurred, including loud banging sounds and large rocks crashing through windows. Plates were tossed across the room by invisible hands, and the father, George Dagg, got a group of employees together to search Dean's property, thinking he might be taking revenge on the farm for being fired. But they found nothing to accuse Dean of the strange events, which continued to the point where Mrs. Dagg suggested a demonic entity was responsible. She was an adherent of Spiritualism, and eventually, she got word to a psychic named Percy Woodstock, who came to the farm and set up a full-on investigation. His conclusion was the family was indeed under demonic attack and suggested the adopted eleven-year-old daughter, Dinah, was the channel for the sinister activity. Dinah confirmed she was in contact with a mischievous spirit that lived out in the old shed. When Woodstock went to the shed to investigate, he was greeted by a deep, guttural laugh that told Woodstock he was the Devil and would break his neck if he didn't leave the house.

Obviously, Woodstock packed up his gear and split. But months later, fires broke out around the house, awful banging could be heard all night, jugs of water were thrown into the faces of the family and guests, and an entity revealed itself as an old man who died on the property. The family children reported the entity appeared sometimes as a devil with a cow's head and hooved feet and other times as a black dog with glowing, red eyes. Another entity appeared in the form of a tall man with flowing, white hair and a brilliant crown of stars upon his head. It was that entity that told the children he was leaving and they would suffer no longer. True to his word, they watched as he floated up into the sky and vanished. The farm and the family experienced nothing but the peace and quiet of normal life afterward.

Maria Jose Ferreira

Imagine being eleven years old and becoming the target of a terrifying poltergeist. That is what happened to Maria Jose Ferreira in Jaboticabal, Brazil, in 1965. Maria was assaulted by an invisible assailant, and stones and bricks would appear out of nowhere and be thrown through the house. Often, Maria would manifest scratches, claw marks, bites, and slap marks on her body, which was constantly bruised. An exorcist from the local church came to the house but to no avail. If anything, it angered the poltergeist even more because now, poor little Maria would be set on fire while out in public.

Maria's family took her to a local medium, who claimed the girl had been an evil witch in a past life and was now being attacked by the spirits of those she tormented. The medium attempted to get the spirts to leave Maria alone, but it failed to work. Maria ended up swallowing pesticides and took her own life. The poltergeist activity ended upon her death, never to return.

A Boy Named Danny

A 1998 story appeared in the *Savannah Morning News* about a haunted antique bed owned by a man named Al Cobb of Savannah, Georgia. The reporter, Jane Fishman, wrote that the bed was vintage 1800s and had been purchased at an auction as a Christmas gift for Al's fourteen-year-old son, Jason. Three nights after the bed was delivered, Jason began to complain of strange sensations of a presence. He said he felt like someone was resting their elbows on his pillow and breathing down his neck. He began to feel sick. The next night, a photo of his grandparents on his nightstand flipped over. Jason stood it back up, and it flipped over again.

In the morning, he found two Beanie Babies in the center of his bed next to a conch shell, a dinosaur made of shells, and a papier-mâché toucan bird. None of these were his, so he got his parents. Al came into the room and asked, "Do we have a Casper here?" He asked the ghost, or whatever was in the room, to tell him its name and age. Al left some lined paper and crayons on the bed, and they left the room.

Fifteen minutes later, when they went back in, someone had written in large, childlike letters "Danny, 7." Al continued trying to communicate with Danny but only when the family was safely away. The ghost child told Al that his mother had died in the antique bed in 1899, he wanted to be with the bed, and no one else was permitted to sleep in it. One of the notes read "No one sleep in bed." Jason had already moved into a different room but one day took a nap on the antique bed. Al was upset, went to check on Jason, and had to dodge a flying terra-cotta pot hanging on the wall that was thrown at him by unseen hands, no doubt belonging to an angry Danny. However, a host of other activity began such as furniture moving on its own, kitchen drawers opening and closing, some invisible hands setting the dining table, chairs being flipped over, and the presence of other spirits the family came to know as Jill, Uncle Sam, and a young girl named Gracie, whose statue sits in the Bonaventure Cemetery. Jason seemed to be the center of the activity, but some paranormal investigators suggested it may have been the bed or the house itself. In other words, nobody knows.

Enfield Poltergeist

The most notorious poltergeist case is the Enfield case, which occurred on a small home in Brimsdown, Enfield, England, from 1977 to 1979. Two sisters, Janet Hodgson, age eleven, and Margaret Hodgson, age fourteen, were at the heart of the controversial story. In August 1977, single mom Peggy Hodgson summoned police to the family home in Enfield after her four children claimed furniture moved on its own and there were strange knocks coming from inside the walls. The female constable sent to the home even witnessed a chair slide across the room. Other activity included disembodied voices, toys and rocks flying through the air, strange noises, overturned chairs, and the children levitating in midair. This went on for over a year and a half and was witnessed by over thirty neighbors, reporters, and psychic researchers. The case received a great deal of media, and Peggy was even accused of creating a hoax as a way to make money.

The activity appeared to end around 1979. The psychic and paranormal investigators on the scene claimed the activity appeared to center around Janet, the younger daughter, and many people claimed she and her older sister faked the activity, allegedly caught on a video camera in the next room. But the faked activity couldn't explain large pieces of furniture moving on their own. The girls admitted their pranks to reporters, although some felt they were forced into the confession. Lead researchers Maurice Grosse and Guy Lyon Playfair from the Society for Psychical Research were humiliated for the admission as well as their peers, deciding that the girls were faking everything and that Janet was an expert at ventriloquism. They apparently did it for media attention.

The girls admitted their pranks to reporters, although some felt they were forced into the confession. Lead researchers Maurice Grosse and Guy Lyon Playfair from the Society for Psychical Research were humiliated for the admission....

For the following few years, believers and skeptics tossed their own pet theories of what happened back and forth, some making good sense but others bordering on the absolutely ridiculous. Like a political debate, the two sides battled back and forth with skeptics refusing to open their minds to the possibility the girls were genuinely telling the truth and the believers refusing to consider the girls might have been faking it from the start. Hollywood jumped on the case and released a movie in 2016 about it, *The Conjuring 2*, and there have been a number of documentaries on the case.

THE COLUMBUS POLTERGEIST CASE

In 1984, the teenage adopted daughter of Joan and John Resch appeared to be the human agent behind a series of poltergeist attacks that garnered widespread media attention. Tina Resch was only fourteen when she saw the movie *Poltergeist*, and soon after, the family reported objects flying about the house and doors opening and closing. The local newspaper, the *Columbia Dispatch*, sent a reporter, Mike Harden, and a photographer, Fred Shannon, to check out the activity. They interviewed Tina and later published the story along with some photos of a telephone flying through the air.

A noted parapsychologist named William Roll asked to stay with the Resch family and document the activity, which resulted in his book *Unleashed:*

Of Poltergeists and Murder: The Curious Story of Tina Resch. Roll claimed there was ample spontaneous psychokinesis but never witnessed it with his own eyes. It often seemed to occur when he had his back to Tina or the room in question or was distracted elsewhere. A television crew that visited later caught Tina on tape kicking over a table lamp and screaming. When they confronted her, she claimed she did it so the reporters would finally leave.

Tina married and divorced twice after those events and changed her name to Christina Boyer. She had a daughter, Amber, who was found dead at the age of three, allegedly beaten to death. Boyer and her boyfriend, David Herrin, were arrested for the child's murder. The cause of death was blunt force trauma to the head. Both Boyer and Herrin blamed the other for the death, and eventually, Boyer was charged with aggravated battery. She agreed to a plea bargain to avoid the death penalty and continued to maintain her innocence. She got a life sentence with no possibility of parole. Herrin received twenty years.

Boyer, aka Resch, continued to maintain her innocence long after the media frenzy faded.

Roll later admitted that while Tina could have staged some of the more minor events, she could not have staged all of them and that there were many witnesses who saw the phenomena and agreed. The house became so uninhabitable from items flying around and breaking, glass shattering everywhere, and appliances starting up and causing potential danger that the case still is open to debate.

The Great Amherst Mystery

A tiny cottage in Amherst, Nova Scotia, Canada, was home to a family who experienced strange and frightening poltergeist activity from 1878 to 1879. The activity was first noted by nineteen-year-old Esther Cox, who lived in the cottage with her family. When Esther was eighteen, she was traumatized by a sexual assault by a male friend. The strange phenomena started shortly afterward.

This house in Amherst, Nova Scotia, is where the teenager Esther Cox became the center of a poltergeist attack on the family, and Esther suffered seizures as well.

One night, she and her sister Olive, who also lived there with her husband, two young children, and three other members of the family, felt something move under the covers of the bed they shared in one room. There was nothing there. Phantom knocking and banging with no discernible origin plagued the house. Esther began having seizures, and objects would then fly about the rooms on their own. Doctors gave Esther sedatives, but the disturbances increased, and when a psychic attempted to contact spirits in the house, there were strange knocking responses.

The activity continued for months, and in December, Esther contracted diphtheria and was bedridden for two weeks. During that time, the poltergeist activity ceased, even when she was sent to recuperate with a family member. But when she returned to the Amherst home, it began all over again. This time, fires broke out all over the house and Esther reported seeing a ghost, who warned it would burn the house down unless she left. Esther went away to stay with a local family, but the activity followed her and was witnessed by several others. Esther began experiencing abuse by the ghosts, including being slapped, pinched, and scratched.

The events were becoming more known outside the local community and Esther went to Saint John in New Brunswick to get away, but the phenomena followed. She was investigated by more researchers, who communicated with spirits via knocking and rapping. The spirits now had identities. Bob Nickle was the ghost of a shoemaker; Peter Cox was a distant relative; and there was a female spirit named Maggie Fisher.

Esther moved again, and this time, an actor who was an amateur parapsychologist, Walter Hubbell, was brought on board to help investigate. He spent weeks with Esther and her family at their summer cottage in Teeds and talked with the spirits, including two new ones—Jane Nickle and Eliza McNeal, although it was never revealed why the spirits were tormenting Esther or if she was indeed the catalyst. He even helped Esther deal with the entities, and she soon went on a speaking tour to talk about the phenomena to mixed audiences. Some welcomed her experiences; others were incredibly hostile and accused her of faking everything. She soon returned to the original Amherst home and worked for a man whose barn burned down mysteriously. He blamed her, and Esther spent a month in prison. At that time, the poltergeist phenomena stopped and never returned.

Esther married twice, had two sons, and moved to Massachusetts, where she died on November 8, 1912, at the age of fifty-two.

A Haunting in San Pedro

Parapsychologist Dr. Barry Taff was involved in another poltergeist case, this time in 1989, when he was asked to visit a home in San Pedro, California. The owner was a young woman named Jackie Hernandez, and she claimed the house was haunted with strange smells, sounds, and apparitions, including a weird, glowing cloud that tried suffocating her in front of witnesses. Even when Jackie tried to leave the house, the activity followed her, and she was terrified.

Taff worked with her and believed she had emotional issues, including a strong romantic attachment to Barry Conrad, the cameraman and photographer he brought with him to document the activity. In fact, anyone the "spirit" deemed a threat to her and Barry was viciously attacked by the unseen entities. However, there were also other entities reported by witnesses in the house, and after Jackie left, the house continued to be haunted, causing any new tenants to bolt within six months of moving in!

Borley Rectory

Over in England, another shocking case occurred and was investigated by paranormal researcher Harry Price. The Borley Rectory was an old, crumbling manor house in Essex County, England. Price read a newspaper report in 1929 about the paranormal activity at the Rectory and went to investigate. The report claimed there were phantom footsteps, ghostly whispers, a headless apparition, a young girl ghost dressed in white, strange lights, and several other identifiable spirits roaming around. It sounded like a classic case of ghosts.

There was also a local legend about the Rectory being built upon the former site of a monastery, where a thirteenth-century monk and a young novice had been killed trying to elope. The monk was hanged to death, and the novice was buried alive in the walls of a convent. In October 1930, Reverend Lionel Foyster and his wife, Marianne, moved into the peaceful building. Suddenly, the place became a hotbed of paranormal activity, and people were locked out of rooms, windows shattered, objects vanished, and furniture moved on its own.

Marianne was thrown from her bed, slapped by phantom hands, had large objects thrown at her day and night, and she was almost killed by a mattress suffocating her. Scrawled messages began appearing on the walls, but they were pleading with Marianne as if needing her help: "Marianne, please help get:" and "Marianne, light mass prayers."

The Borley Rectory, shown here in 1892, was the site of a vicious poltergeist attack in 1930 in which a reverend and his wife were the victims.

Harry Price determined that Marianne was the human agent behind the activity, but he also suggested the ghosts might also be real. Perhaps it was Marianne's kindness and sympathetic nature that caused the ghosts to get her attention. However, no one knows.

Black Monk

Another terrifying English poltergeist case occurred at the forbiddingly named Black Monk House on a quiet street in Pontefract, Yorkshire, England. The small, brick house would be home to Jean and Joe Pritchard, who bought the house to live in with their two teenagers, Philip and Diane, and Jean's mother, Sarah. The activity began in small ways at first, including chalk falling from the ceiling or water pooling on the floor despite no leaks or other sources. Sarah would try to clean up the water, but more would appear after she dried the spot.

Joe and Jean witnessed the ghost of a spirit in black monk robes hovering over their bed one night. The same ghost monk appeared a number of times in the house and on the property. Lights began flickering on and off, heavy plants would fall down the stairs, and family pictures were being slashed by unseen hands. The house began to smell like death at times, and if the family left, they often would return home to find furniture overturned.

After about two years of this type of activity, things began to escalate, and Diane was grabbed by the monk ghost, who had never attempted any such thing before. She said he grabbed her by the neck and dragged her up the stairs. This prompted the family to call in the help of exorcists, who only seemed to make the monk ghost more violent and angry.

Naturally, the media had a field day, and some researchers confirmed that the house was built on land that had been where King Richard II was killed. The land was also the site of former wars, and after the activity ceased, paranormal investigator Tom Cuniff researched the case for years and discovered that a priory had existed near the Black Monk House from 1090 to 1599 and the town gallows had been located across the street. One of the monks hanged there was accused of raping and murdering a young girl, who had been the very same age as Diane Pritchard.

Macomb Poltergeist

In 1948, a disturbed teenager named Wanet McNeil moved in with her father after her parents divorced in 1948. They moved to a farm west of Macomb, Illinois, and Wanet was very unhappy living there. Her emotions were all over the map because of the bitter divorce, and she began to manifest strange poltergeist activity in the form of small fires she set with her mind all over the farm.

The first fire happened on August 7 on the farm of a man named Charles Willey. It began with small, brown spots on the wallpaper inside the home that would then spontaneously burst into flames. Neighbors had to be called upon to come by the house and put out daily fires, and soon, the fire chief was called in to launch an investigation. He had the Willeys strip the wallpaper from their house, and the same brown spots then appeared on the bare plaster beneath, erupting into flames before dozens of witnesses.

The front porch began to ignite along with curtains in each room and one bed. Not even the National Fire Underwriters Laboratory, who were called in to investigate, knew why or how the fires were starting. It got to the point in which over two hundred fires broke out, averaging twenty-nine per day, and eventually, an entire house was destroyed. Willey created a tarp home for his family, but the next day, their barn burned down. Days later, the second barn burned down, along with other structures, and the family fled.

The U.S. Air Force even got involved as more fires broke out, and soon, the farm was filled with over a thousand people coming to see what was happening.

The U.S. Air Force even got involved as more fires broke out, and soon, the farm was filled with over a thousand people coming to see what was happening.

Eventually, Wanet was accused of starting the fires with simple kitchen matches. She confessed to the deputy fire marshal and said it was because she was unhappy and didn't like living on the farm. She missed her mother and had caused the fires to rebel. But that never explained the strange, brown spots and how they turned into fires or the fires that happened on the ceilings of buildings, even when Wanet was nowhere around. But the confession made everyone happy and they closed the case, except for hundreds of reporters and paranormal researchers who believed Wanet was the human agent for poltergeist phenomena.

The fires eventually stopped, and Wanet went to live with her grandmother. Everyone accepted she was guilty of arson. Well, not everyone....

Sauchie Poltergeist

For one year, from 1960 to 1961, the town of Sauchie, Clackmannanshire, Scotland, was terrorized by a poltergeist that focused on the home of the Campbell family. Husband, Thomas; wife, Isabella; daughter, Margaret; and son, Derek, resided with Thomas's sister, Annie, and her daughter, Virginia, who appeared to be the human cause. When Annie and Virginia moved in with the family in the autumn of 1960, that's when the activity began, with objects vanishing and reappearing elsewhere in the house, furniture levitating in the air and moving on its own, pillows and bedding rippling from unseen forces, doors opening and closing, and family members being pinched and poked. The same activity occurred at Virginia's school and at a temporary home she lived in in the town of Dollar. There were many witnesses, including the town's doctor, minister, and a teacher, and no trickery was ever found. Psychic investigator George Owen documented the case and considers it an example of psychokinesis associated with the human agent, Virginia.

San Diego Poltergeist?

This author experienced her own poltergeist phenomena over three decades ago at a large home in San Diego, California. To protect the identity of the family, we will call them the Wilkes family. The activity consisted of objects flying around the house, including clothespins that would hurtle down an upstairs hallway. Pictures were said to move around or topple off their nails. Strange noises and knockings were experienced by the family, all of which seemed to center on a teenage daughter, who was having emotional issues dealing with school and dating.

Though the activity was never hostile, it was dangerous to get hit by a flying clothespin. The family thought the activity came from an antique clock that would ring at odd times, but when the activity ceased after the daughter in question moved out, the clock was let off the hook. At one point, the author of this book stayed overnight and experienced a strange, cold wind moving through her the next morning, at which time the younger daughter said, "Did you feel it?" It felt as though a breeze literally moved through every cell, yet there were no open doors or windows at the time.

The Wilkes family talked to their local church about assisting with stopping the strange phenomena, but because they were Lutheran, exorcisms were not performed. The family ended up moving away after a while, long after the daughter, who appeared to be the human agent, had gone off to college, and the new owners of the home had it razed and rebuilt from the foundation up. No one ever found out why.

The late paranormal investigator William Roll was a psychology professor at the University of West Georgia. He believed poltergeists were the result of what he called "recurrent spontaneous psychokinesis."

An Indianapolis Poltergeist

A suburban street in Indianapolis, Indiana, was the home of Renate Beck, her widowed mother, Lina Gemmecke, and her daughter, Linda, who was thirteen at the time the activity began. Objects moved about the house, glassware and pots and pans were thrown by unseen forces, and pillows and photographs were torn by unseen hands. Lina experienced what looked like bite marks. There was a lot of hostility between Renate and her mother, which created tensions that might have led to the activity, but in this case, the daughter was not around when most of it occurred. The case was investigated by William Roll, who was known for his investigation and subsequent book documenting the Tina Resch case. Along with him was Dr. David Blumenthal, a clinical psychologist who visited the home and witnessed the family over several days. The activity was confined mainly to the two weeks between March 10 and March 24, 1962. The mother, Lina, was reported to have caused quite a bit of trouble and was even seen throwing an ashtray and turning over furniture. She was arrested and later returned to her home in Germany after doing some jail time. When she left, all poltergeist activity ceased.

Another case investigated by William Roll involved a nineteen-year-old Cuban refugee named Julio Vasquez. His family life was stressful, and he attempted suicide shortly after he was hired to work at the Warehouse of Tropication Arts, a wholesaler of novelty items, in Miami, Florida. From 1966 to 1967, when Julio worked there, objects began moving and breaking, ashtrays and glasses were thrown across the rooms, and boxes would be overturned or moved by unseen hands. Julio apparently did not get along well with his boss, and the phenomena only occurred when he was working on-site, but witnesses claim he was nowhere near the items that were thrown or boxes that were overturned. His mere presence at work seemed to be enough. Naturally, when he left the company, the activity ceased but allegedly continued at other places Julio worked afterward.

In many poltergeist cases, the activity starts out small, then escalates to the point where it poses a danger to all involved. Yet, it often ceases after a while on its own and not necessarily when the human agent in question leaves or moves away. Perhaps it ceases when the agent's hormones and emotions level off enough to end the kinetic activity and there is not enough energy left for the phenomena to feed off of and manifest from.

PARANORMAL HOT SPOTS

Imagine a place where just about every possible paranormal anomaly occurs all within a fixed boundary. Known as hot spots, these can be massive desert landscapes, mountain ranges, top-secret military bases, specific bodies of water, or intersections of highways that defy the known laws of reality. In these regions, beasts roam that are rarely seen on the outside, and anomalies occur that challenge gravity and laws of physics. Sometimes, human activities add to the creepy atmosphere such as cults and satanic rituals.

Often, Native American tribes know the lands are cursed and why. It is only natural that the land that once belonged to Native American tribes be filled with legends, lore, and spirits from their vast pantheon of traditions and beliefs. The fact that some of these legends might have a great deal of truth to them chills the bones of the most enthusiastic legend tripper, paranormal enthusiast, and even horror-movie aficionado. The following hot spots are filled with a variety of phenomena, as if these specific areas are marked by otherworldly forces as unique and special. Are they vortices leading to other realities, where life in those realities travels the highways and byways that lead here? Though not all hot spots have a Native influence, they all seem to attract every possible type of anomalous phenomena known to exist.

Black Star Canyon

Southern California's Orange County is known for its gorgeous beaches and suburban neighborhoods, but to the east are the Santa Ana Mountains, filled with trails locals say are haunted by a bloody past. The canyon itself is an archaeological site filled with artifacts of the Shoshone American Indian tribe, and it also serves as a reminder of the violence and bloodshed in the 1800s, when the Shoshone fought white settlers who were encroaching on their land. Trappers who wanted to ingratiate themselves to the Spanish would sneak down into the area called Hidden Ranch and plan their attack, which involved lying in wait and then assaulting the Shoshone with guns, while the Shoshone had mainly arrows to defend themselves. The Shoshone suffered terrible losses, although few of the white men died.

Black Star Canyon in Orange County, California, was once the domain of the Shoshone Indians as well as deadly battles between them and European encroachers. The spirits of the dead are said to still inhabit the canyon trails.

Along with the deaths from the ongoing battles were murders committed on Hidden Ranch during the Wild West's final days, including an actual shoot-out between two horse-ranching families who were feuding that resulted in the death of James M. Gregg and, of course, deaths from the elements and harsh conditions.

The canyon has been haunted ever since by the spirits of those who perished there, and many ghost-hunting groups and psychics have braved the terrain to try to contact the dead. Witnesses in the canyon say they've seen ghosts of men lost in battle, mainly Shoshone warriors, and the spirit of James M. Gregg walks about the land near Hidden Ranch. A dark energy permeates the area, and paranormal groups claim to capture tons of EVP of the dead. But the creepiest thing about Black Star Canyon is the famous—or maybe infamous—winds. The area is eerily quiet and still, but sudden gusts of wind will start up, howling loudly through the canyon. While there are desert winds called Santa Anas that blow fast and hard in the area during the fall months, or fire season, as the locals call it, there are those who believe the howls are coming from the spirits of the dead Shoshone.

TERRORS OF TURNBULL CANYON

Puente Hills, California, is a sunny chain of hills covered in chaparral with ample hiking trails, parks, and open spaces for biking and off-roading. Located just south of the San Gabriel Valley in an unincorporated part of east Los Angeles County, the western hills are often called the Whittier Hills. The terrain mixes desert landscaping with woodsy spots as well as the Puente Hills Landfill, the country's largest landfill, which closed in 2013. The mostly rural and uninhabited hills are filled with a plethora of flora and fauna indigenous to the region and also an incredible number of terrifying stories of paranormal high jinks and just plain creepy human behavior.

One particular spot seems the most "haunted." Turnbull Canyon was the home to an insane asylum in the 1930s and was open for ten years before it burned to the ground in a mysterious fire in the early 1940s. The ruins remain and are said to be haunted by the dark spirits of those who were abused and mistreated while patients, many of whom died. According to "Turnbull Canyon Deaths: Ghosts of the Old Asylum" on the *Haunted Los Angeles* website, in the early 1960s, a group of teenagers were hiking in the canyon and found an old electric shock device among the ruins. One of the young men, who may have been intoxicated, strapped the device to his head, bragging about how he was going to burn—and he did. Even though there was no electricity to be found, the device fired up and sent thousands of volts into his body. His hair, clothes, then eyes and skin burned, and within seconds, while his friends watched in horror, he was dead.

Over the decades, the area has been full of ghostly encounters, including the spirits of children swinging from trees who open their eyes if you stare at them. They may have been victims of satanic cults said to be operating in the remote ruins. The ghosts of Native Americans and patients from the asylum wander the ruins and hills, and huge pentagrams have been found carved into the earth. The Orange County Police Department reported that Richard Ramirez, known as the Night Stalker serial killer, belonged to a cult that met in the canyon.

Locals claim the area is cursed by Native Americans and others claim by witches. UFOs are sighted repeatedly as if the Turnbull Canyon area is some kind of paranormal vortex. Psychics who visit the place hoping to contact spirits of the dead sense strong feelings of panic and dread. Rumors of murders run rampant, and hundreds of years ago, the canyon was given the name Hutukgna, or "the dark place," which refers to the ghosts that reside on this forbidden ground. In fact, when later Spanish settlers arrived, they chose to ignore the warnings of the cursed land and built their San Gabriel Mission nearby. The settlers drove the poor off the land and made the natives convert to Christianity or be slaughtered. Many natives simply chose to die, refusing to give the settlers what they wanted and knowing that in death, their spirits would remain a part of the land, even if their living bodies could not.

Another southern California hot spot is Turnbull Canyon in the Puente Hills, where everything from ghosts to UFOs have been reported.

In more modern years, the canyon locals reported seeing men, women, and children performing strange rituals late at night while dressed in black robes and hoods. A young boy was strapped to a cross as the cultists danced and chanted around him. The cross was lifted, turned upside down, and the boy tried to scream through a rag stuffed in his mouth. The boy was beaten to a pulp, then taken down and whisked away in a wagon. Months later, a rash of missing persons broke out and a posse was formed to confront the cultists, but they were already long gone.

Those who hike and walk the trails will no doubt meet up with some spectral entity of the past, but at least for now, they won't have to worry about being kidnapped by a cult. Turnbull Canyon represents a Bermuda Triangle-like region where people go missing, UFOs are seen in the sky, ghosts and spirits abound, and an eerie sense of doom pervades. There are others just like it, though.

THE ALASKA TRIANGLE

More people have vanished in the area known as the Alaska Triangle than anywhere else in the country. The remote and heavily forested triangle borders Anchorage and Juneau in the south to Barrow on the state's northern coast and is some of the harshest wilderness in the world, covered in Boreal forest, alpine lakes, craggy peaks, and bleak and desolate tundras. Oh, and it gets incredibly cold up there, too. So, it's not surprising many people go missing. What is surprising is just how many are never seen or heard from again, and no bodies are ever found. In fact, nobody knows if they are alive or dead. According to "More People Disappear in the Alaska Triangle Than Anywhere in the U.S." for *themanual.com*, that number is close to sixteen thousand people since 1988, more than twice the national average.

The triangle came on the map of locals and paranormal researchers in 1972 when a small, private plane with U.S. House Majority Leader Hale Boggs on board vanished in the area. Because of his official status, the government launched a massive search and rescue effort with over fifty planes and forty military craft, as well as hundreds of people, focusing on a thirty-two-thousand-square-mile stretch of land where it was believed the plane went down. After thirty-nine days of searching, nothing was ever found. In 1950, a military craft with forty-four passengers vanished without a trace. In 1990, a Cessna 540 with five people on board disappeared, never to be heard from again.

Though the sheer uninhabitable nature of the land and the geography of the area are no doubt to blame in part for the record numbers of vanishings, resulting in hundreds of search and rescue missions every year, rarely do state troopers find any bodies, dead or alive. There are avalanches in the mountains and the terrain is absolutely no place for tourists and hikers, even those with a great deal of experience. There are caverns, caves, and other hidden chambers within the icy glaciers that someone could take shelter in, but the cold, lack of food and water, and isolation would not allow for anyone to survive for long, and surely, bodies would be found, even if only bones left behind.

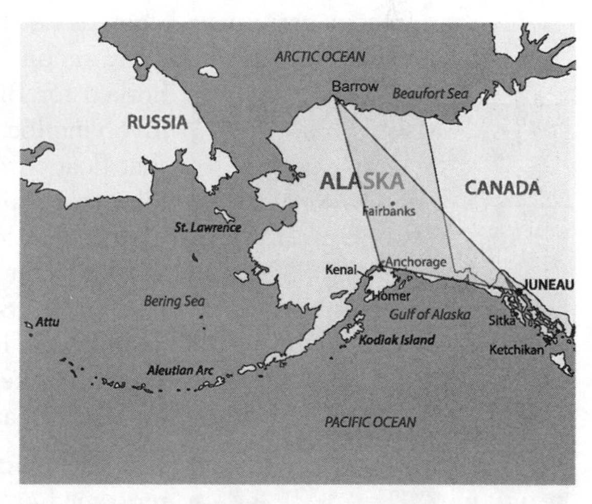

The Alaska Triangle is a mysterious region between Barrow in the north and Anchorage and Juneau in the south.

Which is why local legends hint at a Bigfoot creature that roams the snowy landscape, and indigenous myths speak of shape-shifting entities that kidnap lost humans. According to the Tlingit and Tsimshian tribes that are native to the area, these creatures are called Kushtaka and can take on human form to appear to fellow travelers, often as a relative or a child in need of help, and lead their victims to the river, where they are torn to shreds to be morphed into another Kushtaka. Unfortunately, the only way to prove what is happening out in the Alaska Triangle is to go there and possibly become victim to whatever forces, natural or supernatural, may be at play, and one has to wonder if it's worth the risk.

The Bridgewater Triangle

Some urban legends are combined with ghost sightings, UFO sightings, cryptid encounters, and just about every other type of paranormal phenomenon one could imagine. These places are called paranormal vortexes, and the Bermuda Triangle and Devil's Triangle off the coast of Japan are two well-known examples where ships and planes vanish and no traces of the wreckage or crew is ever found. This particular paranormal vortex exists on land and makes up a 200-mile (322-kilometer), triangular swath of land in Massachusetts, with the three towns of Abington, Freetown, and Rehoboth as its three points. Dead center is the town of Bridgewater as well as nearby towns of Raynham, Taunton, Brockton, Mansfield, Norton, and Easton.

Within this region, mystery abounds. The reports of bizarre activity began as far back as 1760 when a sphere of fire was reported hovering over the area, emitting a bright light that was seen over a large area. Ever since, the area has been rampant with UFO sightings and a host of other ghostly and strange activity, prompting locals and paranormal researchers alike to wonder if this was indeed some strange vortex or a wormhole that linked our world with others, including whatever lives in those other worlds.

Local newspapers and news channels have documented much of the recent activity and there is no shortage of books written on the Bridgewater Triangle, but to this day, no one is really sure why this area in particular is a hotbed for Bigfoot sightings, UFO landings (even some involving local law-enforcement personnel), balls of light that float through the woods, a ghostly, redheaded hitchhiker that haunts Route 44 in Rehoboth, animal mutilations in the towns of Freetown and Fall River that were attributed to a local cult performing ritual sacrifices, a phantom in the Hockomock Swamp near Route 138, a ghostly man who sits upon Profile Rock by the Freetown Fall River, and even a ghostly trucker who speeds on the Copicut Road and honks his horn at passing cars.

Those who have visited and investigated the abundantly haunted locations within the triangle say it is a legend tripper's dream—two hundred miles worth of haunted ground....

The actual name Bridgewater Triangle came from renowned cryptozoologist Loren Coleman, who gave the place its name back in the 1970s. Much of the area is forested, rural, remote, and the perfect spot for cult activity,

Happily Haunted? Sedona's Good Vibrations

Amid all the notorious haunted locations sits a hotbed of positive vibrations and good feelings. In the Arizona desert city of Sedona, nestled amid the massive, red, sandstone formations at the southern end of the Oak Creek Canyon, people flock to experience all types of paranormal, metaphysical, and spiritual activity that is uplifting to the body, mind, and spirt. The warm, beautiful mountain country is not only peaceful and relaxing to look at but houses an alleged vortex that radiates amazing healing energies and draws all sorts of alternative medicine practitioners, yogis, and believers looking to experience contact with a benevolent spirit or alien.

The town of Sedona is named after Sedona Arabella Miller Schnebly, the wife of Theodore Carlton Schnebly, the city's first postmaster. It is filled with unique art galleries, cafes, and gourmet restaurants, and it attracts legions of tourists. Outside the town, people love to hike the stunning natural terrain and go camping, swimming, and biking. But most people are there for the healing vibes and feel-good spirit that permeates the area.

Local Native American legends claim Sedona is in fact a spiritual vortex, and it's not uncommon to see UFOs and benevolent entities, angels, dancing orbs and balls of light, and even spirit guides in the form of animals appear. Those who visit often claim the vortex is a doorway between worlds where all types of higher-consciousness beings come through to make their presence known. The UFOs are most often described as balls of light rather than the colder, metallic, gray objects usually reported.

This New Age Disneyland, as it's often called, is a favorite destination for those seeking a spiritual getaway and for those who want to immerse themselves in the phenomenon that has made this region world famous.

murders, and numerous suicides, all of which add to the spooky reputation of the triangle, which also includes unusual geological features such as Dighton Rock, which contains unidentifiable etchings thought to be from Vikings or ancient Phoenicians, depending on who you ask. Taunton is home to the Taunton State Hospital, once used by satanic cults in the 1960s and a place to see strange orbs and spectral figures that reach out and touch you with phantom fingers.

Those who have visited and investigated the abundantly haunted locations within the triangle say it is a legend tripper's dream—two hundred miles' worth of haunted ground where every possible supernatural spookiness occurs, thus increasing visitors' chances of getting to experience at least a ghost, a UFO, or a run-in with Bigfoot, if not all three.

Yosemite National Park

Over four million people visit Yosemite National Park every year. The U.S. national park, which was designated back in 1864, is filled with some of the most stunning, eye-popping natural scenery in the world. With towering

Most people just consider Yosemite National Park in northern California to be a spectacular, bucolic vacation spot, but it is also home to ancient spirits; bizarre, cryptic beasts; and UFOs.

waterfalls, deep valleys, gorgeous meadows, icy glaciers, rugged mountains, peaceful lakes, ancient giant sequoias, and the tranquility provided by the remoteness of the High Sierras, this 1,200-square-mile (3,100-square-kilometer) park that spans three central California counties is bound to have a dark side. The word Yosemite means "killer" in Miwok and refers to a renegade tribe of Native Americans that were once driven out of the region and slaughtered by the Mariposa Battalion. Prior to that, the natives called it *Ahwahnee*, which means big mouth.

Located at the center of the vast landscape is Grouse Lake, a verifiable hot spot for paranormal phenomena. The otherwise peaceful-looking lake belies the high strangeness that occurs there, including sightings of a dead boy who drowned in the lake. Visitors claim to hear his yelping and crying as he tries, according to native legend, to make others come to his aid so he can trap them on the bottom of the lake and keep him company. Then there is a malevolent ancient spirit, the Po-Ho-No, who draws people to the edge of a large waterfall so it can push them to their deaths. Three people have reportedly lost their lives plunging to the bottom.

Nightcrawlers, a strange, cryptid entity that looks like a walking pair of pants with a tiny head, have been spotted around the lake. Native legends claim they've walked the area for decades. Visitors might also get a sight of Bigfoot roaming near the lake as well as the Wendigo, a hostile cryptid from Native American lore that may be responsible for the park's many missing-persons reports. The Wendigo began as human beings but, because of their sins while in human form, were cursed and forced to take on the appearance of beasts that cannibalize anyone they come in contact with. Unlike the shy Bigfoot, who seems to just want to be left alone, the Wendigo are not afraid and can be rather aggressive.

Between 11 P.M. and 3 A.M. on certain nights, hikers and campers might see the ghost of a camper who hanged himself in the woods or perhaps one of many UFOs that hover in the skies, especially around the notorious top-secret base Area 51, which is said to house crashed UFOs, and above the allegedly cursed Tenaya Canyon area. After the natives were forced out of their homes, Chief Tenaya of the Ahwahnechee Tribe put an angry curse on the area, and since then, hikers and campers go missing on a regular basis, never to be seen again but for a few found alive in some kind of trancelike shock, missing their shoes.

Yosemite is a huge area, and 95 percent of that is wilderness, much of it difficult, if not impossible, to reach by foot or otherwise. It is filled with rumors, legends, lore, and plenty of reportedly real encounters with things that like to hide in the remote, isolated natural setting until some unsuspecting human comes along.

Superstition Mountains

Superstition Mountains may sound familiar from the famous Phoenix Lights UFO wave that happened just to the north for several months in 1997. But the largest of the mountain ranges surrounding the city of Phoenix is home to quite a bit of paranormal activity other than UFO sightings. The range, made of volcanic peaks and boulder-filled, saguaro-covered canyons, rises above the desert to a height of 5,024 feet (1,531 meters), much of which falls within the Tonto National Forest. It is part of the larger Superstition Wilderness Area and, as its name implies, it is a hotbed of high strangeness mixed with native legend and lore and, next to the Grand Canyon, it is the most photographed area in the state.

Superstition Mountain is the focal point of the range and a popular recreation spot for locals and tourists alike, with hiking and biking trails, camping, fishing, and legend tripping for those who hope to encounter something out of the ordinary around the area of the Lost Dutchman Gold Mine. Legend claims the mine is somewhere beneath the vast range of mountains and contains a huge stash of gold. Some lore claims the stash is located below a tall rock known as Weaver's Needle, but nothing has yet been found. The mine got its name from a German immigrant named Jacob Waltz, who found the mine in the nineteenth century and kept its location hidden. Since German men were referred to as "Dutchmen," the name stuck and, along with California's lost Pegleg Mine, has become the most notorious lost mine in the country.

The name Superstition Mountains comes from local farmers in the 1860s, who heard stories from the Pima Indians about strange noises and phantom lights, vanishing people, mysterious deaths, and spirits of the dead. Add to that the legend of a lost gold mine, and you have the perfect mixture of curiosity and greed. Those who set out to find the booty never do, and some perish in the harsh landscape or vanish altogether.

Apache tribes nearby called it the home of the Thunder God and claim there are the faces of spirits seen in the rocks along the Apache Trail. UFOs were often reported during the 1950s and 1960s near the Flat Iron and Bluff Springs Mountains. Spirits of the dead are said to haunt certain canyons and around caves once thought to house lost gold or diamonds. Haunted Canyon is one of those where old native legend and lore mixes with nuggets (pun intended) of truth. Whether any of it is true or not doesn't stop thousands of people from coming to the mountain to search out lost gold or spot a spirit or alien ship in the sky.

The Borderlands

The Colorado–New Mexico border sits along the paranormal hot spot known as the 37th Parallel. Known also as the Borderlands, it's not uncommon to experience everything from a Bigfoot sighting, cattle mutilations and black helicopters, UFOs buzzing the skies, and strange, interdimensional vortexes. Navajo and Ute Native American and Spanish Colonial legends add to the fantastical flavor, as does the amazing landscape, which is a vast, harsh desert edged by the rush of the Rio Grande River and the overlooking snowy, 14,000-foot (4,250-meter) mountain peaks. The region includes the Sangre de Christo Mountain Range, running from southern Colorado to northern New Mexico, that gives off a spooky, red glow at sunset.

One of the most notorious haunted locales in the region is the San Luis Valley, where seeing and hearing all kinds of bizarre entities and activities is normal, everyday happening. This 8,000-square-mile (20,720-square-kilometer) area is home to the world's largest alpine valley, the floor of which is 60 miles (97 kilometers) across at its widest point. There have been upward of twelve Native American tribes that either once inhabited the region or do so now, and they lived off the valley's game and the lake's freshwater fish supplies. But something about this valley prompted theories of electromagnetic fluctuations and anomalies that were responsible for the sightings of atmospheric phenomena, phantom lights, stories of witches and Satan worshippers using the sites for dark ceremonies, black choppers that often showed up after UFO sightings, cryptid sightings, and even a mysterious presence of military vehicles nearby.

Some of the military presence might be related to the Aztec, New Mexico, UFO crash site, which lies about a hundred miles west of the Great Sand Dunes Monument. In March 1948, eight months after the more famous Roswell UFO crash, which was also in New Mexico, a policeman followed a

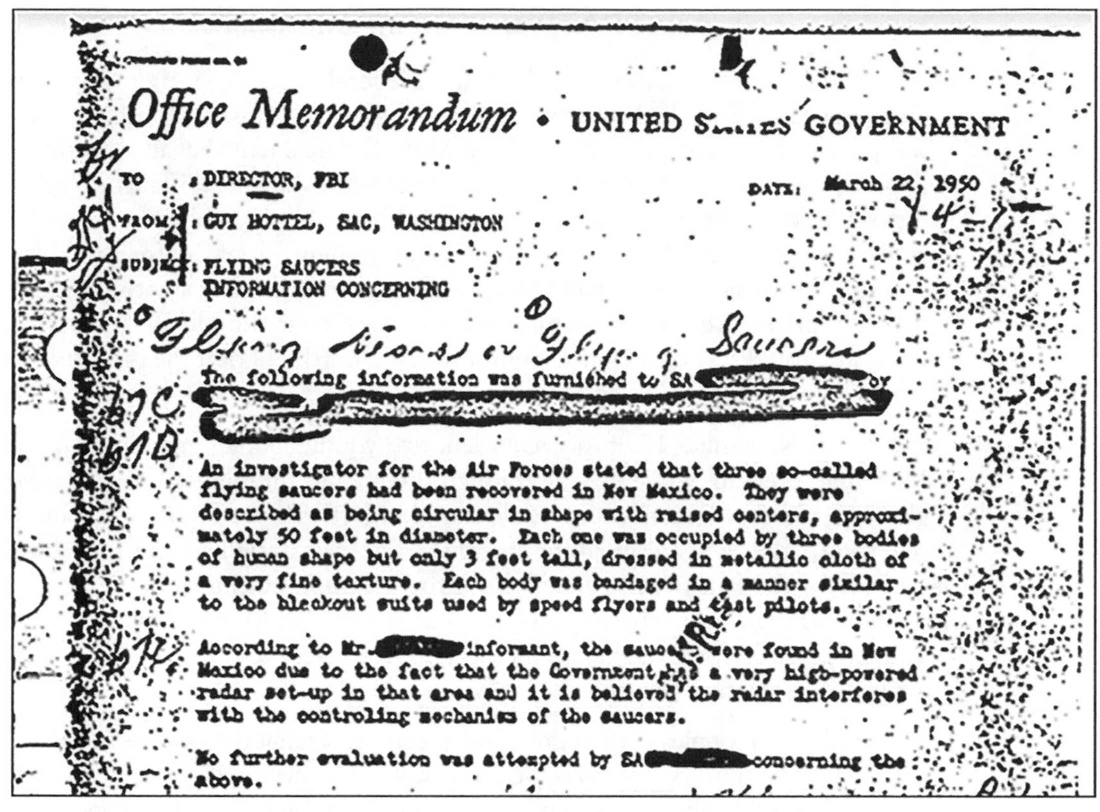

Office Memorandum • UNITED S[illegible] GOVERNMENT

TO : DIRECTOR, FBI   DATE: March 22, 1950

FROM : GUY HOTTEL, SAC, WASHINGTON

SUBJECT: FLYING SAUCERS
INFORMATION CONCERNING

The following information was furnished to SA [redacted] by [redacted]

An investigator for the Air Forces stated that three so-called flying saucers had been recovered in New Mexico. They were described as being circular in shape with raised centers, approximately 50 feet in diameter. Each one was occupied by three bodies of human shape but only 3 feet tall, dressed in metallic cloth of a very fine texture. Each body was bandaged in a manner similar to the blackout suits used by speed flyers and test pilots.

According to Mr. [redacted] informant, the saucers were found in New Mexico due to the fact that the Government has a very high-powered radar set-up in that area and it is believed the radar interferes with the controling mechanism of the saucers.

No further evaluation was attempted by SA [redacted] concerning the above.

This is part of a 1950 memo filed by FBI Special Agent Guy Hottel about the UFO sightings in Aztec, New Mexico. He describes three UFOs about fifty feet in diameter that had been recovered, each containing three alien crewmembers.

strange, erratic craft for hours. A New Mexico highway patrolman was also watching the bizarre craft, as was a rancher nearby who thought he heard a sonic boom. Instead, the craft dropped out of control just beyond his property and crashed to the ground along Hart Canyon Road, where a brush fire broke out. Like the Roswell crash of infamy, there were reports of small bodies inside and, in this case, slumped over the control panel. Soon, military vehicles arrived to interrogate the many witnesses who saw the craft along the way.

Aside from the crash site, there are reports of Bigfoot roaming the terrain, elusive as always, and visits by Star People from Zuni mythology. These Star People are depicted in petroglyphs and rock art found throughout the area and are mirrored in Lakota tales of beings that come down from the skies and take children. Sound familiar? One theory suggests that the UFOs and Bigfoot enter our world via a number of portals hidden in the vast Borderlands and that they go back to their worlds the same way. So much activity occurs here, *gaia.com* dubbed it "North America's Paranormal Disneyland."

POINT PLEASANT, HOME OF MOTHMAN

The story of Mothman is the stuff of legends. Urban legends. But with quite a core of truth. In 1966, the small town of Point Pleasant, West Virginia, was put on the historical map for all eternity when residents began reporting a huge, flying, humanoid entity that would be dubbed "Mothman." The first sighting occurred in Clendenin, West Virginia, on November 12, when five cemetery workers watched as a large, dark-winged creature flew out of the trees into the sky. They described it as far more humanoid than birdlike. The sightings spread throughout the area, with the majority occurring near the old West Virginia Ordnance Works, an abandoned munitions plant north of Point Pleasant known to the locals as the TNT Area.

On November 15 of the same year, two young couples encountered the Mothman creature while driving through the area at midnight. They saw two glowing, red eyes coming from inside the old North Power Plant, and soon, a seven-foot-tall, winged creature emerged. The car stalled in the road long enough for the four to get a good look at the creature, but imagine their terror when Mothman began chasing after their car as it sped down Highway 62 at over 100 miles (160 kilometers) per hour trying trying to get to the city. When they arrived, the creature was nowhere to be seen.

The two couples were stunned and uncertain of what they had seen, so they headed back to the TNT Area and, lo and behold, were accosted again by the creature on Route 62. That encounter triggered a host of sheriff investigations out to the TNT Area, and for the next thirteen months, various locals spotted Mothman. Some claim there were up to one hundred additional sightings. The eeriest was a string of reports claiming Mothman warned them of a pending disaster, which turned out to be the horrific Silver Bridge collapse on December 15, 1967, which killed forty-six people during rush-hour traffic. There are other similar cryptids all over the world that are known to warn of pending disasters. Mothman-like creatures have been sighted around a Freiburg, Germany, mine that collapsed shortly afterward and just before the infamous Chernobyl power plant meltdown in Ukraine. They are always bipedal, winged humanoids with glowing, red eyes and are dark brown, black, or gray in color. They have a wingspan of up to 15 feet (4.6 meters), have been clocked flying at over 100 miles (160 kilometers) per hour, and can lift straight up off the ground like a helicopter.

Witnesses also reported visitations by Men in Black, usually in the form of two men dressed in black suits and hats who appear robotic in their movement and speech and warn people not to talk about anything they've seen or experienced. MIBs are common in UFO reports and have a hypnotic effect on those they question and threaten. Yes, there were UFO sightings in the region during the Mothman activity, which have continued to this day (unlike the Mothman sightings, which tapered off shortly after the initial wave of sightings).

Electrical disturbances have also been reported such as GPS devices not working, landlines giving a fast busy signal, cell phones going dead, batteries draining quickly, and computers not working properly.

There have been people in the area, or traveling through the area, who have reported blacking out and waking up hours later with no known rationale for what happened. There are also numerous reports of cattle mutilations that cannot be attributed to predators or vandals, something often reported in areas of high UFO activity. Could they have been food for a hungry Mothman instead?

There have been people in the area, or traveling through the area, who have reported blacking out and waking up hours later with no known rationale for what happened.

Paranormal researchers, cryptozoologists, and ufologists alike believe that where there is a plethora of one type of sighting, there is often a plethora of others. For example, locations known to be haunted by many ghosts, such as a haunted canyon or ranch, might also experience UFO sightings, and UFO hot spots are often associated with corresponding reports of cryptids or interdimensional creatures. Maybe the vortices and portals like the Bermuda Triangle, Bridgewater Triangle, Alaska Triangle, and others are the roadways traveled by these beings and craft and explain these paranormal clusters of bizarre and varied activity, unlike a haunted house or graveyard that is home only to ghostly apparitions. The idea has been discussed by this author as to the need to widen the umbrella of paranormal phenomena to include far more than just ghosts and spirits. After all, it's all *para*normal.

Point Pleasant today is far quieter when it comes to paranormal activity than it was in the 1960s with no recent reports of the giant entity, but the Mothman presence is felt everywhere: in museums, yearly events, a Mothman festival, paranormal conferences, and the stories witnesses tell their children and grandchildren. Mothman, along with Nessie and Bigfoot, is one of the most famous cryptids ever witnessed and has become the subject of novels, movies, and spooky television shows galore as well as nonfiction books devoted to trying to solve the mystery of who, or what, Mothman truly was and where he came from. Because of the entity's strange interdimensional, yet also physical, nature, it has become one of the most studied cryptids on record.

But while the town of Point Pleasant, and soon the nation, were caught up in the Mothman sightings and other bizarre activity, there were reports of something even stranger coming in—an entity named Indrid Cold, also known as the Grinning Man.

It began the same month and year as the Mothman sightings: November 1966. A sewing machine salesman named Woodrow Derenberger was driving home to Mineral Wells on Interstate 77 near Parkersburg on the cold, rainy

An artist's concept of Mothman, a cryptid being that seems to be based in West Virginia and is associated with UFO activity.

night of November 2. A sewing machine somehow fell out of the back of the vehicle, and Derenberger stopped to fetch it. He got back in the car and drove on. Soon, a set of headlights moved past him at high speed and slowed, pulling itself sideways in front of Derenberger's car. Derenberger had to stop; he had no choice. He stopped in the middle of the road, thinking it was a police car.

The door to the other vehicle opened, and a man stepped out. He had dark hair, swept off his face, and a deep tan. He had a strikingly wide grin and wore a dark overcoat, beneath which was a strange, metallic, green uniform. As he approached Derenberger, the man's vehicle rose forty feet into the air and floated there. When he spoke, the man claimed his name was Indrid Cold and that he was from a place "less powerful than the United States." He claimed he was human and nothing out of the ordinary and asked about the lights of the city and the people who lived in Parkersburg. The creepy man also encouraged Derenberger to report their encounter to the police and that more confirmations would follow. Cold told Derenberger they would meet again. The strangest element of this whole encounter was the fact that the whole conversation took place as telepathy between the two.

The two did visit a few more times. Often, Indrid was accompanied by others, who he claimed were from the planet Lanulos. He even took Derenberger on a trip to the planet. Derenberger went on to tell his story to noted UFO researcher John Keel. During that investigation, Keel himself began receiving creepy phone calls from Indrid Cold or a third party who knew of Indrid. Often, these calls took on a prophetic tone, speaking of events to come.

The same night Derenberger had his encounter, two men reported an object landing in front of their car. They stopped and a man got out, dressed just as Indrid Cold was. He asked them a series of questions that the man said seemed relatively pointless, then got back on the craft and left. Weeks later, two boys, James Yanchitis and Martin Munov, would also encounter the mysterious Grinning Man standing along the fence line across from the Turnpike, a local landmark. The boys claimed the man was staring at them, grinning.

There are those who believe that seeing or encountering Indrid Cold precedes a disaster or bad luck and that he may be one of the Men in Black who confronted witnesses of the Mothman entity that same month. However, a Point

Pleasant reporter named Mary Hyre reported being visited in her office one night in January 1967 by one of those MIBs, and she described him as short and stocky with dark, long, bowl-shaped hair and a speech impediment like a stutter. Nothing like Indrid Cold. Maybe there were different types of MIBs operating after the Mothman sightings. Maybe Indrid Cold was a whole separate phenomenon. Or maybe it was all a part of the cluster of strange activity that engulfed the town of Point Pleasant and nearby locales and is connected in ways we still don't begin to understand.

The Grinning Man has become a part of American urban legend and folklore with reports of a similar entity coming in from all over the country. Either Indrid Cold gets around, or he is but one of many Grinning People that speed past drivers, cut them off, and engage in telepathic Q&A sessions only to smile that spooky, wide smile, turn around, and leave. They have not caused any harm, but would you want to see one?

Skinwalker Ranch

The most notorious haunted hot spot in the country is a 480-acre (194-hectare) cattle ranch in the middle of Utah near the town of Ballard called Skinwalker Ranch (also called Sherman Ranch). It may even be the most terrifying place in the world. But before we find out why, we first need to know what a Skinwalker is. In Navajo Indian culture, there exists a type of shape-shifting witch, and not the Glenda the Good kind that can take on the appearance of, and possess, an animal or even a human being. It does so, according to legend, by removing the victim's skin so it can wear it, taking on their persona—thus the name Skinwalker. The Skinwalker story is nowadays the stuff of modern Hollywood movies, as the Navajo are not open to discussing the lore of the mythological and archetypal Skinwalkers. Outsiders are not permitted to know all the details, which are protected by the tribe, but what we do know is that these are not healing witches or helpful medicine men or women—not by a long shot.

In Navajo Indian culture, there exists a type of shape-shifting witch ... that can take on the appearance of, and possess, an animal or even a human being.

The Skinwalkers are considered evil in Navajo lore and take part in rituals and ceremonies that manipulate dark magic for sinister purposes. They often take on the image of a coyote or other creature that is associated with death. They can, and do, possess animals and humans and literally walk in their skins by locking eyes with them. Usually, Skinwalkers are male, but they have been reported in female form as well. Perhaps we can say that Skinwalkers are medicine men, and women, who have gone to join the dark side.

People driving through Utah heading into Arizona have reported seeing Skinwalker creatures along the desolate roadsides, described as a hairy human or a hairy animal wearing human clothing with yellow, glowing eyes. They have a monstrous appearance and are aggressive with no fear of attacking humans. Just ask the residents and visitors who have been to Skinwalker Ranch. The Ute Indians will not go anywhere near the ranch, which borders their reservation, believing it to be Skinwalker territory. Members are forbidden to trespass on the ranch property that sits in the Uintah Basin in Uintah County, Utah, believing the ranch is on ground cursed by the Navajo Indians. Though most people wouldn't think of Utah being such a vortex of high strangeness, this ranch would prove them otherwise.

In the 1950s, UFOs were sighted regularly over the ranch, and cattle, cat, and dog mutilations have been reported by former ranch owners throughout the last fifty years. The Skinwalker Ranch got its reputation as a notorious haunted location mainly when the Sherman family, often referred to as the Gorman family, took ownership in 1994 only to be driven off the farm two years later by a host of terrifying paranormal activity. Strange, hybrid-like animals often appeared, including a giant wolf the size of a car that could not be killed by bullets fired right into it, birds that glowed in the dark, and a hunched, red-haired, hyena-like creature with a bushy tail that attacked the horses of the original ranch owners one night. These entities were impervious to bullets and, as with the horse-attacking hyena beast, appear and disappear right before witnesses' eyes. There are a host of bizarre lights in the area that people claim have an intelligence, as they have been known to attack people and livestock by zapping them, almost like an electrical shock. Shafts of light emanate from the ground up. The fields sometimes light up as if surrounded by lights on a football field.

People staying on the ranch see apparitions in the fields on and around the ranch and claim they've heard the sound of people speaking alien gibberish or saying the names of those staying at the ranch, yet the origin of the voices remains unexplained except that the voices seemed to be coming from about twenty feet above their heads. Families who once lived on the ranch have reported poltergeist phenomena, voices calling out their names when no one else was around, aliens seven feet tall standing amid the fields' lit-up bright lights, UFOs the size of two football fields, and, of course, the horrifying Skinwalkers. One UFO report claims a craft the size of a refrigerator, with one light on the front and a red light on the back, had hovered over the ranch in the spring of 1995. There were repeated sightings of strange, unmoving clouds that hovered over the property with colorful, blinking lights and the sounds of small explosions coming from inside!

They appeared to be controlled by some intelligence and would dart off when a flashlight beam fell upon them.

In 1996, blue spheres were being sighted almost every day as well as orbs the size of baseballs with bubbling liquid inside. They appeared to be controlled by some intelligence and would dart off when a flashlight beam fell upon them. When Sherman family members saw the orbs, they reported feeling intense fear or panic. One of these blue orbs appeared in May 1996 and led the family dogs out across the field and into thick burrs where the dogs could be heard yelping before falling silent. The next morning, where the dogs were last heard were three round spots of dried vegetation. Inside each round spot was a lump of dark, greasy substance that may have been the incinerated remains of a dog. It was this event that convinced the Shermans they'd finally had enough of the horrifying events surrounding the property.

The Shermans were interviewed by a Salt Lake City news reporter, and the story aired on the local media. The Shermans sold the property in 1996, when it was then purchased by billionaire Robert Bigelow, who owns the Budget Suites hotel chain. He had seen their story on the wire service and purchased the ranch for $200,000. He immediately installed surveillance equipment, turning it into the headquarters for a paranormal research group called the National Institute for the Discovery of Science, which operated there until 2004 and was later replaced by the Bigelow Aerospace Advanced Space Studies. The Shermans stayed on during this time as caretakers but were so plagued by nightmares and identical dreams, they began suffering psychological consequences. They were still seeing apparitions in the house, dark entities peering into the windows at night, and experiencing poltergeist phenomena the whole time the ranch was being investigated for paranormal research.

In 2007, Bigelow received a nice chunk of the $22 million budget of the Advanced Aviation Threat Identification Program, which had undertaken the quest of investigating UFO activity. In 2016, Bigelow sold the ranch to a private corporation, and in 2017, the name "Skinwalker Ranch" was officially trademarked. It is a hugely popular subject in paranormal, UFO, and cryptid research circles as well as movies, television shows, and books.

The ranch is private property and not open to the public at all, although a few researchers have been allowed onto the grounds to investigate and study the ongoing phenomena that continues to make this place the stuff of legends and horror movies. Though Skinwalkers were and still are reported at other locations, the concentration of sightings makes Skinwalker Ranch a true vortex of paranormal phenomena of every type.

Being There

The best stories are always those that come from personal experience. The following are actual experiences people have had while visiting or investigating these haunted locations. What is chilling is that this book contains only a fraction of the innumerable haunted places around the nation, let alone around the world. Ghosts and their like are everywhere, and perhaps, the ground we all stand upon is filled with beings that exist in a dimension beyond ours. The fact that there isn't a culture, region, or belief system on the planet that doesn't embrace the world of the paranormal is telling. Even though scientists insist this type of phenomenon is impossible to prove, this writer counters with the sheer number of reports, sightings, experiences, cases, hauntings, possessions, and encounters people have reported for hundreds, if not thousands, of years.

The unknown scares us, but we are drawn to it like moths to a flame. Our curiosity gets the best of us, and often, we are not prepared for what we might find. But we are drawn nonetheless. Our motives may differ. Some people seek out ghosts and paranormal activity to prove that life goes on after death. Others love the adrenaline-filled rush of coming face-to-face with bizarre cryptids, spirits, or entities. Most of us love the idea that there are other forms of life out there somewhere, even if they terrify us.

Chances are, most of the people reading this book have their own stories to tell, maybe not personally but certainly of family experiences. Our history, individually and collectively, includes the things we cannot prove alongside the things we can because they are tangible, repeatable. Yet, just mention encounters with spirits, cryptids, or ghosts at a large gathering, and no doubt, several people will lean forward, whispering, "It happened to me, too. Want to hear my story?"

Yes. We do.

Being at Gettysburg

By Peaches Veatch

We all know that what happened to soldiers on the battlefield during the Civil War was tragic. Young men perished, and families lost 750,000 fathers, brothers, sons, nephews.... Most of us have a general understanding of the Civil War, but do many know what it felt like to be there? I took a trip there nearly eight years ago with my husband and met some friends in the paranormal community. My husband loves history, especially the Civil War. Me? I love the paranormal and wanted to see what I could find or who I could contact. I sense things ... sometimes, I see things ... things of the paranormal kind. And this trip truly opened my eyes about what it's like during a war.

Soon after arriving for our seven-day stay in Gettysburg, we visited many of the familiar places of the area, including the preserved battlefields. The grounds are vast and well kept, of course, but I wanted to roam and let my senses take over. I wanted to see if anything could be felt there. I was not disappointed.

Late one evening, in an area named Cemetery Hill, the night was damp and quiet. There isn't too much that happens in the evening in Gettysburg. Before summer hours, the parks close earlier, and there isn't much traffic through the town. It was extremely quiet, and as we were on the hill, I just stood there overlooking a field lined with trees. The longer I stood there, the longer I was certain I saw movement on the ground below us—movement of people, hundreds of people. They all appeared to be small, white shadows in the distance, like individual clouds of people moving about. I gathered if they were spirits, they may have been fighting for ground there. Then came the sounds of cannons. As far as we could investigate, we found that no actual cannons were fired that evening, but after speaking to my paranormal friends, I found that they heard it as well. We all heard it the same night, at the same time, but we had been spread out all over town.

The longer I stood there, the longer I was certain I saw movement on the ground below us—movement of people, hundreds of people.

I'm not as keen on some details as my husband when it comes to history. He remembers it all; he's studied it for decades. I'm glad I didn't know the details when we visited because I don't like to have my experiences with the paranormal tainted by already knowing previous events that happened there. A general idea is fine, but knowing what's happened like a movie playing in front of me is not something I need when I want to try to explore things for myself. One of these times was at Little Round Top. I decided to go exploring through the field, and suddenly, I was hit with a flood of emotions. Knowing many men died where

I stood would bring some heavy emotions to anyone, but this was different. I suddenly realized I was feeling what the soldiers felt. They were scared. Many of them had thoughts of not knowing if they would see their mom again, their girl again. And in the instant those emotions washed over me, they were gone, but they left me still and somber. I couldn't imagine feeling what they did, not knowing if you would be alive or dead at the end of the day.

Across the driveway where one of the lookout towers stands, I suddenly began feeling emotions of arrogance, like someone who felt like he needed to prove something, and was sending troops where they shouldn't have been. My husband identified this person as Major Daniel Sickles, who disobeyed orders and nearly collapsed the Union defense line. Not knowing details about this but being able to relay what I felt was an interesting way to approach learning history!

We also spent time in the home where Jennie Wade lived. Jennie Wade was the only civilian to die in the Battle of Gettysburg. Pierced by a stray bullet through her back, she perished on July 3, 1863, as she made bread for the Union soldiers. During the evening I was in the Wade house, I experienced a few things that weren't explainable. Sitting on the floor upstairs trying to communicate with Miss Wade, I felt someone brush past me as if they were wearing a long, full skirt, possibly with petticoats. No one corporeal walked through that doorway. During this time, I also felt a piercing pain through my back near the same area Jennie had been shot. I knew she had been shot there but did not know the area of her back where she'd been hit.

Skeptical or not, Gettysburg holds the imprint of one of the bloodiest times in American history, and it gave me a greater appreciation for what our soldiers, and American people of the time, experienced during the war.

Peaches has been seeking answers to the paranormal since she was a child. After joining a paranormal research group in the 2000s, she has conducted hundreds of investigations and is the director of the California Paranormal Private Investigations (CPPI), located in southern California.

Denver's Wildest Haunted Landmarks

By Jalynn Venis

Denver, Colorado, has been home to gold and silver tycoons, oil barons, and legends of the historic West such as Buffalo Bill Cody. It's a town of big dreams, rich passions, and legendary haunts.

With the Rocky Mountains to the west, Denver lies in the South Platte River Valley—a place of beauty with universal appeal for those who live large, think big, and are rarely ready to exit the good life for an uncertain afterlife. As an intuitive and paranormal investigator, I know that any structure fifty years or older has a good chance of being haunted. The more magnificent the building or remarkable the landscape, the more likely it is that some people just can't say goodbye—ever. Denver is as spirited as any city can be.

Here is a sampling of some of the most delightful stories filed under the heading of Dead in Denver.

The Brown Palace Hotel (1892): 321 17th St., Denver

When walking into the Brown Palace Hotel, a time shift creeps over you as you step through the doors of the sandstone and red, granite walls onto the onyx floors of the atrium lobby. The cast-iron railings with ornate, metal panels and elaborate chandeliers that hang high overhead thrill and delight the senses.

This iconic, western hotel was built in the style of Italian Renaissance by Henry Brown. He made his money in land speculation and once grazed his cow on this triangular plot of land that would become the center of downtown Denver and some of the most expensive real estate in the world. The Brown Palace has hosted almost every president since 1905 along with a pantheon of other notable guests such as Thomas Edison, Desmond Tutu, Andrew Carnegie, and the Beatles.

It's also hosted some guests who simply refused to leave. Louise Crawford Hill was a socialite who lived in room 904 during the 1940s and '50s. Although long since dead, she still calls the switchboard for room service with a static hiss and even did so when the room was under renovation and had no phone or lights. Other long-term guests include an old-fashioned train conductor, a crying baby in the boiler room, a uniformed waiter in the service elevator, and, of course, those pesky children who run up and down the halls of this grand hotel throughout the night. But the most unusual group to haunt the hotel is a ghostly string quartet in formal attire that plays in the restaurant called Ellyngton's. The musicians have been known to tell people that they live there.

Denver's Brown Palace Hotel is home to several spirit guests who refuse to check out.

The Buckhorn Exchange (1893): 1000 Osage St., Denver

The Buckhorn Exchange sits in a building that looks like the finest old saloon in the city, although it was originally built to be a trading post for pioneers, miners, and fur traders, who would occasionally get into gunfights there. It has the distinction of holding Liquor License #1. The walls display more than five hundred wild animal trophies (both head and full body of bear, moose, elk, mountain goat, fox, cougar, and anything else indigenous to North America) and more than two hundred antique weapons that include rifles, hand guns, knives, swords, and arrowhead collections.

The wild game menu is delicious at this popular restaurant, but what people remember best about the Buckhorn is all of the animal eyes staring at them while they dine on buffalo prime rib, elk, salmon, quail, alligator tail, and Rocky Mountain oysters.

Evidently, other eyes watch the patrons and the wait staff, who sometimes see tables move and chairs slide away from tables. Other phenomena include footsteps and disembodied voices, especially conversations heard in the bar area when it's empty.

Byers-Evans House Museum (1883): 1310 Bannock Street, Denver

Built by William Byers, founding editor of the *Rocky Mountain News*, this Italianate structure was bought six years later by William Evans, the son of Colorado's second territorial governor. The home remained in the Evans family for almost ninety years until it was given to the preservation organization History Colorado. Throughout that time, Denver's cultural elite and power brokers of the day attended parties and meetings in the house. They imbued it with a sense of history and purpose that few houses of its era could match.

Today, the structure rests in the shadow of the Denver Art Museum and is open daily for tours. Many feel that because of the Evans family's long history with the home and the fact that many of their belongings remain there, several deceased members of the Evans clan still are attached to the lovely, old house.

Both visitors and docents have heard voices coming from empty rooms and seen ghostly forms dressed in early 1900s clothing moving around the building. Among the other spectral manifestations are doors that open and close on their own, furniture that moves around, and books that appear in different places in the library.

On one visit to the house, I helped clear the spirit of a distraught young woman from a room in the servant's quarters. While there, photographs were made of some large and colorful orbs in the library and in the front sitting room. One large orb followed the investigating party out to the sidewalk and stayed with us as we discussed the house. This was the first time I became aware of a multigenerational haunting that shared visions of the family getting together every Sunday for dinner. It was a beautiful and fascinating experience unlike any other paranormal investigation.

One large orb followed the investigating party out to the sidewalk and stayed with us as we discussed the house.

Cheesman Park (1907): 1599 East 8th Avenue (at Franklin Street), Denver

It's been said that Cheesman Park was the inspiration for the film *Poltergeist* because the park was built over the 1858 Mount Prospect Hill Cemetery. After the cemetery fell into disuse and became overgrown, city leaders thought it would be a good idea to turn the cemetery into a park.

After serving notice to the community of the planned park and giving residents ample time to remove the remains of loved ones, the city hired a man to remove the remaining bodies. After it was discovered that he was cutting up bodies and packing them along with multiple remains into children's caskets to move to another cemetery, public outcry cost him his job. Lacking a better solution, thousands of graves were then left for future gardeners and other workers to uncover the hard way as subsequent years rolled by.

Soon after the park was created, people living in the homes near Cheesman began to report sightings of specters that would knock on their second-story windows at night and wander through their houses.

The Cheesman Memorial was built in 1908 in a Neoclassical style to commemorate the philanthropic work of Denver pioneer Walter Cheesman, known for funding the Colorado Humane Society and aiding children in need. Late at night, the spirits come out to play. People have seen apparitions standing on the marble flooring that fade in and out under the moonlight. Some have heard a man whispering, "Get out!"

I observed an individual walking late one evening in Cheesman Park who vanished into a small tree. People nearby heard eerie noises and "someone talking on the wind." Cheesman Park—beautiful by day, very eerie at night.

Croke-Patterson Mansion (1891): 420 East 11th Avenue, Denver

The Croke-Patterson Mansion was built in the Châteauesque style by Thomas Croke between 1890 and 1891 for just $18,000. Its red, sandstone walls with gables and turrets are representative of a French castle.

The landmark is now known as the Patterson Inn after its second owner, Thomas Patterson. He was an attorney and U.S. senator as well as publisher of the *Rocky Mountain News*. Patterson traded Croke 1,440 acres (583 hectares) of ranchland for the home, which remains one of the most spectacular buildings in Denver.

It's said that Croke entered the finished mansion only once, and he left the house shaken by what he experienced there. He never returned, and he traded it to Patterson just two years later.

The building was used for many things after being sold in the 1930s by Patterson's granddaughter: a boardinghouse, a dance studio, an office building. While being renovated in the 1970s, the house came alive again. Workers returned to find the previous day's work undone on several occasions. Thinking someone was being mischievous, the owner of the building left guard dogs inside the house. The next day, he found his two Dobermann Pinschers dead on the sidewalk—apparently, they jumped from a third-story window.

Later, office workers reported that typewriters and copy machines turned themselves on, and several people witnessed a spectral form gliding up and down the main floor staircase. An apparition that looked like Thomas Patterson was seen many times in the courtyard between the mansion and the carriage house. An apparition of his wife, Kate Patterson, also has been seen inside the house. Occupants who lived there when the mansion was an apartment building often complained of hearing wild parties on the third floor, but when management investigated, the rooms were dead quiet.

I visited the Croke-Patterson Mansion late one night when it was empty and, once again, waiting to be repurposed. Of the three people with me, two of them would not exit the car. Even in the moonlight, the structure had a desolate darkness to it that repelled visitors. Our photos showed clouds of orbs hovering above.

Denver Firefighters Museum (1909): 1326 Tremont Place, Denver

Old Fire Station No. 1 served the city when horse-drawn engines were the norm. It was a working firehouse for sixty-six years. Today, it houses several exhibits from Denver firefighters and caters to museum visitors and paranormal investigators alike.

While on an investigation, I felt energy swirling in the firemen's bathroom and saw orbs streaking overhead. Other paranormal phenomena included the smell of hay in what would have been the horse stables one hundred years earlier, orbs in the main exhibit among the old firefighting equipment, orbs around the firemen's lockers, and an ominous presence in what is known as "Caleb's closet" in the basement.

Other reported haunting high jinks include ringing bells on the engines, shuffling papers, printers that turn on and spit

The Denver Firefighters Museum was established in 1978 and is maintained in a 1909 station that is on the National Register of Historic Places.

paper uncontrollably, ghosts in photographs, disembodied footsteps, laughter, and children's voices.

Molly Brown House Museum (1889): 1340 Pennsylvania Street, Denver

Built in the Capitol Hill district by Isaac Large, a silver tycoon, this beautiful, Victorian home was designed in the classic Queen Anne and Richardsonian Romanesque styles by famed architect William Lang. It had all the luxuries that Mrs. Large wanted—electricity, indoor plumbing, heat, and even a telephone. When the Silver Crash hit in 1893, Mr. Large had to sell his wife's beloved home. The buyers were the very well known James Joseph (J. J.) and Margaret (Molly) Brown—yes, the "Unsinkable Molly Brown" of the *Titanic* disaster.

At the time, the Browns owned a gold mine that was one of the largest in the world. They were generous people who always seemed to have others living with them. It's not surprising that the gregarious Browns, and some of their family members and servants, remain there in the afterlife.

Ghostly activity at the Molly Brown House includes J. J.'s pipe and cigar smoke wafting through the halls and cold spots in Molly's bedroom, where a rocking chair rocks now and then. Many have reported seeing a woman in a Victorian dress going around corners in the house and in the dining room. She is believed to be Molly. The staff reports that she sits at the dining table and has even tolerated people taking photos of her there. Sometimes, she moves chairs around in the dining room. One needy guest claimed that Molly pointed her in the direction of a bathroom.

Other apparitions that have been spotted include a grumpy butler, no doubt wearied of the forty-five thousand people who visit the Molly Brown House each year, a maid in the library, and Johanna (Molly's mother who lived with the Browns after their young daughter died). Johanna lived in the girls' room, and it's reported that the shades in that room rise and lower on their own.

The last time I was in the Molly Brown House, I smelled pipe and cigar tobacco in the halls and, for an instant, I thought I saw a woman in elegant, Victorian attire rounding a corner and glancing back at me. Sadly, I left without taking selfies in the dining room with Molly.

The Oxford Hotel (1891): 1600 17th Street, Denver

The Oxford Hotel and the Brown Palace Hotel argue about being the oldest hotel in Denver. They were built at the same time, and the Oxford opened first. Each was designed by architect Frank E. Edbrooke and built at the peak of the Silver Rush. The Oxford had many amenities, including gas heating, an elevator, and its own power plant.

The Oxford's updated Art Deco style is elegantly functional and worth taking a moment to savor before starting your investigation. The beautiful Cruise Room Martini Bar is a must—there's also a nightly Bourbon Hour to ease paranormal jitters. The Cruise was the first bar in Denver to open after the repeal of Prohibition in 1933. It was a pretty good place to drink back then, and it's even better now.

Paranormal activity falls into the classic category of flickering lights, bathroom sink faucets turning on by themselves, and guests getting mysteriously locked into their bedrooms for a good, old-fashioned ghostly scare.

There's a story that in room 320, Florence Montague bedded a married man in 1898, got jealous when she learned he had a wife, and she shot him and then herself for having done the deed. It's said that she rips the covers off of single men who stay in that room.

A woman was murdered in one of the bedrooms when her husband discovered her there with a lover. Some have seen an apparition of a woman standing in various rooms. People also have reported seeing the face of an extra woman in their photos.

He muttered, "The children, I have to get gifts to the children," and then left.... His decomposing body was later discovered during the spring thaw along with bags of Christmas presents.

One of the saddest stories involves a postal worker who stopped into the bar for a beer in the 1930s to warm up from the snowy outdoors. He muttered, "The children, I have to get gifts to the children," then left. Later, the Oxford staff read the news story of a postal carrier who disappeared en route to deliver Christmas gifts to Central City. His decomposing body was later discovered during the spring thaw along with bags of Christmas presents. The ghost still stops by the bar now and then to order a drink, appearing fully human. Bartenders see him drink, but the liquor level in his glass never goes down.

Red Rocks Amphitheater: 18300 West Alameda Parkway, Morrison

Many people who enjoy rock concerts have visited Red Rocks, the awesome park and outdoor concert venue in the foothills west of Denver. The amphitheater is built between enormous rock formations with magnificent views of city lights. The greatest musical acts that come to Colorado play Red Rocks, and the Colorado Music Hall of Fame is located there.

Before concertgoers were visiting this region, its natural beauty was well loved by Native American tribes, too. For those who are vibrationally sensitive, there is energy around these natural wonders that many identify as soothing and healing. Many people have reported seeing Native American apparitions dressed in ceremonial clothing at Red Rocks.

The most striking legend of Red Rocks is that of the Hatchet Lady, who wanders among the rocks looking for young couples getting intimate at the park. Sometimes she's reported wearing a red cloak and sometimes she's naked, and she's also been seen riding a horse through the rocks headless. The Hatchet Lady appears to people waving a bloody hatchet to scare them away. This story is probably based on reports of a homeless woman who lived in a cave nearby during the 1950s.

An old, weathered miner also has been seen standing in an off-limits area near the Red Rocks stage. He often appears to be drinking from a liquor bottle and is described as grouchy.

Jalynn Venis is an intuitive and paranormal consultant who has lived in five haunted houses. She and Richard Gorey are the coauthors of the supernatural thriller *Ghost Island*, and Jalynn is the author of its nonfiction companion book *Cassandra's Field Guide to Ghostly Encounters*.

Haunted New Jersey Stories

By Gary S. Crawford

Mount Prospect Cemetery

I offered to help clean up an old cemetery in Neptune, New Jersey. My stepfather was donating his time there, and I volunteered to help. The Mount Prospect Cemetery was established in 1881 and was the first area cemetery that was more of a memorial park than a church-owned graveyard. All races and religions were accepted. My stepdad had relatives buried there, the reason he became involved.

Offering my help in the ongoing cleanup, I was asked to become a trustee of the nonprofit cemetery corporation. (I had a pulse, was warm, and showed an interest.) I accepted, and a few years later, the president, now approaching his ninetieth birthday, decided it was time to make that move to Florida. By popular vote, I became the president.

People look at cemetery officials as they see funeral directors—macabre individuals who need to be avoided as long as possible. Weird people who love the dead. The Addams family and the Munsters.

The truth is, the time required to run a cemetery is around 85 percent for landscaping. People aren't crazy about visiting cemeteries, but they expect them to be well groomed and parklike in appearance. Cutting the grass and trimming trees—85 percent. Administration—10 percent. Burying the deceased—5 percent.

Adding to this, my wife created a database listing all the burials—some fifteen thousand. It took her over six years to accomplish this.

Not very creepy, is it?

I also took it upon myself to place American flags at the graves of veterans in time for each Memorial Day. My American Legion Post Color Guard fires twenty-one-gun volleys over this and eleven other cemeteries each year. I place almost five hundred flags here along with another three hundred in other local cemeteries.

Cutting the grass and placing flags, I've easily walked the entire 33 acres (13 hectares) in the course of a year. I knew the names on the monuments and knew some of them personally while they were alive. A place of honor, respect, love, and dignity, although Stephen King might disagree. Working the land, I often saw things from the corner of my eye. You'd almost see someone standing there, but when you turned that way, the figure was gone. It happened almost constantly. Always a shadow, even in the daytime.

The biggest example came when my wife and I were standing up the toppled stone of a Civil War veteran. As we secured the old stone, my wife said she saw someone in a Civil War-style uniform standing nearby. She is a little better at seeing things than I am. I didn't see him, but my wife claimed he looked happy. Maybe it was his headstone?

I get a good feeling when working there, no matter what job I'm doing. A feeling of general content. The same feeling you get in a room full of happy people, that kind of energy.

I've never investigated these "shadows" at night, but seeing them during the day is enough to convince me the place is haunted but not in a bad way.

The *Morro Castle* Ship Disaster

As a historian specializing in local history, I've researched the SS *Morro Castle* ship disaster of 1934 to the point where I'm considered an expert on the event and asked to speak at various group meetings. It began with my walking-history-book grandfather, whose sister was married to one of the ship's crewmen involved in the disaster. A family matter, you might say.

The 520-foot SS *Morro Castle* was a cruise ship launched in 1930, making 172 round trips between New York and Cuba, a very popular, inexpensive vacation, even during the Depression.

On its return trip on September 8, 1934, fire broke out aboard the ship three miles off the Jersey Shore. Chased by a hurricane from the south and heading into another storm to the north, the fierce winds fanned the flames until the entire ship was ablaze. Passengers and crewmembers were caught in the fire, and many jumped off the ship into the raging, twenty-foot seas.

Everything that could go wrong did. The crew was accused of cowardice and dereliction of duty to the passengers, and the crew countered that the passengers panicked and wouldn't follow orders to assist them. Firefighting systems

An aerial photo of the SS *Morro Castle* captures the fateful disaster on September 8, 1934, when the ship caught fire, killing 137 people.

failed, power was lost, and over thirty minutes were wasted before an SOS could be sent. The First Officer, already on duty for thirty hours before the captain died from mysterious circumstances and had to take over, wavered in his command, not sure of what to do.

One hundred and thirty-seven passengers and crewmembers, exactly 25 percent of those 549 on board, died as a result of the fire or from trying to escape the flames.

The burning ship drifted for several hours until beaching itself at Asbury Park, New Jersey, within striking distance of Convention Hall.

The burned hulk of the ship rested in the sand at Asbury Park for six months before it could be pulled free. It was certainly one of the biggest draws to the Jersey Shore. Happening a week after Labor Day, the wreck brought business to the town for months after the summer season.

Asbury Park seems to have more than its share of ghostly apparitions roaming around town. It is believed that many of them are *Morro Castle* casualties seen in and around Convention Hall and the boardwalk where the burned and rusted hulk of the *Morro Castle* rested until March 1935.

The Theaters of Asbury Park, New Jersey

They were all haunted: the Baronet, the Lyric, the Savoy, the St. James, the Mayfair, and the Paramount. Add to that the Palace, later known as the Beach Cinema, in nearby Bradley Beach. I started working as a projectionist in 1972 as a relief operator, giving the regular workers a night off. I was in a different theater each night, an opportunity the other projectionists didn't have, as they were assigned one work location for most of their careers.

The theaters were all old, the first opening in 1913, the last in 1929. All were ornate—some more than others—Golden Age gems of architecture.

After two weeks of training in different venues, I was on my own for the first time in the Paramount, part of the Convention Hall complex on the oceanfront boardwalk. All seemed to be going well for an hour or so. But then, strange things began to happen.

A carbon arc lamp shut off. It didn't just go out; the switch was turned off. No one was there but me, but somehow, the switch was turned off. Then, I got a call from the manager downstairs that I was out of focus. Again, no one was there but me, and the focus knob was moved about a quarter turn. Using two projectors, the other lamp was shut off a little later. Then, a stack of empty film reels fell over. Outside of the projection booth were the catwalks over the ceiling of the auditorium. I heard someone talking out there. I went to see, and no one was there. I felt my skin begin to crawl.

After the show, the local projectionists all met at a nearby tavern for a drink. I came in, white as a sheet as they told me, and demanded a drink. They wanted to know what was wrong. I told them of my experiences of the evening. They all waved me off, saying I was just jumpy on my first night alone. I insisted on what went on. They kept laughing at me. I was starting to get angry. I know what happened.

Finally, one of the guys came over and told me, quite frankly, that the theaters were all haunted. Various employees, from stagehands to projectionists and even patrons, existed in the theaters. A few died while working, but most of the others died naturally but came back to haunt their former jobs. One stagehand was robbed and murdered while walking home from work one night.

One of the ghost hunter TV shows featured the Paramount. They found evidence of spirits along the long corridor of dressing rooms.

As I worked the other theaters, I caught many just-out-of-vision sightings. Shadows. But not all the time. Here and there, one would pass by. One cinema often has the figure of a person in the front row as the place closes each night. Look again, and it's gone. Employees would all claim to have seen some-

As I worked the other theaters, I caught many just-out-of-vision sightings. Shadows. But not all the time. Here and there, one would pass by.

one still sitting in the front row. Some walked down there to see if a patron had fallen asleep. But no one was there.

In a recent theater job, the town was putting on a fireworks show for the Fourth of July. The window in the booth faced the wrong way, so you could only hear the fireworks. This seemed to shake up two spirits I saw running around. Just shadows, but I saw them moving around. They were acting scared, as if hearing the explosions as incoming fire. Perhaps they were war veterans. When the noise stopped, so did they. That was the most activity I had ever witnessed by possible ghosts.

Madame John's Legacy

By Alexandrea Weis

Tucked away at the bend in the Mississippi River, the French Quarter of New Orleans has seen three hundred years of fires, plagues, hurricanes, floods, murder, mayhem, and a lot of drunkenness. Such energy leaves a spiritual residue on the plaster and cypress Creole cottages, keeping the dead tethered to the place they once called home.

Anyone who has visited the Big Easy can tell you about the many spooky mansions. But there is one home famous for a certain vampire movie filmed there, which happens to have several spiritual residents trapped within its brick and wood foundation—ghosts no one dares mention.

How do I know about them? I grew up across the street from Madame John's Legacy.

The current house, built in 1788, sits atop the remains of a first structure destroyed by fire and is one of the few homes to survive the devastating conflagration of 1794 that wiped out most of the French Quarter. The simple, unadorned French West Indies design pales next to romantic iron balconies of the Spanish Colonial homes surrounding it. Named after a story by New Orleans author George Washington Cable, it's one of the oldest structures in the city.

Numerous legends persist about the property and its former owner, Renato Beluche. Ghost tour guides intrigue tourists with tales of the lieutenant in Jean Lafitte's band of pirates and how he purchased the home with treasure earned while sailing with the city's famous hooligan. His ghost is said to whisper in the ears of pretty women who grace the halls of his former residence, enticing them to stay.

No one I knew living around Madame John's ever ran into anyone resembling a pirate. They had encounters with several other apparitions—ones never mentioned on the ghost tours.

The best known by the locals is the woman in black who walks the balcony in front of the mansion. She paces back and forth in a black gown dating to the 1700s. Residents of the 600 block of Dumaine call her Madame Pascal, widow of a sea captain named Jean Pascal who purchased the land in 1727. Neighbors in the know often walk on the other side of the street in front of the cottage where I grew up to not "upset the madame." A few avoided the house altogether, often heading the other way to evade the gaze of the old lady on the balcony.

She wasn't just an apparition; she also got hostile. If she didn't want you close to her home, she would toss pebbles at you. I got hit by a few of them when I played on the sidewalk in front of our cottage as a child. No one was ever on the street behind me. I didn't give it a second thought, but I never liked getting close to the house. An uncomfortable feeling in my gut told me to stay away.

During this time, the state of Louisiana owned the mansion as a registered landmark, but due to its dilapidated condition, no one was allowed inside, and the front was kept boarded up with a padlock on the door—a lock that always seemed to be open every morning before the workmen arrived.

The part about God casting the demon into a bottomless pit had blackened fingerprints on it, blotting out the verse.

My father befriended the workers renovating the home, having them over for coffee on several occasions. In exchange, we often got to roam the building, exploring the main house and courtyard.

With tons of broken boards, glass, cracked brick, and rusted nails, it wasn't the safest place, but it was a museum of artifacts. Even though it had been lived in as a private residence until the forties and used as a museum in the sixties, the closed portions of the mansion, not yet updated, offered glimpses into the past. The kitchen still housed its original hearth and swing hooks to hold cooking pots over an open fire, but the attic was the real treasure trove. Furniture, lanterns, books, and portraits left by previous owners still waited for removal. I got the chance to go through several corners of the cramped space with my father. We never ran across anything sinister—at least not in the attic—but the odd thing I discovered was a family Bible dated to 1867, with all the names and family tree listed in French on the inside cover. The Bible sat open to a page in Revelations on a short, wooden table next to an old-fashioned hurricane lamp. The part about God casting the demon into a bottomless pit had blackened fingerprints on it, blotting out the verse. The fingerprints never went away, no matter how many times we wiped the page to read the passage. Today, the Bible remains on the site, and some say the eerie fingerprints are still there.

The workmen shared stories of the children they encountered when renovating the courtyard. They often ran around the pond and could be seen when people walked on the balconies or heard laughing when they were in other rooms of the house. Neighbors who lived on either side of the home reported children laughing, especially on humid, summer evenings. These ghosts were also mischievous. Workmen recounted strange occurrences. Equipment moved, radios turned on and off, and lights flickered when there was no electricity running to them. One plumber had problems with someone pulling at his shoestrings as he tried to fix the broken pipes under the house.

But there were more than children appearing during the renovations. One day, a terrified painter knocked on our cottage door, spooked by what he had seen in the main living room. A woman in old-fashioned dress had yelled at him in French. He didn't know what was said, but when she vanished before his eyes, he figured out she wasn't real. He swore never to return to the house again.

If ghostly laughter and furious Frenchwomen weren't enough, there was the music. Many people living around Madame John's reported the music. I heard it on several occasions. Sometimes it was a violin, other times a piano, and it always came at night in faint wisps carried on the wind. It was as if the essence of a long-ago party still lingered in the air. Music in the French Quarter is hardly noticeable to many because of the frequent bars and clubs open all night, probably why many people shrugged it off. But this music was very different from the local jazz and upbeat tempos offered on Bourbon Street. It was somber, ethereal, and came when you were all alone on the street, when no one else was around to bear witness, adding to the spine-tingling unease of it. Then as soon as you heard it, it would disappear, making you second-guess your sanity.

Stories about the historic property differed, and neighbors would often gather to debate their creepiest experiences, but despite all the tales, there was one unanimous consensus about Madame John's—it left everyone with an unpleasant sense of sorrow. It was not a happy place, and every time you stepped into its dark rooms, you could almost touch the sadness on the walls.

So, if you ever come to New Orleans, be sure to check out the unassuming mansion at 632 Dumaine Street. And if you see Madame Pascal pacing the balcony, give her my love.

From New Orleans and raised in the motion picture industry, Alexandrea Weis began writing at the age of eight. With twenty-seven published novels to her credit and over a dozen national writing awards, Weis continues to work tirelessly to hone her craft. She has worked with Lucas Astor on the *Magnus Blackwell* series as well as the YA thriller *Death by the River,* with more books planned in the future. Her works include the *Nicci Beauvoir* series, the *Corde Noire* series, the *Cover to Cover* series, *Acadian Waltz, Broken Wings, The Ghosts of Rue Dumaine,* and the soon to be released YA historical epic, *Realm.* A permitted wildlife rehabber, Weis rescues orphaned and injured animals. She is married and lives in New Orleans.

HAUNTED GEORGIA

Lesia Miller Schnur

Henry Greene Cole House, Marietta, Georgia

Henry Greene Cole was a Union sympathizer living in the Confederate South. He was also wealthy. He built a small house on Washington Avenue just outside the Marietta Square. It is told that his father-in-law urged General Sherman not to burn the Fletcher House Hotel because of his relation to Cole. Cole donated the land adjacent to his home for the Union National Cemetery, where over ten thousand Union soldiers are buried. Cole endeavored to build a larger home a block down from his small house. Although he died before it was completed, his family resided in the grand house for many years. Today, the house is a commercial building; however, it still boasts the architectural elements of a Georgian home.

It is also haunted. A local resident, whose grandparents lived down the street, spoke of walking past the house and seeing a woman in the upper left-hand corner. She saw this girl many times over the years. For several decades, the house was home to several law firms. Attorneys and their employees reported feeling cold drafts and hearing voices. One attorney experienced her clock running backward. People walking past claim to see curtains shifting and lights turning on and off at night. The house sits directly across from the National Cemetery.

Kennesaw House, Marietta, Georgia

The Great Locomotive Chase began in Cobb County, Georgia. On April 12, 1862, civilian James J. Andrews and several Union soldiers stole *The General*, the prize steam locomotive, that was essential to the Confederate rail

The Kennesaw House has been restored to look as it did back in 1862. It is home to the Marietta Museum of History.

system. The Andrews Raiders, the name given to the men, stayed at the Fletcher House Hotel the night before commandeering the train.

The Fletcher House Hotel served as the Confederate hospital and mortuary during the Civil War. The Union Army took control of the hotel shortly before they marched toward Atlanta. When the city of Marietta burned, the hotel was spared. Today, it is known as the Kennesaw House and serves as the Marietta Museum of History for the city.

The front-facing, second-floor room where the Andrews Raiders stayed has been reconstructed to look like it did back in 1862. The museum has an extensive military weapon and uniform collection. Visitors have experienced paranormal phenomena within the museum. One visitor described shadows forming on the wall. Others claim to hear the screams of possible Civil War-era patients who linger. A woman dressed in a dress with pink trimmings has been seen by children visiting the museum. These sightings appear to be benign.

Pigeon Hill, Kennesaw Mountain National Battlefield Park, Marietta, Georgia

Five thousand, three hundred and fifty soldiers were killed during the Battle of Kennesaw from June 18, 1864, to July 2, 1864. Most of these casualties were killed at Little Kennesaw Mountain, today known as Pigeon Hill. The Confederacy claimed the small victory here; however, they ultimately lost the Civil War. Today, the souls of both Confederate and Union soldiers haunt the area around the battlefield.

People driving along Old Highway 41 report seeing men dressed in Civil War military uniforms walking among the woods. Some reason that they're seeing actors engaged in the frequent re-enactment activities; however, others look closer to notice the ghostlike appearance of these men. The national park contains several monuments dedicated to different divisions, memorial markers along the hiking trails, and cannons. Reported paranormal activity includes residual hauntings where soldiers repeat prepping the cannons for battle as well as soldiers walking along the woods. Homeowners in several subdivisions surrounding the area also report activity. Some see the ghosts of soldiers walking in their homes and outside along their driveways. Others have claimed to see soldiers hiding and ducking in backyards. None of the reports have indicated malicious behavior.

Reported paranormal activity includes residual hauntings where soldiers repeat prepping the cannons for battle as well as soldiers walking along the woods.

Southern Airways Flight 242 Plane Crash, New Hope, Georgia

Annette "Annetta" Snell just finished recording new tracks for her debut album and was heading home to New

York City on Monday, April 4, 1977. Formerly of the R&B all-female group called The Fabulettes, Snell had secured a record deal with Epic Records and a recording session in Muscle Shoals, Alabama. She boarded Southern Airways Flight 242 carrying the studio session tapes. Unfortunately, Snell and sixty-two other passengers and crewmembers died in a fiery crash along Highway 92 during a torrential hailstorm. The crash was the worst airline disaster in Georgia history.

In total, seventy-two people died following the airline's crash along the highway as the pilot attempted to make an unpowered emergency landing. The wings clipped a gas station and burst into flames as the plane traveled along the highway. The plane broke into five pieces. The highway remains intact today, as does a house that has since been turned into a thrift store. A memorial/historical marker stands outside a cemetery near the crash site.

Annetta's family initially thought they saw her walking dazed in the background on local news broadcasts. Though her body was never recovered, a partial bridge found at the site matched her dental records. To this day, people claim to have seen victims from the crash walking along the highway. Patrons at a local restaurant tell stories of seeing ghosts from the flight. Finally, customers at the thrift store have reported seeing ghostlike people walking in the front yard.

St. James Episcopal Cemetery, Marietta, Georgia

Best known as the final resting place for murdered child beauty queen JonBenét Ramsey, St. James Episcopal Cemetery is located at the intersection of Polk Street and Winn Street across from the Marietta Middle School. The cemetery was established in 1844 and houses the remains of some of the city's most important residents. Surrounded by a beautiful, wrought iron fence, the cemetery has an active nightlife.

Daytime visitors come to pay respects to JonBenét, her mother Patsy, and her half sister, Elizabeth Pasch Ramsey. JonBenét's Christmas Day murder remains unsolved and incredibly popular. Despite tabloid reports, the ghost of JonBenét does not haunt the cemetery. However, others do.

Marion "Mary" R. Meinert died at age thirty-four. The mother of twins, Mary's monument is a young woman holding two babies. Visitors claim to hear a woman crying at night. Others claim to have seen tears coming from the statue's eyes.

Students at the middle school across the narrow street report seeing ghostlike apparitions walking in the small cemetery. Others have heard voices.

The cemetery is owned and operated by St. James Episcopal Church. The gates are usually open daily; however, the city police actively patrol the area at night.

Lesia Miller Schnur is a former librarian who goes by the name "The Haunted Librarian." Her website, *www.thehauntedlibrarian.com* is listed as one of the Top 50 Paranormal

Websites and offers paranormal news, pop culture, and Lesia's investigations into popular theories. She has been on the radio, appeared at Dragon Con and academic conferences, and also writes paranormal mysteries, short stories, and screenplays. She resides in Atlanta, Georgia.

Old Paulding Jail

Kat Hobson

I have been fortunate enough to investigate Old Paulding Jail in Paulding, Ohio, several times. I have been there with an event company group and had some small experiences in various areas of the building. I have been there filming with a much smaller and experienced group and had ghostly fingers placed over my lips in a shushing fashion when I pushed too hard for answers. I have been there to broadcast a live episode of my radio show *Paranormal Experience* and basically caused a ghostly riot to break out in the first-floor cellblock. And I have been there for a birthday/death day party for one of the known spirits who haunts there, who was found hanged in the cellblock area on his birthday. Such sad irony.

With each visit to the jail, my paranormal experiences have escalated. The first two times I felt nothing threatening, heard nothing that would cause a loss of sleep. The owner of the event company and the owner of the jail both shared the history of the facility, and that was interesting, well documented, and matched the experiences well.

When I went to Old Paulding Jail to do a live broadcast for my show, everything seemed to be very mellow, and it felt as though the spirits were not going to react negatively to my presence. I was staying in the jail a couple of nights in an upstairs room that used to be part of the sheriff's living quarters. The owner of the jail, Shelly Burk Robertson, has a bedroom there, as she commutes from her home for events and often stays there. When the activity occurred, she and I and one other member of her team were the only living people present in the building. When we were upstairs on the third floor (ironically, where people will not spend any time alone, including the owner), we tested my equipment and Internet connections to verify that we would be able to broadcast live. Everything was fine. There.

The moment I sat down to test the connection with my producer, all hell broke loose.... Immediately, the settings on my computer started resetting themselves, and it was showing no Internet connection.

We next moved down to the first-floor cellblock, where I set my computer on the only table in the area. It just happened to be where an inmate was found hanged one morning in what could only be described as unusual circumstances. The moment I sat down to test the connection with my producer, all hell broke loose. I believe that to be a literal statement. Immediately, the settings on my computer started resetting themselves, and it was showing no Internet connection. That was an impossibility. While I had wi-fi connectivity with the jail's network, I was using my hardwired connection to their router. There was no way I could have lost connection unless their entire service went out, which wasn't the case. We checked.

The more I tried to understand what was happening with my computer, the louder the cellblock became. There was stomping all around me. The cell doors, while not moving, were making sounds of slamming shut and banging open. The fire doors on all three levels of the building, whose stairs are still enclosed with fencing from when it was an active jail, were being banged on. And meanwhile, my producer is Skype messaging me to just keep going, that I WAS still connected, and he was recording what was happening around me. I became just as irritated with the ghosts as they were with me at that point. It never dawned on me that if they were striking objects, they could strike me too! After struggling with the connections for a bit longer, I got a message from my producer that things were escalating and it would be good idea to wrap up what I was doing and leave that area. He was becoming concerned for my safety.

Shelly and I left the cellblock at that point. She went into the kitchen to make coffee, and I took my computer to the office to see what I could do to get things working properly in order to do my show that night. Once I stepped out of the cellblock, my computer settings immediately corrected themselves. I had a clear Skype connection, I had full Internet connectivity, and everything else was functioning normally as well. I had never experienced anything like that!

I immediately went into the kitchen, where a communication device is always set up to ask the owner to initiate a voice box session. When she did, a very arrogant voice answered her question of who had been messing with my computer settings with "I did!" After about thirty minutes of back-and-forth conversation, including my reasons for doing the show there, all of us seemed calmer. She explained that I was there to help raise awareness for the jail as a paranormal research center and that her projects were how she could keep the jail up and running. Then she asked if we could broadcast from the cellblock. The response? "Absolutely not!" She asked if we could broadcast from the third floor, and the response was "Yeah, sure." So, we did, with no difficulty, but with a lot of electronic voice phenomena and shadow play around us. It was definitely one of the most bizarre experiences I have had to date in the paranormal and the only time I felt threatened as well.

Kat Hobson is the owner of WBHM-DB *Paranormal Talk Radio* and host of *Fate Magazine Radio*, and *Paranormal Experienced Radio*, as well as a paranormal investigator.

Jennie Wade House

By Laurie Hull

Gettysburg is a town with so many hauntings! Thousands of soldiers gave their lives there during the Civil War battle, and many of their spirits are believed to still roam the battlefields. The story I found most compelling is in a location off the battlefield in a small house now called the Jennie Wade House, named after its most celebrated visitor. Jennie Wade (full name Mary Virginia Wade, also known as Ginnie Wade) didn't live in the house named for her. She was born and raised in Gettysburg in a home not far from the Jennie Wade House. At the end of June 1863, Union soldiers were gathering in anticipation of conflict, and Jennie Wade came to stay with her sister, Georgia McClellan, who lived in part of the house. Georgia was about to have a baby, and Jennie Wade occupied her time baking bread for soldiers before and during the battle.

It was during this chore that Jennie became the only civilian killed in the Battle of Gettysburg. A bullet traveled through the house and hit her, killing her instantly as she was kneading bread dough. Her family decided to then take refuge in the basement of the house, and two soldiers helped carry the body with them to the relative safety of the underground cellar.

It is this area where the most spirit activity takes place. I have visited the house on several occasions during regular and ghost tours. The basement always draws me in. There is an uncomfortable feeling, as if you are intruding on someone. Could this be members of the family still mourning Jennie? Once I stayed behind in the basement as everyone else on the tour moved on. As I sat, I felt a cold settle in around me, colder than the air of the basement. Very faintly, I heard a heavy sighing sound like the beginning or end of a crying session. It sounded like someone trying to catch their breath. When I asked the tour guide about it, they indicated that crying and sighing sounds have often been heard in the basement area and are believed to be one the parents mourning their lost daughter.

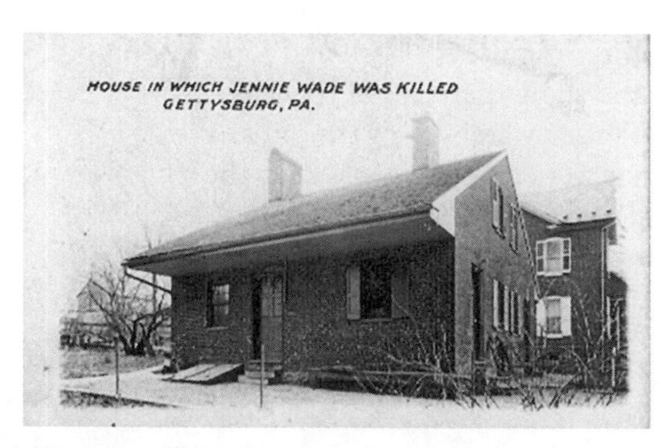

HOUSE IN WHICH JENNIE WADE WAS KILLED
GETTYSBURG, PA.

An early 1900s photo of the house in Gettysburg in which Jennie Wade was accidentally killed by a bullet while kneading bread for Union soldiers.

Some people believe that one spirit that haunts the house is Jennie Wade herself. Often, people who pass away suddenly or in a violent manner tend to linger at the site of their death. She was only twenty years old when she was tragically killed. She could be waiting to hear the fate of her fiancé, Jack, who was fighting for the Union. Jack was taken prisoner and died from his wounds at Winchester. Sadly, she never found out his fate, and he never found out hers. The ghost of Jennie Wade has been seen by visitors and guides, who have also caught the scent of her favorite perfume, Rose Water.

In addition to these ghosts, the spirit of a young boy has been reported. He is known to run about the house and cause the chain in the upstairs bedroom display to swing on its own. During one of my visits to the house, I saw a flash of a young child run up the kitchen stairs out of the corner of my eye. As we went upstairs to the bedrooms, I noticed the chain on the toy display was swinging, even though there was no one in the room.

The ghost of the young boy is not believed to be connected to Jennie Wade's family but is likely a previous resident. Mortality rates among young children were very high in the early 1800s, and many children did not live to adulthood. He seems to be having fun with the visitors to the house, as many have reported having their hands touched and clothing and jewelry tugged on. If you visit the house, make sure to take lots of photos! I have several photos of the interior of this house that contain unexplained misty shapes.

Laurie Hull is an author, psychic, and paranormal investigator from Springfield, Pennsylvania and has had a lifelong interest in ghosts and the supernatural that began while she was growing up in a haunted house. She is the founder and director of Tri-County Paranormal Research, which can be found at *www.tricountyprs.com*.

Children Ghosts of St. Augustine, Florida

By Sara Harrison

During the first of many visits to Florida's St. Augustine, I went on a ghost walk to see for myself if the town lived up to its reputation of being the "most haunted" city in America.

The guide was a black-cloaked woman with a black hat and lighted, antique lantern. Taking some pauses at locations along the way, she wove intriguing yarns about the town's origins and its spectral events. Just in case, I took photos to record any unusual phenomena.

Halfway through the tour, we came to a large set of limestone pillars. As we passed through, I saw a girl in a dress scampering along the top of one wall. I was instantly judgmental. Why would any parents allow her to do that? When I turned my attention back to the guide, she explained that there had once been a guard at the city gate whose job it was to keep newcomers out of the city due to an outbreak of typhoid fever. The disease had hit the city hard and caused the deaths of so many residents that they were eventually buried in mass graves, and some were accidentally buried before they had even died. By the time we reached the mass grave area, she explained that the gatekeeper did his best but eventually succumbed to the illness, so his daughter, Elizabeth, took up his post in the absence of anyone else to do the job. (She also fell ill and died shortly thereafter.) I was chilled when our guide revealed Elizabeth had always accompanied him at the gates, often playing atop the stone wall to pass the time. That was the girl I had seen! I had never thought a ghost would look so three-dimensional.

At the end of her presentation, the guide explained that a child named James was often seen in the graveyard, looking for relatives who, unfortunately, were buried elsewhere.

When we reached another graveyard that was from a more recent time—the Civil War—the tour guide's candle mysteriously went out. She asked if anyone had a lighter. Because I stepped forward to give her mine, I was allowed a closer view of the cemetery. Inside, I saw a huge tree that seemed pretty cool; the child in me wanted to break into the cemetery and climb it. At the end of her presentation, the guide explained that a child named James was often seen in the graveyard looking for relatives who, unfortunately, were buried elsewhere. His remains were buried just under the tree I was enamored with, one he had had great affection for and often climbed. I then knew that his spirit and mine had connected, but I didn't know how attached he was to me until I was leaving for the trip home and drove past the Civil War graveyard. Upon reaching the entry gate, my car stereo crackled and changed from rock to nineteenth-century orchestra music, the music of James's lifetime. I recognized his desire to get my attention and was grateful.

"Goodbye, little James," I said aloud.

Once home again, I examined my photos on my computer and realized there were many with odd light anomalies. I made a slideshow with them and inserted the DVD into my player, but soon, it refused to work—it would not release the slideshow. When I tried to reburn the slideshow on my computer, that machine, too, crashed and would not start again. Both electronic devices were ruined beyond repair, and the ghost walk photos were gone forever. Perhaps the experiences were meant for me and me alone. For my part, I no longer needed concrete proof that ghosts existed because I had more than enough evidence to be convinced.

Sara Harrison, M.A., B.Ed., is a freelance writer, artist, and evidential medium. She lives with her soul mate, Lee, in Napanee, Ontario, Canada. sara.lee@cogeco.ca.

The Lady of the Lake

By Dennis Waller

Growing up in Dallas, Texas, our home was just a few blocks from White Rock Lake. My father, who loved to fish, practically lived on the lake. During the fall, our routine was to run to the lake before work and school to check his trot lines. We could be from front door to water in five minutes and most times be back home within the hour.

I was seven years old when, on one of these fall mornings, I came face-to-face with the Lady of the Lake. On this particular morning, the weather was cold and blustery, so my father suggested that I stay onshore while he went out on the boat. Even staying onshore, I still had my duty to man the ropes, tying off the boat to the dock when he came in. I kept an eye out across the water, straining to see my father's boat when, out of the corner of my eye, I caught movement. Turning to my left, I saw a beautiful woman in a long, white dress walking on the water, and she was walking toward me! I stood there, unable to move, while I watched her walk. There was something melancholy about her gait and expression. As she approached me, she gave me one of those crooked smiles, the kind that was civil but masked some sort of pain. She came within ten feet of me, then slowly turned and, as she walked toward the road, I heard my father call out to me. I turned to see that he was almost to the dock. When I looked back to the road, the lady was gone, simply vanished. It couldn't have been a second, but she was gone.

Frustrated at me for being distracted, he asked what I was doing. I told him, "I was watching the lady." Of course, he replied, "What lady!?" During the process of storing away the boat and loading the truck, I told my father what I had seen. He sternly said that he was watching me from the boat and that there was nobody else there but me, to stop my daydreaming and get in the truck.

I soon forgot about the incident until a few weeks later, my father came back from the morning trip to the lake. It was too cold and windy for me to go, so I had stayed home. I'll never forget the look on his face. I can count on one hand the times I had seen my father visually shaken. Being a very stoic man, not much could get to him. But this morning was different. He sat down next to me while I ate my breakfast. To be honest, I was scared, not knowing what brought on this change in behavior. With his arms resting on the table, he leaned in and asked in a soft voice, "Tell me about the woman you saw at the lake." Revived, knowing that I was in the clear, I recounted the story down to the color of her hair and the color of her eyes. As I told my story, I noticed that he started tapping his fingers on the table in a rapid manner while he seemed to be staring out into space. At one point, he stopped me and said, "Let's keep this to ourselves; let it be our secret."

There was never another word spoken about the incident, nor his admission to seeing the Lady of the Lake, but I am convinced that my father had come face-to-face with the strange, eerie woman like I had.

It wasn't until years later that I heard the alleged stories about the famed "Lady of the Lake." Some say she was a heartbroken bride-to-be who committed suicide upon her groom leaving her at the altar. Others say she was a socialite who drove her car into the lake in distress.

Over the years, the story has become an urban legend, one that is brought up every year around Halloween. Those who claimed to have seen her are often ridiculed and mocked. Keeping my word to my father until now, I haven't spoken of my experience on that day. What I have learned, though, is that it doesn't matter what people think is true or not, whatever they believe, none of it matters because it doesn't change the fact that my father and I have both seen her, the woman in the white gown walking on the water, the Lady of the Lake.

Brian Keith Ellis Has an Amazing Experience at Gettysburg

This is where I died.

As I stepped out of the tree line, I stared across the stretch of open ground. Aghast. There, almost a mile away, was the fence line where ten thousand Union guns waited for the Confederate charge to commence. For a moment, I wasn't sure if I was still in 2010 or if this was July 3, 1863. The emotion was so charged in me, so raw and clear, that I fell to my knees and dug my hands into the dirt beneath the early grass of spring.

Gettysburg.

The name itself is so mythical now. Legends and stories of tides of battle and outcomes of single events that would shape the future of a nation. For me, though, this moment was so intensely personal that all of that lore, all of that intriguing history that I had learned was gone.

Because this is where I died.

I've always been inexplicably drawn to Gettysburg. I remember a friend talking about past lives and telling me, "Think of places and times that draw you, over and over, for an unknown reason—these are where and when you lived."

Visiting the Gettysburg Battlefield, author Brian Keith Ellis had a profound experience, a sense that, in a previous life, he had died there.

At the time, I wasn't really a "past lives" guy. But that explanation kept gnawing at me as I thought of a place like Gettysburg. I'd never been there. Until Ken Burns's Civil War documentary, I knew only that it was a turning point in the war. Why, then, was I so drawn to it? Now I knew.

This is where I died.

I got up and walked farther out into that field where General George Pickett had led us out toward the Union lines. I closed my eyes and let myself immerse into the moment, trying to connect with those valiant soldiers who knew, *knew*, the slaughter that was coming. I could *feel* the emotion of that moment. Time enough in battle to know that the upcoming action was not in our favor. Looking in each others' faces, seeking encouragement to find some shred of belief that the outcome might be a successful one. Each one of us knowing that this action was as hopeless as one could imagine. But we'd been there before. So many times, we'd faced an enemy of far superior numbers and equipment and, time after time, we'd whupped them. It was with that mix of fear, grimness, and hope that we stepped out onto that field.

I'd finally come to Gettysburg for the history, not knowing that I would find this incredible well of feelings under the surface. Driving along the road that passes through the trees where the massive Confederate Army emerged, I was suddenly overcome with emotion at the location of the Tennessee memorial. It was there that I got out of my car and walked out onto that expanse of grass. I ran my fingers over the engraved monument, connecting to the notes of the Tennessee 14th Regiment.

Now, partway across the open ground, it was as if I could hear sounds not there on this April morning. Shots. Booms of cannon. Shouts of pain and bravado. Heat and bugs and crunching grass as we, against all odds, moved closer and closer to the fence line. All for naught. The 14th Tennessee got close enough that Union soldiers were able to dart out and capture the flag, but that was as far as they got—as far, it turns out, as the Confederate Army got during that war. As far as I got before the dark.

I continue to try to research who I might have been. I keep thinking that if I find the right photo of the men of the 14th Tennessee, I'll know the body I inhabited for a short while. Or perhaps I'll never know. What I do know is that in that moment, on that field, I felt, saw, and heard things that I can't explain in traditional "scientific" terms. Emotions that really shouldn't exist in a dude from southern California visiting an old, historic battlefield. Perhaps it's just because:

This is where I died.

Brian Keith Ellis is a screenwriter and producer with a number of film projects in development.

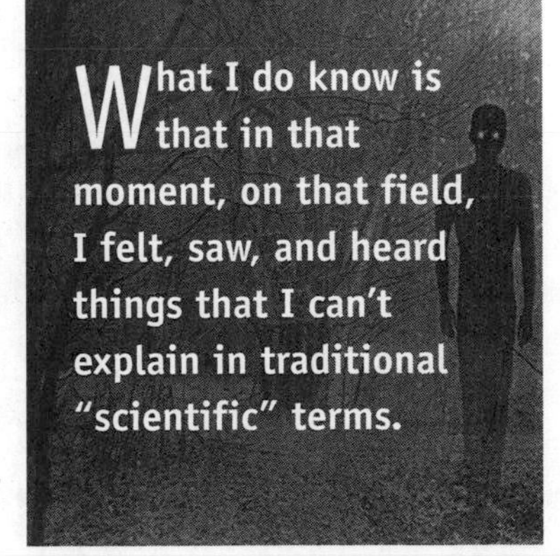
What I do know is that in that moment, on that field, I felt, saw, and heard things that I can't explain in traditional "scientific" terms.

The Forum Theater

Jason Roberts

Having spent the last twelve years investigating and researching the paranormal, there is one building that always comes to mind as possibly being the most haunted location our team has ever encountered. The Forum Theater, which is what we'll keep with calling it since that is what it was turned into during the years we were able to investigate, is located on the east side of Wichita, Kansas. The building is three stories, including the basement, not to mention the creepiest organ room, hidden high above the stage. It was built in 1926 and has massive, stone pillars out front, a school built on the side over the years, and had been a church for different religions for decades. The church is hard to miss driving along the road, and it was a popular place for Sunday mornings. That is, until the congregation abandoned their place of worship.

The new owners, Janet and Grant, were the eleventh to make an offer when the building was finally up for sale. They thought it was strange that a building of this size and beauty was just left behind. Hymn books laid on the seats, dishes were still in the sink in the downstairs kitchen, and so many random things were stored everywhere inside from the basement on up past the main floor and filtered to the third floor. Grant wanted to make it into a place for auction, but Janet wanted a theater for stage performances; Janet won the argument. So, they hired a crew to redesign the complete inside of this former church to prepare for theater acting, weddings and dinners in the reception hall downstairs, and anything else that could entertain guests. Everything seemed to be going well until Grant wanted to work on the old pastor's study. That is the time everything took a turn they never expected and opened their eyes to the thought that they were not the only ones who were there. One day while Grant was working in the study, he noticed the door kept closing. Years of being abandoned had left the old church victim to vagrants who broke in and stole the brass doorknobs, parts of the balcony railings, and anything else they could find. So, Grant kept getting locked in the room every time the door closed, and he had to pry the door open with tools. He finally had enough and took the door off its hinges, placing it upright in the hall. About that time, he saw his wife and the foreman walking his way, so he turned and stepped forward to them, and just as he did, the door went slamming past him to the other side of the hall. The door just missed him and shocked them all so badly that they knew they needed help.

The spirits started off being little kids peeking around doors watching the workers, and, knowing there were no children in the building, it began to upset everyone.

Our team was called in to check the old church out, which excited us all since it has such a history and, well, investigating old churches is exciting in itself. We walked in, and the place was more than we expected. It was huge inside, with different staircases, multiple rooms, and closets everywhere. Janet began to explain that they and the construction crew were experiencing giggling, footsteps, equipment being moved, crying in the main auditorium, the sound of a full orchestra playing, and seeing full-body apparitions. The spirits started off being little kids peeking around doors watching the workers and, knowing there were no children in the building, it began to upset everyone. The most frightening of the spirits were the angry man upstairs and the woman who screams. I wanted to find out the history of this place, but it was very difficult to find any information. So, we began our investigation by setting up the DVR and cameras along with other tools that we hoped would be able to communicate with the spirits. Splitting up into small groups, we went all over trying to find some good spots to start. Three of us went to the study to start with and noticed a strange closet just outside the study. We assumed it was merely the door to a closet, but it just had a weird vibe. We got comfortable in the room and started asking questions of who was there and if they could help us out with what was happening. Some taps here and there, possibly some activity, but it was mostly quiet, so we started the knocking game. One of the investigators said that we'll go around the room and knock, but the last person cannot knock until whoever was there made a noise or knocked themselves. We had three handheld recorders in the room and started our game. When it came time for the spirit to make a knock, it did, and it was very clearly in the room, and we were hooked with this location. The team also moved downstairs to check out the kitchen and other offices down there. We got up to the office on the south side of the basement and went to open the office door to see what was inside. As soon as the door opened, we were greeted by the loudest scream right in our faces, making each of us almost drop to the ground. It was female and, after checking ourselves for a change of underwear, we searched the office for any clues or signs to indicate whether it was fake or real. Nothing was found, and the scream was recorded on all three levels of the building.

Checking over evidence, we listened to the recordings from the pastor's study and were shocked at what we heard. On two of the recorders, we caught the knock we asked for, but on the third recorder, we caught a voice instead of a knock. It was a name, but we had no idea who it could be. We had just been asking who was in there, and the voice said Ernest. Over the next few weeks, we pored over the evidence to find answers of who he was and why he was there. Why was there a woman screaming in the basement? Finally, Janet called and said she had found a book of history on the old church. She said, "Jason, you'll never guess who the first pastor was! His name was Ernest." I was excited to put a name with the voice, but it seemed confusing why he was still there. Nevertheless, we continued to work inside the church that was transformed into a beautiful theater that put on large performances of classic theater and dinners downstairs.

One investigation turned into four years of research and investigations with several hours of evidence of the hauntings inside. We have caught the

Some were touched, whispered to, and locked in closets and changing rooms as well as seeing Ernest himself watching people angrily, as if he did not want people inside there.

sound of children running the stairs, the giggling in the hallways, crying, and even heard a little girl singing "Jesus Loves Me" in the old classrooms. We often encountered the sounds of growling coming in and around the old study as if possibly, Ernest did not like us up there near his room or the creepy closet next to it. Often, we wondered if there was a connection between him being there and the children crying but never could find the answer. On the last night I was ever inside there, I took an old friend that had heard the stories and wanted to see or hear for himself. While walking along the balcony just talking, we were startled to hear loud orchestra music coming from near the stage. It was 1:00 A.M., and no one was there but us. Janet and Grant had to sell the Forum Theater after working so hard to get it going, which ended our time inside there as well. To this day, we are told by people who went to the plays or worked for the production company of all the scary things that happened to them while there. Some were touched, whispered to, and locked in closets and changing rooms as well as seeing Ernest himself watching people angrily as if he did not want people inside there. Many have even driven by the old church and have seen a man in the window staring out as if lost to the past.

Jason Roberts has been a member of Everyday-Legacy Paranormal and a tour guide for the Wichita Ghost Tour, which is owned by Ghost Tours of Kansas, since 2009. He took ownership of Road Trip Paranormal in 2013 and provides public events all over Kansas. Go to *www.everyday-legacy.com* to hear some evidence from the forum or *www.roadtripparanormal.com* to learn about our events.

Paranormal Investigations

Paranormal View's Henry Foister

Waverly Hills Sanatorium

When I started doing *The Paranormal View* radio show on *para-x.com* and CBS Radio, I was able to travel to some of the famous haunted places in America. The first place was an event with Para-X at Waverly Hills Sanatorium in Louisville, Kentucky. It was a very large building, five floors, and had very long halls. On the fifth floor, I witnessed a doppelganger of one member in our group, and on the fourth floor, I heard footsteps behind me, but when I turned around, they stopped, and no one was there. I could only capture unintelligible EVPs.

Hillview Manor

Hillview Manor is located in New Castle, Pennsylvania. This is one of the most active places I have ever been. We caught good EVPs of a man who worked in the boiler room. He was trying to get our attention by saying "hey" very softly. When we were on the third floor in the Hairdresser Room, I caught an EVP saying "go on in there" in a very hushed voice.

We went into the caretaker's apartment to the private bathroom. Two members of my group, Tim and Kerri, were in the bathroom asking questions. I was just coming from the Hairdresser Room and entering the caretaker's room, and as I turned to go down the hall to the private bathroom, I heard two very loud stomps as Tim and Kerri started hollering "What the heck!" They came out and asked me if I had seen anyone come out. I had not, but my recorder caught the whole episode.

The next time we were at Hillview Manor, a docent took our crew to some of the known active spots. We were shown where the servers had been and how the patients came along in line to walk in front of the counter to get their food. The docent said EVPs had never been gotten on the servers' side but had been heard on the patients' side of the line.

In the evening, we did our Internet radio show *The Paranormal View.* I felt very sick and feverish during the show. Afterward, we did an investigation and also returned to the cafeteria. There, I said, "I am sick. I have a fever and sore throat. Do you have any coffee?" Later, when I listened to my recording, a man's voice could be heard softly answering my question: "Yeah."

The David Stewart Farm, Gettysburg

I have been on location in Gettysburg many times for *The Paranormal View.* On one occasion, we were at the David Stewart Farm, which was used as a Confederate field hospital during the retreat from the Battle of Gettysburg. The barn on the property was known to be active with the ghosts of Confederate soldiers. There were about ten of us inside the old barn standing at one end looking toward the other end. As I was listening and asking questions, some of the mediums there were talking to some of the spirits, and I noticed seven or eight red dots at the far end of the barn. The lights appeared, got brighter, then dimmed out. After a few minutes, more red dots would come on, brighten, then go out. I could discern no source of reflection or cause for the lights. After observing for about fifteen minutes, I finally asked, "Does anyone else see those red lights?" and in unison, they all said, "Yes." So, I asked, "What are they?" and the others said they were the lights from cigarettes the Confederate soldiers were smoking.

The Bell Nursing Home

The Bell Nursing Home, located in Kimbolton, Ohio, was a very interesting place to investigate. When the nursing home closed, all the patients were moved to another facility in Cambridge, Ohio, but all the beds, equipment, records, staff logs, and calendars were left behind. Some spirits who did not want to leave also stayed behind.

We did *The Paranormal View* radio show live from the Bell Nursing Home one evening. After the show, a group of seven of us were eager to make contact with the "residents." We broke into two groups. My group included Kat K. and Tim Foister. Our group started with the north wing day room and patient rooms. As I walked into one room, I heard a low, audible sigh, and we could feel a presence.

While we were sitting at the nurses' station on the south wing, we heard bed curtains being pulled open and closed in one room. When we checked the floor in that room, it was evident that the curtains had not been moved because tape had been placed on the floor to mark their original position. The light in the room across from the nurses' station came on by itself at times, and we heard footsteps on the stairs. The best piece of evidence we caught was an EVP in the day room. Kat and I were there talking, and on the recorder, we heard a little girl's voice say, "Please wake up." We speculated that she was either trying to wake a sleeping patient or that a patient had passed away and she was trying to wake the person.

FURTHER READING

Alexander, Bryan. "The True Story Behind 'The Conjuring.'" *USA Today*, July 22, 2013.

Argie, Theresa, and Eric Olsen. *America's Most Haunted: The Secrets of Famous Paranormal Places*. Berkeley, CA: Berkeley Books, 2014.

Baley, Anne. "The Story of the Hollywood Tower Hotel." *USA Today*, March 21, 2018.

Burke, Patrick. *Ghost Soldiers of Gettysburg: Searching for Spirits on America's Most Famous Battlefield*. Woodbury, MN: Llewellyn Publications, 2014.

Clark, Jerome. *Unexplained! Strange Sightings, Incredible Occurrences, and Puzzling Physical Phenomena*, 3rd edition. Detroit, MI: Visible Ink Press, 2013.

Coleman, Christopher. *Ghosts and Haunts of the Civil War: Authentic Accounts of the Strange and Unexplained*. New York: Thomas Nelson Books, 1999.

Dowd, Katie."Everything You Think You Know about the Winchester Mystery House Probably Isn't True." *Houston Chronicle*, February 4, 2016.

"Former FBI Employee Saw Angels Guarding Flight 93 Site after Deadly Crash." *Daily Mail*, July 3, 2012.

Gage, Joan. "Ronald Reagan's White House Ghost Story." *Huffington Post*, December 31, 2013.

Galloway, Stephen. "Guillermo del Toro on Seeing a UFO, Hearing Ghosts and Shaping 'Water.'" *Hollywood Reporter*, December 21, 2017.

Holzer, Hans. *Famous Ghosts: True Encounters with the World Beyond*. New York: Black Dog and Leventhal, 2004.

———. "*Murder in Amityville*." New York: Tower Publications, 1979.

Horrocks, Alyson. "The Lizzie Borden House: Tour the Macabre." *New England Today*, October 24, 2017.

"Is Myrtles Plantation the Most Haunted Home in America?" *Country Living*, October 11, 2017.

Jacobson, Laurie, and Marc Wannamaker. *Hollywood Haunted: A Ghostly Tour of Filmland*. Angel City Press, 1999.

Jeffries, Benjamin. *Lost in the Darkness: Life Inside the World's Most Haunted Prisons, Hospitals, and Asylums*. Schiffer Publishing, 2013.

Jones, Marie D. *Demons, The Devil, and Fallen Angels*. Detroit, MI: Visible Ink Press, 2018.

———. *PSIence: How New Discoveries in Quantum Physics and New Science May Explain the Existence of Paranormal Phenomena*. Franklin Lakes, NJ: New Page Books, 2007.

Jones, Marie D., and Larry Flaxman. *The Grid: Exploring the Hidden Infrastructure of Realty*. San Antonio, TX: Hierophant Books, 2013.

Jurica, Jenny Webster. "The Devil's Backbone: The Most Haunted Stretch of Texas Highway." *Hill Country News*, October 24, 2017.

Keel, John A. *The Mothman Prophecies: A True Story*. New York: Tor Books, 2002.

Kreps, Daniel. "Unexplainable Photo Snapped at Jim Morrison's Grave." *Rolling Stone*, October 16, 2009.

Myers, Arthur. *Ghosts of the Rich and Famous*. Chicago, IL: Contemporary Books, 1988.

Nesbitt, Mark. *Ghosts of Gettysburg: Spirits, Apparitions and Haunted Places on the Battlefield*. Second Chance Publications, 2015.

Ogden, Tom. *Haunted Hollywood: Tinsletown Terrors, Filmdom Phantoms and Movieland Mayhem*. Los Angeles: Globe Pequot, 2015.

O'Hagan, Sean. "I'm Still Haunted by Belushi." *Guardian*, September 27, 2003.

Pappas, Stephanie. "Oscar Psychology: Why Celebrities Fascinate Us." *LiveScience.com*, February 24, 2012.

Pramis, Joshua. "Hotels Haunted by Celebrities." *Travel & Leisure*, October 5, 2015.

Price, Lydia. "Celebrities Who Have Had Actual Ghost Encounters." *People*, August 16, 2018.

Ramsland, Katherine. "Serial Killer Ghosts." *Psychology Today*, October 17, 2016.

Roll, William, and Valerie Storey. *Unleashed: Of Poltergeists and Murder: The Curious Story of Tina Resch*. New York: Pocket Books, 2007.

Seaburn, Paul. "Jimi Hendrix's Ghost and His UFO and Alien Encounters." *Mysterious Universe*, April 6, 2017.

Spitznagel, Eric. "Q&A: Dan Aykroyd on Sleeping with a Ghost, Aliens, Vodka and Doctor Detroit." *Esquire*, October 30, 2013.

Tejeda, Valerie. "Is the Hollywood Sign Haunted?" *Vanity Fair*, October 31, 2014.

Vogels, Russell. *Hunting Ghosts: A Paranormal Investigator's Guide*. Amazon Digital Services, 2014.

Willin, Melvyn. *Ghosts Caught on Film: Photographs of the Paranormal*. New York: David & Charles Books, 2007.

Index

Note: (ill.) indicates photos and illustrations.

A

Aaliyah, 59
Ackergill Tower (Caithness, Scotland), 230
Adams, Abigail, 92
Adams, John, 92
Addiscombe Railway Station (England), 131
Adkins, Avril, 241
Air Force One, 242
airplane crashes, haunted, 275–77, 354–55. *See also* airports, haunted
airplanes, haunted, 129
airports, haunted, 277–81. *See also* airplane crashes, haunted
Alabama
  haunted cemeteries, 173
  haunted plantations, 102–3
  haunted universities and universities, 268, 269 (ill.)
  sports ghosts, 196
  urban legends, 291–92
Alaska, paranormal hot spots, 323 (ill.), 323–24
Alaska Triangle, 323 (ill.), 323–24
Alberta, haunted mines, 155–57, 156 (ill.)
Albright, Jesse, 258
Alcatraz (San Francisco, CA), 238 (ill.), 238–40
Alexander, Jane, 44
Alexandria Hotel (Los Angeles, CA), 71–72
Allen, Jack, 85
Alley, Daniel, 223
Alley, Lucy, 223
Altadena Haunted Gravity Hill (Rubio Wash Debris Basin, CA), 149–50
alternate dimensions, 12–13
Alton Mental Health Hospital (Alton, IL), 250–51
Alton Mine (Drumheller, AB, Canada), 155–57, 156 (ill.)
Amargosa Opera House and Hotel (Death Valley, CA), 209, 209 (ill.)
American Flight 191 crash (Chicago, IL), 275–76, 276 (ill.)
Amherst poltergeist (Amherst, NS, Canada), 313 (ill.), 313–14
The Amityville Horror (1979; 2005), 180
The Amityville Horror (2005), 55–56
Amityville Horror House (Amityville, NY), 301–4, 304 (ill.)
amphitheaters, haunted, 345–46
amusement parks, haunted, 173
Anaheim Cemetery (Orange County, CA), 170
ancient Indian burial grounds, 180
Andersonville Civil War Prison (Andersonville, GA), 242
Andrews, James J., 353
Anson, Jay, 56, 301
Antietam Battlefield (MD), 160
Aokigahara Forest (Japan), 145–46
Apache, 328
apparitions, 7
Aquia Episcopal Church (Stafford, VA), 177
Arbuckle, Roscoe "Fatty," 81
Archer Avenue (Chicago, IL), 143–44
Archerfield Airport (Brisbane, Queensland, Australia), 279–80
Arizona
  haunted caves, 152
  haunted high schools, 271
  haunted landmarks, 190–94, 191 (ill.), 194 (ill.)
  haunted prisons, 245–46
  haunted railroad tracks, 132
  haunted roads, 145
  paranormal hot spots, 327–28
  sports ghosts, 197
Arkansas
  haunted hotels and motels, 203

haunted sanatoriums, 251–52
urban legends, 292–93, 298
Arkansas Tuberculosis Sanatorium (Booneville, AR), 251–52
Arnall, Roland, 84
Arnaz, Desi, 67
Arthur, Prince, 18
Arundel Castle (West Sussex, England), 228–29, 229 (ill.)
Aspect, Alain, 14
asylums, haunted, 252–54, 256–58
Athens Mental Hospital (Athens, OH), 250, 250 (ill.)
Atherton, Frances, 266
Atherton, George, 266
Austin, Laurence, 74
Australia, haunted airports, 279–80
Austria, haunted castles, 229, 232
automobiles, haunted, 130
Avalon Theater (Hollywood, CA), 73–74
Aykroyd, Dan, 46–47
Aylesford, Philip, 9

B

Babcock, Elisha, 206
Bachelor's Grove (Midlothian, IL), 170
Bagans, Zak, 187, 188–89
Baird, Spencer, 184
Baker, Norman, 203
Bakers Island Light (Salem Harbor, MA), 122
Baldwin, Alec, 54
Ball, Lucille, 31, 67
Ballyseede Castle (County Kerry, Ireland), 230–31
Bannerman's Castle (New York, NY), 226–27
Bannockburn, SS (ship), 117–18
Bardsley Road (Tulare, CA), 144
Barker, Arthur "Doc," 238
Barker Ranch (Death Valley National Park, CA), 149
Barkulus, George, 49
Barnegut, New Jersey, lighthouse, 122–23, 123 (ill.)
Barney's Beanery (Los Angeles, CA), 87
Barnsley, Godfrey, 102
Barnsley, Julia, 102
Barnsley Gardens (Adairsville, GA), 102
Baron, Rhonda, 40
Baron Falkenberg (ship), 119
Baronet Theater (Asbury Park, NJ), 349–50
barracks, haunted, 169
Barris, George, 49
Bash Bish Falls (Mount Washington, MA), 146 (ill.), 146–47
Baskerville Hall (Powys, Wales), 225
Battery Carriage House Inn (Charleston, SC), 211 (ill.), 211–12
Battery Point lighthouse (Crescent City, CA), 123
battlefields, haunted, 159–67, 338–39, 354, 362 (ill.), 362–63, 367
Batts, Kate, 294
Baumeister, Herb, 51
Baychimo (ship), 120
Beatles, 37–38, 340
Beck, Julian, 61
Beck, Renate, 318
Beetlejuice, 54
Begunkodor Railway Station (West Bengal, India), 131
Belgium, haunted battlefields, 165–66
Bell, Betsy, 294–95, 295 (ill.)
Bell, John, 294–95
Bell family, 286
Bell Nursing Home (Kimbolton, OH), 367–68
Bell Witch urban legend (Adams, TN), 294–95
Beluche, Renato, 350
Belushi, John, 46, 71
Berkley Square monster urban legend (London, England), 297–98
Bermingham, Thomas, 59
Bern, Paul, 30
Berry, Halle, 58
Berry, William Jan, 78
Bessels, Emil, 184
Bettis, Gerald, 298
Beverly Glen (CA), 86
Beverly Hills Bermuda Triangle, 77–78
Beverly Hills Hotel (Beverly Hills, CA), 71
Bierce, Ambrose, 290 (ill.), 292
Big Bay Point Lighthouse (Big Bay, MI), 123
Big Bopper (J. P. Richardson), 39–40
Big Bull Tunnel (VA), 134
Big Thunder Mine (Keystone, SD), 154
Bigelow, Robert, 335
Bigfoot, 329
Bird Island lighthouse (Sippican Harbor, MA), 123
Bisbee Courthouse (AZ), 193
Bishop, Bridget, 208
Bishop, Leonard, 113
Bishop, Raymond, 307
Bither, Doris, 308, 309
Black Angels, 175
Black-eyed girl urban legend (Chase, England), 297
Black Monk House poltergeist (Pontefract, Yorkshire, England), 315–16
Black Star Canyon (Orange County, CA), 320 (ill.), 320–21
Black Volga, 130
Blair, Linda, 59
Blatty, William Peter, 59, 306–7, 307 (ill.)
Block Island Southeast Lighthouse (RI), 123
Bloody Mary, 186
Bloody Mary Haunted Museum (New Orleans, LA), 186
Bloody Mary urban legends, 294
Blue Ghost Tunnel (Thorold, ON, Canada), 133
Bluff Mountain Appalachian Trail (VA), 147
Blumenthal, David, 318
Blunden, Edward, 297–98
Blymire, John H., 295
Bobbie Prince Charlie, 165

Bobby Mackey's Music World (Wilder, KY), 197, 199–200
Bogart, Humphrey, 80
Boggs, Hale, 323
Boleyn, Anne, 95–96
Bonaventure Cemetery (Savannah, GA), 170–71, 171 (ill.)
Booth, John Wilkes, 90 (ill.), 90–91, 211
Borden, Abby, 219–20
Borden, Andrew, 219–20
Borden, Lizzie, 219–20, 249
Borderlands (CO-NM), 328–29, 329 (ill.)
Borley Rectory poltergeist (Essex County, England), 315, 315 (ill.)
Borman, Frank, 277
Boston, Massachusetts, lighthouse, 124
Boston Strangler, 265
Boston University (Boston, MA), 264–65
Bourbon Orleans Hotel (New Orleans, LA), 203–4
Bowaker, Elijah, 155
Bowdern, William, 307
Boy Scout Lane (Stevens Point, WI), 144
Boyer, Christina, 313
Bozoniere-Marmillion, Edmond, 101–2
Bradley, Mickey, 195
Brazil, poltergeists, 310
bridges
  crybaby, 138–39
  haunted, 135–39
  suicide, 136–37
Bridgewater Triangle (MA), 324–25
British Columbia
  haunted hotels, 208, 210
  haunted railroad tracks, 132
British Museum (London, England), 190
Brody, Sam, 84
Brolin, James, 55, 56, 302
Brougham, Allen Ross, 113
Broughton, Richard S., 15
Brown, Molly, 344
Brown Lady of Raynham Hall, 19, 19 (ill.)
Brown Palace Hotel (Denver, CO), 340, 340 (ill.)
Brunvand, Jan Harold, 283, 284 (ill.)
Bryan, Pearl, 199, 200
Buard, Julia, 100
Buckhorn Exchange (Denver, CO), 340–41
Buffalo Child Long Lance, Chief, 81–82
Bulloch Hall (Roswell, GA), 102
Bundy, Ted, 50
Bunker, Edward, 226
Burke, T. C., 223
Burkhart, J., 196
Burns, Ken, 363
Burnside, Ambrose, 160
Burr, Aaron, 93, 94 (ill.), 95
Burr, Eliza Jumel, 95
Burr, Theodosia, 94
buses, haunted, 130
Bush, Barbara, 208
Bush, George H. W., 208
Byberry Mental Hospital (Philadelphia, PA), 251
Byers, William, 341
Byers-Evans House Museum (Denver, CO), 341

C

C. E. Byrd High School (Shreveport, LA), 272
Cable, George Washington, 350
California
  haunted airports, 278
  haunted barracks, 169
  haunted bridges, 137, 137 (ill.)
  haunted castles, 226
  haunted caves, 152–53
  haunted cemeteries, 80–81, 170, 172
  haunted elementary schools, 273–74
  haunted high schools, 271
  haunted hiking trails, 147
  haunted hospitals, 247–48, 248 (ill.)
  haunted hotels and motels, 70 (ill.), 70–72, 79 (ill.), 79–80, 202, 202 (ill.), 204, 206–7, 207 (ill.), 209, 209 (ill.)
  haunted houses, 212–14, 213 (ill.), 214–16, 215 (ill.)
  haunted landmarks, 69–70, 76–88, 79 (ill.), 82 (ill.)
  haunted lighthouses, 123, 124–25, 126
  haunted missions, 178–81, 181 (ill.)
  haunted museums, 277
  haunted roads, 139–40, 144, 148, 149–50
  haunted sanatoriums, 254
  haunted theaters, 72 (ill.), 72–76, 75 (ill.)
  paranormal hot spots, 320 (ill.), 320–22, 325–27
  poltergeists, 314–15, 317–18
  urban legends, 287–88
Calueche (ship), 121
Campbell, John, 120
Campbell family, 317
Canary Islands, haunted airports, 281
Canyon Diablo, CA, 152–53, 153 (ill.)
Caobao Road Subway (China), 131
Capone, Al, 238, 241, 246
Captain Tony's Saloon (Key West, FL), 200
Caray, Harry (baseball announcer), 195
Carey, Harry (actor), 33
Carnegie, Andrew, 340
Carpenter, Jennifer, 57
Carpenter, Karen, 64
Carpenter, Liz, 91
Carroll A. Deering (ship), 118–19
cars, haunted, 130
Carter, Jack, 34
Carter, June, 41
Cash, Johnny, 41
Cashtown Inn (Gettysburg, PA), 164
Casper the Friendly Ghost, 53
Cassady, Neal, 226
Castel Reszel (Poland), 234
Castle, William, 62
Castle Air Museum (Atwater, CA), 277

Castle Leslie (County Monaghan, Ireland), 231
Castle Mont Rouge (Rougemont, NC), 226
Castle of Frankenstein (Darmstadt, Germany), 232 (ill.), 232–33
castles, haunted, 225–35
Cat & Fiddle, 87
Cathedral High School (Los Angeles, CA), 271
Catherine the Great, 97
caves, haunted, 150–53
Caviezel, Jim, 60
Celebrity Worship Syndrome (CWS), 24–25
cemeteries, haunted, 80–81, 169–76, 178, 205–6, 338–39, 346–47, 355
Chaleur Bay fireship, 121
Chandler, Harry, 69
Chaney, Lon, 33, 65
Chapel of the Cross (MS), 178
Chaplin, Charlie, 35, 64, 65, 66, 67, 80
Chapman, Mark David, 37
Char-Man urban legend (Ojai Valley, CA), 287
Charles II, King, 97
Charlie Chaplin Studios, 64
Charlie No-Face urban legend (Piney Fork, PA), 290
Chase, Philander, 264
Chasen, Ronni, 78
Chateau Marmont, 70 (ill.), 71
Cheesman, Walter, 342
Cheesman Park (Denver, CO), 342
Chicago Cubs, 195
Chickamauga Battlefield (GA), 160–61, 161 (ill.)
Chilnualna Falls Trail (Yosemite National Park, CA), 148
China, haunted railroad tracks, 131
Chloe (slave), 99
A Christmas Carol, 53
Christoffer, Count of Oldenburg, 234
churches, haunted, 176–78. *See also* missions, haunted
Churchill, Winston, 71, 91, 111
Ciro's/Comedy Store, 83
Clan O'Bannon, 231
Clanton, Billy, 191
Clanton, Terry Ike, 19
Clark, Blake, 83
Cleveland Museum of Art (Cleveland, OH), 187
Clift, Montgomery, 29, 70
Clinton, Hillary, 45, 45 (ill.)
Clinton Road (West Milford, NJ), 142, 142 (ill.)
Clown Motel (Tonopah, NV), 205–6, 206 (ill.)
Cluskey, Charles, 128
Cobb, Al, 311
Cobb, Charles, 149
Cobb, Jason, 311
Cobb Estate trail (Altadena, CA), 149–50
Cohen, Larry, 78
Cold, Indrid, 331–33
Cold Harbor Battlefield (Mechanicsville, VA), 161–62
Cole, Henry Greene, 352–53
Coleman, Loren, 324
colleges and universities, haunted, 261–70. *See also* elementary schools, haunted; high schools, haunted
Collins, Floyd, 151
Colorado
- haunted airports, 277–78
- haunted amphitheaters, 345–46
- haunted cemeteries, 173
- haunted hotels and motels, 201–2, 340, 340 (ill.), 344–45
- haunted houses, 341, 342–43, 344
- haunted landmarks, 340–41
- haunted museums, 341, 343 (ill.), 343–44
- haunted parks, 342
- haunted roads, 141, 145
- haunted tunnels, 133–34
- paranormal hot spots, 328–29, 329 (ill.)

Colorado Street Bridge (Pasadena, CA), 137, 137 (ill.)
Columbus poltergeist (Columbus, OH), 312–13
Colville Covered Bridge (Bourbon County, KY), 138
Combermere, Lord, 19
The Conjuring, 56–57
Connecticut
- haunted castles, 227, 227 (ill.), 228
- haunted cemeteries, 176
- haunted hospitals, 254–55, 255 (ill.)
- haunted houses, 305
- haunted lighthouses, 124
- haunted museums, 186–87
- urban legends, 289–90, 296–97

Connolly Station (Dublin, Ireland), 131
Conrad, Barry, 315
consciousness, 13–14
Constellation, USS (ship), 113
Conyngham, John, 267
Coolidge, Grace, 91
Corbin, Anna, 226
Corden, James, 44
Corey, Giles, 172
Coronado Bridge (San Diego, CA), 137
Corwin, George "The Strangler," 222–23
Corwin, Jonathan, 223
Cory, Giles, 222–23
Cotent, Don, 270
Cotton, John, 172
County Road 675 bridge (Anderson, IN), 139
Cox, Esther, 313–14
Cox, Peter, 314
Crawford, Christina, 31
Crawford, Gary S., 346–47
Crawford, Joan, 31–32
Crescent Hotel (Eureka Springs, AR), 203
Croke, Thomas, 342
Croke-Patterson Mansion (Denver, CO), 342–43
Cronkite, Walter, 208
Crookes, William, 18
Cropsey, the Child Hunter urban legend (Staten Island, NY), 291
The Crow (1994), 57
Crown, Henry, 85

crybaby bridges, 138–39
Crystal Cave (KY), 151
Culloden Moor Battlefield (Scotland), 165
Culver Studios, 65–66
Cuniff, Tom, 316
Cunningham, James, 169
Curless, Dick, 144
Cusack, John, 180, 211
Cyrus, Miley, 43
Cyrus, Noah, 43
Czech Republic, haunted castles, 233–34

D

Dagg, Dinah, 310
Dagg, George, 310
Dagg haunted farm (Clarendon, QC, Canada), 309–10
Dahmer, Jeffrey, 51–52, 52 (ill.), 53
Daltrey, Roger, 47
Dandridge, Dorothy, 58, 58 (ill.)
Dannemann, Monika, 42
Danson, Ted, 62–63
Danvers Lunatic Asylum (Danvers, MA), 252
Darby, Christine, 297
The Dark Knight, 56
David Stewart Farm (Gettysburg, PA), 367
Davidson, Elizabeth, 230
Davies, Marion, 66, 81
Davies, Paul, 13, 14 (ill.)
Davis, Ann, 126
Davis, Bette, 208
Davis, Geena, 54
De Niro, Robert, 208
Deacon Richard Hale House (Coventry, CT), 186
"dead body under the bed" urban legends, 298
Dead Children's Playground (Huntsville, AL), 173
Dean, James, 48–50, 48 (ill.)
Decken, Hendrik van der, 116
DeFeo, Ronald, Jr., 55, 301, 302, 304
del Toro, Guillermo, 37
Delaware, urban legends, 298
Delaware and Hudson Company mines (Taylor, PA), 155
DeMille, Cecil B., 66, 80
demons, 8, 11–12
Denmark, haunted castles, 234–35
Denver Firefighters Museum (Denver, CO), 343 (ill.), 343–44
Denver International Airport (Denver, CO), 277–78
Depot Theater (Dodge City, KS), 198–99
Derenberger, Woodrow, 331–33
DeSalvo, Albert, 265
Devil's Bridge (San Antonio, TX), 136
Devil's Den (Gettysburg, PA), 162–63
Devil's Highway (Four Corners region), 145
Devil's Hopyard State Park urban legend (East Haddam, CT), 289–90
Dickens, Charles, 53, 211
Dighton Rock (MA), 325
Dillard, James, 276
Ding Dong School (1953), 64
Dodge, Grenville M., 175
Doe, Roland, 306–7
dog boy urban legend (Quitman, AR), 298
dogmen urban legend (Norton, OH), 292
Doheny, Ned, Jr., 84–85
Doheny, Ned, Sr., 84
Doheny Mansion, 84–85
Donkey Lake Bridge (San Antonio, TX), 136
Donner, Richard, 60
Doyle, Arthur Conan, 18, 228
Dragna, Jack, 77
Dragsholm Castle (Denmark), 234–35
Drayton, John, 104–5
Drayton Hall Plantation (Charleston, SC), 104–5
Drish, John, 102
Drish, Sarah, 102–3
Drish House (Tuscaloosa, AL), 102–3
Drum, Richard, 169
Drum Barracks (CA), 169
Duchess of Windsor, 35
Dudley, Edmund, 296, 297 (ill.)
Dudley family urban legend (Cornwall, CT), 296–97
Duke of Gloucester, 97
Duke of Windsor, 35
Dunbar, George, 169
Dunn, Dominique, 61
Durante, Jimmy, 30
Dusseault, Sheri, 24
Dwarka Sector 9 Metro Station (Delhi, India), 131
Dybbuk Box, 188, 189

E

Earhart, Amelia, 35, 267
Earl of Kildare, 231
Earnhardt, Dale, Jr., 46
Earp, Wyatt, 191
Eastern Air Lines Flight 401 crash (Everglades, FL), 276–77
Edbrooke, Frank E., 344
Edgar Allan Poe House (Baltimore, MD), 186
Edgewood Plantation (Charles City, VA), 104
Edinburgh Castle (Scotland), 230
Edison, Thomas, 35, 340
Edward I, 229
Edward V, Prince, 97
Edward VIII, King, 71
Egg Hill Church (Potter Township, PA), 177
Egypt Road Bridge (OH), 139
Eisenhower, Dwight, 91, 93
Eisenhower, Mamie, 93
El Campo Santo Cemetery (San Diego, CA), 172
El Paso High School (El Paso, TX), 270–71, 271 (ill.)
electronic voice phenomena (EVP), 17
elementals, 6
elementary schools, haunted, 272–74. *See also* colleges and universities, haunted; high schools, haunted
Elfman, Danny, 37
Elizabeth V. Edwards School (Barnegat, NJ), 272
Elliot, Cass, 46, 84
Ellis, Brian Keith, 362–63
Ellis Hotel (Atlanta, GA), 208

Emerson, Ralph Waldo, 211
Emily's Bridge (VT), 137–38
Empire Mine Road (Antioch, CA), 148
Empson, Richard, 297 (ill.)
energy, 12
Enfield poltergeist (Brimsdown, Enfield, England), 311–12
England
- haunted airports, 278–79, 279 (ill.)
- haunted battlefields, 167
- haunted castles, 228–29, 229 (ill.), 230, 231 (ill.)
- haunted landmarks, 224–25
- haunted museums, 189–90
- haunted railroad tracks, 131
- poltergeists, 311–12, 315–16
- urban legends, 297–98

Entity House, 79
Entwistle, Peg, 69–70
environmental conditions, 12
Essex Mountain Sanatorium (Essex County, NJ), 255–56
Estep, Sarah, 17
Evans, William, 341
Ewell, Isaac, 163
The Exorcism of Emily Rose (2005), 57
The Exorcist (1973), 58–59, 306–7

F

Fairbanks, Douglas, 35, 66, 80
Fairmont Empress Hotel (Victoria, BC, Canada), 208, 210
Fallsvale Elementary School (Forest Falls, CA), 273–74
Fantasy Island, 81, 82
Farmiga, Vera, 57, 306
farms, haunted, 309–10
Farnam, Stephen Head, 218
Farnam Mansion (Oneida, NY), 218–19
Feldevert family, 175
Fenton, Roger, 18
feral children urban legend (Holland, MI), 289
Ferreira, Maria Jose, 310
Ferry Plantation (Virginia Beach, VA), 103 (ill.), 103–4
Fidler, Peter, 156
Figueroa Hotel, 71
Fisher, Carrie, 32, 32 (ill.)
Fisher, Lavinia, 246
Fisher, Maggie, 314
Fitzgerald, F. Scott, 35
Flagler, Henry, 241, 268
Flagler College (St. Augustine, FL), 267–68
Fleming, John, 178
Florida
- haunted airplane crashes, 276–77
- haunted churches, 178
- haunted colleges, 267–68
- haunted hospitals, 249
- haunted houses, 214
- haunted jails, 241
- haunted landmarks, 200
- haunted lighthouses, 126, 127
- poltergeists, 319

Floyd, Charles "Pretty Boy," 245
Flying Dutchman (ship), 116–17, 117 (ill.)
Flynn, Emma, 284
Flynn, Errol, 80
Foister, Henry, 366–68
Fokke, Bernard, 116
Fonda, Henry, 48
Fonda, Jane, 48
Ford, Arthur, 35
Ford, Harrison, 66
forests, haunted, 145–46, 289
Fort Concho (San Angelo, TX), 168–69
Fort Fisher (Wilmington, NC), 167–68
Fort Meigs (Toledo, OH), 167
Fort Warren (Boston, MA), 167
Fort William Henry (Lake George, NY), 169
Fort Worth Museum of Science and History (Fort Worth, TX), 189
forts, haunted, 167–69
Forum Theater (Wichita, KS), 364–66
Foster, Gloria, 59
Four Oaks Restaurant, 85
Fox, Katie, 286 (ill.), 286–87
Fox, Leah, 286 (ill.)
Fox, Maggie, 286 (ill.), 286–87
Fox Hollow Farm, 51
Foxx, Redd, 36
Foyster, Lionel, 315
Foyster, Marianne, 315
Francis, John, 95
Frankenstein, Knight, 233
Fred Harvey Hotel (Dodge City, KS), 198–99
Freeman, Morgan, 56
Friedan, Betty, 261
Friedkin, William, 59
friendly ghosts, 23
Friske, Elias, 138
Frontier Baseball Field (Rochester, NY), 196
Fulkerson, Dan, 144
Furnace Creek Inn and Ranch Resort (Death Valley, CA), 209

G

Gable, Clark, 29, 71, 77
Gabor, Zsa Zsa, 34
Gage, Joan, 92
Gage, Mary Jones, 166
Gaineswood (Demopolis, AL), 103
Gallagher, Liam, 38
Galloway, Stephen, 37
Garbo, Greta, 71
Gardiner Bay phantom fighters, 122
Garthright House (Mechanicsville, VA), 162
Garton, Ray, 305
Garwell, Bob, 38
Gates to Hell (Antioch, CA), 148
Gaynor, Kerry, 308
Gehman, Anne, 93
Gemmecke, Lina, 318, 319
Gemmecke, Linda, 318
Genna Brothers, 246
George IV, King, 225
George V, King, 116
George House (Gettysburg, PA), 164
Georgia
- haunted airplane crashes, 354–55
- haunted battlefields, 160–61, 161 (ill.), 354

haunted cemeteries, 170–71, 171 (ill.), 355
haunted hotels, 208
haunted houses, 217 (ill.), 217–18, 352–54, 353 (ill.)
haunted landmarks, 212
haunted lighthouses, 127–28
haunted mountains, 354
haunted museums, 353 (ill.), 353–54
haunted plantations, 102
haunted prisons, 242
poltergeists, 311
Germany, haunted castles, 232 (ill.), 232–33
Gettysburg Battlefield (Gettysburg, PA), 162–64, 163 (ill.), 338–39, 362 (ill.), 362–63, 367
Gettysburg College (Gettysburg, PA), 262–63
Ghost (1990), 53, 57
The Ghost and Mr. Chicken (1966), 54
The Ghost and Mrs. Muir (1947), 53
Ghost House Trail (Big Ridge State Park, TN), 147
ghost hunting, 2
Ghost Lake (Warren County, NJ), 143
Ghost Road urban legend (Scotland), 288–89
The Ghost Whisperer, 57–58
Ghostbusters, 53
ghosts
apparitions, 7
demons, 8, 11–12
electronic voice phenomena (EVP), 17
elementals, 6
fame and celebrity, 23–26
famous, 27–28
friendly, 23
haunted houses and objects, 9–11, 10 (ill.)
haunting at night, 20–22
historical, 6
imprints/residual, 4
living, 3
malevolent, 23
neutral, 23
origins of, 1–3, 11–13
personalities, 22–23
photography, 18–19, 22
poltergeists, 7
preference for sad places, 5–6
reticular activating system (RAS), 16–17
science surrounding, 13–16
sentient/intelligent, 4
tulpas and thought forms, 8–9
types of, 3–9
Ghosts of Christmases Past, Present, and Future, 53
Gibraltar Point (Toronto Island, ON, Canada), 124
Gibson, Brian, 61
Gibson, Mel, 60
Gillette, William Hooker, 228
Gillette Castle (East Haddam, CT), 228
Gipp, George, 262
Glattke, Helen, 243
Glenn, Margaret, 104
Glenn, Paul, 240
Goat Man urban legend (Bowie, MD), 287
Goatman's Bridge (TX), 135–36
Goddard, Victor, 19
Godfrey, Linda, 292
Gold Brook Bridge (VT), 137–38
Golden Gate Bridge (San Francisco, CA), 137
Golden Lamb Inn (Lebanon, OH), 210
Good, James, 185
Goodman, Steve, 195
Gordon, Dan, 195
Gorey, Richard, 346
Gorin, Frank, 151
Grace Episcopal Church (Alexandria, VA), 177
Graham, Steam Train Maury, 189
Grand Canyon Caverns (AZ), 152
Grande, Ariana, 43–44
Grant, Cary, 77
Grant, Ulysses S., 92, 161–62
Grauman, Sid, 75
Graves, Rob and Vicky, 51
Green Man urban legend (Piney Fork, PA), 290
Gregg, James M., 321
Grenier, Volney, 280
Grey, Orrin, 213
Gribble, Eliza, 217
Gribble House (Savannah, GA), 217, 217 (ill.)
Grierson, Edith, 169
Griffith, Griffith J., 80
Grimes, Charlie, 195
Grinning Man, 331–33
Grosse, Maurice, 312
Grouse Lake (CA), 326
Guinness, Alec, 49
Guinness, Belle, 50
Guttenberg, Steve, 63

H

Hagerty, James, 91
Haggard, Merle, 226
Hale, Deacon, 186
Hale, Nathan, 186
Hall, Carl Austin, 245
Halloween decorations/hanged woman urban legend (Frederica, DE), 298
Hamilton, Alexander, 93, 94 (ill.), 95
Hamilton-Parker, Craig, 47
Hamilton-Parker, Jane, 47
Hamlet, 53
Hampton, John, 74
Hannigan, Alyson, 45
Harbin, Joseph, 104
Harden, Mike, 312
Harding, Warren G., 84
Hardy, Corin, 59–60
Harlow, Jean, 30
Harris, Emmylou, 41
Harrison, George, 37
Harrison, Rex, 53
Harrison, Ronnie, 84
Harrison, Sara, 359–60
Harrison, William Henry, 167
Harrow, Joey, 38
Harvey, Robert, 293
haunted bed poltergeist (Savannah, GA), 311
Hawthorne, Nathaniel, 222
Hawthorne Hotel (Salem, MA), 208

headless ghost urban legend (Blue River, IN), 287
Heady, Bonnie, 245
Hearst, William Randolph, 65, 66, 81
Hearthstone Castle (Danbury, CT), 227, 227 (ill.)
Heathrow Airport (London, England), 278–79, 279 (ill.)
Heceta Head (Yachats, OR), 124
Hell's Bridge (Algoma Township, MI), 138
Hendrix, Jimi, 42 (ill.), 42–43
Henry, Joseph, 184
Henry, William, 105
Henry Greene Cole House (Marietta, GA), 352–53
Henry II, 229
Henry VII, 296, 297 (ill.)
Henry VIII, 95
Hepburn, James, 234–35
Hernandez, Jackie, 314–15
Herrin, David, 313
Hershey, Barbara, 79, 308
Hewitt, Jennifer Love, 57–58
Hickman, Edward, 304
Hicks, Steven, 52
High Bridge (Chicago, IL), 136–37
high schools, haunted, 270–72. *See also* colleges and universities, haunted; elementary schools, haunted
Highway 87 (Great Falls, MT), 142–43
hiking trails, haunted, 146–50
Hilchey, Eugene, 66
Hill, Faith, 39
Hill, Louise Crawford, 340
Hillview Manor (New Castle, PA), 366–67
Hilton, Conrad, Jr., 34
Hindenburg, 280–81
Hinton, Eddie, 42
historical ghosts, 6, 89–97
Hitchcock, Alfred, 63, 66
Hitler, Adolf, 95, 234
Hobson, Kat, 356, 357
Hockey Hall of Fame (Toronto, ON, Canada), 197
Hodgson, Janet, 311–12
Hodgson, Margaret, 311–12
Hoia Baciu Forest urban legend (Romania), 289
Holly, Buddy, 39 (ill.), 39–40
Hollywood, CA, theaters, 72 (ill.), 72–76, 75 (ill.)
Hollywood, CA, tourist spots, 76–88, 79 (ill.), 82 (ill.)
Hollywood Forever Cemetery (Hollywood, CA), 80–81
Hollywood hotels, 70 (ill.), 70–72, 79 (ill.), 79–80
Hollywood Pacific Theater (Hollywood, CA), 74
Hollywood Roosevelt Hotel (Hollywood, CA), 70
Hollywood sign (Hollywood, CA), 69–70
Hollywood Tower Hotel (Hollywood, CA), 79 (ill.), 79–80
Hollywood Wax Museum (Hollywood, CA), 76
Holmes, James Eagen, 56
Holmes, John, 76
Holmes, Oliver Wendell, Sr., 211
Holy Terror Mine (Keystone, SD), 154
Holzer, Hans, 95, 113, 303
Hooper, Tobe, 60
Hoosac Tunnel (MA), 134
Hoover, Herbert, 91
Hopkins, Patrick, 224
Horton, Hank, 221
Horton, Johnny, 41
Horton Grand Hotel (San Diego, CA), 207
Horton Mine (Humboldt-Toiyabe National Forest, NV), 154–55
hospitals, haunted, 247–51, 254–55, 256, 258–59
Hotel Del Coronado (San Diego County, CA), 206–7, 207 (ill.)
hotels and motels, haunted, 70 (ill.), 70–72, 79 (ill.), 79–80, 198–99, 201–12, 340, 340 (ill.), 344–45
Hottel, Guy, 329 (ill.)
Houdini, Bess, 35
Houdini, Harry, 34 (ill.), 34–35, 41, 82–83
Houdini Mansion, 82–83
Houran, James, 24
House of Seven Gables (Salem, MA), 222
houses, haunted, 9–11, 10 (ill.), 212–25, 295, 301–4, 304 (ill.), 305–6, 341, 342–43, 344, 350–54, 358 (ill.), 358–59, 366–67
Houska Castle (Blatce, Czech Republic), 233–34, 288 (ill.), 289
Houston, Jean, 45
Howard Street Cemetery (Salem, MA), 172
Hubbell, Walter, 314
Hughes, Howard, 72–73, 77, 78 (ill.)
Hull, Laurie, 115, 358–59
Humperdinck, Engelbert, 83, 84
Hunt, Kenneth Dean, 63
Hunter, J. C., 217
Hunter, Maggie, 217
Huntingdon College (Montgomery, AL), 268, 269 (ill.)
Hure, Mary, 333
Hyams, Joe, 31

I

Idaho, haunted high schools, 270
Identity (2003), 180
Illingworth, Hallie, 148
Illinois
- haunted airplane crashes, 275–76, 276 (ill.)
- haunted bridges, 136–37
- haunted cemeteries, 170, 173
- haunted elementary schools, 273
- haunted high schools, 272
- haunted hospitals, 250–51
- haunted jails, 246–47
- haunted roads, 143–44
- haunted universities, 269
- poltergeists, 316–17
- sports ghosts, 195

imprints, 4
Ince, Thomas, 65–66
India, haunted railroad tracks, 131
Indian burial grounds, haunted, 180
Indiana
- haunted bridges, 139

haunted colleges, 269–70
haunted jails, 244–45
haunted landmarks, 51
haunted universities, 262
poltergeists, 318–19
sports ghosts, 197
urban legends, 287
Indianapolis poltergeist (Indianapolis, IN), 318–19
Ingersoll, Samuel, 222
Ingersoll, Susan, 222
The Innkeepers (2011), 58
The Innocents (1961), 53
Introducing Dorothy Dandridge (1999), 58
Iowa
haunted cemeteries, 175
haunted houses, 220–22, 221 (ill.)
Ireland
haunted castles, 230–31
haunted railroad tracks, 131
Iron Goat Trail (Stevens Pass, WA), 147

J

Jackie (*Queen Mary* ghost), 109, 112
Jackson, Andrew, 92
Jackson, Freddie, 19
Jackson, Michael, 47, 47 (ill.)
Jackson, Oren, 222
Jackson, Peter, 36 (ill.), 36–37
Jackson, Scott, 199
Jackson Five, 73
Jacobson, Laurie, 72, 83, 85, 86
jails, haunted. *See* prisons, penitentiaries, and jails, haunted
James, Jesse, 153
James, William, 13
James I, King, 96
Jan and Dean, 77–78
Japan, haunted roads, 145–46
Jeddo Mine (Lancaster, PA), 155
Jefferson, Thomas, 91, 93
Jennie Wade House (Gettysburg, PA), 358 (ill.), 358–59
Jenny Jump State Forest (Warren County, NJ), 143
Jesus Christ, 150
Jim Henson Studio, 64
Jiminez, Luis, 278
John Lawson House (New Hamburg, NY), 218
Johnson, John, 114
Johnson, Lady Bird, 91
Johnson, Lynda Bird, 92
Johnson, Lyndon, 92
Johnson, Robert, 141
Johnston, Warden, 239
Johnstone, Helen, 178
Jolie, Angelica, 66
Jones, Frank, 222
Jones, John Treasure, 111
Jones, Myra, 63
Jones, Robert H., 210
Joplin, Janis, 38
Joseph, James, 344
Josephson, Brian, 14, 15 (ill.)
Joshua Ward House (Salem, MA), 222–23

K

Kaiser, Mr., urban legend (Miltonsburg, OH), 290–91
Kalthenpacher, Paul, 232
Kane, Don, 68
Kansas
haunted cemeteries, 174
haunted high schools, 271
haunted hotels and motels, 198–99
haunted theaters, 198–99, 364–66
sports ghosts, 197
Karloff, Boris, 79
Karsavina, Jean, 95
Kaufman, Phil, 41
Keaton, Buster, 30
Keaton, Michael, 54
Keel, John, 332
Kelly, George, Reverend, 221
Kelly, George "Machine Gun," 238
Kennedy, John F., 29, 211
Kennesaw House (Marietta, GA), 353 (ill.), 353–54
Kennison, USS (ship), 116
Kentucky
haunted bridges, 138
haunted caves, 150–51
haunted hospitals, 258–59
haunted hotels and motels, 204 (ill.), 204–5
haunted landmarks, 197, 199–200
haunted sanatoriums, 366
Kenyon College (Gambier, OH), 264, 264 (ill.)
Kerr, Deborah, 53
Kevorkian, Jack, 188
Kidd, Captain, 172
Kidder, Margot, 55, 302
Kidman, Nicole, 53
Kilgore, Merle, 41
Killian, Victor, 75
King, Edmund, 268
King, Joey, 57
King, Martin Luther, Jr., 245
King, Richard, 205
King, Stephen, 53, 64, 180, 201–2, 211, 243, 249
King, Tabitha, 201
King's Chapel Burying Ground (Boston, MA), 172, 172 (ill.)
Kingston, Kenny, 81
Kinison, Sam, 83
Knickerbocker Hotel (Hollywood, CA), 71
Knight, Curtis, 43
Knotts, Don, 53 (ill.), 54
Koller, Paul Jacob, 229, 232
Kollerin, Barbara, 232
Komeda, Krzysztof, 62
Ku Klux Klan, 273
Kubrick, Stanley, 53
Kushtaka, 323–24

L

La Llorona legend (NM), 195
Lady Gaga, 44
Lady in Black, 167
Lady in White, 139–40, 161, 170, 293–94
Lady Lovibond (ship), 119
Lady of the Lake (Dallas, TX), 360–62
Lafitte, Jean, 350
Lake County Jail (Lake County, IN), 244–45
Lake Morena Campground (San Diego, CA), 147
Lake Shawnee Amusement Park (Rock, WV), 173

Lakehurst Naval Air Station (Lakehurst, NJ), 280–81
LaLaurie, Delphine, 216
LaLaurie House (New Orleans, LA), 216–17
Landis, John, 63
landmarks, haunted, 76–88, 79 (ill.), 82 (ill.), 190–95, 197, 199–200, 224–25, 340–41, 360–62
Lang, William, 344
Lanier, Melanie, 167
Large, Isaac, 344
Laurel and Hardy, 30
Laveau, Marie, 173–74, 186
Lawler Ford Road (Glencoe, MO), 140–41
Lawrence, Jennifer, 208
Leap Castle (Ireland), 231
Lecomte, Ambrose II, 100
Ledger, Heath, 56, 56 (ill.)
Lee, Brandon, 57
Lee, Robert E., 162
Lee, Samuel F., 249
Lee, Walter, 276
Lee Williams High School (Kingman, AZ), 197, 271
Leigh, Janet, 64
Lenin, Vladimir, 97
Lennon, Cynthia, 38
Lennon, John, 37–38, 62, 71
Leonardi, Lillie, 275
Leslie, Lady Marjory, 231
Leslie, Normal, 231
Letchworth Village (Thiells, NY), 148–49
Leyden, John, 116
Liberace, 39, 47
lighthouses, haunted, 122–28, 165
Lincoln, Abraham, 90 (ill.), 90–92, 93, 129, 211
Lincoln, Mary Todd, 91, 92
Lincoln, Willie, 92
Lincoln High School (Sioux Falls, SD), 271
Lincoln phantom train, 129
Linda Vista Community Hospital (East Los Angeles, CA), 247–48, 248 (ill.)
Lindbergh, Charles, 35
Linn, Darwin, 222
Linn, Martha, 222
Linney, Laura, 44
Liszt, Franz, 47
live burial urban legends, 298–99
living ghosts, 3
Lizzie Borden House (Fall River, MA), 219 (ill.), 219–20
Lockwood, Bob, 41
Loft, Robert, 276–77
Lombard, Carole, 29
Lone Sentinel, 263
Long, Sylvester Clark, 81–82
Long Beach Bar Lighthouse (Orient, NY), 124
Long Path (Thiells, NY), 148–49
Longfellow, Henry Wadsworth, 211
Lorre, Peter, 80
Los Angeles County Arboretum and Botanical Gardens, 81–82, 82 (ill.)
Los Reyes, Alvina de, 170
Louisiana
  haunted cemeteries, 173–74
  haunted high schools, 272
  haunted hotels and motels, 203–4
  haunted houses, 216–17, 304–5, 350–52
  haunted museums, 186
  haunted plantations, 99–102, 101 (ill.)
Lovato, Demi, 43
Lovecraft, H. P., 151
Ludwig, Gregory (Ghost), 189
Lugosi, Bela, 79
Lumley, Lily, 230
Lumley Castle (County Durham, England), 230
Lutz, Daniel, 303
Lutz, George, 55, 302, 303–4
Lutz, Kathy, 302, 303–4
Lyric Theater (Asbury Park, NJ), 349–50

M

MacDonald, John, 116
Machen, Karen, 277
MacKenzie, Ranald, 169
Mackey, Bobby, 200
Macomb poltergeist (Macomb, IL), 316–17
Mad River and NKP Railroad Society Museum (Bellevue, OH), 189
Madame John's Legacy (New Orleans, LA), 350–52
Madison, Dolley, 92
Madison, James, 92
Magnolia Plantation (Natchitoches, LA), 100–101
Maine
  haunted lighthouses, 125–26, 127
  haunted roads, 144
Major, Union, 100
malevolent ghosts, 23
Malone, Nancy, 72
Mammoth Cave (KY), 150–51
Man in Gray urban legend (Pawley Island, SC), 289
Manassas National Battlefield (Prince William County, VA), 164
manifestations and perceptions, 12
Mansfield, Jayne, 83–84
Mansfield, William, 222
Manson, Charles, 30, 62, 76, 149, 257
Maple Hills Cemetery (Huntsville, AL), 173
Marietta Museum of History (Marietta, GA), 353 (ill.), 353–54
Mariposa Elementary School (Redlands, CA), 273
Markle family, 267
Marmillion, Charles, 102
M·rquez, James, 209
Martin, Alexander, 35
Martin, Robert, 297–98
Marx, Harpo, 71
Marx Brothers, 30, 149
Mary Celeste (ship), 115, 119, 119 (ill.)
Mary I, Queen, 109, 294
Mary Queen of Scots, 234
Maryland
  haunted battlefields, 160
  haunted cemeteries, 174, 176
  haunted lighthouses, 126

haunted museums, 186
urban legends, 287
Massachusetts
haunted asylums, 252
haunted caves, 151
haunted cemeteries, 172, 172 (ill.)
haunted forts, 167
haunted hiking trails, 146 (ill.), 146–47
haunted hospitals, 249–50
haunted hotels and motels, 208, 211
haunted houses, 219 (ill.), 219–20, 222–23
haunted lighthouses, 122, 123, 124, 126
haunted tunnels, 134
haunted universities and colleges, 261–62, 264–65
paranormal hot spots, 324–25
Matheny, Sarah, 267
Matilda, Empress, 229
The Matrix, 59
Matthew Whaley Elementary School (Williamsburg, VA), 272
Maurice, Father, 149
Max the Security Guard, 263
Maxwell Street Police Station and Jail (Chicago, IL), 246–47
Mayer, Louis B., 77
Mayfair Theater (Asbury Park, NJ), 349–50
Mayo, Edward, 104
McCartney, Paul, 37–38
McClaughry, M. W., 222
McClellan, Georgia, 358
McGraw, Gracie, 39
McGraw, Tim, 39
McLean, Don, 40
McMaugh, James, 117
McNeal, Eliza, 314
McNeil, Wanet, 316–17
McQueen, Steve, 85
Meek, Fielding, 184
Meinert, Marion, 355
Meisner, Brett, 40
melatonin, 21
Memorial Stadium (Indiana University), 197
Menger Hotel (San Antonio, TX), 205
Merritton Tunnel (Thorold, ON, Canada), 133
Mexico, haunted railroad tracks, 131–32
Michel, Anneliese, 57
Michelini, Jan, 60
Michigan
haunted bridges, 138
haunted lighthouses, 123, 125, 125 (ill.), 126–27, 128
haunted railroad tracks, 132
urban legends, 289
Midway, USS (ship), 120
Mignola, Mike, 37
Mihaly, Robert, 226
Miller, Frank, 150
Miller, Jim, 189
Milliken, William Mathewson, 187
Minardos, Deborah Ann Montgomery, 81
mines, haunted, 153–57
Miranda, Carmen, 80
missing farmer urban legend (Selma, AL), 291–92
Mission San Buenaventura (CA), 180–81, 181 (ill.)
Mission San Diego de Alcala (CA), 178–79
Mission San Gabriel (CA), 179–80
Mission San Miguel (San Luis Obispo, CA), 179
missions, haunted, 178–81. *See also* churches, haunted
Mississippi
haunted churches, 178
haunted plantations, 104
Missouri
haunted penitentiaries, 244 (ill.), 245
haunted roads, 140–41, 141–42
urban legends, 292
Missouri State Penitentiary (Jefferson City, MO), 244 (ill.), 245
Mist Trail (Yosemite National Park, CA), 148
Mitchell, Lisa, 72
Mitchell, Sarah, 138
Moaning Cavern (Vallecito, CA), 152
Molly Brown House Museum (Denver, CO), 344
Monet, Claude, 187
Monroe, Marilyn, 29, 39, 70, 71, 207
Montague, Florence, 345
Montalbán, Ricardo, 81
Montana, haunted roads, 142–43
Montgomery Biscuits stadium (Montgomery, AL), 196
Montz, Larry, 75
Moon, Keith, 47
Moon River Brewery (Savannah, GA), 212
Moonville Tunnel (Vinton County, OH), 132–33
Moore, Demi, 53
Moore, Henry Lee, 221
Moore, John, 60
Moore, Josiah, 220–22
Moore, Liz, 60
Moore, Mary Katherine, 220, 221
Moore, Ross, 220–21
Moore, Sarah, 123
Moore, William, 123
Moores, Amanda, 38
Moosham Castle (Unternberg, Austria), 229, 232
Morgan, Jeffrey Dean, 62
Morgan, Kate, 207
Morris, Raymond, 297
Morrison, Jim, 40
Morro Castle, SS (ship) (Asbury Park, NJ), 347–48, 348 (ill.)
Morrow, Vic, 63, 63 (ill.)
Moses, William Stainton, 18
Moss, Thelma, 31
Most Holy Trinity Church (Brooklyn, NY), 176
motels, haunted. *See* hotels and motels, haunted
Mothman, 330–33
Mount Prospect Cemetery (Neptune, NJ), 346–47
Mount Rubidoux (CA), 150, 150 (ill.)
mountains, haunted, 354

movie and TV sets, 55–64
Mulholland Drive (Hollywood, CA), 86
Mullaly, Katie, 192–93
Mullaly, Mikal, 192–93
Muller, J. P. Radan, 124
multiverse, 12–13
Mumler, William H., 18, 91
Munov, Martin, 332
murdered peddler urban legend (Hydesville, NY), 286 (ill.), 286–87
Museum of Shadows (Plattsmouth, NE), 185
museums, haunted, 183–90, 277, 341, 343 (ill.), 343–44, 353 (ill.), 353–54
Myers, Arthur, 38, 88
Myrtles Plantation (St. Francisville, LA), 99–100

N

Nash, Eddie, 76
Nash Road (Columbus, MO), 141–42
Nathan Hall Homestead (Coventry, CT), 186
National Battlefield Park (Marietta, GA), 354
National Cathedral (Washington, DC), 177, 177 (ill.)
Native American lands, 319–35
Navajo, 333–34
Navajo County Courthouse (AZ), 194, 194 (ill.)
Nebraska
  haunted caves, 153
  haunted museums, 185
Neff, Wallace, 35
Nelson, David, 85 (ill.)
Nelson, Harriett, 85 (ill.), 86
Nelson, Ozzie, 85 (ill.), 86
Nelson, Ricky, 85 (ill.)
Neshannock Township, PA, coal mines, 155
Neufeld, Mace, 60
neutral ghosts, 23
Nevada
  haunted cemeteries, 205–6
  haunted hotels and motels, 205–6, 206 (ill.)
  haunted mines, 154–55
  haunted museums, 187, 188, 188 (ill.), 189
New Jersey
  airports, haunted, 280–81
  haunted cemeteries, 346–47
  haunted high schools, 272
  haunted lighthouses, 122–23, 123 (ill.)
  haunted roads, 142, 142 (ill.), 143
  haunted sanatoriums, 255–56
  haunted theaters, 349–50
New London Ledge Lighthouse (CT), 124
New Mexico
  haunted landmarks, 195
  haunted roads, 145
  paranormal hot spots, 328–29, 329 (ill.)
New River George Bridge (WV), 137
New York
  haunted asylums, 256–57
  haunted battlefields, 164–65
  haunted castles, 226–27, 228
  haunted churches, 176–77
  haunted colleges, 263
  haunted forts, 169
  haunted hotels and motels, 210–11
  haunted houses, 218–19, 301–4, 304 (ill.)
  haunted lighthouses, 124
  haunted roads, 148–49
  sports ghosts, 196
  urban legends, 285–87, 291
Newley, Anthony, 32
Nichols Canyon (Hollywood, CA), 79
Nicholson, Jack, 56, 201
Nickle, Bob, 314
Nickle, Jane, 314
Night Stalker, 322
nightcrawlers, 326
nightcrawlers urban legend (Fresno, CA), 295–96
Nimoy, Leonard, 63
Noftsger Hill Inn Bed and Breakfast (Globe, AZ), 192–93
Norman, Michael, 92
North Carolina
  haunted castles, 226
  haunted forts, 167–68
  haunted roads, 148
Northumberland ghost ship, 121
Norton Creek Trail (Great Smoky Mountains, NC), 148
Norwich State Hospital (Preston, CT), 254–55, 255 (ill.)
Nova Scotia, poltergeists, 313 (ill.), 313–14
The Nun (2018), 59–60
Nurmi, Maila, 50
nursing homes, haunted, 367–68
Nyberg, Leo, 251

O

Oak Alley Plantation (Vacherie, LA), 100, 101 (ill.)
Oakland Cemetery (Iowa City, IA), 175
objects, haunted, 9–11, 10 (ill.)
O'Carroll, Charlotte, 231
O'Carroll, Emily, 231
O'Connor, Donald, 32
Ogden, Tom, 30, 71, 83
Oglethorpe, James, 128
Ohio
  haunted bridges, 139
  haunted colleges, 264
  haunted elementary schools, 274
  haunted forts, 167
  haunted hospitals, 250, 250 (ill.)
  haunted hotels and motels, 210
  haunted museums, 187, 189
  haunted nursing homes, 367–68
  haunted prisons, penitentiaries, and jails, 242–43, 356–57
  haunted tunnels, 132–33
  haunted universities, 261
  poltergeists, 312–13
  urban legends, 290–91, 292
Ohio State Penitentiary (Columbus, OH), 243–44
Ohio State Reformatory (Mansfield, OH), 242–43

Ohio University (Athens, OH), 261
Ohlander, Carrie, 217
O.K. Corral (Tombstone, AZ), 190–91, 191 (ill.)
Oklahoma, urban legends, 292
Old Alton Bridge (TX), 135–36
Old Charleston Jail (Charleston, SC), 246
Old Coaly, 265, 266 (ill.)
Old Green Eyes, 161
Old Jail (St. Augustine, FL), 241
Old Lady's Field (Garnerville, NY), 285
Old Milton School (Alton, IL), 273
Old Paulding Jail (Paulding, OH), 356–57
Old Point Loma Lighthouse (San Diego, CA), 124–25
Old Presque Isle lighthouse (Presque Isle, MI), 125, 125 (ill.)
Old Tooele Hospital (Tooele, UT), 248–49
Olympia, USS (ship), 114 (ill.), 114–15
The Omen, 60
Omni Parker House (Boston, MA), 211
O'Neill, Eugene, 265
Ono, Yoko, 38
Ontario
  haunted battlefields, 166
  haunted lighthouses, 124
  haunted tunnels, 133, 133 (ill.)
  sports ghosts, 197
Oregon, haunted lighthouses, 124
O'Rourke, Heather, 57, 61–62, 67
Osborne, Frederick, 128
Osment, Hayley Joel, 53
The Others (2001), 53
Ourang Medan (ship), 118
Owen, A. R. G., 9
Owls Head Light State Park (ME), 125–26
Oxford Hotel (Denver, CO), 344–45
Ozark howler urban legend (Ozark Mountains), 292

P

Pahuk Bluff (Lincoln, NE), 153
The Palace (New Orleans, LA), 304–5
Palatine (ship), 119–20
Pantages, Alexander, 72
Pantages Theater, 72 (ill.), 72–73
Panteones Metro Station (Mexico), 131–32
Pappas, Stephanie, 23–24
Paramount Pictures Studios, 66–67
Paramount Theater (Asbury Park, NJ), 349–50
paranormal hot spots, 319–35
Parc des Buttes-Chaumont bridge (Paris, France), 137
Parker, Marion, 304
Parker, Perry, 304
parks, haunted, 342
Parks, Lillian Rogers, 91
Parris, George, 125
Parsons, Gram, 41
Parsons, Louella, 65
Pascal, Jean, 351
Pascal, Madame, 350–51, 352
Passchendaele Battlefield (Belgium), 165–66
The Passion of the Christ, 60
Patterson, Kate, 343
Patterson, Thomas, 342, 343
Patterson Inn (Denver, CO), 342
Peabody, Charles, 210
Pearl Jam, 57
Peck, Gregory, 60
Peck, Walter, 152
Peckham, Mary, 220–21
Pecos Bill, 168
Peel, Simon, 119
penitentiaries, haunted. *See* prisons, penitentiaries, and jails, haunted
Pennhurst Asylum (Spring City, PA), 252–54, 253 (ill.)
Pennsylvania
  haunted airplane crashes, 275
  haunted asylums, 252–54, 253 (ill.)
  haunted battlefields, 162–64, 163 (ill.), 339, 362 (ill.), 362–63, 367
  haunted bridges, 137
  haunted cemeteries, 339
  haunted churches, 177
  haunted hospitals, 251
  haunted houses, 295, 358 (ill.), 358–59, 366–67
  haunted mines, 155
  haunted penitentiaries, 241, 241 (ill.)
  haunted universities and colleges, 262–63, 265–67, 266 (ill.)
  sports ghosts, 196, 196 (ill.)
  urban legends, 290, 295
Pennsylvania State University (PA), 265–67, 266 (ill.)
Perron, Andrea, 306
Perron, Caroline, 56
Perron, Roger and Carolyn, 306
Perron house (Burrillville, RI), 306
Perry, Rebecca, 105
Pet Sematary, 180
Peterson, Roger, 40
phantom ships, 113, 115–16
Philadelphia Eastern State Penitentiary (Philadelphia, PA), 241, 241 (ill.)
Philip Experiment, 8–9
Philippines, haunted airports, 280
photography, 18–19, 22
Pickett, George, 363
Pickford, Mary, 35
Pigeon Hill (Kennesaw Mountain, GA), 354
Pima Indians, 327
Pink Lady, 170
Pink Palace, 83
Pippo, 129
Pirate's House (Savannah, GA), 217–18
Plank, Eddie, 196, 196 (ill.)
plantations, haunted, 99–105
Plath, Sylvia, 261
Playfair, Guy Lyon, 312
Plume, Michael, 197

Plunkett, Hugh, 84
Plymouth Lighthouse (Plymouth, MA), 126
Po-Ho-No, 326
Poasttown Elementary School (Cincinnati, OH), 274
Pocatello High School (Pocatello, ID), 270
Poe, Edgar Allan, 174, 185–86
Poe, Elizabeth, 186
Poe Museum (Richmond, VA), 185 (ill.), 185–86
Poinsett Bridge (Greenville County, SC), 138
Point Lookout (Scotland, MD), 126
Point Sur Lighthouse (CA), 126
Poland, haunted castles, 234
Polanski, Roman, 62
Poltergeist (1982), 60–62, 180
poltergeists, 7, 307–19
Poor Bear, Thomas, 296
Port Boca Grande lighthouse (Gasparilla, FL), 126
Porter, David, 168
The Possession (2012), 62
Potter Street station (Saginaw, MI), 132
Powell, Colin, 208
Powell, Ottie Cline, 147
Power, Tyrone, 80, 81
Power, Tyrone, Jr., 81
presidents, U.S., 90–93
Presley, Elvis, 28 (ill.), 28–29, 66
Presley, Gladys, 29
Preston, Stuart, 264
Preston Castle (Ione, CA), 226
Price, Harry, 315
Price, Vincent, 85
Princess Augusta (ship), 120
Prior, William, 123
prisons, penitentiaries, and jails, haunted, 237–47, 356–57
Pritchard family, 316
Priteca, B. Marcus, 72
psi phenomena, 15
Psycho (1960), 63–64
Purgatory Road (Texas Hill Country, TX), 144 (ill.), 145
Purple Masque Theater (Kansas State University, KS), 197

Q

Quebec, haunted farms, 309–10
Queen Anne Hotel (San Francisco, CA), 202, 202 (ill.)
Queen Elizabeth, RMS (ship), 110, 111
Queen Mary, RMS (ship), 109–12, 110 (ill.)
Questhaven Road (San Diego County, CA), 139–40

R

Rabindra Sarobar Station (Kolkata, India), 131
Rachmaninoff, Sergei, 71
railroad tracks, haunted, 131–32
Raleigh, Sir Walter, 96–97
Raleigh Studios, 67–68
Ramirez, Richard, 322
Ramone, Johnny, 80
Ramsey, Elizabeth Pasch, 355
Ramsey, JonBenét, 355
Ramsey, Patsy, 355
Rand, Andre, 291
Randall, Monica, 88
Rappe, Virginia, 81
Rattenbury, Francis, 210
Ray, James Earl, 245
Raynham Hall (Norfolk, England), 224–25
Reagan, Maureen, 91, 93
Reagan, Nancy, 93
Reagan, Ronald, 92–93
Red Castle Inn (Nevada City, CA), 204
Red Coach Inn (Niagara Falls, NY), 210–11
Red Garter Inn (Williams, AZ), 191, 194
Red Ladies, 268
Red Rocks Amphitheater (Morrison, CO), 345–46
Reed, William, 179
Reeves, George, 33
Reeves, Keanu, 45, 59
Rehmeyer, Nelson, 295
Rehmeyer's Hollow urban legend (Stewartstown, PA), 295
Repo, Donald, 276–77
Resch, Joan and John, 312
Resch, Tina, 312–13, 318
residual ghosts, 4
Resurrection Cemetery (Justice, IL), 173
Resurrection Mary, 173
reticular activating system (RAS), 16–17
Reynolds, Henry, 268
Reynolds, Ryan, 55
Rhode Island
  haunted houses, 306
  haunted lighthouses, 123
Richard, Duke of York, 97
Richard II, King, 316
Richardson, J. P. "Big Bopper," 39–40
Richardson, John, 60
Ricks, Bernard, 41
Riklis, Meshulam, 36
Ringsby, Gary, 152
Riverdale Road (Thornton, CO), 141
roads, haunted, 139–45
Roberts, Jason, 198–99
Robertson, Raymond, 290
Robertson, Shelly Burk, 356, 357
Robins, Oliver, 61
Robinson, Bertram Fletcher, 190
Robinson, James W., 214
Robinson, James "Yankee Jim," 213
Robinson, Sarah, 128
Robinson, William, 128
Robinson-Rose House (San Diego, CA), 214
Rockne, Knute, 262
Rodriguez, Christian, 74
Roelant, Peter, 85
Roenigk, Elise, 203
Roenigk, Marty, 203
Rogers, Buddy, 35
Rogers, Millicent, 33
Roll, William, 312–13, 318 (ill.), 318–19
Rolling Hills Asylum (East Bethany, NY), 256–57
Rolling Stones, 73
Romania
  haunted forests, 289
  urban legends, 289
Roosevelt, Eleanor, 45
Roosevelt, Franklin D., 35

Roosevelt, Martha Bulloch, 102
Roosevelt, Theodore, 70, 71, 91, 102, 205
Rosemary's Baby (1968), 62
Route 491 (Four Corners region), 145
Route 2A (Haynesville, ME), 144
Rowland, Lizzie, 104
Roy High School (Roy, UT), 271–72
Rubenstein, Zelda, 61
Rubidoux, Louis, 150
Russ, Joseph, Jr., 214
Russ House (Marianna, FL), 214
Russell, Dan, 88
Russia, haunted battlefields, 166, 166 (ill.)
Ryan, John, 246

S

Sach's Bridge (Gettysburg, PA), 137
Sacramento Airport (Sacramento, CA), 278
Saginaw River Rear Range lighthouse (Bay City, MI), 126–27
Saint Mary of the Woods College (Terre Haute, IN), 269–70
Salem Witch Trials, 208, 252
Salton Sea ghosts urban legend (CA), 287–88
Sampson, Will, 61
San Diego poltergeist (San Diego, CA), 317–18
San Francisco Plantation (Garyville, LA), 101–2
San Juan Mission railroad tracks (San Antonio, TX), 131
San Luis Valley (CO-NM), 328
San Pedro poltergeist (San Pedro, CA), 314–15
Sanford, E. Starr, 227
sanatoriums, haunted, 251–52, 254, 255–56, 366
Sasa Airport (Davao City, Philippines), 280
Sauchie poltergeist (Sauchie, Clackmannanshire, Scotland), 317
Savalas, Telly, 45–46
Savoy Theater (Asbury Park, NJ), 349–50
Schilling, Margaret, 250
Schnebly, Sedona Arabella Miller, 325
Schnebly, Theodore Carlton, 325
Schnur, Lesia Miller, 355–56
Schoellkopf, William, 210
Schwab, Charles, 265–66
Schweiger, Jennifer, 291
Scotland
  haunted battlefields, 165
  haunted castles, 230
  poltergeists, 317
  urban legends, 288–89
Scott, Beth, 92
Scott, Walter, 116
Screaming Tunnel (Niagara Falls, ON), 133, 133 (ill.)
Seaburn, Paul, 42
Seaman, Jonas, 210
Sebring, Jay, 30
Sedgwick, Kyra, 62
Sedona, AZ, 325
Seelbach, Louis, 204
Seelbach, Otto, 204
Seelbach Hilton Hotel (Louisville, KY), 204 (ill.), 204–5
Seguin Island Lighthouse (Bath, ME), 127
Selleck, Tom, 63
Seltzer, David, 60
Senkowski, Ernst, 17
Sensabaugh, Edward, 133
Sensabaugh Tunnel (TN), 133
sentient/intelligent ghosts, 4
serial killers, 50–52, 54
serotonin, 21
Serra, Junipero, 150, 178, 179
Seul Choix lighthouse (Gulliver, MI), 127
Shades of Death Road (Warren County, NJ), 143
Shafter, William, 168
Shakespeare, William, 53
Shannon, Fred, 312
The Shawshank Redemption, 242–43
Shelley, Mary, 233
Sherman, Charles R., 210
Sherman family, 334–35
Sherwood Point Lighthouse (Manistique, MI), 127
The Shining (1977), 53, 64, 180
Shiprock (Four Corners region), 144 (ill.), 145
ships, haunted, 107–22, 347–48, 348 (ill.)
Shoshone, 320–21
Shotgun Annie, 285
Shumaker, John F., 24
Shutt, Tim, 264
Shyamalan, M. Night, 53
Sickles, Daniel, 339
Siegel, Bugsy, 77, 80
Sierra Sky Ranch and Resort (Oakhurst, CA), 254
Silent Movie Theater, 74
Silver Cliff Cemetery (Silver Cliff, CO), 173
Silverpilen, 130
Sinatra, Frank, 38–39, 67, 77
Singapore, haunted railroad tracks, 131
Singaporean MRT station (Bishan, Singapore), 131
The Sixth Sense (1999), 53
Skinwalker Ranch (Ballard, UT), 333–35
Slender Man, 283–84
Slimer, 53
Smiley, George, 194
Smith, Carl, 189
Smith, Edward J., 113
Smith, Will, 24 (ill.)
Smith College (Northampton, MA), 261–62
Smithson, James, 184–85
Smithsonian Institution museum complex, 184–85
Snedeker, Allen and Carmen, 305
Snedeker house (Southington, CT), 305
Snell, Annetta, 354–55
Snidow, Conley T., 173
Sommer, Elke, 31, 85
Soto, Dwayne, 73–74
sound stages and studios, 64–68
South Carolina
  haunted bridges, 138

haunted hotels and motels, 211 (ill.), 211–12
haunted jails, 246
haunted plantations, 104–5
urban legends, 289
South Dakota
haunted high schools, 271
haunted mines, 154
urban legends, 296
Southern Airways Flight 242 plane crash (New Hope, GA), 354–55
Spanish Military Hospital (St. Augustine, FL), 249
Spearfinger, 148
Spelling, Aaron, 81
Spielberg, Steven, 60, 63, 66, 180
spirits of the dead, 1, 11
sports ghosts, 195–97
Spruce Railroad Trail (Olympic National Park, WA), 148
Spungen, Nancy, 41
St. Andrew's Episcopal Church (Staten Island, NY), 176–77
St. Augustine, FL, children ghosts, 359–60
St. Augustine lighthouse (St. Augustine, FL), 127
St. George's Episcopal Church (Fredericksburg, VA), 177
St. James Episcopal Cemetery (Marietta, GA), 355
St. James Theater (Asbury Park, NJ), 349–50
St. Louis Cemetery (New Orleans, LA), 173–74
St. Louis Light (AB, Canada), 130
St. Mary's-in-Tuxedo Church (Tuxedo, NY), 176
St. Paul's Cemetery (Key West, FL), 178
St. Paul's Episcopal Church (Key West, FL), 178
St. Simons, GA, lighthouse, 127–28
Stalin, Joseph, 97
Stalingrad Battlefield (Volgograd, Russia), 166, 166 (ill.)
The Stand (King), 249
Stanley, F. O., 201–2
Stanley, Flora, 201
Stanley Hotel (Estes Park, CO), 201–2
Star of India (ship), 120–21
Starkey, Zak, 45
Starr, Ringo, 37, 45, 83, 84
Steinem, Gloria, 261
Stevens, John, 128
Stevens, R. Gregory, 32
Stewart, Mrs., 100
Stilley, Frank, 223
Stilley, Minerva, 223
Stilley-Young House (Jefferson, TX), 223–24, 224 (ill.)
Stillinger, Lena, 221
Sting, 44, 48
Stoney Creek Battlefield (ON, Canada), 166
Stony Point Battlefield (Rockland County, NY), 164–65
Stony Point Lighthouse (Rockland County, NY), 165
Story, H. L., 206
Stovepipe Hat Bigfoot, 296
Strickland, Nicole, 109, 112
Stubbersfield, Joe, 284
Stull Cemetery (Stull, KS), 174
Styler, Trudie, 44
submarine, spectral, 122
suicide bridges, 136–37
Suleyman, Prince, 304–5
Sullivan, Bridget, 219
Summit Elementary School (Amarillo, TX), 273
Sundher, Taj, 76
Superstition Mountains (Phoenix, AZ), 327–28
Sutton, "Slick Willie," 241
Suvarnabhumi Airport (Thailand), 280
Swallow Cave (Nahant, MA), 151
Swanson, Gloria, 35
Swayze, Patrick, 53
Sweeney, John, 61
Switzer, Carl Dean, 81
Syme, Jennifer, 59

T

Taff, Barry, 86, 308–9, 314
Taft, William Howard, 71, 92
Taku-he, 296
Tate, Sharon, 30, 62
Taunton State Hospital (Taunton, MA), 249–50, 325
Taylor, Elizabeth, 34
Taylor, Lily, 57
TCL Chinese Theater, 75 (ill.), 75–76
Tebb, William, 298
Tehrani, Jamie, 284
Tejada, Valerie, 69
Tenerife Airport (Canary Islands), 281
Tennant, Neil, 47–48
Tennessee
haunted high schools, 270
haunted hiking trails, 147
haunted tunnels, 133
urban legends, 294–95
Tennessee, SS (ship), 115–16
Tennessee High School (Bristol, TN), 270
Texas
haunted bridges, 135–36
haunted elementary schools, 273
haunted forts, 168–69
haunted high schools, 270–71, 271 (ill.)
haunted hotels and motels, 205
haunted houses, 223–24, 224 (ill.)
haunted landmarks, 360–62
haunted museums, 189
haunted railroad tracks, 131
haunted roads, 145
haunted universities, 269
urban legends, 292
Texas State University (San Marcos, TX), 269
Thackray Medical Museum (Leeds, West Yorkshire, England), 190
Thailand, haunted airports, 280
theaters, haunted, 72–76, 72 (ill.), 75 (ill.), 198–99, 349–50, 364–66
Thomas, Dylan, 41
Thomas, Hannah, 126
Thomas, John, 126
thought forms, 8–9
Three-legged Lady, 141–42

Three Men and a Baby (1987), 62–63
Tibble, Derek, 278
Tierney, Jean, 53
Titanic, RMS (ship), 107–8, 108 (ill.), 112, 113
Todd, Dewey, Sr., 80
Todd, Thelma, 30, 30 (ill.)
Tonopah Cemetery (Tonopah, NV), 205–6
Topeka High School (Topeka, KS), 271
Torquay Museum (Devon, England), 189–90
Torrence, Dean Ormsby, 78
Tower of London (London, England), 96 (ill.), 96–97
Townshend, Dorothy Walpole, 225
Towton Battlefield (Towton, England), 167
trains, haunted, 129–30
Trans-Allegheny Asylum (Weston, WV), 257 (ill.), 257–58
Travers, Jerome E., 64
Trimble, Marshall, 245
Truman, Harry, 91, 92
Truman, Margaret, 91
Trumbauer, William, 268
Trump, Donald, 45
Tucciardo, Fran, 88
Tulloch Castle (Ross-Shire, England), 230, 231 (ill.)
tulpas, 8–9
tunnels, haunted, 132–34, 133 (ill.)
Tunnels One, Two, and Three (central CO), 133–34
Tuomi, Steven, 52
Turnbull Canyon (Puente Hills, CA), 321–22, 322 (ill.)
Turner, John, 222
Turner-Ingersoll Mansion (Salem, MA), 222
Turnupseed, Donald, 49
Turpin, Dick, 278–79, 279 (ill.)
Tutu, Desmond, 340
The Twilight Zone (1983), 63
Two Guns, CA, 152

U

ubasute, 146
Udovich, Alfred, 276
UFOs
  Aztec, NM, 328–29
  Phoenix, AZ, 327–28
  Point Pleasant, WV, 330–31
  Skinwalker Ranch (Ballard, UT), 334
  Yosemite National Park, CA, 327
Union Cemetery (Easton, CT), 176
Union Station (Phoenix, AZ), 132
United Airlines Flight 93 crash (Shanksville, PA), 275
Universal Studios, Stage 28, 65, 65 (ill.)
universities, haunted. *See* colleges and universities, haunted
University of Illinois (Urbana-Champaign, IL), 269
University of Montevallo (Montevallo, AL), 268
University of Notre Dame (Notre Dame, IN), 262
Unterweger, Jack, 54
urban legends, 283–99
Urbana High School (Urbana, IL), 272
U.S. Grant Hotel (San Diego, CA), 207
U.S. presidents, 90–93
Utah
  haunted high schools, 271–72
  haunted hospitals, 248–49
  haunted roads, 145
  paranormal hot spots, 333–35

V

Valencia, SS (ship), 118
Valens, Ritchie, 39
Valentino, Rudolph, 33–34, 67, 71, 80
Vallee, Rudy, 83
Van Sickle, James, 74
vanishing hitchhiker urban legends, 293
Vasquez, Julio, 319
Veatch, Peaches, 338–39
Venis, Jalynn, 339–40, 346
Vermont, haunted bridges, 137–38
Vesey, Denmark, 246
Vicious, Sid, 41
Victoria, Queen, 18
Villisca Axe Murder House (Villisca, IA), 220–22, 221 (ill.)
Virginia
  haunted battlefields, 161–62, 164
  haunted churches, 177
  haunted hiking trails, 147
  haunted museums, 185 (ill.), 185–86
  haunted plantations, 103–4
  haunted tunnels, 134
Vogue Theater (Hollywood, CA), 75

W

Wade, Jennie, 339, 358–59
Waldeck Mine (NV), 154
Wales, haunted landmarks, 225
Walke, Sally Rebecca, 104
Walker, Clifford, 217
Walking Sam urban legend (Pine Ridge Indian Reservation, SD), 296
Waller, Dennis, 360–62
Walling, Alonzo, 199
Walpole, Lady Dorothy, 19 (ill.)
Waltz, Jacob, 327
Walworth Castle (County Durham, England), 230
Walz, John, 171
Wan, James, 56
Wanamaker, Marc, 72, 85, 86
Warboys, Robert, 297–98
Warehouse of Tropication Arts poltergeist (Miami, FL), 319
Warm Springs Canyon Road (Death Valley National Park, CA), 149
Warner, Sam, 74
Warren, Ed, 57, 187, 303, 305
Warren, Lorraine, 57, 187, 303, 305, 305 (ill.)
Warrens' Occult Museum (CT), 186–87

Washburn, Oscar, 135
Washington, D.C.
haunted churches, 177, 177 (ill.)
haunted museums, 184–85
Washington, George, 93, 162
Washington (state), haunted roads, 147–48
waterfalls, haunted, 146–47
Waterfront Station (Vancouver, BC), 132
Watson, Gracie, 170–71
Watson, Margaret Frances, 171
Watson, Wales, 171
Waverly Hills (Louisville, KY), 258–59
Waverly Hills Sanatorium (Louisville, KY), 366
Waverly Mansion and Gardens (West Point, MS), 104
Wayne, Anthony, 165
Webb, Clifton, 81
Weber, William, 303
Weis, Alexandrea, 350, 352
Welles, Orson, 32–33
Wells, H. G., 32, 35
Wells, Henry, 263
Wells College (Aurora, NY), 263
Wendigo, 326–27
Wengert, Cyril S., 187
West, Ti, 58
West Virginia
haunted amusement parks, 173
haunted asylums, 257 (ill.), 257–58
haunted bridges, 137
haunted penitentiaries, 240–41
paranormal hot spots, 330–33
West Virginia Moundsville Penitentiary (Moundsville, WB), 240–41
Westminster Hall and Burying Grounds (Baltimore, MD), 174, 176
Whaley, Anna, 213
Whaley, Matthew, 272
Whaley, Thomas, 212–13
Whaley, Violet, 213
Whaley House (San Diego, CA), 212–14, 213 (ill.)
White, Gaylord, 173
White, John, 96
White, Leslie T., 84
White River lighthouse (Whitehall, MI), 128
White River Monster urban legend (Newport, AR), 293
Whitehead, Mae, 30
Whittier, John Greenleaf, 120
Wiestling, George, 267
Wilde, Oscar, 48
Wilhelmina, Queen, 92
Willey, Charles, 316–17
William Kehoe House (Savannah, GA), 217
Williams, Hank, 42
Williams, JoBeth, 61, 61 (ill.)
Williams, Robbie, 45
Williamson, Orion, 291–92
Williamson, Thomas, 104
Willin, Melvin, 91
Willis, Bruce, 53
Wilson, Ellen, 92
Wilson, Patricia, 204
Wilson, Patrick, 57, 305
Wilson, Woodrow, 71, 177
Winchester, Sarah, 215–16
Winchester, William Wirt, 215
Winchester Mystery House (San Jose, CA), 214–16, 215 (ill.)
Winfield Hall, 88
Winter, William, 99–100
Winthrop, John, 172
Wirz, Henry, 242
Wisconsin, haunted roads, 144
Witch House (Salem, MA), 223
Witch Wonderful, 151
witching hour, 20–22
Wonderland Murders House (Hollywood, CA), 76
Wood, Rose, 93
Wood, William, 199
Woodstock, Percy, 310
Woodward, Bob, 45
Woolworth, Frank Winfield, 88
Wrigley Field (Chicago, IL), 195
Wutherich, Rolf, 49
Wyckoff, Clarence, 228
Wyckoff, William O., 228
Wyckoff Castle (Cape Vincent, NY), 228
Wyoming Coal Fields (Scranton, PA), 155

Y

Yanchitis, James, 332
Yorba Cemetery (Yorba Linda, CA), 170
Yosemite National Park (CA), 325–27, 326 (ill.)
Young, Charlie, 224
Young, George Hampton, 104
Young, Leslie, 223
Yuma Territorial Prison (Yuma, AZ), 245–46

Z

Zadora, Pia, 36
Zak Bagans' Haunted Museum (Las Vegas, NV), 187, 188 (ill.), 188–89
Zdunk, Barbara, 234
Zevon, Warren, 40
Zombie Road (Glencoe, MO), 140–41
Zvikov Castle (Czech Republic), 233